WITH E. B. WHITE: "Farewell to the Model T"

Maud (EDITOR)

Richard L. Strout

TRB

VIEWS AND PERSPECTIVES ON THE PRESIDENCY

Macmillan Publishing Co., Inc.

NEW YORK

Collier Macmillan Publishers

LONDON

*Macmillan Publishing Co., Inc.
866 Third Avenue, New York, N.Y. 10022
Collier Macmillan Canada, Ltd.*

*Library of Congress Cataloging in Publication
Data
Strout, Richard Lee, 1898–
TRB, views and perspectives on the Presidency.
TRB columns reprinted from the New republic.
Includes index.
1. United States—Politics and government—
1933–1945—Collected works. 2. United
States—Politics and government—1945—   —
Collected works. 3. Presidents—United States
—Collected works. 4. Executive power—
United States—Collected works. I. New
republic. II. Title.
E806.S825   320.9′73′09   79–9318
ISBN 0–02–61530–8*

Carroll Kilpatrick's Introduction to this volume was originally published in the March 18, 1978, issue of *The New Republic*.

First Printing 1979

Designed by Jack Meserole

Printed in the United States of America

Contents

THE EISENHOWER YEARS [1952–1960]

THE KENNEDY YEARS [1961–1963]

THE JOHNSON YEARS [1963–1968]

THE NIXON YEARS [1968–1974]

THE FORD YEARS [*1974–1976*]

THE CARTER YEARS [*1976–1978*]

Introduction

More than a half century ago a young and eager newspaperman arrived in Washington. At about this time Bruce Bliven, then editor of *The New Republic,* was taking one of his weekly subway rides from his office in Manhattan (where *TNR* was then published) to Brooklyn to deliver copy to the printer. Bliven had in his pocket a new political column from Frank R. Kent, a Washington correspondent of the *Baltimore Sun.* The column was to be anonymous and Bliven had puzzled over how to sign it. As he rode the lurching train and pondered his problem, his eyes fell on a placard bearing the subway name—BRT, for Brooklyn Rapid Transit. Bliven reversed the initials and signed the new column TRB. It has been a fixture in *The New Republic* ever since. Today it is one of the most widely read and respected columns of opinion in America, and is reprinted in sixty newspapers.

Frank Kent was a fighting liberal in those days. After all, he fought Prohibition and he regularly attacked Calvin Coolidge. He was a slashing writer who believed that nearly all government was bad and all bureaucrats were miserable sinners. When Franklin Roosevelt reached Washington, Kent, in the *Sun,* became one of the New Deal's most acid critics, as might be expected of a good friend of Henry Mencken.

Other writers also were called in to contribute the TRB column. Kenneth Crawford, later a columnist for *Newsweek,* was one of the notable contributors in the late 1930s and early 1940s. Then, in 1943, the young man who had left New England for Washington about the time Bliven launched the column tried his hand. It has been his ever since, except for times off for vacation, for travel, and for covering the Normandy invasion.

Every editor knows that the enthusiasm and imagination of youth make a newspaper or magazine sparkle. Richard L. Strout, who writes TRB every week on long sheets of white paper, is that youthful person. His long legs propel him about Washington every day with a speed that many of his colleagues find exhausting. Few can match his ability to digest masses of government documents and to see through every false argument. If Dick Strout has one outstanding characteristic it is his youthfulness. His enthusiasm for life and for the drama of Washington politics is as alive as it was the day he came to the city the first time. Not long ago, in the issue of February 25 [1978], he wrote one of his sprightliest columns on, of all things, the statistics he, and he alone, dug out of the President's economic report.

"There's nothing more agreeable on a winter evening than to curl up before a good fire with the tables of statistics of the president's Annual Economic Report," the column began. "Let the gale howl. Let the snow fall. I have here Table B-28." That beginning might have sent many of his readers out into the snow for a breath of fresh air. But, knowing TRB, the majority must have kept on reading. There followed a dramatic and entertaining interpretation of those figures in human terms. Dick Strout did not see the dull statistics. He saw the human beings, the farmers, the workers, the blacks, the women, whose biographies were encompassed in those figures. He found sex, humor, sadness, and hope in what he read. Did any other reporter find so much and report it with such style?

One day early in the Nixon administration, John Ehrlichman invited Strout to his office to ask for advice. Ehrlichman is a Christian Scientist who had come to appreciate Strout's factual reporting in the *Christian Science Monitor*. Strout has been working for the *Monitor* since 1921 and has been a member of its Washington bureau since 1923. He is a reporter on the *Monitor*, a commentator in *The New Republic*. Perhaps Ehrlichman did not know of the second Strout. He asked his gangling visitor with the somber eyes and bushy eyebrows what he thought the Nixon administration should make its first goal. Why, to build the kind of social democracy and equality that one finds, for example, in Sweden, Strout replied, confidently. Needless to say, the interview was short, and it was the only time the Nixon administration sought Strout's advice.

Later, when he was covering Watergate, other reporters asked Strout how it compared with Teapot Dome, his first big Washington story. During both investigations, Strout wrote, many readers charged that the press was "carrying things too far." Many voters, he said, "shrugged and said both parties were alike and it was all just politics." But there was a crucial difference between the two scandals, he said in one TRB column. Watergate was "more disturbing and dangerous" than Teapot Dome because it was "a special kind of corruption without greed. No sex, no dollars. Just power. It doesn't strike at oil leases, it strikes at democracy." Unlike some who have seen the same sort of argument or event time and again, Strout is never blasé about the story he is covering. He sees the drama every time and reports it in a way that makes it come alive to the reader.

Long before Johnson and Nixon, Strout expressed concern about the growth of presidential power. As he once said, "there's a feeling that once you sleep in Lincoln's bed, you become deified. It's a dangerous thing." He is convinced that the presidential system is structurally muscle-bound, and he has long believed that the parliamentary system is both more effective and more responsive to the people's needs. No amount of argument has swayed him from that conviction, nor has he been persuaded that it is idle to think the United States will move from the presidential to the parliamentary system.

Another campaign of his that failed was against the televising of presidential news conferences. In 1954, when parts of the Eisenhower conference first were opened for television, Strout wrote an unusual signed article for *The New Republic*, arguing that verbatim recording of a press conference "turns what has been an extremely handy, carefully evolved, semiofficial, and unique contrivance into a theatrical performance. The press conference becomes a show. Its informal, easygoing nature is changed into a self-conscious half-hour broadcast." He argued that the informal mood that helped make it possible to pry out information would be lost "if each reporter knows that his boss, the world, and his wife will listen to what he is about to say." Now there are as many prima donnas in the press as in the United States Senate. But to argue against television's intrusion was to try to turn back the tide.

Nevertheless, Strout was right about what television would do to press conferences and to the press. Some of FDR's press conferences lasted five or ten minutes, some forty-five minutes or an hour, depending upon the questions and the news developments of the week. Now a presidential conference must fit into television's rigid schedule and appearances often are more important than substance. On television, a president's every word is guarded; informality and give-and-take are held to a minimum, as Strout feared. Even in the Senate debate has degenerated because a senator would rather use his oratorical skills to obtain a half minute on television than to explore an issue in floor debate. "The communicating medium is television, not the ornate Senate chamber," Strout has written.

Where some writers make a complex subject more complex and even dull, Strout with his marvelous light touch and clarity engages the reader's attention. The reader quickly senses Strout's sturdy principles. His convictions have never led him to color a news story. But these convictions are strongly expressed in TRB. Today there is no more respected writer in Washington, none with more warm friends. His views have never been more pertinent or more up-to-date than now.

CARROLL KILPATRICK
Former White House
Correspondent for the
Washington Post

TRB

THE ROOSEVELT YEARS
[*1943-1945*]

Strout's First Column

MARCH 8, 1943   I wonder how well the country understands the pessimism that broods over Washington these days? This is not merely the pathological gloom of the chronic reformer soured by the world's ills, but the considered view of the would-be optimist who hopes against hope that something worthwhile will be won from the present war, but who remembers the last one.

That Congress is now in a state of blind revolt anybody can see. When these notes appear the Seventy-eighth Congress will have been sitting two months. What is its record? Acrimony, rebellion, and, above all, disorganization. It is striking out fiercely at the president, labor, and "bureaucrats" (a "bureaucrat" is anybody you dislike), but in doing so it is not offering a constructive program of its own but is injuring the war effort. Mischief-makers like Burt Wheeler, who have kept quiet since Pearl Harbor, are making themselves leaders of the fight to prevent the army from drafting those fathers of families who are not in essential occupations. The farm bloc is so bent on keeping the hired man down on the farm that it, too, threatens to interfere with the army's plans, while it is always quite willing, of course, to upset inflation controls. Just how far these twin revolts will go is anybody's guess, but they mean, if successful, that Congress has intervened in a vital point of war strategy and taken control away from the commander in chief and the military experts.

Even more dangerous is the possibility that one of these "midterm deadlocks" is developing, which might well last until the next presidential election. Nobody has ever quite figured out how to meet this dread situation, unique to the American form of government under our constitutional separation of powers and rigid two-year elections.

5

If presidential policies are repudiated at midterm and a hostile party takes over, the president must keep office till his term expires, whether he can accomplish anything or not. Such a deadlock between president and Congress occurred in the 1929 depression under Hoover. Now New Dealers have little influence in Congress, and the coalition of Republicans and poll-tax Southerners have it, for the time being, their own confused way.

This would not be so bad if the coalition had something constructive to offer, but so far the revolters have distinguished themselves chiefly by showing that they hate labor with a keener, more intimate relish than they hate Hitler. A crusade against "absenteeism" is succeeding the earlier attack over the so-called "forty-hour week" issue, and once more the threat of antistrike legislation is being injected into a fairly healthy situation where strikes amount to only about one-tenth of one percent of total time worked.

The aimlessness of the revolt is best illustrated in the shotgun action of the House Appropriations Committee last week. Manpower Chief McNutt asked for a minor $2,454,000 item to equalize the pay of the demoralized United States Employment Service, where discontent is so rife that there was a 90-percent labor turnover last year. This agency must bear the brunt of the new national manpower-placement problem. The item was rejected. Frances Perkins had a modest request for $337,000 in the same bill to promote a state-aid program against absenteeism. Despite all the shouting about absenteeism, that was thrown out too. So were half a dozen similar home-front requests. And having turned down, on smug grounds of procedure, the request of the Children's Bureau for a preliminary $1,200,000 to help states provide medical care for newborn babies and prematernity care for wives of $50-a-month doughboys, the House turned its eager attention this week to the "millionaires' relief bill"—the Disney rider on the bill to increase the debt limit, to revoke the president's executive order limiting salaries to a miserable $25,000 net, in wartime.

There are indications that the congressional revolt is going too far, even for its own purpose. Conservative newspapers are beginning to protest certain actions, including the latest McKellar raid on the merit system. Mr. Roosevelt is biding his time, inviting "freshmen" congressmen to a get-together, making compromises on the farm-party bill (which mean higher food costs for all of us), and holding his hand. Is this wise? I don't know. Some people advocate a head-on clash with the rebellious congressmen. But what does a president do in wartime when faced by a revolt that threatens the war effort?

The real danger in the situation is that isolationist leaders will turn the revolt to their own end and swing the congressional majority to what might ultimately result in a quiet sit-down strike against an all-out war. There are some indications that the situation is headed that way.

To meet the situation the president needs popular support. But here, if Washington correspondents are any judge, he runs into another problem. Is the president's franchise running out? There is a strong belief that it is, and that Mr. Roosevelt doesn't know it. From this distance, at any rate, 1944 doesn't look like a Democratic year.

The country's basic dissatisfaction, I think, lies not in petty irritations over sugar and shoe rations, or sectional or even group interests, but in a feeling of helplessness about the peace after the war. Again and again the argument comes back to that. The feeling is growing that maybe this is just another war. In the administration nobody but Wallace is saying much about things like postwar collective security, or associations of nations. The war is being fought against something, but not for something. The Four Freedoms are all right, but they have never been dramatized. The phrase does not warm the heart. Something more concrete is needed, some bolder stroke. Maybe the Sumner Welles speech at Toronto outlining plans for immediate postwar discussions means the start of something more specific. The mood of America reflected in Washington today is like that in the Civil War, before the Emancipation Proclamation.

And so, to be brief about it, I think the war needs a shot in the arm. What the country craves is a moral tonic. Announcement of specific, idealistic, postwar aims, or some approach to it, would help Mr. Roosevelt in Congress; it would help the men in the factories; it might give the boys in the trenches a lot of help, too. Laugh if you want. But when a man dies, he wants to die for something important.

The Trouble with Congress

MAY 31, 1943   Here are seven reasons I can think of, offhand, for disliking this Congress. I could probably think of more if I put my mind to it. Let me set them down and then generalize from them. This is really a big problem, Congress, and I have to go about it systematically.

1. The one basic need for meeting inflation is more taxes. There are other remedies but, come hell or high water, taxation is the biggest one. Mr. Roosevelt in January asked for $16,000,000,000 of extra taxes. In five months, in the midst of desperate war, with the domestic front menaced more by inflation, rising prices, black markets, consequent wage demands, and a loss of morale generally, than by any other single factor, Congress hasn't even yet touched the president's basic budget recommendation. This Congress is reckless.

2. This Congress is inefficient. Most of five months it has debated the Ruml plan which, even at best, is a technique for tax collection, not a bill for new taxes. Most of this time it has been helplessly deadlocked.

3. This Congress is parochial. After more taxes, a strong, unyielding hand at the price-control throttle is the thing most needed today on the domestic wartime front. Not this Congress, but the last, undermined Leon Henderson. This Congress has continued the sabotage with its farm and other local blocs, making effective control almost impossible.

4. This Congress is improvident. When the war ends, 30,000,000 workers and soldiers, at a conservative estimate, are going to be demobilized, close together. It will be America's major unemployment threat. Advance planning will save the public millions, indeed, almost certainly, billions. Congress isn't doing the planning itself, and it proposes either to kill the National Resources Planning Board, or to make an economic zombie out of this, the one agency that has been doing the job.

5. This Congress is ruthless. The whole world cries for food. Starving children in China are eating the bark from trees. The agency in America that has shown itself outstandingly able to increase food production, from low-bracket farmers, is the Farm Security Administration. Congress has attacked it from the start, and threatens its life. Also, Congress fights, tooth and nail, against farm subsidies to boost production.

6. This Congress—the House anyway—is lawless. In passing bills of attainder singling out Lovett, Dodd, and Watson it has revived something specifically forbidden by the Founding Fathers.

7. This Congress—the House anyway—is indecent. In naming Gene Cox (D) of Georgia to try the FCC when the FCC offered evidence that Cox had received $2,500 for helping a Georgia radio station get an FCC license, the House, in effect, put a judicial wig and robe on an accused man to try his own accusers.

And yet, when I have said these things, another, larger question arises; one which I must face if I am honest. What business have I to criticize Congress at a time when democratic legislatures all over the world are under attack? Men are dying—better men than I—giving their lives in malarial jungles and among Arctic snows to safeguard this Congress, this institution, these very Gene Coxes and Ham Fishes —God help us—and, above all, the tradition of free government. Where does that leave my attack?

It takes the matter back several stages and to higher ground. Personalities drop out. I must then talk about Congress, and not just this Congress. It brings up a personal conclusion I have come to after watching the legislature for some fifteen years. I do not think the caliber of men and legislation in Congress can be very much improved until the congressional system itself is improved. The trouble in Washington goes deeper than the men.

Judging by a column last week, I believe that Mr. Arthur Krock of the *New York Times* agrees with me in part. Mr. Henry Hazlitt, who writes *New York Times* editorials and is probably more conservative than Mr. Krock, agrees with me. Read his indictment of the Washington separation of powers in his book, *A New Constitution Now.*

Mr. Krock was impressed, as I was, by the speech of Winston Churchill to Congress. I looked down from the press gallery on Mr. Churchill's bald head and thought, as Mr. Krock indicates he did, what tragic folly it is that we do not have a system like that of the British, which brings the president and Congress, the executive and the legislative, automatically into closer contact. This speech of Churchill's would have been, for the House of Commons, just the usual routine normal affair from the majority leader. Why, asked American observers, can't we have the same thing here? Why not end the everlasting deadlock, delay, and rivalry between executive and legislative?

The answer is, of course, because of the rigidity of our governmental system. Under our separation of powers, antagonism between Congress and the executive is chronic. The basic fact in Washington under the division of powers is the absence of final responsibility. You can never fix the blame. And the delays are interminable.

Let us take the Ruml-plan debate. The House has a veto. The Senate has a veto. So does the president. Each one can deadlock the others but none has the corollary power of being able to enforce its own plan. And this happens again and again. It is true of the tax program, the action on NRPB and FSA. It is true of almost any measure you can think of.

Only a nation supremely gifted in self-government could make a system like this work for 150 years. But now it is in competition with tiger-swift dictatorships. On the answer to the question, can we have efficiency and still have Congress, may rest the future of democracy in America.

I hope I have made it plain that I don't care for this particular Congress. I think it is reactionary. But basically I think the fault lies deeper, and overwrought critics who simply let fly at Cox, Fish, Smith, Dies, et al., miss the point.

Put it this way: I have an old conduit on the roof of my house. Water collects there and stagnates. I have two possible methods of procedure. I can go up periodically and sweep the thing clear, down to the drain, or I can elevate one end of the conduit and it will drain itself out every time it rains. One reform deals with the symptoms, the other with the cause.

The War vs. "Normalcy"

November 15, 1943   President Roosevelt sat behind his desk. With his cigarette pointed at the eagle molded in the ceiling, he answered questions and told of the Chungking conference. Only at the end came the question uppermost in many minds, "How about the election, Mr. President?" The president was ready. Smilingly, he offered a neat gag line. He had enjoyed listening to the returns election night, he said, laughing—returns from the Russian front, Italy, and the Southwest Pacific! The reporters went out, grinning.

But for Democrats it wasn't so funny after all. Not even for Willkie. The returns proved the Republican tide is still coming in. And they reverse the old political formula that you can't beat somebody with nobody. The Republicans did that in half a dozen places. To Washington political writers the Kentucky result was most significant. Conservative reporters gave Democratic Donaldson a rock-bottom minimum of 25,000 votes—but the bottom caved in. Kentucky's four-year gubernatorial election has faithfully forecast for decades the presidential election in the year following.

The elections strengthened Dewey, weakened Willkie. Willkie's chief appeal has been that you need a positive point of view, intelligence, and liberalism to beat the New Deal. Republican politicians are going to cite the 1942 and 1943 elections to prove you don't. More than ever, Dewey can have the nomination—if he wants it. Here in Washington the indications are that observers' expectations are swinging from a Democratic to a Republican victory, probably going too far in the new direction as they did in the old.

The war still holds the answer. The war—and the jacked-up automobile in John Smith's garage. When the war ends, the tug of the car, and "normalcy," will be well-nigh irresistible. The letdown of morale and the lessening of tension that will come with victory are ready to play into the hands of Republican reaction. Will victory come before the next election? It is the great political imponderable.

I was one of the reporters who waited that long Sunday evening after Pearl Harbor on the pillared White House portico, watching a half moon climb the bare elm boughs on Pennsylvania Avenue, while members of the Senate Foreign Relations Committee entered and left. I shall never forget the breathless silence as Hiram Johnson arrived, passed silently through the path we made, and entered the glass doors, followed by all the ghosts of 1920. . . . Last week Hiram Johnson, an old, old man, got to his feet in the Senate and, in a voice so low that members crowded to surrounding desks, uttered a broken, choked prayer for America, joining a minute later with four others—Wheeler, Reynolds, Langer, and Shipstead—in the minority side of the 85-to-5 vote passing the amended Connally resolution.

It would be nice to believe that Hiram Johnson's prayer marked the passing of the old order. But I doubt it. Not after watching the preceding fortnight's debate. When all allowances are made for the historic importance and the implicit moral pledge in the Connally resolution, the fact remains that it has no legal or binding effect, and that the very size of its majority shows the vagueness of the gesture. Its control over senators is about like that of the Kellogg Pact's over aggressor states. Again and again as the Senate discussion progressed, amendments were brought up of the very pattern of those old "reservations" whose cumulative effect was to kill the League of Nations under the archaic two-thirds rule. The Revercomb amendment, for instance, stipulated that any future American international action should be taken by the orthodox treaty route. It was defeated 54 to 28 (less than two-thirds). Each reservation like this is capable of knocking off one or two disgruntled supporters in a close fight.

A Look at the Seventy-eighth Congress

J ANUARY 3, 1944   When President Roosevelt goes before Congress in about a week to give his formal report on the Stalin-Churchill-Chiang talks there are now indications that he will also give vent to a growing irritation over the domestic front, for which Congress is very largely responsible. And it is just possible that by the time Congress reconvenes on January 10, after talking to the voters, it may be in a slightly chastened mood. The plain fact is that Congress has been going too far; even for reaction there is a limit.

The story of the first session of the Seventy-eighth Congress is now complete. Here is a brief recapitulation, for the sake of the record. It killed the National Youth Administration, the National Resources Planning Board, the Home Owners' Loan Corporation; it let the Guffey coal act expire, and slashed funds of the OPA [Office of Price Administration] and the OWI [Office of War Information]. It stripped rural resettlement and crop insurance from the Farm Security Administration, emasculated grade labeling, and is now gunning for the FCC. It repealed the president's $25,000 salary-limitation order, slashed the Treasury's tax program to one-fifth, and proposed to emasculate the contract-renegotiation law, opening the sluice to huge war profiteering.

Until it was halted by a national outcry, Congress seemed bent on ending all food subsidies and on preventing soldiers from voting. As the servile puppet of pressure groups, it has voted favors to the petroleum interests, the dairy interests, and many others. It passed bills of attainder against Goodwin Watson, William E. Dodd, and seventy-three-year-old Professor Robert Morss Lovett, who gave a son in World War I.

Even more significant is the fact that this Congress is almost wholly negative; it has shown no leadership for constructive planning in world crisis. It killed the federal aid-to-education bill, halted the prescribed increases of old-age and unemployment-security funds, and met the recommendation for an "American Beveridge Plan" by ignoring the report and killing the National Resources Planning Board, which offered it.

Congress has set up its own bottleneck "committee on postwar planning" under Chairman George, which did nothing from March to November, and now seems only interested in freezing the big profits in war contracts. Last April President Roosevelt appealed to Congress for a $7,700,000,000 federal-state-local postwar public works program; last May he asked for an initial $85,000,000 to get the program into the blueprint stage; in September, in a letter to Majority Leader McCormack, he asked for quick action on a river and harbor bill of postwar projects. He hasn't yet had any response on any of these matters.

There are signs that the public is getting fed up with Congress. It isn't that the administration is getting popular by contrast, but that the sheer ineptitude, partisanship, and cowardice of Congress are beginning to worry the home folks, the kind of family that has a service flag in the front window. And the queer thing about it is that all this time a breath of liberalism is running through many of America's fighting allies. The Chinese and Russian masses know that victory holds better prospects for them. New Zealand and Australia have Labor governments which came through autumn elections with flying colors. In Canada the successes of the radical CCF (Cooperative Commonwealth Federation) are scaring the life out of the older parties and forcing a new approach to postwar problems. In Britain, the common man's demand for a better postwar world has taken shape in the Beveridge Plan. Only America is fighting under the lusterless banner of "Status Quo"; only America has "peace panics" on the stock market; only America has the Seventy-eighth Congress.

Mr. Roosevelt's implied criticism of Congress in his Christmas broadcast, following his rather ostentatious scrapping of his "New Deal" label, is interpreted by some here as the start of the fourth-term candidacy. Without going that far, it is still possible to say that rarely has a Congress made such an opening for executive jibes and that if Mr. Roosevelt wants to, he will know what to do.

Barkley Resigns

MARCH 6, 1944   The Barkley resignation episode was good drama, whatever else it was. Reporters were on the Senate floor at five minutes to twelve for their customary chat with the majority leader. Mr. Barkley brushed in stormily with Leslie Biffle, secretary of the Democratic majority. "Don't argue with me, my mind is made up!" he ejaculated. The secretary withdrew, crestfallen. Mr. Barkley had baffled Biffle.

As the session began, Mr. Barkley paced nervously through the preliminaries, sending a Senate page for the wooden lectern from which to read his speech. As in most really great scenes in Congress, the public galleries were about two-thirds empty. The press gallery, however, was jam-packed, and as the word spread, members of the House trooped over and stood all around the rear.

Mr. Barkley normally has an easy, extemporaneous delivery, but in this case, because he stuck to text, he stumbled badly. There was no doubt of his emotion, however, and the Senate was dead silent. Nobody had ever heard a majority leader denounce his own party president before.

Barkley started his speech with only about six printed pages of text, and elderly, fusty, Senator McKellar "ran copy" for him as he continued, bringing in freshly typed pages on two occasions just as Mr. Barkley seemed on the point of running out. A tempestuous Washington day sent alternating shadows and sun through the translucent double-glass roof as Barkley proceeded—a wonderful melodramatic effect worthy of Hollywood. Newsmen had their bulletins—"Barkley resigns"—all written, for the word of his determination was generally known by now. When Mr. Barkley actually uttered the word, there was a tremendous uproar in the press gallery, transcending all decorum, as copyrunners sprinted up the steps and swept through the rear swinging glass doors with the "flash." All their lives that stampede of feet will haunt newsmen who heard it. Following this, members on all sides rose and applauded, in defiance of Senate rules, while Barkely sat, flushed and heavy and a little anxious: a normally mild, easygoing, gum-chewing, and likable politician, strung up now to the greatest scene of his life.

What did it all amount to? Primarily, I think, that a phony issue had been substituted for a real one. The phony issue is Mr. Roosevelt's alleged "usurpation of powers." The real issue is what columnist Ernest Lindley trenchantly describes as "full mobilization v. moneymaking and politics-as-usual." For the smudging of the real issue I think Mr. Roosevelt must take part of the blame.

If the reader will go back and study the texts of Mr. Roosevelt's annual message, budget message, soldiers'-vote appeal, and now the two veto messages (all five since the first of January), he will find a definite pattern running through them. The commander in chief is trying to rouse the nation to measure up to its responsibilities—to fight a "hard" war. But Congress wants a "soft" war. In no place is the issue drawn more sharply than on taxes. Mr. Roosevelt is overwhelmingly right on taxes. The country can and should pay more revenue, and the failure to do so may be measured in a host of problems now and later.

But it is not sufficient for a political leader, who is also commander-in-chief, to be merely right on a subject; he must also, alas, be successful. In this tax veto Mr. Roosevelt took a bad licking which seemingly might have been avoided. The defeat was in two parts. First, the veto itself was overridden, almost certainly as a result of the Barkley speech, the most important permanent effect of this being the probable "freezing" of social-security contributions for keeps, which means a radical alteration of the whole fiscal setup. The second result was the bigger danger to Mr. Roosevelt's own prestige as war leader, and the obfuscation of the basic issue of backing up the boys at the front, on which the president may be basing his fourth-term campaign.

Personally I do not question Mr. Barkley's good faith. He is an easygoing conservative, and one of the instruments upon which a president must lean. Mr. Barkley tried to protest the veto message at the preceding Monday legislative conference at the White House. Mr. Roosevelt certainly did not realize the depth of Barkley's emotion. Mr. Roosevelt is slightly deaf in his left ear, and occasionally declines to listen out of his right. From what I gather, this seems to have been one of those times. Changes in phraseology here and there would probably have made Barkley's protest perfunctory.

Mr. Roosevelt was also handicapped in this fight by his failure to pave the way for it by proper militancy over taxes in the past. His sound tax proposals have generally cried in vain for hard-hitting defense. One reason has been an excessively timid secretary of the treasury who, like some other cabinet members, is a political liability rather than an asset. It wasn't like this in Ogden Mills's time.

The chief thing to note is that the fight isn't over yet. Mr. Roosevelt may be staking his war leadership on it. He is backing a "hard" war, and the question is whether the public will support him. With the cross-channel invasion and the worst casualties of the war just ahead, Mr. Roosevelt may once more prove himself a better judge of public sentiment than a halfhearted Congress.

War and the Future

APRIL 3, 1944   The forsythia bush outside the White House is as yellow as a pat of butter. President Roosevelt is recovering from another in a succession of head colds. He looks pallid and wan. An election, a world war, and a head cold—it is enough to bog down any man. It doesn't bog down Roosevelt. He has an elastic humor in small things. There is a laugh in nearly every press conference: as when he said with mock helplessness that Steve Early had "edited" both Lowell Mellett's informal letter of resignation and his own racy reply. Grinning Early and Mellett were both present. Roosevelt reaches for these laughs like a stratosphere flyer for an oxygen mask when the strain gets too great.

Yes, it's spring again in Washington. And here is a World Boxscore as the robins sing.

War.—A million, or maybe more, men are posed for invasion in England. . . . Russians have pushed the southern front back to the border where it started. . . . The Allies are bogged in Italy. . . . German cities and air forces are being ground down. . . . The outer Jap defensive ring has been pierced.

Diplomatic.—Signs of disunity are appearing among the Allies. . . . Stalin has recognized Badoglio in what appears to be a fit of pique. . . . Both Churchill and Hull-Roosevelt feel the need of satisfying growing democratic restiveness over the interpretations of the Atlantic Charter.

Domestic.—The third wartime presidential election in history is now warming up popular passions. . . . Dewey accumulating strength by saying nothing. . . . Willkie making some of the best speeches in his career. . . . Bricker busily looking backward. . . . MacArthur being used to spearhead isolationist and nationalist groups that will switch later, probably to Dewey. . . . Roosevelt, with an aging cabinet, still the hope of most liberals, holding his fire in what looks to be his hardest race.

Future.—All sorts of traps stand in the way of World War II's meaning anything. . . . There is the trap of Allied disunity. . . . Of inability to work the constitutional division of powers between president and Congress. . . . The trap of the Senate two-thirds treaty rule. . . . Of postwar inflation, with Eccles testifying last week that the "inflationary potential" will be $194,000,000,000 as of next June 30.

Thought.—What a sardonic joke it would be for the inspired inventors of that social satire, the game called Monopoly, to bring out now its sequel, called Victory, with the stakes reckoned not in terms of token dollars but in batches of ten thousand, a hundred thousand, a million human lives. If the Senate and president couldn't agree on a peace treaty, say, the player would move back 20 years and lose 100 tokens, representing a million lives.

The Senate revolt over the TVA will probably be blocked in part by the House, but it is symptomatic. During a war the growing resistance of Congress is directed at the executive. In the best of times, under the divided system of constitutional control, the powers of the president and of Congress are in an uneasy balance. But in wartime, power automatically gravitates to the president. Like it or not, the Congress has to go along on military matters. Congress bides its time. When the war ends there is normally a great explosion of pent-up irritation. Such an explosion spoiled the peace after the Civil War; it hamstrung Wilson's peace after World War I. It is one of the reasons why America is better at making war than at making peace. Thus far, Mr. Roosevelt has managed to placate Congress in many particulars. But more and more Congress has tended to kick over the traces on domestic matters. The Senate TVA battle is the latest example of the mood. Under vindictive McKellar, the upper chamber voted to throw 27,000 federal jobs into the political grab-bag, by requiring senatorial confirmation (something the House will reject not, alas, from lofty motives, but primarily because it increases Senate, not House, patronage); it ordered the TVA to come annually to Congress for financing; it voted to wipe out Mr. Roosevelt's Fair Employment Practice Committee, designed to promote racial fairness; and took a vicious swipe at a dozen other agencies.

Meanwhile, over on the House side, the Foreign Affairs Committee inserted "restrictive" amendments into the Lend-Lease-extension bill, designed to prevent this agency from effecting postwar commitments without specific congressional approval. These and other developments show the present congressional mood. It is apt to be increasingly belligerent as peace draws nearer.

An argument for Dewey, and one that is almost certain to be strongly urged if he is nominated, is that his election would reconcile legislature and executive, and avoid the unfortunate postwar congressional explosion. This would be true, however, only if (a) Dewey, or the Republican incumbent, carried along with him decisive party majorities in both houses, and if (b) the so-called honeymoon period had not expired before the war came to its close. If there were any insurance that president and Congress could really work in harmony for constructive goals after this war, almost any candidate would be worth ardent support. Unfortunately, constitutional and political experience shows there is no such guarantee.

Fala Speech

O c t o b e r 2 , 1 9 4 4   The Roosevelt speech of last Saturday was given to the press at 7:00 P.M. As reporters skimmed through the advance, shouts of glee and excited exclamations of enjoyment went up and were called from typewriter to typewriter. "Have you got to that part about Fala?" somebody would cry. "Yes—but did you see what he says about John L. Lewis?" The feeling was best summed up by a correspondent who has followed the president since his first swing around the circle: "He's back in the old 1932 groove."

The question was, would he put it over? As I write this I am just back from the ballroom of the Statler Hotel. The last member of Dan Tobin's brotherhood whom I saw was battering a tablespoon against a silver-plated cake-holder in an ecstasy of enjoyment.

The interesting thing about Mr. Roosevelt is the pleasure he him-self seems to get out of these affairs. I have watched him give speeches now for twelve years and I never saw him enjoy one more than this. It was the Old Maestro himself, past master of the various platform arts of which perhaps, when all is said and done, laughter is as effective as any. There have been few politicians in America who have been sure enough of themselves to use laughter and keep their dignity, and Mr. Roosevelt is one of them; and here he used humor against a humorless opponent, which made the contrast all the more striking.

From where I was, just beneath Mr. Roosevelt, it was fun to look up and see him put over a special bit. His face would become deadpan, he would catch the right degree of emphasis (often interpolating a word or two), he would lead into his gag line, time it just right, and then come out with it with inexpressible drollery and relish, as when he answered Representative Knutson's absurd charge about Fala: "I think I have a right to object to libelous statements about my dog!"

Well, well, this has little to do with the solemn matters of the day, but one has to admit that campaigning with Mr. Roosevelt is fun. And Republicans who charged that the Bremerton address was "po-litical" ought to be able to tell the difference between a Roosevelt political and nonpolitical speech, after this.

The anxious observer of national affairs finds considerable danger in all this electioneering and must constantly ask himself how much bitter-ness it will leave, and what effect it will have on the nonpartisan American cooperation which is so vital when the campaign is ended. The lines of the forthcoming Senate struggle over League of Nations No. Two, for example, are already appearing. Make no doubt about it, isolationism has not disappeared; it has merely been transformed into "nationalism" and the double line of attack on the Dumbarton Oaks international-security agency is already pretty clear. In the first place, the Senate's Wheelers, Bushfields, Bridges, et al., will object to having the nation join any league until the main body of the peace settlement is written and approved. The latter, as Senators Ball and Burton have pointed out, cannot possibly please everybody. Suppose some senator demands that India be freed and this is not included in the world settlement—then will he argue that America shall not join a new league on that account? The second line of attack will be to seek to delay permission for America to answer the international fire-alarm, if a new military conflagration is threatened by some aggressor, until a formal debate has been held and a vote taken. Germany crushed Poland in twenty-six days, and such a Senate debate might be protracted by isolationists for three months.

What particularly impresses this writer is the shortness of notice the next war is going to give. I have seen the robot bombs flaming in the sky over London, and felt the earth shake when they hit near me. War, my friends, has been utterly transformed. I do not see how this can be too much stressed. After, say, about ten years—if what may be man's last chance at setting up a workable league fails—emplacements for robot bombs may be set up all over Europe, bombs of new and deadlier varieties, pointed across international boundaries at all the principal cities of the Continent. The next war will be fought by automata. And when war comes, it will not be by diplomatic formalities; somebody will just press a button and all the opposing cities will go up in the air at once—whoosh! This is not a nightmare: the robot bomb is here, and has come to stay.

Roosevelt–Dewey

NOVEMBER 13, 1944 I watched the president give all of his big campaign speeches. I suppose I heard half of Dewey's radio talks. Here are things I remember:

Stumbling from our chilly Cadillac at Ebbets Field, Brooklyn, running through pouring rain and sodden leaves to the park, discovering the president, in an open car, smiling, rain streaming from his glasses and wind whipping down the sleeve of his upraised right arm, addressing the crowd . . . then thinking about the wet, cold, smiling man up ahead as we continued the fifty-mile ride; the vast crowd at Soldiers' Field, Chicago, the stadium holding 100,000 people—heads with no bodies—the strange, glaring, unnatural lights on the thick, green lakefront grass, the feeling of never having been so lonely as in that strange, vast human backdrop; the rollicking enjoyment of Roosevelt's teamsters' speech, after a good meal in the glitter and comfort of the Statler, the feeling that in virtuosity and delivery it was the best technical performance he ever put on; the dawning disappointment at Dewey's first radio speech at Philadelphia, hoping for a man worthy of the times and listening to the embittered prosecuting attorney's charge that the administration was plotting to keep boys in the army; the sonorous, cold perfection of the Dewey delivery night after night on the radio, running the gamut of emotion from A to B and possessing all a speaker should have except warmth, humor, and fellow feeling; the smother of reporters round Joe Ball's Senate office desk, and the slow, half-hesitant, earnest replies as he staked his political future on the belief that the soldiers' hopes should be placed above party regularity. . . . Well, well, well! Quite an election, quite an election.

I have trouped with Roosevelt since '32. The newest gadget is the loudspeaker system inside the train, and the evolution of the work car for the press, with long shelves on the sides for typewriters, like lunch counters, and the rear-platform speech piped back on amplifiers, right into the car.

In contrast to the dislike of Dewey on his special train, the correspondents with Mr. Roosevelt generally favored him. Only eleven out of forty polled by Don Pryor thought Dewey the better man; all but two (despite Gallup) bet Mr. Roosevelt's reelection. I know only one with a venomous hatred—a correspondent who was proceeding to Hyde Park on the off chance that he could be the one to put that suave, final, fatal question to the defeated candidate, "And what, sir, are your future plans?" . . . Incidentally, most of the Dewey correspondents didn't think he could survive a defeat politically, that the GOP would bob up with an ex-general, or war hero, in 1948.

The campaign is over, or at least it will be when the soldiers' votes are counted, and a good many editorial writers (who might have favored Mr. Roosevelt but for the business office) will comfort their egos by maintaining that at any rate Democracy has been Vindicated, the Great Republic has shown its Fundamental Strength, by holding a peaceful referendum in the midst of War. The old pap. What are the facts? In the midst of an agonizing struggle, the object of which is to win our second and perhaps final chance to work out a world order, we are forced by an inflexible constitution to take time out to fight an internal battle which only a minority of rabid Roosevelt-haters could have wanted at this particular time. This battle unleashed ugly and dirty partisanship, bound, in a close contest, to weaken either successful candidate.

To be frank about it, friends, from this Washington viewpoint, I take no rosy view of the affair. True, both candidates endorsed the world security organization, and here Mr. Dewey deserves credit. But latent isolationism clearly revealed itself and many GOP pledges of internationalism carried the half-threat that they were invalid if Dewey lost.

Another thing must be set down frankly. Neither candidate—and this specifically includes Mr. Roosevelt—met the full-employment issue squarely. Governor Dewey doesn't know the answer; President Roosevelt may know it, but is afraid to give it. The brutal fact is that the public is enjoying a war boom and won't be disturbed. Its preference for economic sleepwalking is parallel now on the home front to the time when Mr. Roosevelt gave his prewar "quarantine" speech and then backed away from it, because the public didn't want to hear the truth about foreign aggressors. Most modern economists agree that we must pass bold tax, social-security, fiscal, public-works, federal control, and relief measures if we are to do what no free-economy nation has ever done hitherto—stabilize a boom. But Congress won't hear of it, no matter who's president. Governmental instru-mentalities to handle a mixed economy (to take over, let us say, the $15 billion of government-owned war factories) have not yet been evolved in the United States, although they are the commonplace of Scandinavian and British democracies. America must seemingly have Depression No. 2 as she had World War II, before she convinces her-self that playing ostrich doesn't solve problems—and gets sand in the eyes.

Once more this presidential campaign showed curious examples of the news blackout imposed by the overwhelmingly Republican press.

Baltimore, Boston, Detroit, Pittsburgh, Toledo, Cleveland—to name a few—had no Democratic newspapers. Lack of funds hampered the Democrats, many of their radio programs being cut short for financial reasons. Roosevelt made only eight major speeches; Dewey made three times that number, many expensively rebroadcast next day. Probably the 1940 ratio will be exceeded this year; then the GOP spent $15 million for Willkie and senatorial candidates, according to the Gillette Committee, the Democrats only $6 million.

FDR's Death

> Now he belongs to the ages. EDWIN M. STANTON, *April 15, 1865, speaking of the assassinated Lincoln.*

APRIL 13, 1945   As these lines are written, the balmy air of a soft spring night comes into my open office window. Up and down the corridors of the Press Building, shirt-sleeved newspapermen are writing desperately against morning-paper deadlines. Below me, across the alley comes the rumble of the big presses—the newspaper across the way has just started out its "bulldog" edition with the great black headlines.

I have just come in here from the White House. The sidewalk in front has been roped off. It was like this on the night of Pearl Harbor. The people stand across the street and look at the building. They don't do or say anything—just stand and look. The crowd has been here since shortly after 6:00 P.M. It was here as the sun was setting behind the new verdure of the elm trees that arch the great Pennsylvania Avenue. You would think a parade was coming down the street. But only cars with silent people drive up to the White House; and away again.

Inside the executive wing, it recalls again that Pearl Harbor afternoon. Correspondents and radiocasters are standing, working, feverishly writing, telephoning, or talking into the microphones that the big radiocasting companies have set up. They are friends, and I know them all. Every now and then one stops, and speaks in a quiet voice. A queer, bewildered look comes into his face. It seems impossible for anyone to realize what has happened. It is easier to dash back into work again, to get rid of that empty feeling.

A little after 7:00 P.M. Mrs. Roosevelt left the White House. We saw her go—tall, erect, in black—leaving by airplane for Warm Springs. She is, I think, a brave woman. When given the news, she said, "I am more sorry for the people of the country and the world than I am for us." She sent telegrams to her four sons, all in the armed services. She told them in her message, according to Steve Early, that their father had done his job to the end, as he would want them to do. She added, "Bless you all and all our love." She signed it, "Mother."

Now I am back here at my desk, thinking what to say about Franklin Roosevelt. I followed him through most of his election trips. I was with him in 1932, in 1936, in 1940, and again in 1944. I think I heard nearly every campaign speech he ever made, every speech in Congress, every inaugural. And I have seen him countless times in the past dozen years at press conferences, and watched the lines deepen in his face.

I think the time I admired him most was on the occasion in the last campaign when—to silence charges about his health—he rode four hours in an open car, in and out of the boroughs of Greater New York, as the cold, intermittent rain came down, sometimes pelting him with sodden leaves, sometimes turning to a drizzle.

The six of us in Car 24 climbed in and sat shivering. We were all reporters. Every one of our papers was supporting his opponent, Governor Thomas E. Dewey; two were bitterly vindictive against Mr. Roosevelt. But I remember how we got into our particular press car, after watching Mr. Roosevelt stand ten minutes in the drenching rain at Ebbets Field, Brooklyn, as he delivered a talk, and looked at one another. It was cold and damp enough in our closed car, huddled together for warmth. How could that sixty-two-year-old man, up there in front, out in the rain, smiling and waving to the knots of people huddled under newspapers to protect their hats—how could he stand it?

"Well, you got to admire him. . . ." growled his most savage critic.

Before I came down tonight to write this story, the telephone rang. A friend had called to tell the news. It seemed like Pearl Harbor again, monstrous and unbelievable—this time without the exhilarating excitement. She told how the United Press "ticker," out of the clear sky, suddenly had begun to ring its little alarm bell. People came running to get the "flash." That was 5:48 P.M.

It was a queer sensation for my whole family, trying to adjust ourselves to the new world. "I think I know how how they felt," I said, "in this same city, when Walt Whitman wrote his poem about Lincoln."

I was surprised that both my daughters had learned it at school. This is the way it went:

> O Captain! my Captain! our fearful trip is done,
> The ship has weathered every rack, the prize we sought is won.
> The port is near, the bells I hear, the people all exulting,
> While follow eyes the steady keel, the vessel grim and daring.

And then the rest of it; they repeated it very solemnly:

> The ship is anchored safe and sound, its voyage closed and done.
> From fearful trip the victor ship comes in with object won.

But where is the captain who brought the great ship into port?

That was in this same month in this same city, eighty years ago lacking three days.

I first met Mr. Roosevelt when I joined his presidential campaign train in the fall of 1932 for the *Christian Science Monitor*. Paul Leach of the *Chicago Daily News* and I were taken back to the last car on the candidate's special train. There we met a large, smiling, self-confident, magnetic man, sitting in a big chair. From time to time, he would wave out of the window as the train slowed down, to crowds outside. Leaning on the shoulder of his bodyguard or son James, he would appear at station stops.

It was my first discovery that the man who was to be four times elected president could not stand or walk without braces. They were painful, and could not be used without practice. Yet I have seen Mr. Roosevelt time after time since then walk in those trying affairs—

before a joint session of Congress or some great gathering—in long, unnatural steps supported on either side in a position that never failed to bring a startled hush to the audience, only to be broken in a sudden burst of applause that came from political friends and foes alike—applause that I never heard given to any other man, and that was as much as anything a tribute to his gay, indomitable courage. Unfailingly he responded with a grin and a characteristic throw of his head, then later, when he got his hand free, a cheery wave.

I know Mr. Roosevelt had many political foes. I was far from an admirer of him myself when I met him, and I have disagreed with many of his acts since. But to the best of my recollection, I know of only one or two who had personally met Mr. Roosevelt who did not like him, however much they may have differed with him. He was gay, at least in his outward contacts; nobody ever enjoyed being president more.

Last year at the Quebec Conference, Mr. Roosevelt's open automobile waited as the big special train pulled in with Prime Minister Winston Churchill. Circumstances and the crowd pushed me right up against the Roosevelt car as the British prime minister, followed by a little cluster, strode forward to see his old friend. I was so near as practically to be taking part in the conversation. What I remember most was the look of affection on the faces of the two men as they clasped hands and the discovery that they addressed each other—at least in the excitement of this greeting—by their first names. "Hello, Winston!" "Hello, Franklin!"

Steve Early tells me that the prime minister has been careful, under normal circumstances, to address the other as "Mr. President." But in this moment it was a more intimate salutation. Who knows but that history was changed by the fact that at a moment of crisis the two leaders were on a first-name basis? He told me, too, in the warmth of recollection at Quebec, that the same look of liking—call it affection if you like—came into Premier Joseph Stalin's eye when he talked to the president. It was one of Mr. Roosevelt's great achievements that he kept the grand alliance of forty nations in being throughout the war; it was largely the feat of one man.

The great fact about Mr. Roosevelt, I think, was that he worked under a sense of history; he was conscious of history at all times. No reporter who covered Washington can fail to remember the change in atmosphere in the electric spring of 1933. "The only thing we need to fear," he said, "is fear itself." He was aware of what he did and said; he shrewdly dramatized his position.

My two favorite estimates of Mr. Roosevelt are both by historians, seeking to appraise him. The first, by Morison and Commager, in their *Growth of the American Republic*, describes him as "a liberal rather than a radical . . . with a confidence in the common man as instinctive as that which Bryan cherished, and as rationalized as Wilson professed." He was no revolutionary, they point out; he worked within the constitutional pattern. "With shrewdness he combined audacity and courage; he was tenacious of ultimate ends, opportunistic as to means, and preferred compromise to strife."

Another famous historian, Charles A. Beard, declared Mr. Roosevelt had taken up "more fundamental problems of American life and society than all the other presidents combined.

"Whatever else may happen, it seems safe to say that President Roosevelt has made a more profound impression upon the political, social, and economic thought of America than any, or all, of his predecessors."

It is just midnight now, and I must stop writing. All this time the news ticker in the next room has been jerking out copy on yellow paper—an effort to grasp what has occurred, about Mr. Truman's taking office, the new plans, and page on page of comment and eulogy. Secretary of War Stanton said it all eighty years ago: "Now he belongs to the ages." But Senator Arthur H. Vandenberg gave a comment to newspapermen earlier in the evening that should be added. With all past differences put aside, it is as true of Mr. Roosevelt as it might have been true of Lincoln. It is brief, very brief, half hope, half prayer, and who will not agree with it?—

"A successful peace must be his monument."

[Since TRB went to press before the news of FDR's death, Strout wrote this article for the *Christian Science Monitor*.]

THE TRUMAN YEARS
[*1945-1952*]

The Greatest Scientific Gamble in History

AUGUST 20, 1945   When wars come to an end people have to start thinking again. If they don't—more wars. Up to a fortnight ago the great unanswered postwar riddle was: Can capitalist United States and communist Russia cooperate? Now there is the new riddle: What shall we do with the atomic bomb?

It is the measure of President Roosevelt that he had the audacity and imagination to invest secretly close to two billion dollars in the greatest scientific gamble in history. In a vague way, newspapermen heard what was going on. There were censorship requests not to discuss three, among several other, subjects: (1) radar, (2) whether and how soon Russia would join in the Pacific war, and (3) the mysterious matter of atomic disintegration. In this column of July 23, I included the comment that, in bombing, "the evolution of destructiveness is still accelerating, and the Japanese have something new to learn." But the revelation, when it came, was incomparably greater than anyone had expected. In a short week man learned that he had at last found how to blow himself up. I do not mean to strike any pose of gloom, but what is there in past history to encourage a cosmic insurance company to take out a policy on the Earth? The next big war may very well blow us out of the solar system. At any rate, we now have our choice.

The terrible moral decision to use the atomic bomb was made by a few people. I suppose its use was inevitable. Once you invest two billion dollars in a firecracker you have to light it. Personally, I am sick and tired of decisions like this being made in secret, including those at Potsdam; of all the restrictions to be relaxed by peace I think it is most important to relax the practice of having great decisions made by a few people. For the atomic bomb, it could justly be argued that in the short-range view it shortened the war and saved lives, though from the longer view we may all regret that it was ever employed. I understand the group of international scientists and advisers, which included Secretary Byrnes, originally recommended against its use. When it was used it was dropped on two crowded cities, obliterating two-thirds of the first, and a considerable part of the second.

The fantastic situation is now presented of the United States and Britain possessing a potentially world-destroying invention which, for the time, anyway, we are not going to share with other countries, meaning Russia. If this is not melodrama I don't know it. We are an optimistic people and must assume that some international machinery will be set up to handle the bomb. Among my friends I find a curious new sense of insecurity, rather incongruous in the face of military victory. If it is felt deeply enough to make for world action, maybe it will save us all yet.

Russia entered the war punctually ninety days after V-E Day, and censorship restrictions are consequently lifted on that subject. It turns out that President Roosevelt had attended to that matter, too, at Yalta. Most informed correspondents here, I believe, had understood Russia would come in.

As to radar, the censorship has also lifted the wraps on that this week. Radar accounted for some of the startling events of the war, for example, the defeat of the U-boat; it provided the slim margin of Allied victory again and again in the early days of the struggle, notably the Battle of Britain, the victories over the Italian fleet in the Mediterranean, and our success off Guadalcanal. Now the secret is out, and the story can be told. Only second to the atomic bomb, radar was the most dramatic and decisive weapon of the war. A revolution in our patent system seems likely in the peacetime efforts to exploit these two great new lines of invention, both of them developed by scientific collectivism.

As the orchestra plays and the curtain goes up on history's next epoch, President Truman becomes a party leader. When peace comes to the Pacific it means political war in Washington. All these months we have pointed to the staggering problems of reconversion. Well, we shall now see how well we are prepared. To date Mr. Truman's popularity has rested largely on public sympathy extended to him in his heavy role, and to the fact that on many domestic issues he has not strongly committed himself. He has remained all things to all men. Now he must come out of his wraps. Censorship is going to be unveiled on Mr. Truman, too. He has got to choose sides, he has got to stop writing nice notes to Congress on crucial domestic issues that divide conservatives from liberals, and begin throwing his weight around. Mr. Truman has done a good job on international affairs. He has shown modesty, common sense, and a considerable gift for leadership in the emergency period. Meanwhile some of his appointees at home have been disappointing. The real test begins now.

Envoy Winant in London gets $17,500, the sum fixed for ambassadorial salaries by Congress in 1856 and never since changed. It is subject to income tax. In addition he gets tax-free allowances to cover such matters as rent and some entertainment, amounting to $12,080.

Envoy Halifax in Washington, on the other hand, gets a tax-free allowance of $70,000 a year. He receives no salary, to free him from the burden of income tax.

This contrast in Anglo-American diplomatic pay illustrates the singular parsimony of rich Uncle Sam when it comes to foreign representation. Entertainment costs are heavy, and Americans of low income just can't afford the job. To a lesser degree the low salary scale is true of subordinate ranks in our foreign service. Peru's ambassador in Washington gets about half as much again as does the United States envoy in Peru.

Secretary of State Byrnes is about to give his department a shake-up, on top of the one that Mr. Stettinius administered. The facts indicate that something more is needed than a change in personnel. We should not debar the use of first-class middle-income and poor men from the diplomatic career service at a time when the atomic bomb has made the need of competent international handling all the more apparent.

The First Six Months

OCTOBER 15, 1945   Impeccably dressed Harry S. Truman, standing alert behind his White House desk, with three neat folds of a matching handkerchief protruding, just so, from his breast pocket, has now been president six months this Friday, October 12.

Each president's burden seems impossible at the time, and Mr. Truman's is no exception. Roosevelt was free from international problems for a long enough time at the start of his twelve years to put through a reform program. Mr. Truman has had no such interval; his task is all mixed up: reconversion and world affairs, atomic-energy control and Lend-Lease—they all overlap. Peace has brought him immediate problems perhaps as great as those of war, without the same national unity to help solve them.

Outstanding in six months' development was Mr. Truman's message to Congress, a long, humdrum document which nevertheless placed him definitely on the liberal side and picked up most of the Roosevelt New Deal reforms. It ended the political honeymoon, finally dispelled conservative illusions, and ensured opposition from the Right. Now Mr. Truman faces growing opposition from the Left because he has not yet shown adequate vigor in pushing his program. In general, six months have confirmed Mr. Truman as a well-intentioned, politically minded middle-roader, of higher caliber than some feared and of weaker leadership than some hoped. In fairness to the president, however, it should be said that the evidence is not yet all in. He is still trying to establish his ascendency in his own party, and he is feeling out the temper of the conservative Congress.

The British debt negotiations illustrate the importance of the presidential role. Public opinion polls show the man-in-the-street ignorant of the critical need of bailing out the British, and unaware of the disaster to global trade if the world's dollar and sterling areas are blocked off into rival and antagonistic elements. I think it is fair to say that the team of American debt negotiators here are aware of the situation and are sympathetic to the British. But they are tempted to follow the old line, not of what is the right solution, but what is the solution that Congress (reflecting the voters' current ignorance) will approve. This is what happened after World War I, when politicians lacked the courage to face facts on debts and reparations, and instead left a festering controversy to poison Allied relationships and foster isolationism for twenty years. It is encouraging that in the past week powerful voices like the Luce publications, and middle-road columnists like Lippmann, George Fielding Eliot, and others, have begun to speak out militantly on the matter. Roosevelt never got around to explaining Lend-Lease to the masses, as he intended. According to the actual Lend-Lease agreement, for example, help in winning the war might be considered sufficient payment for America's aid. The problem is really up to Truman. Like a good many other things, it is a test of political courage. He alone has the public's ear and can tell the story simply and candidly. The time has nearly come when he must do it.

The St. Lawrence Seaway bill has a pretty good chance of passage—thirty years late. It would have been of inestimable value in World Wars I and II; it was blocked, of course, by the Constitution. A great majority of the people and the states have wanted the seaway—a glance at a map is the best argument for it—but the constitutional requirement of a two-thirds Senate majority for approving a treaty has hitherto put it in the power of a minority of senators to block it. They did that in 1934. Opponents are the railroads, the power companies, and dog-in-manger rival seaports. The two-thirds treaty provision is probably embedded in the Constitution for keeps, but more and more, as its undemocratic and harmful nature is realized, means are being found to circumvent it. In this instance a resolution has been drawn up utilizing a prior agreement with Canada, by which the waterway can come to both houses of Congress for a direct majority vote, rather than by the cumbersome treaty route. It should pass.

Unfortunately, the seaway will be late. The cost of the whole thing, I am told, would have been paid for by lower transportation rates in the past war, if the seaway had been dug earlier. But better late than never. Surplus power from contemplated hydroelectric developments will be no mean benefit. Seaway advocate Senator Aiken of Vermont tells me that New England and New York are now paying $300 million more annually in electricity bills than they would under TVA rates.

Senator O'Mahoney and others have put a brake on what looked like one of the biggest spoils grabs of public property in years. Just as the Departments of Justice and the Interior had worked out a court test to decide which—state or federal government—had sovereign title to fabulously rich underwater oil deposits in tidelands, an oil lobby rushed a bill through the House guaranteeing the title to the states. The bill went through without a record vote, almost unnoticed, 108 to 11. What it meant was that instead of letting the courts decide the matter, Congress would hand title over to the states, which, in the case of California, are already committed to turning the whole domain over to private oil companies. If a court decides that the undersea oil land is federal property, then the oil belongs to you and me. The House proposes to give it all away, without even letting a court decide whether you and I have an interest. Fortunately a fight has developed in the Senate to block HR 344. Last year the fire-insurance-company lobby tried to do the same thing: push a bill through Congress in its own interest after the matter had come before a federal court for decision. O'Mahoney blocked that move, and he and others are now insisting on public hearings in the tidal-lands issue. This is a victory, so far as it goes, but unless there is extremely strong public pressure, the Senate may ultimately follow the decision of the House.

Reuther vs. GM

JANUARY 7, 1946   Walter Reuther is talking. He is presenting the case of strikers walking the picket line in Detroit as the new year begins, in zero weather. He is addressing the president's three-man fact-finding board, across the table from white-haired Charles E. Wilson, head of General Motors, while fifty reporters watch the scene with bated breath.

Reuther is thirty-eight, his salary $7,000. White-haired Wilson, flanked by respectable dignitaries of GM, is sixty-five, his remuneration last year, in salary and bonuses, $459,000. General Motors has 426,000 stockholders. But they merely own the company. They have little to do with its management. Even provided they sympathized with Reuther's workers, which they probably don't, there is almost no way for them to intervene against the duPont minority, but controlling, interest.

The room is a government chamber, a green and gold affair with forty-foot ceilings; I laid my coat and hat on a gilt piano on my way in. At one end sits the three-man panel, ruddy-faced, balding chairman Lloyd K. Garrison; Milton Eisenhower, Kansas college president, a spectacled, strong-jawed younger version of his brother; bow-tied Judge Stacy, chief justice of the North Carolina Supreme Court, deep-voiced, reflective, head thrust forward in a peering look. They are the jury in this strange case.

Walter Reuther is talking. Your first impression is of youth. He has brownish red hair, almost pitch-black eyes. His voice is high and loud, he is speaking easily and excitedly. His hands are in action . . . or else hooked into his vest pockets . . . or else thrust into his trousers. This is no lawyer working for a fee, his voice has fervor and emotion; his answers to panel questions are needle-sharp. "Our boys are walking the streets in zero weather," he is saying. "For they know that everything that's good and decent, somebody had to fight for." His eyes are narrow, like a plainsman's. He is self-confident, young, and sure of himself; he is talking extemporaneously, without notes; he sounds like all the New Deal economists who helped Franklin Roosevelt in the past twelve years. And that is the point your mind finally fixes on. This is a new kind of strike, a new kind of leader.

Reuther is emphasizing again and again the concept that workers have got to have high pay to buy the goods they produce. In the midst of this strike he has set his ideological sights far and away beyond those of any past leader of a big labor group. The communists oppose Reuther; he isn't their kind. Reuther took three years off and worked in Germany, Russia, and the Orient. He came back more of a native product than ever, with a remarkable comprehension of domestic and world issues. What he is saying and what he implies is that this isn't a strike, it's a crusade; furthermore, whatever happens here —it's just a beginning. Something new has happened in the labor movement.

Walter Gordon Merritt rises to give GM's rejoinder. GM head Wilson, with his $459,000, doesn't trust himself to do the talking. He has brought down this New York attorney, specialist in labor cases. What a contrast! Walter Gordon Merritt is sixty-five, old enough to be this whippersnapper's father. His voice is bland, suave, sensible. He wears a double-breasted black suit, might be a respectable undertaker, but he has taken care of that, too—there is a single splash of orange in his black tie. He belongs to the New York Harvard Club ('01); his experience with anti-union cases goes right back to the Danbury Hatters, that classic of injunctive repression. He is the very picture of rectitude, soundness, probity. His tone is carefully couched to contrast with Reuther's impetuosity; it is a quiet, conversational voice, better adapted to his immediate audience. He engages in a little courteous byplay about his young antagonist; he takes the three-man panel into his confidence; his voice is that of an indulgent parent talking to equals about some difficult neighborhood boy. He emphasizes the words "radical" and "revolutionary." And he tells the panel baldly that giant General Motors does not want the government messing around with its books: "If the fact-finding board rules otherwise," he says, "General Motors will withdraw from the proceedings. . . ."

Now, even as he is talking, President Truman calls his bluff. He tells the panel to go ahead; look into GM's data on prices and profits. Chairman Garrison reads the president's statement aloud as a messenger rushes it to him, and all the faces on labor's side break into grins. And GM decides not to withdraw—not for the time anyway. Not, perhaps, until it can think up some more good full-page advertisements for the newspapers. . . .

Well, folks, there you are. To me it was a pretty impressive performance. I have known Reuther before, but have never seen him in action like this. This present strike may make him, or break him, in the labor world. But I have an idea we are going to see a lot more of him, and young men of his type, in the next generation or two. And I had another queer feeling as I watched: the sense that here in the room something was being born, something pretty important was happening: that a man and a time were coming together, that an Idea was finding a Leader.

I think we shall look back after a year or two and say that it was some time in the past few months that Congress took the decision to have another inflation. It took it in a negative sense, by deciding to do nothing about it. Certainly the elements of inflation are infinitely greater now than after World War I, when the dollar's purchasing power dropped to forty cents; and Congress is still knocking off controls. In the Christmas buying rush, for shoddy goods at outrageous prices, millions of Americans suddenly realized what is happening to their dollar. Perhaps for the first time some of them lost confidence in the government's ability to hold the line. The Senate helped it along when, just before recess, by a vote of 31 to 30 (with thirty-five Senators not voting), it beat the amendment to extend the president's war powers (including price stabilization) a year, and substituted a six-month deadline. And so all controls may end June 30 and another incentive be given for holding goods off the market until midsummer brings higher prices.

Vandenberg

MARCH 11, 1946   Senator Vandenberg is bald on top and wears his hair plastered over his head from the side. He is a good speaker because he puts his heart into it, while still knowing the value of self-restraint. I watched him deliver his speech on Russia in the Senate last week, and there was no doubt about it, he struck a popular chord.

Mr. Vandenberg, among other things, was needling the State Department—and particularly Messrs. Byrnes and Stettinius—for failure to take a firmer stand at London. The sequel came quickly: Mr.

Byrnes altered his New York address to put more zip into his definition of American foreign policy, especially in regard to Russia. As reflected here in Washington, there has been a substantial shift going on,
I think, regarding the USSR. More and more I hear officials reluctantly asking whether we can rely on Russia's good faith. Mr. Vandenberg's speech which, in effect, called upon the United States to "be
tough" with Russia, was undoubtedly popular; the only trouble was
that he did not indicate any means of carrying it out or, indeed, seem
to recognize the implications involved. Watching the senators line up
and walk in front of Mr. Vandenberg's desk after he concluded, I had
an odd feeling. There was quite a little scene. There could be no
doubt the speech made an impression. But Walter Lippmann's acerb
comment helped to put the eloquence in perspective. Some of these
senators who applauded the proposed manifestation of America's
strength and "moral leadership" have been the most vociferous in
demanding that the boys come home. It is easy to make faces at
Russia; but just how far will senators go in supporting the sacrifices,
disciplines, self-denials required in even a friendly duel with communism?

American world leadership demands a lot of things, many of them
coming up for discussion here in Washington right now. There is the
British loan and the question of financial advances to the rest of the
world. There is food and famine relief. There is the question of
whether America is going to shake a fist at Russia while demilitariz-
ing herself. There is the question, too, whether we really believe
firmly enough in democratic capitalism to take the economic steps
necessary to make it work, to prevent a new boom-and-bust. Mr.
Vandenberg's speech would have been a good deal stronger if he had
gone into some of these little details.

Bilbo

M AY 6 , 1 9 4 6   Down below you, as you look from the
gallery, Bilbo is talking about the British loan—Bilbo is "defending"
the Senate. It seems *Life* magazine has appraised thirty-two senators
up for reelection and called him the worst man in the chamber. So
Bilbo is being funny. Other senators walk about uneasily with self-
conscious smiles; girls in the press gallery giggle hysterically as Bilbo
calls himself "the nigger's best friend." Representative Rankin has
come over from the House to see the fun. All the newspapers tomorrow will treat this as a great joke. Bilbo attacks "Papa and Mama
Luce," and that is funny, isn't it? He is ingenious in bringing in all
his phobias: references to Catholics in connection with Mrs. Luce; the
"communism" of *Life* magazine, because it attacks high-ranking officials (Bilbo); the charge that the Luces are "nigger-lovers," because
their magazine prints photographs of stage hits about Negro life.

There is something ignoble and contaminating in the scene, like
listening to a buffoon making nasty jokes. Why doesn't somebody
get up and answer him, you ask; why doesn't somebody redeem the
dignity of the Senate, of America, by crying out upon him? Nobody
does; "senatorial courtesy," you know. Bilbo sits down. . . . You go
out to the men's room and wash your hands.

The administration probably has enough votes in the Senate to put
the loan through, but a narrow margin would be almost as bad as
defeat. That is because there is more opposition to the loan in the
House than the Senate, and the psychological effect of a big majority
in the Senate is almost necessary to get it through the lower chamber.
There is danger of postponement. The curious thing is that, on April
10, the Senate committee favorably reported the loan with a thumping majority, 14 to 5. All danger seemed past. But since then the outlook has definitely darkened. What has happened? Nothing that bears

directly on the loan. But the pressures tending to postwar confusion and irresponsibility in America's approach to domestic and international affairs have been coming closer to the climax toward which they seem heading. The big revolt of Congress against the administration is continuing, reflecting a growing mood to throw off war disciplines and restraints, and with this goes the temptation to lighten the burden of responsibilities abroad. The fate of the loan is a good barometer of what America really means to do in world affairs.

I listened to Senator Taft's attack on the loan. Taft looks so wise, so solemn, so reasonable, he talks statistics so glibly, his references are so perfect and cross-citations to financial international dealings so apt, that it seems impossible to refute him. And yet what he says is often plain silly. Few men have such a knack for figures and such an inability to use them right. According to Taft, America is making available to foreign countries in one year "$21 billion," a preposterous estimate; in the same speech he said (a), Britain probably couldn't repay the loan and (b), "the condition of Great Britain today is not so serious as the advocates of this loan claim." Obviously one statement or the other is wrong.

Taft's speech was really in answer to Vandenberg's, made earlier in the same week. These two men are fighting for the soul of the Republican Party on international affairs. Vandenberg supports the loan but he has gone to Paris with Byrnes just when his personal influence would be strongest on wavering GOP senators. There was no doubt that Taft's speech was effective. He proposed an outright "gift" to the British of $1,250 million, as a substitute for the loan. There are few better devices for defeating something you don't like than to offer a reasonable-sounding alternative that confuses or divides your opponents. Taft has done this before. The "gift" proposal has little or no chance in Congress.

Postwar Internationalism

MAY 13, 1946   This morose reporter—who started out a gay and carefree lad twenty years ago but whose "covering" of the Senate since then has dried his inner juices of geniality like the blight of those unfortunate Manhattan trees that are bathed continually in another kind of exhaust miasma—this reporter, I say, watched the so-called debate on the British loan conscientiously for three weeks and sickened at the sight. "What!" he was asked time and again by astonished friends, "You mean the British loan is in danger?" To which this now-misanthropic reporter repeatedly replied, in the colloquialism of an earlier day, "Kid, you said a mouthful."

A dreary spectacle, my masters. Here was the showdown on America's practical application of postwar internationalism. Here was the test of the new cooperation. Here was the debate at home while Secretary Byrnes, at Paris, proposed a four-power, twenty-five-year treaty to keep Germany disarmed. Foreign diplomats said little at Paris but kept their eyes peeled for the Senate. And what was going on there? Day after day, repeated quorum calls that failed to get, or later to hold, quorums; set speeches, read from manuscript, hours in length, while only five or six senators lolled in their chairs; an approaching deadline created by the need to act on the draft-extension bill; purposely dilatory tactics that always began with the mawkish statement, "I am not anti-British, but—" and that went on into such filibustering digressions as Senator Langer's reading of the account of the Crucifixion.

We get about as good a government as we deserve, I suppose. We tolerate a Senate where cloture is next to impossible. We permit a bedridden octogenarian to remain a member, who has not been in the chamber for years, and whose absentee vote is directed by his wife and secretary. We allow, too, such another sight as I shall not soon forget: an aged member, too deaf and misty-eyed to get the chairman's recognition without assistance from his party whip, too infirm to make his poor old piping voice heard beyond the next chair, mumbling the words of an isolationist antiloan speech—which he has not written—to an audience of half a dozen senators who pay no attention to what he says. Well, maybe the British will get their loan, even so; and maybe someday we shall have a better method of handling these matters.

Alert, Quick, Breezy

SEPTEMBER 23, 1946 President Truman was dressed in a double-breasted brown suit. His tie and handkerchief matched. The crowd of reporters lagged in entering because Secret Service men inspected each White House pass meticulously. Other Secret Service men tried to hurry them into the circular study where the president waited. "All in!" came the announcement finally. Mr. Truman rose.

Most of the newspapermen had read Wallace's foreign-affairs speech to be delivered that night in Madison Square Garden. The reporter who asked the question started badly. He referred to "Secretary of State Wallace," then quickly corrected himself. Truman did not allow him to finish. Was he referring to a speech still to be delivered—? Yes. Well then, he couldn't comment on an undelivered speech. The president adopts an alert, quick, breezy attitude at press conferences. In half a dozen cases this pose has betrayed him: it has been shown later that his impulsive replies are based on insufficient knowledge. In this instance, the reporter explained, Wallace referred to Truman himself, that's why he asked. Having made his sparring point and shown no weakness or hesitation, Truman now good-naturedly agreed to hear the question.

Had the president endorsed the entire Wallace speech or just the paragraph to which specific endorsement was noted? asked the reporter.

Quickly, breezily, alertly, the president replied: his endorsement applied to the whole speech.

Correspondents looked at each other. He might have guarded himself with a brief "No comment." The question came up again. "Do you feel that Wallace's speech represents a departure from Byrnes's foreign policy?"

Quickly and alertly, Truman again responded; no, he didn't: the two speeches were exactly in line. His manner implied that he was dismissing a frivolous question, that reporters ought to ask him something harder. The reporters trooped out. Well, if Truman hadn't understood the implications of the Wallace speech, or hadn't read it (as many still believe), they had. The fat was in the fire.

On Saturday reporters were called in again to watch the interesting spectacle of a president eating his own words. It was a "natural misunderstanding" . . .

In his twelve-point program for a GOP Congress, Republican Chairman Reece declares as point 10 that he will fire "about two-thirds of the three million civilian employees of the federal government." Of course the Republicans won't do any such thing; the danger is, however, that they might try. Federal employees now total 2,705,014, of whom 423,000 are abroad. Since the latter are chiefly connected with defense or diplomatic work, Reece would probably concentrate on the 2,282,014 at home (a drop from over three million, incidentally, at wartime peak). If Reece fired two-thirds of the employees it would mean that America could keep only the Veterans' Administration, Post Office, and Treasury: all other departments would close.

It is the fashion now for economy-hunters to attack public employees, whether federal or local. In Norwalk, Connecticut, teachers went on a successful nine-day strike to get better pay. The National Education Association, with offices here, underlines the disgraceful predicament of teachers caught by inflation. Public-school teachers number 900,000; there's been a turnover of 660,000 in the past eight years. In 1920, teachers' colleges enrolled 22 percent of all college students, now only 7 percent. Many cities seem unwilling to levy taxes high enough to pay teachers more than street sweepers or garbage collectors.

Who ordered dropping of the atomic bombs on Hiroshima and Nagasaki? Admiral William Halsey unreservedly charged last week it was the atomic scientists; they "had this toy and they wanted to try it out, so they dropped it." Actually, on June 1, 1945, two months before Hiroshima, a committee of Chicago scientists sent a report to the secretary of war declaring America would lose her moral position by loosing the bomb in a surprise attack on Japan, and advocating a demonstration on an uninhabited locality. On June 11, a petition to the same effect, signed by sixty-four Chicago scientists, was sent to Truman. Dr. A. H. Compton polled 150 participating scientists, three-quarters of whom voted against all-out use. Responsibility for using the bomb, whatever Halsey says, lies on the Joint Chiefs of Staff in consultation with Truman and his special board of advisers. One hopes that the agreeable president really understood the implication of what he was doing and did not, "by a natural misunderstanding," say one thing and mean another.

Time for Leadership

MARCH 10, 1947   The international test is almost here. The time has come for leadership. Can Truman give it? The story started back with World War I, but reached its decisive point in a recent snowstorm in Britain. Britain has given up her position in Egypt; she is dropping out of Burma, will quit India a year hence, plans to turn Palestine over to the United Nations. Now, in a formal little note, she tells the United States that she cannot maintain her financial responsibilities in Greece after March 31. The note dumbfounded Secretary of State Marshall, who considered its implications far more grave and pressing than even the issue of Germany at the Moscow Conference.

The snowstorm revealed that Britain's imperial burden is beyond her means. Next comes the question of whether Britain can sustain her part of the German occupation costs. How about the value of the pound sterling, and its effect on Canadian currency? Britain must produce to keep her head above water, and yet her internal weakness is such that a snowstorm stopped her plants: her total overall loss will be equivalent to one month's production, or a twelfth of a year's work, it is estimated here.

The Greek issue is the one immediately critical in the international power vacuum opened up by Britain's decline, and in the consequent jagged juxtaposition of the two world giants, Russia and America. Truman and Marshall called a hush-hush conference of legislative leaders last Thursday, laid the facts before them with brutal frankness, pledged them to solemn secrecy. The result was that twenty-four hours later the story was all over Washington. Simultaneously Hoover, back from Europe, was mentioning the need of spending $475 million to get Germany running again; $350 million for relief in liberated areas.

Neither Hoover nor Congress will yet face the facts. Hoover urges that relief to bankrupt Europe be made as a "loan," not a gift. He wants desperate Britain to match the proposed $475 million American item to Germany. This is almost funny. If you want to see how funny it is, go back and read about the Hoover war-debt "moratorium" to our Allies after World War I. The nation couldn't face facts then, and now Hoover wants us to make the same mistake again. On balance, however, Hoover's documented statement is immensely valuable in its effect on Republicans.

Congress shows no disposition to face facts either. For a fortnight it has been going through its fantastic fairy-tale egg dance over whether to use hypothetical and unhatched budget savings for debt reduction or for tax cuts, and growing quite bitter about it. It is hard to think of any parallel to this for unreality. The world's wants are going to exceed anything proposed in Truman's budget. Furthermore, a breath of business recession at home, which most economists now expect, would wither a budget surplus. The whole "surplus" thesis is postulated on the hope that the biggest national income in history will grow still bigger next year. A decline under the estimate by so much as 5 percent, it is thought, would knock $4 billion out of Treasury tax revenues. Yet Taft and Taber are already "spending" the surplus on a 20-percent tax cut.

So now the time has come for Truman to show his hand. He will discuss the international crisis soon, probably this week. Secretary

Marshall, either himself, or through Dean Acheson, will speak shortly, too. This is the time of decision. After we have lived behind the security of the British Empire for a century, with all the attendant fun of criticizing it, the buffer is coming down. What the United States does now will set the pattern for a long time to come.

This column emphatically opposes the proposed constitutional amendment limiting future presidents to two terms. The Constitution needs flexibility, not more rigidity, and this is just one more effort to tie the hands of future generations by the supposed superior wisdom of the present. Safety against a dictator does not lie in the words written in a formal document but in the faith implanted in the hearts of citizens. If, in some future world crisis, Americans want another third-term Roosevelt, this proposal would block it, just as it would have halted Theodore Roosevelt from running as a third-term "Progressive." It is pleasant to record that even the conservative *Washington Star*, which apparently has just had a hormone injection in its editorial page, attacks the proposal as an example of "political immaturity."

Dewey vs. Truman in '48

APRIL 14, 1947   The political prospect in brief is: Dewey will run against Truman in 1948, and win. The qualifications are two: Taft may deadlock the convention, when he or a dark horse might be nominated; and Truman might beat Dewey. Neither of these chances seems overlikely now.

Truman's Jefferson Day dinner speech indicates his campaign platform. His popularity has been increasing. Short of death, he will be the Democratic candidate. Undoubtedly his position has improved, but Washington observers still think Dewey would have the edge. However, the Republicans seem bent on knocking themselves out, and we must never underestimate their capacities in that direction. More seriously, Truman can't win without the independent voters. Democratic advisers know this. Liberals probably hold the balance of power.

Dewey is an opportunist. Neither GOP politicians nor correspondents like him much. But he is hard, efficient, effective. He didn't get far against Roosevelt; Truman might be easier.

Taft, of course, is a possibility. As Taft introduces his new labor bill he will share the Washington spotlight. But the Lilienthal fight really showed Taft up. Call it what you will, his opposition to internationalizing the atom bomb, his attack on the Acheson-Lilienthal-Baruch program, are really isolationism. It's hard to conceive of the public taking him.

Does Vandenberg have a chance? His development is fascinating. Three years ago he was an isolationist, as conservative as Taft. Then something happened. Vandenberg grew; Taft didn't. But again it's hard to see the GOP picking Vandenberg. Take the Lilienthal fight: most Republicans (thirty-one) voted for recommittal with Taft; only eighteen supported Vandenberg. Taft still has pretty much of a mortgage on the Senate Republicans.

In Chicago a Democratic reform candidate for mayor, Martin H. Kennelly, has beaten the GOP party hack put up by Colonel McCormick. Observers have long wondered when the improvement in municipal politics that struck New York a quarter-century ago would finally reach Chicago. Kennelly may help it along if the Kelly Democratic machine isn't too powerful. Meanwhile the state GOP is further weakened by the apparent participation of Republican Governor Green in the shakedown of coal operators prior to the Centralia explosion. These are not decisive political factors. But they all illustrate two things: the '48 presidential race may be closer than anybody expected and the power of the independent, progressive vote is thereby tremendously enhanced.

It isn't considered polite to mention corporation profits in Washington news dispatches, and we approach the delicate subject with natural hesitation. As the *Wall Street Journal* noted in a modest paragraph last week:

> Corporation profits climbed to an annual rate of $15 billion in 1947's first quarter, the Commerce Department calculates. That's $3 billion above 1946 profits. Field offices report businessmen are worried about public reaction to these profits and continued high prices.

You can see that the whole thing is pretty darn embarrassing. First of all, Congress knocked off the excess-profits tax. That was almost its first reconversion measure. It meant billions for corporations. Then the OPA and the price-control system went overboard. That meant present high prices and more billions. Meanwhile generous tax refunds from the Treasury (intended to help business reconvert to peace) were paid out to corporations and actually met a large share of their 1946 strike losses. Now comes the new House tax bill to aid millionaires. More billions here. And all this time the richest market in the world, and profits never before known in war or peace! Well, the thing can't last. A new wage-price-profits relationship must come. The Easter sales weren't up to expectations, some goods are piling up, and retailers like Macy's are swinging over to support consumers against exorbitant manufacturers' prices. What comes next? A big shake-out. How big we don't know, but certainly some unemployment.

Don't think, however, that conservative congressmen are licked. One genial GOP leader in a relaxed moment explained to us all about it. It's going to be a "stabilizing recession," he said. (Isn't that a cute phrase?) There will be maybe eight million unemployed, and that will make labor behave. The real crack-up, however, won't come for five or ten years. And when it does—why, it will be high time to think of increased tariffs. Workingmen must be taught the danger of foreign goods flooding American markets. Our man seemed quite chipper about the whole affair. And why shouldn't he be, with most newspapers still attacking labor and as blushingly timorous about the word "profits" as a Sunday-school teacher is of the word "sex"?

Full Dinner Pail for Europe

MAY 5, 1947   Secretary Marshall and Congress are coming to grips on the Russian question. A major shift in emphasis has taken place in State Department strategy toward Russia, which Marshall must now try to sell to Congress. It will be harder to sell than the Greek-Turkish loan. It is the thesis that the USA must build up and revitalize Western Europe as the best answer to Communist infiltration, and second, that the USA must have allies in its diplomatic duel with the Kremlin. Marshall went to bat with congressional leaders on restoration of funds for broadcasts to Russia almost immediately on getting home. Marshall's prestige is immense. He'll probably win the specific battle on broadcasts.

The other issue is bigger, harder to sell, because basically it means granting loans, food, and relief on a large scale. There is no limit to what State Department top leaders want. They are already talking about a second big loan to Britain. The question is, what can they get through a reluctant or hostile Congress? The Greek-Turkish program is regarded primarily as "defensive," a step which had to be taken but which can't win by itself any more than can aid to Korea. They declared that something more positive is needed. In a sense, State Department strategists have now come around, in part at least, to the point a good many "visionaries" have been urging all along—that one way of combating communism is to give Western Europe a full dinner pail. Secretary Marshall is sold on this idea; the question is, can he sell Congress?

Information regarding the new Marshall high-level policy board, headed by George F. Kennan, has just leaked out. The board will direct its attention almost wholly to Russia and will formulate the new American drive to strengthen Western Europe. But that will take loans, cost money. There are two international enigmas in the postwar world: the Kremlin and Congress.

Truman was right on the OPA; he didn't want it abolished, predicting the inflation that punctually arrived. Truman was right on housing, too; he asked Congress for aid that it refused. Truman was right about the recession; he said it would come unless business mended its ways, and it is here. Truman was right on these things, and he can make his appeal to 1948 voters on that record.

The trouble is, Truman didn't make a real fight on any of these issues. He didn't carry through on the OPA struggle; he failed to support Wilson Wyatt on housing; he saw and predicted the recession but let Congress and business have their way. Truman has won the argument all right, but that isn't quite enough in politics. Cassandra couldn't carry the Sixth Ward. Truman had the option of making a real, knockdown fight on any of the above or other issues.

A lot of well-meaning people, who recognize the normal deadlock between a president of one party and a Congress of another, urged him not to fight, to go along, to "cooperate." We have a bipartisan foreign policy, they said—why not a similar domestic policy? So Truman did; he appeased. What is the result? Well, down to date, anyway, a stalemate has been avoided and nobody hates Truman the way they hated Roosevelt. But we have inflation, the housing program has collapsed, and recession (we trust a mild one) is at hand.

This doesn't mean we dislike Truman. He has our affection. Back in the Senate now he'd probably be voting on our side. He's an attractive, oh-so-human figure, trying hard, but without much of a talent for leadership. After a banquet the other night, and skits which the president, Mrs. Truman, and Margaret all enjoyed, the question rose among the womenfolk whether they would stay on and stand in the receiving line. Mrs. Truman, a friendly, gracious woman, proposed staying. But the president looked tired. Her face cleared; she would put the decision up to the chief executive himself. She said simply, "I'll go ask Papa." They didn't stay, but who could resist a family like that?

Herbert Hoover

JUNE 23, 1947   In the face of the onrushing world dollar crisis, the outlines of the vast new American aid program begin to take shape. This is what the Truman Doctrine should have done at the outset. The administration's crucial job of "selling" the program is now under way. Each new official speech carries the affair one step further. Marshall at Harvard cited the need for European self-aid; Truman carefully declared that Russia is invited to participate, if she'll cooperate; State Department counselor Ben Cohen on the West Coast indicated the size—"As much as $5 or $6 billion a year for another three or four years." Hints are being dropped of a special session this fall, devoted to foreign affairs alone.

Will Congress balk? The world must have this aid ultimately, and America's own prosperity depends on it. It is probably fair to say that the big test of our times is now approaching. How difficult the task is under our system can be seen in the wool bill. Higher wool tariffs will aid only a fractional percentage of America's industrialists and will wreck the whole drive for freer world trade. Yet the high-tariff wool bill passed the House, 151 to 65, without a record vote and with only half of the 435 members present—and Senate-House conferees now approve it. Can our cumbersome, divided system of government really cope with world problems? We solemnly record that, as of this date, we can't guess the answer.

Good old Herbert Hoover is back. It seems that American inflation isn't due to ending the OPA at all, but to sending too much abroad, just as Taft said. In his letter to Senator Bridges (R, N.H.), Hoover (who seemed to be advocating separate peace treaties the other day) now says we must cut down exports to save our own economy. Otherwise, he adds (self-contradictorily), we must put it all on a charitable basis. Some people, Hoover acknowledges, want to restore price and export controls to meet the crisis, but that is "totalitarian."

It has always been pretty hard for us to follow poor, dear Hoover. In this case we fear a great many conservative Republicans are going to hail his letter as a challenge to Marshall. At heart, though, Hoover is an honest, soul-searching humanitarian. He wants to be rehabilitated as the Good Gray ex-president. If the Truman-Marshall program is to go through, men like Hoover have got to be convinced. Maybe it is folly, but this column recommends that Hoover be put on the top-level, bipartisan council which Vandenberg proposes to advise the president and Congress on multi-billion-dollar spending. Then all the other council members can work on Hoover. We might as well face it—the new program must have Republican support. If Hoover will go along, then anybody ought to go along.

The Taft-Hartley labor bill is an interesting barometer of the political weather in this year of a Republican Congress. More than that, as a piece of legislation it was bound to be an old-fashioned hell-raiser.

Two statements describe the measure, both by its friends. Senator Ball (R, Minn.) said the bill was designed to "put the risk back into striking." Representative Hartley (R, N.J.) said (winking), "There is more in this bill than meets the eye." Truman's advisers on labor matters detect half a dozen "jokers" planted in the bill, one of which would (it was hoped) practically end industrywide bargaining. It was all pretty queer.

Here is one example. The bill heaps economic problems on the enlarged labor board, and then specifically says the board shouldn't employ "economic analyzers." Just why, we don't know. The new chief counsel of the revised labor board will be something to watch. Such a job creates America's first labor czar, with the board losing all control over him.

But it is provisions like the one forbidding trade-union journals from discussing politics, or even running the voting record of a candidate at election time, that inflame labor leaders. Good old Ed Keating, editor of *Labor* (the organ of the railway brotherhoods), says he would go to jail proudly rather than obey that provision. Who wouldn't? It seems likely that this bill could finally do what nobody had quite thought possible—put the AFL into politics, with its own political subsidiary. We have a feeling that the Taft-Hartley labor bill is going to be remembered for a long, long time.

Taft-Hartley

JULY 7, 1947   Confusion in Washington? Oh, nothing more than usual. Senator Taft, who said killing the OPA would promptly reduce prices, now says the new labor law will reduce strikes; one day after the Taft-Hartley Act to solve labor problems was passed, Representative (there-ought-to-be-a-law) Hartley urged enactment of another law; with the fuel crisis turning on how much coal there is aboveground, it develops that for the first time in twenty years the Bureau of Mines has discontinued compiling statistics on soft-coal supplies, because of the GOP economy drive; and President Truman, having declared the Taft-Hartley Act "unworkable," is now entrusted with trying to make it work. Confusion in Washington? Nothing unusual.

Having enthusiastically urged the Taft-Hartley labor bill as a panacea for six months without bothering to read its provisions, most editorial writers are now secretly trying to find out for themselves whether it's a milestone or a millstone. That accounts for the current rash of articles explaining what's in the law—it's the editors boning up on the thing themselves. A week after passage many grudgingly admit the law is "not perfect." In private, some who were played for suckers on the "kill-the-OPA" drive are uneasily preparing themselves for a new year-long set of explanations. This column has always found itself comparing labor-management relations with those between husband and wife. The two may quarrel, but they can't live alone. Now Congress has passed a law ordering mama to love papa—or else. Well, we'll wait and see.

What is actually known about the Marshall "plan"? First, it has never been formulated. About six months ago it became frighteningly obvious to certain high government officials that dollar shortages threatened ultimate European disaster. The Greek-Turkish loan crisis suddenly intervened. It was largely extraneous to the first problem. Washington has had four secretaries of state in three years, and Byrnes, we gather, had simply forgotten to inform Marshall of the immediacy of the British retirement from Greece. To get the emergency Greek-Turkish appropriation through, as the London *Economist* wryly observed, the US practically had to declare war on Russia. Well, that matter was settled, but meanwhile the bigger issue of threatened European economic collapse came closer.

When Marshall returned from Moscow things started to happen. High government officials began to tell newsmen the real situation, off the record. Then a carefully planned series of State Department speeches started. They emphasized the immensity of the needed program. Dean Acheson passed the ball to Ben Cohen, and others joined in.

The crescendo reached a climax in Marshall's Harvard speech on June 5. Most of the Marshall suggestion was implied, not explicit. If Congress is going to be sold a big program, he virtually declared, then Europe must crash through with a daringly imaginative plan of its own. Marshall indicated that what he wanted was an agreement on a self-liquidating reconstruction program, the diminishing deficits of which the US will underwrite. Doubtless the general outline of what Marshall will try to get through Congress was taken abroad by Will Clayton.

Hollywood Red Probe

NOVEMBER 3, 1947 America took off war controls too fast and is now faced with an inflation which is beginning to scare the daylights out of economists while threatening to ruin our foreign-aid program. After months of delay, Truman has finally proposed action and the Ship of State is beginning to make headway—the best news out of Washington this season.

Truman's delay was agonizing. He didn't cry "Fire" till the flames were almost singeing the hair of the congressmen's heads and till the exasperated public was yelling at him almost as much as at Congress. Now it is all yelling at Congress.

Insofar as international aid goes, it must be said in Truman's behalf that his tactics seem likely to be successful. The Vishinsky speeches, the bad state of Europe, and what pop-eyed traveling congressmen actually saw for themselves, indicate something will be done for Europe.

But the second Truman idea on prices—the thought that we actually have got to do something to save ourselves in addition to saving the world—is like a bombshell to legislators. What—don't we have the free enterprise system? Isn't everybody employed? Aren't profits and dividends the highest in history?

To which Truman (and the able Nourse Economic Council behind him) says, "Yes, and if we get much more of this kind of inflation prosperity we'll be broke; the nation is pricing itself into a position where people can't buy the goods they produce, and this just can't go on."

Six motion picture cameras whir in the Hollywood Red probe; six monster floodlights blind you for thirty seconds if you so much as glance at one; the sound men test their amplifiers, "One, two, three; one, two"; the crowd is big, the mood electric; and newsreel men take pictures of other newsreel men taking pictures. A flying squad of twenty-five still photographers, snapping celebrities, dashes around the great carpeted hall, whose walls rise up thirty-five feet, with highly prismed candelabra hanging from the ornate ceiling. And inside, in all this commotion and excitement and hubbub, chairman J. Parnell Thomas of the House Un-American Activities Committee makes mincemeat of America's traditional rules of evidence.

"Where has Bill gone?" we heard one reporter ask another. "Guess he's just gone out to throw up," was the gag answer, and they both laughed. Well, we felt that way, too.

We are pretty certain from our own information that the Commies have been active in Hollywood studios, particularly in the Screen Writers' Guild, and personally we have no use for them; but for our own money the Thomas committee is the worst agency to ferret them out. It draws no more distinction between mild liberalism and Communism than it does between evidence and hearsay.

We begin to see why top writers in Hollywood sometimes go Communist: it is either that or go nuts. We heard witnesses brand films as "un-American" because they were slow-moving, morbid, "in the Russian manner." And we like the UP's simple account of the question put by investigator Robert Stripling to movie director Leo McCarey: Asked by Stripling what he thought of films that showed bankers, for example, in an unfavorable light, McCarey said he thought they were un-American. That tells it all.

We tantalized a rapt maiden who sat behind us at the all-star Hollywood Communist probe by turning around periodically and asking her whether Robert Montgomery was a script writer or director, and what Gary Cooper's first name was. She got so she was almost as much interested in us as in the screen stars. We shall always treasure her information that Robert Taylor is really *very* well known.

Politics last week had some new developments, including the announcement by Bob Taft that he is a candidate. Well, you could knock us over with a feather. It is significant that he says he will not make any contest in the primaries save in Ohio. This is a definite sign of weakness. We have a genuine affection for Taft and like his courage and candor; we have only two things against him—his record on foreign affairs and his record on domestic affairs.

Colonel Robert R. McCormick, of the *Chicago Tribune*, is hurling all the smears he's got against Eisenhower, and seems to be genuinely frightened by the prospect. Actually it may get so bad that Ike will withdraw further than he has yet from the race, saying everything but an absolute no. We like Eisenhower, but we warn now that a victorious general on the GOP ticket would almost certainly mean an accompanying landslide of the reactionary Republican elements in Congress, riding in on his coattails, just as they did on poor dear Hoover's in 1928.

As for Truman, he's running for the presidency, too, and the latest Gallup Poll boosts his stock, alleging that as of today the Democrats would have a 56-to-44-percent edge over the Republicans. We can't believe the figures. But it is true that there's a tendency of the public to sympathize with the man in the White House, not in the sense of pitying him, but of identifying itself with him in all the difficulties and problems he is facing. Maybe Truman doesn't know the answers, but at his best he seems conscientious, humble, and patriotic. He hasn't a single oratorical trick, but in last week's broadcast, when he said he knew the difficulties of the breadwinner and housewife, skimping and scared by rising prices, listeners remembered the bankrupt haberdasher in Missouri and caught the note of sincerity in his voice.

Five Decisions for '48

J A N U A R Y   5 ,   1 9 4 8   Nineteen forty-eight will be a year of great decisions in Washington, following a year overshadowed by a kind of blight. What put its stamp on nearly everything here in 1947 was the fact that the GOP overpromised itself in the preceding election.

Republicans never caught up with their own pledges. They are still trying; they will try in '48, and it will continue to gum things up. They promised to cut federal bureaucracy and controls—just before prices started to rise, as a result of killing the OPA. They promised a great slash in taxes—just before inflation began to blaze, which means that a tax cut now will throw gasoline on the flames. They promised to slash federal expenditures—just before the Marshall Plan. Rarely has a party ridden to victory on such reckless and ill-timed pledges; if they don't carry them out now they look silly; if they do, they are unpatriotic.

Never in 1947 could House and Senate GOP leaders agree on the figure they would try to cut from the Truman budget; they ended in a blur of phony economies which, like boomerangs, are now coming back one after another to hit them on the back of the neck. As inflation mounts, the promise to give the nation a planless Utopia without controls is causing a revolt even among the freshmen GOP senators, who are really beginning to get scared at where the Taft-Knutson leadership is taking them. And the aim of balancing budget, reducing debt, and cutting taxes, all simultaneously, is running smack into the fiscal demands of the Marshall Plan.

President Truman through 1947 has had one secret weapon, the GOP Congress. If his popularity has risen on Gallup polls it is due less to what he has done than to his opponents. It will be harder for Truman in 1948, when opposition is personified in an election campaign. Truman won organized labor cheaply, with one veto—a powerful one—of the Taft-Hartley bill. On foreign policy there was rarely a major issue between him and Congress, save over amounts. On economic matters, one of the most fascinating experiences of the past year has been to sit here in Washington and sense the American public gradually making up its mind that the high cost of living is more the fault of Congress than of the President, and that if anything is to be done about it, the hope does not lie in the Republicans. In one sense it has been an easy situation for Truman. He knew Congress would reject almost anything liberal he proposed. He could coast along, putting responsibility on his rivals.

To write a column like this, we read, we suppose, a dozen newspapers a day, and we don't know how many individual commentators.

With some of them we sometimes violently disagree, but we couldn't get along without them. At this New Year's season we extend our thanks to the list. They are so much a habit now that to omit them means a feeling akin to going unshaved and unwashed. If we couldn't steal from them we don't know where we'd be.

Our favorite columnists are Tom Stokes, Mark Childs, Lowell Mellett, Ernest Lindley, and the brilliant crew that gets out the *New York Post*'s "Washington Memo." We want to know every day what the Alsops and Walter Lippmann are saying. If Scotty Reston has a piece in the *New York Times* we try to read it. We like to follow Doris Fleeson on politics; J.A. Livingston, Keith Hutchison, and Sylvia Porter on the business outlook; and, on the radio, Elmer Davis (ABC), Joe Harsch (CBS), and Al Warner of Mutual.

We begin our day on the magnificent news columns of the *New York Times,* and sigh to see the gradual hardening of its editorial arteries, while the excellent *Herald Tribune* remains so much spryer and open-minded. From them, we turn to *PM* for the other side. Our New Year's greetings also to the *St. Louis Post-Dispatch*, which still seems to fire as heavy a broadside as any other editorial page in the country. And we have an affectionate attachment, too, for the hard-hitting *Washington Post*, including Herblock's cartoons.

The best all-round news coverage of Congress we know is the *Baltimore Sun*'s superlative team, Bill Knighton, Joe Short, and Rodney Crowther. It's rare that we can't pick up an idea from the Railway Brotherhoods' excellent weekly, *Labor.* And in this mellow mood of appreciation, let us extend gracious New Year's greetings and hearty thanks, too, to the NAM [National Association of Manufacturers], to Representative J. Parnell Thomas, to columnist Henry Hazlitt of *Newsweek,* to Sam Pettengill, and to all the Neanderthal Men both in and out of Congress, too numerous to mention. How much easier they make our weekly stint!

It isn't just that the US has one simple and uncomplicated decision, like the Marshall Plan, to make in 1948. It has five, and they are all treading on one another's toes. This is an election year, which makes choice Number One, and the presidential race will almost certainly become involved in everything else. Then there is Number Two, the Inflation Issue, and the question whether those who want us to "Sell Capitalism" abroad are prepared to do anything realistic in its behalf at home. There is also, of course, the continuing Soviet-American diplomatic duel. Fourth, there is ERP [European Recovery Program] and the question whether Congress in this year of great decisions will pass "the" Marshall Plan or merely "a" Marshall Plan which probably won't work. Fifth, there is a still bigger question whether America can adjust herself to her new, overall role of world power and responsibility, in view of the isolationism left in the country. Yes, 1948 should prove interesting.

Truman Will Be Licked

MARCH 29, 1948   Frankly and candidly, we think Harry Truman is licked. We don't think any "crisis atmosphere" will elect him. There immediately appeared, of course, charges that his play to Congress on UMT [Universal Military Training] was an election maneuver. But the simple fact is that Truman isn't the type of strong man to whom folks turn in time of national danger. The idea of Truman as a "man on horseback" is just funny. People are much more likely to turn to General MacArthur—God help us!

Another plain fact is that Secretary Marshall is not politically minded. He is not trying to elect anybody. He may be wrong about Russia, but he is playing the part of devoted national servant. Truman, to him, is just incidental.

Marshall sees America gravely threatened. All the democratic prime ministers of Europe are appealing to him, though, of course, it doesn't get into the papers. On foreign-affairs statements, it is Truman's bad delivery, but it is Marshall speaking.

Marshall has taken an extremely hazardous risk. He has put it up to Congress to do something, to show Moscow we are in earnest. But suppose Congress won't do anything, stalls, delays . . . ? What then? Marshall's answer is simple and soldierly: every time you enter battle you take a risk. He believes at this juncture of history the political risk is justified. Russia has somehow got to be made to feel that America means business.

As for Truman, and we say it with some regret, we think he is sunk. He has stood out against a lot of dreadful Republican legislation. Southern Democrats also think he is defeated. They feel they, and the party, have nothing particular to risk in taking a crack at him now in protest against recommendations which they accepted, without blinking, from victorious FDR. We fear the Truman campaign special next fall will be like the Hoover funeral train in 1932, which we remember gloomily. Indeed, we have about decided to cast a protest vote this year—for Our Harry.

The big television spotlights bored through the faintly smoky air of the House of Representatives. Outside there were signs of Washington spring: a forsythia bush was turning yellow, and John L. Lewis had started his regular vernal coal strike. In the chamber, at the emergency joint session, the president was speaking. The gloom and oppression that sat on the legislature when Truman made his Greek-Turkish speech was absent; this time, an air of nervous excitement prevailed.

As Truman urged UMT, there was a definitely self-conscious look on the faces below: politicians were weighing their chances with that unpopular measure, just before an election. When the president finished, there was applause that quickly petered out on the Republican side. Truman entered the chamber in a postwar atmosphere. He left it in a prewar atmosphere.

We constantly get intimations of what life in Washington will be like next January, under the Republicans. There won't be any little man in the White House then, with a big veto. Here are some current samples from the Republican-dominated Congress:

Sixteen Republicans and Democrats in the House Agriculture Committee outvoted ten Democrats to shelve legislation repealing the federal taxes on margarine.

The reactionary House Rules Committee has pigeonholed the O'Mahoney-Kefauver bill plugging up a loophole in the antitrust law, a bill forbidding corporations to swallow smaller ones by buying up all their assets. (The present law merely says they mustn't buy up their stock.)

The Republican House passed a phony rent "control" law, which would remove the federal veto and turn control back to local boards, which in many cities are annexes of real-estate lobbies.

Republicans in Congress have just taken another crack at the long-suffering Labor Department, rejecting a Truman executive reorganization proposal to let it handle federal job-finding and unemployment compensation.

Well, these are just samples. Wait till an all-GOP administration gets it hands on the Hull tariff agreements!

Campaign Special

On the Truman Special Train

JUNE 14, 1948   With the record Congress has made, Roosevelt could have knocked the GOP at this election into a cocked hat. The question is whether it is bad enough to give even Harry Truman a chance. Everybody else has given the fight up by proxy. Truman hasn't. With dogged determination, he is plugging ahead on this trip, giving good speeches with a poor delivery, winning friendliness but no enthusiasm. But he is drawing a sharp line between what he asked and what Congress granted, between mild liberalism and insolent reaction.

Call it anything you want, what we are getting from Congress now is isolationism. European radicals for some time have been fearful of United States "intervention." Personally we have always felt this to be ironic. With a century and a half of isolation tradition behind us, a revival of it sooner or later was bound to occur. It seems to have come now, with Stalin's removal of some of the tension by a "peace" offer, whether genuine or propaganda.

For the last couple of years the US has been doing the right things for the wrong reasons in foreign affairs. For example, it was hatred of

Stalin that put through the Marshall Plan. But now that Stalin has pro-
vided a little breathing space, the House at once cuts the first year's
ECA [Economic Cooperation Administration] amount 26 percent.
The Senate is bound to restore some of this money, maybe all, and
Vandenberg will once again be the hero.

The fiction that Truman's trip is "nonpolitical" lasted only until the
back-platform address the second day, when the president was appealing for a Democratic governor of Ohio and a more sympathetic legislature.

With an outdoor temperature of 92°, Truman emerged from his
air-conditioned rear car to listen to the Central Catholic High School
band play "Hail to the Chief" at Fort Wayne, Indiana. Then he set
echoes ringing from the walls of the Lincoln National Life Insurance
Company building across the way as he challenged Congress to restore
the slash in Marshall Plan funds. At Gary, he told the same Congress
that it would rather listen to the National Association of Manufacturers
than to the president on price control, and blamed it for high living
costs.

At Chicago, Truman said what a lot of us wanted to say after the
Stassen-Dewey Oregon debate over the Mundt bill. Dewey, you recall, favored the bill because it didn't outlaw communism, Stassen because it did. And Truman just said he didn't favor it. He opposed it,
he said, because that wasn't the way to deal with communism—you
can't stamp it out by driving it underground; you met it, if you were
honest, by making the lot of the poor man better, by housing legislation, health legislation, social security, education, anti-inflation legislation. And why didn't Congress get a move on?

Truman said this, and it was rousing stuff in type. He read his
speech through thick lenses, hardly looking at his audience, and with
never a gesture. Even so it was generally agreed among the sixty-five
news and radio men aboard our train that for Truman he said it pretty
well. Some of us, listening to him, have to restrain ourselves all the time.
This columnist found himself stressing words that Truman elided,
pounding the press table at climaxes he missed.

There is a certain temperamental strain in traveling with Harry
that must be acknowledged. A man who could have a spot like that
in the huge Chicago Stadium, with a dramatic entrance, spotlights, and
a great band, and then not rise to the occasion, with the 25,000 audi-

ence and all, must be lacking in imagination. Truman did not botch the affair. There was a real note of earnestness and sincerity in his voice, but it was like listening to a well-meaning amateur church organist trying to play Chopin.

Pardon us, however, who have lived with the Eightieth Congress for two miserable years, if we give credit to the little man who is telling the public now just what he thinks of Congress. At Omaha, Nebraska, he had a few pertinent comments about the long-range farm program. "The Congress has considered it, and studied it, and weighed it, and pondered it," he observed, "but the Congress has not acted upon it."

Congress has been viciously anti-public-power, too, and the West Coast and flood areas have given Truman a dramatic opportunity to show what its restrictions on the Interior Department's reclamation work and power projects have meant.

It is good that many of the things which Truman is saying should be said. The custom of a president's getting out and seeing the folks is an excellent one, and he is meeting signs of full respect for his office. Probably that isn't enough.

Truman's basic fault is, perhaps, that he hasn't enough enemies. He is trying to make some on this trip, but his principal antagonist still seems to be indifference. It is our painful duty to report that he has been received so far in his trip with something like a polite and friendly yawn. At Chicago, the Cook County boss, Jake Arvey, didn't join the party, indicating that his hostility is unquenched. The rush-hour crowds on the streets were apathetic.

But it was in Omaha that the blow really fell. Truman walked into an auditorium with 10,000 seats and not more than 2,000 persons. It was a brutal and chilling experience. Being inside the streamlined, functional Coliseum was like being inside an egg. The crowd was huddled in front with a few hundreds in a gallery on either side. We shall never forget the highlights on those acres of freshly polished, empty seats.

The stage management was dreadful—it was absurd to take Truman virtually out into the country on a Saturday night with a speech that anyone could have heard by radio at home. As reporters surveyed the place, an awful chill seemed to rise from it. Finally, the implacable motion-picture cameras from the perch above took notice.

The hearts of the members of the official party must have sunk as the spotlights were turned slowly and deliberately from Truman to the empty seats. Then the direction of the cameras was reversed and the scene rendered for posterity. As the mile-long parade moved back to the hotel, it felt like a funeral procession.

Can Dewey Snoot Truman?

AUGUST 2, 1948   Governor Dewey is going to try to snoot Truman's candidacy. Why should he stoop to argue about a sure thing? Harding took that line to Cox, Coolidge to Davis, Hoover to Al Smith. There was a GOP landslide each time. Just maintain a detached tone of dignified condescension, say Dewey advisers, and let the rival wings of the Democratic Party do the work for you.

On paper it looks like a Republican cinch. There will be losses of Democratic electoral votes in the Solid South. Wallace's Progressives probably hold a balance of power in some big industrial states such as New York, California, and Michigan. Almost certainly that will throw those states to the Republicans. Why should Governor Dewey soil his hands in the sordid fray?

This seems to be the strategy behind the statement of Herbert Brownell, Dewey's campaign manager, referring to the "rump" session, and saying the Republicans will not be bound by their own platform pledges during it. Lofty detachment is the motto. Truman is just "playing politics" in calling Congress back. Let us raise our aristocratic noses and look the other way.

We have an idea, somehow, that Truman is a hard man to snoot. We are settling back to watch the election with considerable interest. There is a lot of drama in Truman's going before Congress. What friends has he there? The Republicans who sit silent as the little man speaks are outright opponents. The Democrats who applaud vociferously now are the ones who overrode his veto on taxes, the Taft-

Hartley Act, social security. It is a topsy-turvy situation. Truman is the candidate on a Democratic platform that makes it practically a labor party, but the majority of the members of his party in Congress are conservative.

Another difficulty for the "snoot-Truman" movement is the high cost of living. Prices are at an all-time high. The aloof Dewey camp must have uneasy moments. Can it really depend on the voters to understand that the price of pork chops is all due to the New Deal bungling in Washington which two years' Republican control of Congress has not yet been able to extirpate? It still looks as though the pork-chop issue will be a big one in this election.

Actually, we believe inflation has reached a point where any real attempt to check it in Washington will bring a recession damaging to either party. That's why we can't see any major action being taken till after election, if then. Both parties share the blame for the situation. But Truman has rather faithfully followed his Council of Economic Advisers once he understood what they were trying to tell him. On their advice he stubbornly and heroically resisted lowering taxes. And he has advocated partial reimposition of excess-profits taxes, after originally making the awful mistake of permitting their repeal.

The Republicans are bankrupt on the subject except for the proposal to cut government costs. This obviously can't be done while Marshall Plan aid and the cold war continue. And there is one damaging thing on the Republican side. It is all that silly stuff they put out two years ago about sending living costs down by restoring "free competition." They joined the NAM in this nonsense when they killed OPA. Voters are apt to resent those full-page NAM ads, with their glowing promises of cheaper prices, when they are reminded of them. And Truman is the kind of man to bring them up.

At the Progressives' revivalist convention in Philadelphia last week, we watched the right and left wings of Roosevelt's old coalition fly at each other's throats. James Loeb, executive secretary of Americans for Democratic Action, in a discouraged seersucker, defied suave, supercilious Rexford Tugwell, whose black silk ribbon twitched angrily from the right side of his pince-nez. Dr. Tugwell was chairman of the platform committee. The ADA, of course, defends the Marshall Plan; the Progressives denounce it.

Another sight we shall not soon forget was Wallace striding along from the Broad Street station to his hotel on the morning of his arrival. He came on foot, with fourteen big Philadelphia cops in silver shirts, eight-cornered white caps, and heavy revolvers jangling in holsters, running interference for him in a sort of football rush. Wallace proceeds at four miles an hour, city traffic or not. Behind him trailed a thousand ardent followers, the banjo-carrying young men and bobbed-haired girls trying somewhat pantingly to sing the Progressives' campaign song, "A Dollar Ain't a Dollar Anymore," while they bucked traffic.

Harry's Gallant Fight

NOVEMBER 1, 1948 A slight but unmistakable Democratic revival set in during the final days of the campaign, not enough to save Truman but enough to help dozens of borderline Democratic congressmen. Harry's gallant fight was paying off. It seemed as though the public were flinching before its inevitable decision between Truman, the man who can make friends and not influence people, and Dewey, the man who can influence people and not make friends.

We found it so, right on Dewey's own train in the press car: a really rather striking dislike of Dewey. The mechanical smile of the man who always seems to be under television and his bland refusal to deal with issues, have got under everybody's skin. Then there are the contrasting attractiveness and never-say-die spirit of likable little Harry Truman. He deserves well of the nation. In a hopeless battle, he stayed game to the end, and is going down fighting, both popguns smoking.

The most important speech of the campaign was Dewey's at Salt Lake City. He has a lofty conception of a "United States of Europe" and will use ECA funds to stimulate it. He said frankly that he would "prod" Europe with this financial stick, and that foreign aid which doesn't assist this objective is wasted.

If you want to know Dewey's European goal, you must read this speech. Furthermore, it was much stronger in its original form, before editing. Dewey's closest advisers make no secret of it: Dewey intends to act tough, and make ECA funds conditional on the recipients' aiding a unified Europe. Now this is strong medicine. Can a rather ruthless man like Dewey manage to wield the big stick over countries like Britain and France? Will he endanger the very objective for which he is working?

Dewey, the impatient prosecutor, found his sweetness-and-light role hard to take. In the candor of his rear car, he blew off steam in contemptuous references to Truman. Wasn't it harder in politics to defeat a fool, say, than an abler man? All Dewey's instincts were to get in there slugging. This showed again in the press conference which Dewey held in Albany after issuing the seventy-four-word statement on the Vinson-to-Moscow mission. His uncensored private views on Truman were vigorous. From these same surroundings came the ambiguous and alarming phrase that the Politburo is only three votes short of war. No one has yet explained what this means.

Dewey tells visitors who penetrate to his rear car that America has been given the Democratic version of history for the past sixteen years; it is now his necessary duty to set the record straight. He intends to educate the masses back to Republicanism. He started off rather unfortunately at Louisville, Kentucky, by taking personal credit for "founding" the nonpartisan US foreign policy, and by charging that ECA was "just another foreign handout" till the Republicans fixed it up. Cordell Hull and the *New York Times'* James Reston dropped on his neck for these extravagant claims.

Senate control is in doubt. Bob Wagner is probably too ill to take his seat again, even to cast his vote from a stretcher in case of a tie. This means the Democrats need a net gain of five rather than four to organize the upper chamber. Again, Democratic candidate Lyndon B. Johnson, Texas, and Robert S. Kerr, Oklahoma, if elected, will be challenged by the GOP for alleged election irregularities. They could be deprived of votes till organization is effected, though this would be unusual.

We still can't understand the importance some people attach to who organizes the Senate. If senators voted along straight party lines, that would mean something, but they don't. Republican conservatives plus reactionary Dixiecrats will vote together on most domestic issues that have any real social significance. Most Democrats will support Dewey if he presents an enlightened foreign policy, as against those very isolationist Republicans whom he's now doing his best to elect.

"The Dewey Victory"

NOVEMBER 15, 1948 We must clear the litter off our desk now that the election is over. Here are the crystal-ball readings of soothsayers Gallup, Roper, and Crossley. Out they go! Here is that *Newsweek* survey of fifty Washington political writers all predicting Dewey. (Make a note, Mabel, to try to get us invited when *Newsweek* awards its prize for the best forecast.) Let's see, here is *Life* with its photograph of "the next President" crossing San Francisco Bay. It's the man with the dimples. Throw away that *Time* indicating a GOP sweep. Now here's the preelection survey of the Sunday *New York Times* from correspondents in forty-eight states indicating Dewey 345 electoral votes, Truman 105. There's a good diagram, too, of the next Republican Congress. Toss that out. Here are those columns about the Dewey administration by Drew Pearson, Mark Childs, Walter Lippmann, the Alsops, and others. Guess they'll be no use to us now.

We rather think we'll keep that thirty-two-page edition of *Kiplinger Magazine* mailed out just before the polls closed. There it lay in the post office, irrecoverable, while the tortured editors gaped at the incredible returns. Here's one we certainly shall keep, lovingly and affectionately: the Home Edition of that sprightly old *Chicago Tribune* with the banner "Dewey Defeats Truman" over the top, and the lead article by Arthur Sears Henning, beginning, "Dewey and Warren won the presidential election yesterday by a large majority of electoral votes."

What's that, Mabel? What shall you do with last week's TRB column explaining Dewey's victory? Don't be impudent, girl! Burn it, burn it, and all the others. And stop in at Woolworth's as you go to lunch and buy us a new crystal ball, dearie; this one seems to have a slight crack in it.

No political writer who sat through the astonishing returns last week will ever forget them. There was personal humiliation for us as a prophet, but a glowing and wonderful sense that the American people couldn't be ticketed by polls, knew its own mind, and had picked the rather unlikely but courageous figure of Truman to carry on its banner.

As the Truman trend became unmistakable, all those anonymous reports from obscure communities seemed to join together in one voice: "We aren't conservatives, as you thought, but liberal. We are less easily fooled than you supposed. The New Deal is not dead; it is the great living reality of our times."

So now we have in the White House a man with the most radical platform in presidential history. On the basis of two months of campaign speechmaking, Truman is well to the left of the Roosevelt New Deal. On the negative side, we have a president who will certainly block outrageous drives by special interests, like the tidelands-oil grab. On the .positive side, Truman at many places in his speeches went beyond Roosevelt.

Take power, for instance: Truman advocates government ownership and operation of transmission lines from government dams right up to the consumers' electric stoves. "Public distribution of publicly produced power" was what he repeatedly told the West. In the field of health insurance, Truman formulates an extension of the Roosevelt policies that goes well beyond the New Deal. In general, Truman made his campaign on the idea that what used to be called "socialism" needs to be extended. Instead of recoiling from the awful proposal, the public elected him and gave him a Democratic Congress.

Can Truman carry such a program through? We have our fingers crossed. Such men as Joe Ball, Harold Knutson, Curly Brooks, and other troglodytes have disappeared from the legislature, but there is the same latent conservative coalition lying in wait in Congress, scared but powerful. Truman's own victory bears analysis. It was the smallest popular plurality in thirty-two years. The turnout of voters was way down in one of the most apathetic contests in years, however electrifying its outcome.

There is some evidence that Gallup and the others really turned the election by lulling Republicans into blissful overconfidence while energetic labor leaders got out and worked. This, of course, is Dewey's postelection position, and it makes a nice alibi. As against it, there are three shattering facts. The power of organized labor to act politically, when united, can no longer be discounted. A whole slew of pro-Taft-Hartley Representatives were knocked off. Second, the farmers voted Democratic. For our money, Iowa's going Democratic is the single most astonishing thing in the whole election.

What does it mean? That farmers no more want to go back to laissez-faire GOP economics than do other voters. Finally one more political dogma is knocked higher than a kite: that a small vote aids Republicans. The theory was that the low-income group was politically less self-conscious than the upper groups. Like the idea that prosperous farmers "always vote Republican," this one just doesn't seem to be true any longer.

For the fifth time in succession the voters have contemptuously disregarded the presidential candidate whom the American editorial writers picked for them. This time, between 80 and 90 percent of all the daily newspapers were on the minority side. It makes one wonder. Isn't it possible for a newspaper to make money and still represent the majority? It wasn't only Dewey who got a black eye on Election Day; the American press is also sporting a shiner.

Victorious Harry

DECEMBER 13, 1948 Victorious Harry Truman waited until 200 or more reporters, scanned by Secret Service men, shuffled into the packed circular study of the White House. Then he stood up behind his big, flat-topped desk and grinned. Everybody grinned back. It was his first conference since the election miracle.

On April 17, 1945, a humble and rather frightened little man had held his first press conference as president in this same room, and had asked reporters to pray for him. There was nothing of that in the Truman mood now. He had the lively, alert, quizzical expression of a fox terrier with its head cocked, as he invited questions. The titters of the White House secretarial claque which attends these conferences, and of the public-relations agents from all the various federal bureaus and agencies, soon rose to a guffaw. Reporters joined in. It was essentially the same simple, modest, average man from Independence, Missouri, standing behind the desk, but he had been right and nearly everybody else in the room had been wrong. It was the reporters who were chastened.

Was this a "new Truman"? Not that we could see. There was a new note of good-natured contempt for "columnists" in what the president said. There was also a new Truman desk mascot reproducing the famous *Chicago Tribune* postelection headline, "Dewey Beats Truman." There was sudden firmness and grimness when the president repudiated a story that he would accept the Thurmond "Dixiecrat" electoral votes, and said he was proud that he had succeeded in winning with neither New York nor the Solid South. There was a conscious effort to stop and think before answering reporters' loaded questions, but this (in our judgment) didn't go very far. There was also the self-assurance that comes to a man who now feels he can appeal over the head of the hostile, prejudiced, American publicity machine to the other plain people of the country.

But Truman is already caught between divided counsel of Left and Right among his own intimates. Secretary of the Treasury Snyder, White House Assistant Steelman, Budget Director Webb, and gentle, scholarly Dr. Nourse urge a conservative fiscal course. The heart of the problem is the fact that the Republicans cut taxes $5 billion. No longer can an expanded social program at home, and the defense and economic-support program abroad, be financed out of a surplus. More money is needed. Compulsory federal allocation controls for such tight materials as steel are needed. Truman faces what may be the most important decision of a four-year term right at the outset. He must decide this month whether to be bold or timid, carry out his mandate or continue with business-as-usual.

Pale, conspiratorial Robert E. Stripling, counsel of the House Committee on Un-American Activities, saw his chance last week. Committee morale was at a low ebb. Chairman Thomas was accused of taking salary kickbacks from his secretaries; two other GOP committee members had been defeated for reelection; "lame-duck" Republican control would soon end. But off-the-record, preliminary court hearings in Baltimore in the $75,000 slander suit brought by Alger Hiss against the self-confessed ex-Communist spy Whittaker Chambers had produced startling new evidence.

Once again the quiet, careful court procedure was bringing out facts that the sensationalism of the Thomas committee had completely missed. Chambers now admitted that he still had documents taken from State Department and other files. Chambers, it appeared, was at last in a mood to "tell all." It was Stripling's chance. Quickly he descended on his former witness with a subpoena. And to the committee which had given him such friendly prominence in the past, Chambers yielded up hundreds of feet of microfilm concealed in a hollowed-out pumpkin on his Maryland farm.

Committee member Karl Mundt (R, S.D.) was in ecstasy. He rushed back to Washington issuing statements. The mimeograph machines of the committee began to hum. Press conferences and confidential tips for the favorite Stripling correspondents began again. Washington had a new sensation to make people forget the election. Once more the quiet process of law was interrupted. Trial by jury was superseded again by trial by headline.

The State of the Union

JANUARY 17, 1949   We caught ourself musing the other day. Come the revolution, shall we recognize it? Consider what President Truman told the Eighty-first Congress in his State of the Union Message under klieg lights, while the world looked and listened. He called for extension of government authority beyond anything Roosevelt ever proposed, and set forth plans for federal intervention in private business that would have been harder to get through a past congressional committee than it would be to open an oyster with a wet bus ticket. And what happened? When the breathtaking speech was over, the stock market went up. Do we ever really know a revolution when we see it?

By craning hard in our press-gallery perch and shifting our ponderous weight to one foot, we could look down on Truman's pink left cheek as he faced the senators, representatives, members of the cabinet, foreign envoys, and crowded galleries. We could also see the left lens of his spectacles and one shoulder illuminated by movie spotlights. The president parts his hair on the left side, so we could see that, too. Truman seemed to be having a better time than anybody else. He came in beaming. Maybe he remembered the last time he stood on this dais—and the time before that—when Congress yawned in his face. It listened raptly this time.

Looking down over the presidential shoulder, we could see the manuscript in the three-ring loose-leaf notebook—about ten very black, short lines to the page, typed like poetry, with wide margins. We watched the presidential right thumb insert itself under the next page, ready for the turn, while his left hand waved in a sort of time-beating gesture. There were eight movie cameras focused on him, a couple of television machines, a dozen spotlights, and five mikes on his desk.

There were thirty-two separate interruptions of applause. But as we listened from our precarious vantage point (between a large Scripps-Howard man and a woman who kept saying she couldn't see a thing) it seemed to us that the applause was pretty humdrum and perfunctory. Truman was giving the speech everything he had. For greater emphasis, he wiggled his shoulders (at least the left one). But the reception of his near-socialist proposals was matter-of-fact rather than excited. And that to us was most interesting.

With Roosevelt, it would have been a crusade. This man had none of FDR's magnificent presence. His startling ideas sounded like Main Street commonplaces. And in its way, it is a gift to be able to make the revolution sound as casual as shopping at the Safeway. So far as we could judge, most congressmen accepted it in the same spirit. Harness the business cycle? Sure, why not? National health insurance? Ho-hum, maybe it's about time. Government transmission lines to the homes to carry government power? Okay, boss, if you want it that way. That was the mood of one of the most memorable events of our topsy-turvy times. It was, in part, a tribute to Truman; even more, perhaps, to the man, now dead, who made the New Deal seem natural and commonplace.

Congress is gathering momentum. What might be described as a Truman "streamroller" is coming into being. Deft, professional hands are taking over. How strange it seems for a change to hear the screams of rage coming from the conservative side! The first of various far-reaching events was the closed-door caucus of Senate Republicans. Some tart observations were exchanged as to why Dewey lost the election. Newspapers described the "crushing" of the anti-Taft rebels in the 28-14 vote.

Actually, of course, the real significance is on the other side—the fact that the revolt is under way at all, and continuing. When you get such Republicans as Saltonstall, Lodge, and Ives calling the party leadership too conservative, it is worth noting.

The House Democratic caucus was similarly significant. Again it was in secret, but news quickly leaked that the Rankin-Smith-Cox trio of Dewey-Dixiecrats had been soundly spanked. Next came the first big test vote on the House floor, on the proposal to curb the autocratic Rules Committee. This administration victory—275-142—really told the story. In a quiet way, the result was spectacular. Only thirty-one Southerners deserted Truman at the shrill call of Cox and Howard Smith (D, Va.). And to counterbalance them, forty-nine Republicans left the GOP and came over to the administration. Even Republicans couldn't stomach a repetition of the arbitrary Rules Committee of the Eightieth Congress—a single forty-watt bulb that could hold up the whole nation's legislative traffic behind one stoplight.

The Two-Headed Turtle

MARCH 28, 1949   Just about the time of the cherry-blossom festival and the DAR's annual raid on Washington, the foreign ministers of the twelve Atlantic Pact countries will show up (April 4) for signature. Winston Churchill, like the first robin, has already arrived, though his business is different from the others'. Well, the dignitaries will see at first hand the operation of one of the most curious and subtle governments on earth, where a mandate in November doesn't look so good in March. We have been through these striped-pants influxes before and know the bland queries put to newsmen by Distinguished Visitors. "How's Truman doing?" they will ask suavely at cocktail parties, and try to hide their interest in the answer. The answer is, "Not so hot, Excellency, not so hot." ·

We modestly suggest that each Foreign minister find time between formal functions to pay a visit to the famous two-headed turtle still alive at the Commerce Department's aquarium. The visit won't take five minutes and will help to explain our government. The turtle is just an ordinary little turtle except that it has two heads. Neither head can understand what the other's doing in its shell. The two heads fight over food, though it's all channeled to the same stomach. They can't ever agree; it's a case where two heads are not better than one. Scientists say a thing like this happens only once in a million times; the chances of its happening in a capital where government is divided into two rival and equal parts are evidently much greater. Keepers have got to calling the two turtle heads "Executive" and "Congress."

The Atlantic Pact promises to go through the Senate all right, probably in May or June. It looks a good deal more like an old-fashioned military alliance to us than one of those regional agreements which is authorized under the UN Charter. The heart of it is Article 5, which discusses military force to resist an aggressor. This has been neatly devised. It is as full of loopholes as a Senate cloture rule, and senators can point to it with perfect truthfulness and say that it has no advance legal binding effect whatsoever.

Actually, of course, it is a moral commitment and binds us to our first European alliance in history and to go to war under certain circumstances. The danger is that Russia will now reply in kind and that the process of daring each other will lead to its inevitable dread conclusion. A military alliance never yet—by itself—succeeded in preventing war.

Where Congress may be difficult is over the little twin brother of the Atlantic Pact, the proposal to rearm Europe. Nobody yet knows what this will cost, though reporters have been loosely saying "one to one and a half billions." This column has pointed out that the US now seems headed straight back into deficit financing. Congress pretty surely isn't going to pass Truman's higher taxes, but will increase his budget (note House action last week pushing the good old seventy-group-plane program ahead again). National income also seems to be coming down, which means lower tax returns.

The Treasury is going back into the red. This genuinely alarms many conservative congressmen who aren't prepared to do anything about it, however, except cry "economy" and perhaps cut Marshall Plan aid (which would leave the new military pact without those constructive accompaniments which alone justify it). Congressmen might also balk at supplying European military aid. This would seem to have the effect of stirring Russia up without taking adequate precautions for the trouble that might follow. Our forecast is that Marshall Plan aid, the Atlantic Pact, and military lend-lease will all go through substantially as the administration proposes.

We keep asking ourself, "Were the Republicans really smart in teaming up with the Dixiecrats on the filibuster?" You can see the temptation they had. It was great fun while it lasted and it made the administration look sick. But does a party win presidential elections that way? The GOP has lost five times straight. It couldn't win last November even with the aid of Dr. Gallup. It will never win again unless it has affirmative policies. And now it has gone and linked itself in an intrigue with that *femme fatale*, the Belle from Dixie.

This may not be a permanent union, but it certainly was soft dalliance while it lasted, as any observer of last week's filibuster noted. The offspring is a curious creature, suh, a cunning little moppet of a sixty-four-vote cloture rule with only one eye. The blind eye is to be turned on any future filibuster directed against strengthening the Senate rules themselves. Well, we are getting all mixed up in our metaphor but you catch our meaning.

Some GOP members, on second thought, were worried over their Dixiecrat alliance. Langer (R, N.D.) rose at one point and ominously told fellow Republicans that he had written the names of three on a slip of paper and put it into a sealed envelope. He predicted all three would lose their seats in 1950 as a result of the filibuster fight, but he didn't mention names.

Majority Leader Lucas wisely said he would give the new GOP cloture rule a tryout on civil-rights legislation before the session ends. The arithmetic seems to us to be against getting the necessary sixty-four votes, but in the present uneasy Republican mood our guess is that they will at least attempt to put something through, perhaps an anti-poll-tax measure.

Are You Now or Have You Ever Been?

MAY 16, 1949   Senator Eastland takes a long drag at his big cigar. "Thank you," he said. "Next witness." "Do you swear to tell the truth, the whole truth, and nothing but the truth, so help you God?" asks the clerk. "I do," says the woman. "Now, Mrs. Jackson," the clerk continues, "in the light of the policy laid down by the chairman of the judiciary subcommittee considering the Mundt-Ferguson bills to curb subversives, I ask the following: 'Are you or have you ever been a member of the Communist Party?'"

"No."

"'Are you now or have you ever been a member of or affiliated in any way with any organization which has been cited by any governmental agency as a Communist organization, a Communist-front organization, or one substantially controlled, dominated, or infiltrated by Communists?' "

"No," says witness. She comes from Brooklyn, she says, representing the Bethel Baptist church and the Congress of American Women. The clerk pounces. The "Congress" is on the attorney general's subversive list. Mrs. Jackson looks genuinely surprised. She says she didn't know it. We look at her more closely. She is a self-possessed Negro. She defends the "Congress." "There's a difference between what a thing really is and what people say about it," she says.

The chairman hesitates. These test questions of Communist affiliation are put to each witness. The second one would seemingly incriminate anybody who ever got into the same room with a Communist, including certain members of the Supreme Court. There is an unmistakable attitude of tension in the room. The big cops stand in the small chamber, looking ready for anything. We don't mind cops— like 'em, in fact—but these seem unnecessarily large, somehow. We don't like Commies, but we must say the scene at the administration of this loyalty test gives us the creeps. Eastland relaxes, takes a long drag at his cigar. "No use ar-goo-ing," he tells the clerk. Witness proceeds. Later in the morning a spokesman for the anti-Communist ADA gives strong testimony against both bills. He charges that such measures aid rather than injure Communists.

Scene II. This is the Senate Foreign Relations Committee. Only once or twice have these much-heralded hearings on the Atlantic Treaty filled the hall. There is significance in the apathy; the public takes approval for granted. A shrunken little man in a brown suit is testifying; gracious, this is former Ambassador to Germany, James W. Gerard, now eighty-two. How time flies. Like anyone who has written for Hearst most of his life, Gerard talks in headlines. "Not to sign that pact means war in a year!" he croaks into the amplifier.

Antipact Senator Donnell tries to interrogate him. His amplified voice thunders from the marble walls. "What, what, what?" says Gerard. Questions are read back to him in his ear. "The need of the Senate to ratify the pact?" he repeats. "Just a technicality!" Donnell froths and fumes. But Gerard has blurted it out. Once the treaty was signed last month, the Senate had little choice but to go along. That is no doubt one of the reasons why the spectator seats are so empty now.

Scene III. A carafe and tumbler sit at the right of picturesque, white-haired Senator McCarran, chairman of the appropriations sub-committee considering State Department funds. He looks pleased, and why not? He is holding Secretary of State Acheson captive below him. The hard-boiled committee occupies the semicircular dais in a scene that illustrates legislative supremacy. Once a year executive department heads must appear before each chamber to justify proposed expenditures. They sit below, humble petitioners.

Few questions are put now to Acheson; his assistant, John E. Peurifoy, handles these matters. But McCarran insists on Acheson's presence. He must sit and hear his policies attacked. He was here yesterday, too. McCarran swells with power. Yesterday he demanded to know why we didn't recognize Spain?

He started to threaten. Unless Spain is recognized, he said, he will see that department appropriations are gone over with a fine-tooth comb. Few people in Washington are quite so crass and crude as McCarran, the Nevada silver-knuckle man. Delighted Republicans chime in: Wherry, Gurney, Bridges. They want aid to Spain, aid to Nationalist China, aid to German industries. Why isn't the State Department aiding all three?

Questions are thrown at Peurifoy about "subversives" in his department. They are aiming through Peurifoy at Acheson. He sits imperturbable. Peurifoy is quick and smiling. McCarran rumbles a demand for the names of everybody in the department connected with formulating Far Eastern policy "since 1930." Gracious, that's eighteen years; quite a chore. Peurifoy quickly promises it.

McCarran glances covertly at Acheson. The latter sits bland and impassive; this won't do at all. Can the secretary come back again this afternoon?

The secretary replies that, well, there are engagements. . . . Well, then, will the secretary hold himself in town from now on, ready for a call? Unfortunately, in two weeks he must leave the country, Acheson suavely explains; there's a little foreign ministers' meeting over in Paris. . . . McCarran looks as though this was a put-up job by the UN to evade him. "We'll have you up here again, before then," he says grimly.

Acheson

AUGUST 8, 1949   Rarely has a congressional committee room been so crowded. Its sides measured 25 × 50. Five movie cameras stood in the corner and whirred like summer locusts as witnesses testified. Their attendant klieg lights from four big dishpan reflectors, tacked under the domed ceiling, canceled out the air-conditioning system and turned the chamber into a blinding oven. Incongruous photographs of national parks lined the walls. A long oblong table with twenty-five committee seats filled the chamber like a ship in dry dock, but fifty folding chairs, of the body-racking variety, were nevertheless squeezed against the walls and here listeners squirmed. This was the unveiling of the administration's historic $1.45 billion arms program before the House Foreign Affairs Committee.

Elegant, ruddy-faced Secretary Acheson came first, his upper-class voice heard above the strident cameras. Knowing the legislative revolt against the plan, he yet gave no sign of it; his display of unswerving confidence was impressive. Defense chiefs and military brass followed; their keynote was calmness and conviction. There was no tub-thumping. The committee listened noncommittally but was obviously flattered that it, not the Senate, was the center of the show. The outcome?—Congress appears to agree with the principle of the military project; the catch is they don't want to pay for it.

The basic paradox of the Truman administration is the difference between the president's almost radical words and the men advising him. The difference between the men around Roosevelt and the men around Truman, as John Fischer said in last month's *Harper's*, is about eighty pounds around the paunch. Now Truman has named Tom Clark to the Supreme Court. The importance of the new member is shown by the court schism now existing. In the last three years there have been eighty-six five-to-four decisions. Cases with dissenting opinions have steadily risen and reached the high mark of 74 percent in the recent session. Murphy's death reduced the Black-Douglas-Rutledge liberal bloc to three against the Frankfurter-Jackson-Burton conservative bloc and the two "swing" men, Vinson and Reed, who frequently hold the balance of power.

The court is a third legislative house that can block progress for years. This column regards Clark as a conservative. His choice at this juncture is a bitter disappointment. In all calmness and candor we submit that it indicates Truman does not have an intellectual grasp of the difference between conservatism and liberalism in the judicial sense.

The word, folks, is "oligopoly." That's what we have in America, not "monopoly." Under monopoly you are gypped by just one big trust; under oligopoly you are gypped by a few trusts acting more or less in concert. The first system is illicit, the second perfectly legal. The small competitor has as much difficulty under the second system as the first. This information is coming out before the Celler committee in the House, which is making a quiet survey of monopoly practices.

The most fascinating testimony so far came from Adolf Berle, who said that the top corporate giants in the US are growing two or three times as fast as all other corporations. The reason we had never fully realized it before: they generate their own capital. Small company AB&C has to go out on the open market and hire money in stock and bond issues; big company XY&Z, on the other hand, simply takes the capital it needs out of current income. Instead of distributing profits as dividends, it retains them for investment.

From 1919 to 1947, says Berle, more than 34 percent of the total American financing came from money earned by corporations and not distributed as dividends. We consider this one of the most important little old statistics we have heard in a long time. What it means is that once a corporation has snowballed into gianthood it almost can't help staying big.

"That's Our Harry"

JANUARY 9, 1950   Harry Truman stands before Congress this week—the little man from Independence, Missouri, to whom the world listens. The scene is the refurbished chamber of the House of Representatives. Seats for the senators are reserved in front. The Speaker raps his gavel, the House members arise and clap politely, and from the rear swinging doors the senators troop in two by two, some tall, some short, some homespun, some pompous; they come in smiling and waving like seniors entering for the first assembly after the holidays. They are seated, and then are ushered in the members of the Supreme Court—four of them Truman appointees and including, many people think, some of the weakest members in the high tribunal's history.

Finally, a voice cries: "The President of the United States." Yes, that's our Harry—entering with his joint escort and coming down smiling, in double-breasted suit and neat handkerchief while the spectators in the galleries crane and the good-natured applause rises from all sides, and every congressman casts a searching look to get a quick appraisal of the man who will be theoretical leader and chief antagonist till next summer. Then the actual election campaign starts.

And what is the situation as Truman starts the new political year?

Superpower USA is pitted against Superpower USSR. We have done fairly well in Europe and taken a bad defeat in Asia. With the struggle going full tilt, there is some doubt whether bipartisan foreign policy can be preserved. As he speaks, Truman can pick out the Wherrys and the Capeharts below him who are isolationists—but he doesn't; he is too busy with his collar and his speech.

He faces a Congress nominally run by his own party. Owing to rotten boroughs, overrepresentation of farm areas, and predominance of local issues in choosing representatives, it is really a Congress upon which he cannot count. He and they know he is trying to establish a record for next autumn's election, a record on key issues like the

Brannan farm plan, Taft-Hartley, health insurance, federal aid to education, and civil-rights legislation by which the voters can judge.

Well, that's the way the political year starts. Truman lacks stature, tends to surround himself with party hacks, can never quite bring himself to cooperate fully with the GOP on foreign policy, fears fast-talking men with brains. On the other hand, if Truman were a bigger man he probably would have more trouble with Congress than he does; he doesn't frighten it the way FDR did.

This year's census will shift about fourteen House seats from state to state. The spectacular development will be the eight seats California will gain. New York loses three seats, Pennsylvania two, and North Carolina, Georgia, Kentucky, Tennessee, Mississippi, Missouri, Illinois, Arkansas, and Oklahoma, one each. Six states will probably gain one seat each: Florida, Texas, Indiana, Michigan, Washington, and Oregon. Significance? There will be all sorts of new gerrymandering of districts; the rural South will be a little less powerful; the energetic West Coast will have ten more seats. This means greater emphasis on reclamation and power projects, greater interest in the Orient, more importance for usually Democratic California in presidential elections.

Early next month the three chiefs of staff will discuss the "battle of Formosa" direct with General MacArthur. The issue is complex, but crucial. India has recognized the new pro-Communist Chinese government; Britain will do so any day now. The Chiang residue government is entrenching itself on Formosa, and pro-Chiang Republican Senators like Taft of Ohio, Knowland of California, and Smith of New Jersey, plus the Scripps-Howard and Luce press, want him supported there. The strategic question is whether Formosa is vital to American defense.

Back of the immediate issue of Formosa is the long-range problem. Secretary Acheson believes it folly to think that Asiatic nationalism can be halted—that, in fact, cooperation with the national governments of India, Indonesia, Pakistan, and the like is the key requirement of combating the spread of communism. Last-ditch American support of the ousted Chiang regime in Formosa would leave the US isolated, not only from India and Indonesia, but from Britain, Australia, New Zealand, and probably Canada. The State Department is being badly hammered on this issue; indeed, it is not certain that the bipartisan foreign policy can survive the controversy.

J. Edgar Hoover

APRIL 10, 1950   At 4:23 in the afternoon of March 27 the five big klieg lights switched on and the six movie cameras on tripods began to whir like crickets as J. Edgar Hoover took the oath and began his testimony. He is a formidable figure, with a round, florid, bulldog face, strong jaw, and rather pop eyes. His thickset torso seems a little out of proportion with his short legs. This is the mysterious head of the FBI testifying in the McCarthy case. We have never had so good a chance to examine him before. He talks fast in a deep, confident voice, obviously a man who may sometimes be wrong but is never in doubt. At fifty-five, his crisp, wavy hair, combed back and held in place by lotion, is hardly touched by gray.

The essence of Hoover's testimony was that FBI files should not be made public to "smear" innocent men. We confess that we were impressed by the way he said it. There was warmth and conviction in his voice. In effect, Hoover damned the whole McCarthy probe.

It was Haldore Hanson's turn next day. He is a State Department official, charged by McCarthy with "a mission to Communize the world." McCarthy charges this former AP correspondent with having been with the Communist armies in China four years, with having written a pro-Communist book on his experiences, and with making pro-Communist policies in the State Department.

Again the crowd leans forward, the six cameras whir, the spotlights beat down pitilessly. McCarthy's charges are all right, it appears, except that it was "four months," not four years; his book (as excerpts show) is a balanced presentation; and he doesn't make State Department policies. Will McCarthy repeat his charges outside the shield of congressional immunity? Hanson demands. No answer. McCarthy isn't there.

Next scene, the Senate floor last Thursday. The galleries are packed as we have rarely seen them, the corners of the Senate floor crowded with visiting representatives come to see the big show. The McCarthy documents occupy the tops of two desks and two chairs.

The atmosphere is something to remember. No one who sees this show will ever underestimate young Mr. McCarthy again. He is the most formidable figure to hit the Senate, we think, since Huey Long. He has the galleries with him. The Republicans around him beam. Taft and Bridges exchange enthusiastic smiles as he sidesteps hostile questions again and again. To read what he says in cold print makes the affair look silly, as in one way, of course, it was: his horrendous charge, for instance, that Owen Lattimore carried "two cameras" on a recent trip to Point Barrow, Alaska, and has a home equipped with darkroom! But here is a new, coolly calculating Martin Dies, fully aware of what he is doing, gambling for the highest stakes, bold and daring and elusive and slippery and already the darling of the Taft-Wherry-Bridges-Gabrielson forces. It would seem easy to pin down the preposterous utterances, but no; McCarthy is as hard to catch as a mist—a mist that carries lethal contagion.

Executive Order on Korea

J U L Y 1 0 , 1 9 5 0   Korea, of course, has changed everything. It started with what is now known technically as The Night of the Big Gloom. On the evening of Monday, June 26, anybody who was Anybody in Washington knew what Truman was going to do; he was going to appease. Weak, vacillating Truman was going to pass the buck to the United Nations and offer them, as someone sardonically put it, "all aid short of help."

This sounds funny in view of what happened, but the gloom was real and, for some, tragic. Informed observers were saying, "*This* is the test. The time will not come again. Nations that do not read history repeat history. If we do not take a stand against this flagrant affront to the United Nations now, nothing will ever stop Russia or World War III."

At 12:07 Tuesday noon, when Truman's executive order hit the wires, Washington took a new look at the president. It found that he had fooled them even more than he did on Election Day, 1948.

It is queer how Truman is constantly underestimated; we can't try to explain it now. Maybe it is his congenital mildness, his buoyancy and shopkeeper affability. Any president's popularity soars, of course, if he takes a strong stand in a foreign crisis, but unless we completely misjudge the man, partisanship was the last thing he thought of. The mood of pathetic fatalism vanished as America came together in an almost unprecedented moral unity, and watched member after member of the United Nations fall in behind her. So Woodrow Wilson's dream came true.

Probably it was Acheson, the man some called pro-Communist, who turned the tide. He knew what the world stakes were and had the president's ear. Suave, aristocratic, elegant—there have been few such figures as secretary of state. We made note that at his momentous press conference last week Acheson wore a dashing yellow bow tie, studded with brown polka dots like an overenthusiastic speckled trout. Well, in its great crisis the American government is not dressed in funeral black. Indeed, there is some indication of a conscious assumption of calm and nonchalance in the official manner. Truman is carefully relaxed. Wall Street may have the jitters, but not Acheson. It is a time for national strength and steadiness. Maybe a bow tie is as symbolic of customary mood and American aplomb as anything.

In one sense the Tuesday pronouncement was a diplomatic masterpiece, sterilizing Formosa and the Republicans simultaneously. The political opposition was left to the *Daily Worker* and the *Chicago Tribune*, and it is not the first time that this strange couple has shared a bed. Bob Taft was unhappy about it all, too, and why not?—where were the GOP arguments that were to win the election?

Washington experiences the profound psychic satisfaction of replacing hesitation with vigorous action. There is some question whether uncomfortable realities in the Korean situation are not being disregarded in the first exhilaration. What Koreans, North and South, seem to want above all else is unity; the arbitrary line along the Thirty-eighth Parallel is one of the most cruel and preposterous in history. It is not America's fault, but it is there, and it makes the sundered southern republic an economic monstrosity. Furthermore, if reports are correct, Russia in the North has had better propaganda success than America has had in the South. It is hard for us to face up to the difficulty a capitalistic democracy faces in trying to prose-lytize a primitive people. Can we win the world and keep free enter-prise, too? Sooner or later we must recognize the fact that wars are not won merely by guns but by ideas.

McCarthyism may take another form in the war crisis; it may fasten, for instance, on the proposed Mundt-Nixon bill, which is as obnoxious a measure as has popped up for a long time. This is the streamlined antisedition bill calling for the registration not merely of all Com-munists but of all so-called front organizations and their membership, too, whether subversive or just gullible. Republicans are seeking des-perately for an issue, Truman's popularity has jumped, McCarthyism is away back on page 36, resistance to higher taxes is ameliorated by patriotic impulse, Taft-Kerr-Wherry isolationism is exposed for the silly thing it is—what is there left? Well, there is left the possibility of great patriotic breast-beating and Red scares. The Mundt-Nixon bill has been indorsed by the GOP Senate Policy Committee. Senator Kilgore (D, W. Va.) says this bill could be used against labor, could in fact be twisted by a hostile prosecutor to cover almost anyone.

The MacArthur-McCarthy Team

NOVEMBER 20, 1950 Russia has everything to gain, the Free World everything to lose, by entrapping the US in the bottomless quagmire of a proxy-war with China. The situation is really quite terrifying. Chinese reinforcements are crossing from Manchuria into Korea, and what happens after the buildup we don't know. It might be World War III. The strained nerves of Europeans have cracked.

They are shrieking warnings at us, and no wonder. Their press has served up raw and ragged from America isolationist yawps, jingo demands for preventive war, McCarthy attacks on Acheson, and now victory-flushed Taft's brutal query, "Can Europe be defeated?"

A frightening aspect is General MacArthur's conviction that he knows the oriental mind, that it respects only force, and that he is running his own Asiatic foreign policy. Everybody in Washington knows this. When you see the cabled phrase "a high Tokyo spokesman," substitute MacArthur. MacArthur wants to bomb hell out of Chinese concentrations behind the border right away, and he is fuming over restraints from the Pentagon, Acheson, and the UN.

There is really a prowar party in America today. It is much bigger than the preventive-war crackpot group. It includes men like Harold Stassen who would give MacArthur full rein. It includes senators like William Knowland and Joe McCarthy who are demanding immediate use of Chiang Kai-shek's Formosan troops against the mainland. It includes the patrioteer primitives who dance and howl at Acheson for resisting immediate retaliation against the Chinese. (On the side, most of them want to cut taxes.) It includes isolationists like Taft who torpedo West Europe's morale. These groups would deny they are the war party. But their actions look to war, and, above all, to the supreme folly of proxy-war all over the globe at the same time.

The importance of the Democratic election defeat was less quantitative than qualitative. Historical averages looked to a loss of about twenty-five to thirty House seats for the majority party in the customary midterm recession, and that is what happened. Both parties, of course, secretly hoped to alter this midterm rule in their own favor. What the Democrats weren't prepared for, however, was the selective elimination of liberals and progressives. Congress has moved strongly from left to right.

It must be said, too, that McCarthyism was almost universally underestimated. We listened to McCarthy's last election speech. Beyond doubt he is the most dangerous man to appear in public life for many a year. Every former falsehood, every past slander was repeated in the Big Lie with a hypnotic, repetitive presentation whose effectiveness cannot be denied. It must have been a great moment for the GOP Respectables who urged him on. We are somehow reminded of the hopeless comment of an old German artist watching the rise of

Hitler: "Every time I hear him I want to throw up, and the worst of it is I want to eat more and more so I can throw up more."

If you ask us, we honestly don't think there will be a major change in foreign policy because of the election. On the domestic front it looks like the return of that characteristic stalemate which is a built-in part of the American Constitution. It is funny how few Americans really understand that White House–congressional eye-gouging is the rule rather than the exception. Republicans will be able selectively to block the president without taking any responsibility in turn. But on the foreign front we are inclined to believe that Joe Stalin still makes our foreign policy and that if the MacArthur-McCarthy team can be restrained, things may go along much as before. The new Gordon Gray report indicates the direction. Isolationists, of course, will try to block this and there may be cuts in foreign aid. We are still counting on Uncle Joe.

Tariffs are coming up again. It is in such details that the increased GOP strength may affect foreign affairs. Under the headline "Tariff Hope Seen in New Congress" the *New York Times* quotes a customs broker right after the election to a big chemical manufacturers' association. He told them to take heart, the new GOP Congress might junk the ITO [International Trade Organization], the proposed tariff simplification program, and even, maybe, the trade agreements act which comes up for renewal in April. The process of controlling inflation proceeds slowly, paralleling the education of the orthodox-minded conservatives in charge.

General Eisenhower and Senator Taft

JANUARY 15, 1951 Years from now we shall remember last week in the contrasting personalities of two men, General Eisenhower and Senator Taft. We watched each man do his stuff—Ike starting off to Europe to raise morale, Taft on the Senate floor tearing it down. It spoiled our sleep for a couple of nights afterward, thinking about it.

Ike looked pretty good to us back in uniform again, we have to admit. This was particularly true after he started talking. He is a simple, direct, unpretentious speaker with none of the spur-jangling rhetoric of MacArthur, thank heaven. There is a fervor about him, too. There he was, with his grin and his pink, bald dome covered with just about as much brown fuzz as it wore back in London in the black war days. In London he was the rallying point of quiet strength. And quite consciously he was going back to Europe now in a new and possibly more difficult kind of crisis, trying to lift hearts, unify spirits, and breathe life into a paper army. He talked at the Pentagon; it was a sudden springlike day and through the window there were fleecy clouds in a blue sky, the placid Potomac, and beyond it the distant white Capitol. The chests of Ike's two assistant generals were hardly big enough to hold all their service ribbons, but Ike's simple five-star uniform carried only a line of three. He struck us as one of the country's precious national assets, standing solidly there and radiating quiet confidence. Hard-boiled reporters seemed to have the same feeling as we came away. We all felt more cheerful and encouraged. He was above politics and malice, and he expressed basic faith in America. It took courage for Ike to throw his reputation into a risky venture like this, and he did it unhesitantly.

It took some courage, maybe, for a politician like Harry Truman to send a potential rival on a great throw of the dice like this from which Ike might someday reach the presidency. If we know our little man in the White House, he didn't hesitate either.

So now we come to Taft on the Senate floor the next day declaring that "We had better commit no American troops to the European continent at this time." Taft spoke earnestly and sincerely. He read his 10,000-word speech and read it fast. Sometimes he grew so intent he got ahead of himself and had to repeat. He swayed rhythmically, holding the pages in his left hand. The speech ranged all over the foreign-policy lot and was partly self-justification and legalistic criticism of the administration and partly reiteration of the theories that made Taft and a handful of others vote originally against the Atlantic Pact. Our spirits fell lower and lower as we looked down, fascinated.

This was not isolationism like Hoover's; it was defeatism. Taft was telling the young men and the taxpayers and the mothers that it wasn't worthwhile, really, to employ big US armies: (a) we couldn't afford it, (b) we could do everything cheaper and easier with air and sea power, (c) Russia probably wasn't going to attack anyway, and (d) if it did, we could do little to stop them in Europe. "But isn't this defeatism?" demanded Senator Paul Douglas (D, Ill.). Taft didn't deny it, just repeated that Russia could move in anytime and that trying to create a big army would probably provoke Moscow to strike. When Senator Fulbright (D, Ark.) used the word "shocking" in describing this thesis, Taft heatedly replied that the destruction of Europe's industrial potential wouldn't come from advancing Russians: it would be destroyed, he observed cheerfully, from the atom bombs of retreating Americans dropped to render the plants useless. What a billet-doux to send along with Eisenhower to Europe! We can imagine nothing so calculated to curdle the blood of the nerve-torn people Ike is trying to unite with us.

There was an undercurrent of partisan bitterness in what Taft said, but of his sincerity and earnestness there could be no doubt. Well, the big debate has started in Congress. Taft was notably more extreme in his answers to floor questions than in his prepared comments; he was back on the cautious side again in his "Meet the Press" radio interview next day.

Truman partly answered Taft in his State of the Union address Monday; Taft came on again in his National Press Club speech Tuesday. Truman was back again in his economic report to Congress scheduled for midweek.

Congress met in refurbished chambers as sprig and fresh as new Easter hats. The Senate Democrats picked, as majority leader, genial, dogged, beefy McFarland of Arizona.

While we think of it, we should note the absence of practically all national columnists and Washington newspaper bureau chiefs while Taft was speaking. There is a tendency among the Washington "Deep Thinkers" in the press corps to ignore the difficult job of covering Congress. Some of them regard Congress as rather nasty anyway. We hold no brief for Congress, God knows, but the columnists' idea that Messrs. Dewey and Dulles are formulating foreign policy, and not Congress, is carrying things to extremes.

"Truman Can't Avoid
Firing MacArthur"

APRIL 16, 1951   We don't see how Truman can avoid firing MacArthur. It may cause a row with Republicans, but that is
inevitable anyway. Our own idea is that MacArthur's supposed political strength is a myth built up by the very failure of Truman to
deal with him. The present contemptuous insubordination of Mac-
Arthur can't go on. Truman has been trying to avoid the showdown,
knowing that when the new Japanese peace treaty is signed, General
MacArthur's role of "emperor-by-proxy" will end anyway. Mac-
Arthur is forcing the issue now. He has adopted a deliberately mis-
chievous attitude without parallel in our history. Truman's slowness
to act is a cause of humiliation to Americans abroad while it is practically suicidal to his own prestige here at home.

Meanwhile, the draft bill comes to a vote in the House this week.
Efforts to "scare" Universal Military Training through the chamber
appear to have failed. First it was Secretary Marshall, passionate advocate of UMT, who warned the country that the nation's peril is
equal to that at the height of the Korean crisis. Then Speaker
Rayburn, coming from the White House, told the House that "We
stand in the face of terrible danger and maybe the beginning of the
third world war." Then Truman told his press conference that the
danger is just as great as ever.

There can be no doubt that relaxed effort and complacency hang
like a cloud over Washington. The administration wants to counteract
it. Again, men like Marshall, who have seen the US enter every war
unprepared and tear its armies to bits when the war ended, feel that
permanent preparedness under UMT is vital for self-preservation. But
in the face of all this, the House is still in no mood for the program.
It is likely to accept instead a face-saving, make-believe UMT proposal under which decision is reserved until some further crisis does
(or does not) occur. If the new Vinson compromise is approved, it

will mean protracted bargaining with the Senate which approved full UMT at the height of our retreat in Korea.

Many observers believe that the proposed deferment of bright college students from the draft won't pass Congress. The idea looks all right to Director of Selective Service Hershey and some educators, but it runs counter to deep instincts that in a democracy draft service is a universal duty. The contempt and dislike that would fall on brainy youths from their fellows if they accepted privileged status must also be reckoned with.

Marshall, Rayburn, and Truman were mysteriously ambiguous about the supposed new dangers confronting America. Were they simply talking for political effect? Probably not. The Chinese Communists seem about ready for their counteroffensive. It may be the supreme test in Korea. Hostile air power has increased there, almost certainly manned and supported by Russians in Manchuria. If Russia does intervene now to any degree with planes and naval vessels, it is difficult to see how general war can be avoided. The Soviet Union may suppose that it can fight a limited war in Korea—as Japan did along the Amur River before World War II. But limited wars are possible only with dictatorships and autocracies. Public opinion in a democracy would hardly permit such a neat little packaged struggle. One reason top administration leaders are issuing solemn warnings of peril now may be to emphasize that point for Moscow.

Russian Aggression and the "Middle Way"

A U G U S T   6 ,   1 9 5 1   Can Russian aggression be curbed without major war? That is the midcentury's supreme question. It goes to the heart of all Washington issues. America will fight to block aggression; but can we block it without fighting? The wisest and ablest men whom we know in Washington think that we can if we follow the "middle way" outlined by Truman at Detroit. It requires resoluteness, sacrifice, planning, above all international cooperation.

But the enemies of the "middle way" are not merely the Russians. They are here at home, the demagogues, the partisans, the fanatics, the primitives. They are the isolationists and all those who oppose coolness, self-discipline, and steadfastness. They are those who would grab the wheel and skid us into war's end. This is not child's play anymore; over the edge lies atomic war. The scared world watches the Washington drama—a drama with no repeat performance.

General MacArthur at Boston said that the government had "no foreign policy." This is almost identical with the Taft line. Both men regard the UN war in Korea as "useless." MacArthur's oratorical style is a thing of wonder; it is rich and thick and overwhelming like a double ice cream sundae laced with molasses. One spoonful gives some unfortunates intellectual diabetes. And always Mac and Taft oppose the "middle way" or deny it exists. They have a better proposal: spend less money and take greater military risks. Who cares about a third world war? They make a powerful team for 1952.

Truman told the story of the reporter from the Madison, Wisconsin, *Capital Times* who spent July 4 trying to get signatures to a "petition" containing quotations from the Declaration of Independence and the Bill of Rights. Out of 112 persons, 111 refused. Americans were afraid to sign.

Truman at Detroit also mentioned the St. Lawrence Seaway. "There never was a project in the history of the country more badly needed," he said. The program was tabled (killed) in the House Public Works Committee last week. Democrats voted 10 to 5 for the Seaway; Republicans voted against it 10 to 2. The vote symbolizes the difference between the parties and also the coalition, 15 to 12, that is killing most progressive legislation.

Next liberal item on the GOP-Dixiecrat agenda for defeat is a little decision by the Supreme Court. The Court holds that oil and mineral wealth off the shores of the continental US belongs to all the people; the conservative coalition in the House expects to reverse this and turn so-called tideland back to adjacent states for quick, private exploitation. The Senate may block the move. Truman would almost certainly veto such a measure.

Pat McCarran was starting the open hearings of the Senate's Subcommittee on Internal Security. He called visiting Senator McCarthy up to

the table. He began to read the mimeographed, mouth-filling statement which somebody had prepared. He read in a high, portentous
voice. There were ornate lapidarian phrases like "successful conspira-
tors are often consummate dissemblers." There was a long pause before
"consummate." Reporters waited. McCarran tried it with his tongue,
ventured out on it like an elephant on a bridge, feeling it syllable by
syllable. "Dissemblers" was a hard one, too, but McCarran made it.
Everyone sighed with relief. The latest hunt for subversives was on.

Ike Didn't Say No

SEPTEMBER 24, 1951   All Ike had to say was no. Former GOP
Chairman Hugh Scott went to Paris to sound him out. Ike could have
stopped his candidacy then and there. He did not. Scott reported back
enthusiastically, and immediately hardheaded politicians, led by Tom
Dewey, announced Ike would run. Ex-Senator Harry Darby will manage Ike-GHQ in Washington. Over and above Scott's information,
this column is positively assured Ike has made up his mind. He will
not play coy. His answer is yes, and he will resign as supreme commander and take off his uniform the instant he announces his intent.

This means a showdown battle with Taft as to who runs the
Republican Party. The fight has started and it could be as exciting as
the subsequent presidential race itself. Behind Taft are the Midwest
isolationists, the reactionaries, the *Chicago Tribune*, the Hearst press,
and Joe McCarthy. The Dewey-Saltonstall-Eisenhower Republican
group on the other hand represents moderate conservatism at home
and, abroad, the internationalism of Vandenberg, Stimson, and Elihu
Root.

At San Francisco last week Republican Governor Earl Warren told
reporters he would welcome a showdown Republican convention
floor fight to decide once and for all who owned the party. He says

flatly that McCarthy is killing the GOP and that Taft can't beat Truman. That is just what Democrats here believe.

Funniest thing is the transformation of Acheson to a popular hero since his TV performance against Gromyko. Probably it won't last. But those very qualities in Acheson that infuriate congressmen—imperturbability and steely good manners—helped squelch the Russians. It seemed to millions of Americans watching the TV show in California that instead of being "soft" to communism as McCarthy has monotonously charged, Acheson was knocking the daylights out of Soviet delegates and doing it with an icy politeness that made it all the more galling and devastating.

On the world front we are reaching a climax. Five years after World War II we pledged ourselves never to let our enemies rearm; we are now making their rearmament the condition for taking them back into respectability. First Japan, now Germany. Aside from the tragic irony of the situation, the fact is that it is forced upon us by Moscow, and Moscow is now given another invitation to end the cold war. The Big Three foreign ministers fear that piling the German agreement on top of the Japanese Treaty may bring Armageddon. So they made a gesture of conciliation at the end of their Washington conference.

Columnist Joseph Alsop shows that professional ex-Red Louis Budenz contradicted himself under oath about the political affiliations of John Stewart Service, one of the State Department China desk officials the McCarran committee is trying to picture as a Communist plotter. When Senator Lehman (D, N.Y.) sought to put this and other Alsop columns into the *Congressional Record*, Republicans objected. The McCarran evidence so far is almost wholly hearsay, and the victims of the attack have not been permitted to testify. Meanwhile the China Lobby goes uninvestigated. But a big new development has occurred, the charges of graft and corruption against Nationalist China by high officers of its own purchasing mission here. Even Senator Knowland (R, Calif.), an uncomplicated extrovert, is a little daunted in his support of Chiang. The defense of Chiang has become so passionate and personal, however, among the pro–China Lobby, anti-Acheson crowd that it could lose us the cold war. Fifty-six senators have signed a round robin against taking Mao's China into the UN under any circumstances. This comes as impartial experts on the Far East plead for a flexible policy and stress the possibility—remote though it may be—of weaning China away from Moscow.

The A-Bomb and McMahon

OCTOBER 1, 1951   Two years ago this week, President Truman announced that there had been an atomic explosion in Russia. The frightened leaders of the Western world knew that the Soviet Union had solved the nuclear riddle which it was not supposed to solve for three years more. America's security sense of A-bomb monopoly was suddenly exploded. Now Senator Brien McMahon (D, Conn.), in one of the most important Senate speeches in a generation, has carried the cat-and-mouse spiral around another turn. That old sense of security is returning. American atomic knowledge, he reveals, has proceeded so far, so fast, as to call for a fantastic revolution in military weapons. Fissionable material promises to become so cheap that the prospective atomic shell may cost no more than a modern tank.

Washington immediately asked itself (as it does for most congressional speeches) was the senator speaking from knowledge or through his hat? Research at the Pentagon immediately revealed impressive support for McMahon: he was voicing the military view, even though it means dropping the present-type armies and navies down the drain in a few years. The prospect is for an interval in which some of the old sense of A-bomb security may be restored (providing, of course, Moscow will wait for the new weapons).

Moscow's choice comes in Korea. The Chinese can't win without major Russian aid, which might bring on the big war. Failure to give such aid is probably driving a wedge between Peking and Moscow. Tentative resumption of Kaesong peace talks shows the Communists' desire to liquidate the bloody struggle. A fluid diplomatic policy on our side might still detach Peking and cancel out Moscow's single biggest victory since World War II. The chances, of course, are slim, but they are altogether nonexistent if Congress treats any attempt by the State Department even to explore the matter as subversive. There is never a better time to carry an olive branch than when you have an A-bomb in the other hand, as Senator McMahon knows.

Congress is hell-bent for home, and it is rather good fun to watch it. It spent nine months haggling over the first $13 billion of the taxpayers' money but will toss out the next $70 billion quick in the fortnight ahead because it wants to quit. Its dreary record shows almost as many investigations (130) as laws passed (140). After beating breasts for "economy," Congress cynically overrode the president's veto last week in order to pour out more millions to the veterans' lobby. There were only nine senators brave enough to vote against overriding. The session is winding up with an amusing exposure of the conservatives' pretensions in favor of a balanced budget. Conservatives are fighting tooth and nail against the higher taxes necessary to balance it. For generations liberals have been taunted with being "unsound money" men, a characterization which, now the chips are down, seems to apply much more to inflation-bent tories.

Truman's argument that a national chairman of a political party is here to do unpaid favors for friends and that this is ethical and proper won't hold water. It is true that Washington's ambiguous moral climate has permitted such intervention, and both parties have followed it. But it is hypocritical make-believe to pretend that a telephone call from the White House or Democratic GHQ about a loan, an appointment, or similar favor isn't "pressure." It is pressure of the strongest kind. No judge would countenance such political telephone-calling about a pending case for a moment. Democratic headquarters, or E. Merl (mink coat) Young, called up the RFC [Reconstruction Finance Corporation] on the Lithofold loan almost daily. An ironic feature is that the GOP has been caught in the same game. The probe of Democractic Chairman Boyle is likely to lose GOP Chairman Gabrielson his job. He appears to have been working hard with the RFC for a client of his, the Carthage Hydrocol Company. This may take some of the wind out of the Republican sails. Unfortunately it will also tend to leave the present vicious system just as it is.

Everybody in Washington is debating "whether Ike could beat

Truman." At first sight, Ike would seem a certain winner in such a presidential race. A lot of correspondents are not so sure, however. They argue: "It's hard to unseat an administration in time of prosperity; Democrats have been increasing their relative proportion to Republicans for fifty years and now outnumber them; Truman is a tough campaigner and won in '48, despite the loss of New York, because of the left wing, and four southern states because of the right. Also, Ike would have to come out of the clouds and take positive stands on issues with accompanying loss of his military glamor role." Whatever the accuracy of the foregoing, Truman has never acted more confident than now.

Organized labor faces its worst threat in years from Mexican "wetbacks" now pouring illegally over the border. They are undercutting wages and hours worse than old-fashioned "scabs" because they have no legal rights and are wholly at the mercy of employers. A half million wetbacks were apprehended and sent back last year, and it is assumed as many more got in. Wetbacks are invading such northern cities as Chicago, Detroit, and New York. Congress will do little or nothing about this problem for the simple reason that it primarily favors the employer interest, and this means lower wages and longer hours for US workers and fatter profits for influential constituents. In signing the emasculated Ellender-Poage bill regulating Mexican immigration Truman implored Congress for quick action on a stronger law. Without the strongest pressure from trade unions Congress won't do anything.

Cabot Lodge

JANUARY 14, 1952 Squatted on the carpet of the elegant Shoreham Hotel suite with the camera light crisping our back hairs, we could look up the pinstripe of Cabot Lodge's trousers to the smile of the personable senator. From that angle we noted what good teeth he has. As our glance raised to head level, however, we kept catching the eye of the six-foot, blown-up photograph of Eisenhower on the back wall who had embarrassingly singled out us, of all the 150 reporters present, for his direct personal grin. At that proximity it is a little overpowering. We tried ignoring him and kept our mind on the announcement that Ike's name would be entered in the New Hampshire GOP primary. We got the intuitive feeling that Ike would win the primary—and maybe the presidency, too. The most fun was when an intrusive congressman tried to ask a question and the tense reporters, hammering Lodge with questions, with a perfectly unanimous howl of rage demanded what he was butting in for. He made noises like a man who had received a direct head-blow from the speaker's gavel. We got away finally without looking, Ike still grinning at us.

Washington's sluggish season is over and suddenly there is more news than you can follow. It will be like this until June, when Congress will quit early to campaign. Winston Churchill arrived by air. He looks older. Congress is back and Truman gives them the works in a series of three messages. The election preliminaries are gathering steam: Eisenhower's candidacy is announced by indirection. Truman will probably make his own intentions known within a month. Governor Earl Warren is resisting the efforts of Taft's managers to stampede the GOP. Young, liberal Senator Kefauver (D, Tenn.) is making known his own availability. On top of that there is foreign news. Washington is whirling at top speed again.

We repeat what we have said several times before: our best information from the State Department and Pentagon is that the active war stage in Korea is about over; however, long truce-talk haggling continues. It is not too early to calculate the historical consequences of Korea; there are three in particular whose importance can't be exaggerated: It has removed the doubt that the West would tolerate further Russian aggression. We won't. It has put America in a posture of defense so that, for the first time in history, American strength will be available immediately if war breaks out without any two-year wait —a condition that might have averted World Wars I and II. Thirdly, we and Russia now know, almost certainly, that any similar act of aggression will precipitate full-scale war, not limited war; the narrowness by which extension of the Korean War to China and Siberia was averted, which came in the row between MacArthur and Washington, proved that.

A lot of people think that when and if the Korean truce is signed they can breathe freely and relax. Already signs contradict this. Moscow is developing a post–Korean War strategy. There was Stalin's New Year's message to Japan; there is a Kremlin campaign for an East-West trade conference in Moscow this spring: there is prospect of stiffer pressure against the French in Indochina once Korea quiets down.

If Moscow reopened East-West trade, it would have the most far-reaching consequences. Moscow's postwar trade blockade has driven Western Europe into the North Atlantic Alliance and the arms of the USA. If Western factory products could once more be exchanged for Kremlin raw materials, Europe's economic recovery would be swift. It would probably do more to solve Britain's woes than any other one thing. Washington dollars would no longer be lifesaving. Moscow's move would save Washington money—and it would also probably knock the economic foundations out from under the NATO.

Churchill and Sir Walter Raleigh

JANUARY 28, 1952   It will be our grim duty in weeks to come to record the progress of Eisenhower's descent from national hero to partisan politician. Many political innocents won't be aware for another couple of months that this process is inevitable if Ike is to get nominated, for he won't get it by acclamation. Already GOP newspapers are urging ruthless Taft forces for God's sake to go easy— they are destroying the party! What they don't understand is the passionate fervor of Taft leaders. The leaders' mood comes from Taft himself: he has the moral strength of absolute certainty that he is right. He is peddling a brand of salvation, and the mood of his saints is one of consecration. They are elderly, upper-bracket Republicans who deplore liberal deviationists and have a big hold on party machinery. They are not going to tolerate any five-star interloper. Another five-star hero, General MacArthur, will get to work on Ike shortly in Taft's interest. The most urgent kind of pressure is being put on Ike to come home and fulfill tentative speech appointments like that in Philadelphia, mentioned in this space last week. He is soon going to be cruelly told that if he doesn't, he can't win. We rather pity Ike because he is a nice chap, naive in politics, and suffering badly as he now finds out the facts of life. We rather guess that he will come home.

Somebody last week said that Churchill's speech to Congress may not have been his greatest, but it was the best Congress has heard since he was last here. Deep down in everybody's heart was the feeling that this was the kind of thing Congress itself might have if it only would. The immeasurable uplift that would come to American public life under a parliamentary system of united powers where the party leader stands in the well of the legislature, facing a responsible opposition, is self-evident. In the House of Commons it is forbidden to read from a prepared text except by special permission. There are not five men in Congress today who would dare to review, officially, the world's delicate problems without a prepared advance text, as Churchill did. So confident was the Associated Press that it would get the inevitable prepared text an hour after the speech started that when no text appeared, the New York office was frantically trying to get a recording, not having bothered to transcribe the speech itself. Winnie spoke from a sheaf of notes. It was the spontaneity that made all the difference. (We smiled at one point, when he praised Vandenberg's bipartisan foreign policy, at Taft's dainty fingertip applause below.)

Next day the elderly, cherubic prime minister spoke at an off-the-record press lunch before an immense throng. The audience rose and cheered as he entered, the band boomed, and the official party moved down the cleared aisle. Just across from us a dashing young lady from *Newsweek* had dropped her napkin in rising. What a gesture for him in this moment of adulation to pick it up; the actor in him found it irresistible. It was a bad ten seconds for his jittery entourage as the smiling Winnie somehow creased his roly-poly body—one anxious attendant started a dive of his own. But Winnie—with the courtliness of a Marlborough—retrieved the miserable hotel drape. What an air! Bless us if we didn't see—as he passed—the gartered shade of Sir Walter Raleigh in the crowd, waving his plumed hat on sword point and shouting in the tumult, " 'Swounds and oddsbodkins'; good show, old boy, good show!"

Margaret Chase Smith

APRIL 21, 1952   We can't help feeling that liberals who are trying to support Eisenhower are in for bitter disillusionment. Last week we pointed out that Truman would veto the $40 billion states'-rights offshore oil grab and asked what Ike would do. Now we know. The answer is official and definitive; Ike would sign the bill. Ike wrote Jack Porter, Texas campaign manager, March 28, in a letter printed by the *Dallas News,* April 7, that "federal ownership in this case, as in others, is one that is calculated to bring about steady progress toward centralized ownership and control, a trend which I have bitterly opposed." Mr. Porter explained, "There has never been any doubt in my mind as to the position General Eisenhower would take."

Let us see what this means. The Supreme Court has ruled four times that the offshore mineral rights belong to the federal government and all the people. Ike attacks this theory as "centralized ownership . . . a trend which I have bitterly opposed." By the same logic Ike would give away all public lands. The bipartisan American Council on Education, representing tens of thousands of schools and school-teachers, endorses the Hill-O'Mahoney bill to earmark the revenue from offshore oil for federal education. The Senate defeated this bill, 50 to 35. Ike says the majority did right. Truman will fight for federal control and the oil-for-education bill so long as he is president and will veto the alternative states'-rights grab that would turn over so much of the nation's property to the three states of California, Texas, and Louisiana for private exploitation. Ike says he would approve the grab. People ask where Ike stands. Well, here is one answer. He stands far to the right of the FDR-Truman New Deal.

Last week we predicted Ike's resignation would reach here "this Saturday (April 12)." Actually the news broke a day earlier, on Friday. We apologize. *Time* and *Newsweek* will have the story any day now.

Before coming home, Ike will make a farewell tour to Brussels, The Hague, Oslo, and Copenhagen, April 16–23. This journey will be the first presidential campaign trip on European soil in history. Thought of it makes Taft leaders froth at the mouth. Ike today is probably at his all-time peak of postwar military popularity. One can't help sympathizing a bit with the Taft boys as they see him, in absentia, campaigning in uniform while they fight bitter primaries in New Jersey, New York, and Pennsylvania, April 22, and in Oregon, May 16. There is great danger here. Hitherto "internationalism" has been predominantly bipartisan, even in the GOP. There is every indication that from now on Taft forces will try to pin the onus for every hardship, miscalculation, and prejudice relating to world affairs on Ike, and in so doing will involve the nation in a raging foreign policy free-for-all. The House has just cut the $52 billion defense budget to $46 billion. It will be a wonder if the GOP family row does not extend into this, too.

Senator Margaret Chase Smith (R, Maine) wore a red rose on her left shoulder as she vindicated the Senate's honor against McCarthyism. While the swarthy, saturnine senator from Wisconsin paced the floor restlessly last Thursday with a fixed smile, the little gray-haired woman from Skowhegan did what everybody has been wanting to do for two years—she gave him a tongue-lashing, couched in polite parliamentary terms, and she wound up with a 60-to-0 vote against him. For the lucky correspondents on hand it was the happiest day in 1952. McCarthy had slipped. Instead of denouncing helpless outsiders he had made the mistake of attacking as thieves and pickpockets the five-member Senate subcommittee of his colleagues set up to investigate him. Not one member of the ninety-six stood up to defend McCarthy's charges. He had advocates, it is true—Dirksen (R, Ill.) and Hickenlooper (R, Iowa)—but the best his pals could do was to pooh-pooh the whole affair. Indomitable Mrs. Smith, who seemed fairly to tower on the Senate floor, repeatedly asked the uncomfortable Hickenlooper if he had ever been called a "thief" by a colleague, and why he thought the charges unimportant?

The scene left a curious nightmare impression on us: that sinister smiling figure of McCarthy pacing restlessly, jumping up and down to interrupt others, making a bravura exit before the vote, was like an evil force that had somehow got loose amidst tumult and confusion and which some discomfited senators were trying to hustle back into its box while others pretended it wasn't there.

Ike in Abilene

JUNE 16, 1952   Abilene is still a nice town—the kind you would like to raise children in—and in the memory of Dwight Eisenhower it is still nicer. He left it forty years ago, in 1911, to enter West Point. He has carried the memory with him around the world. There have been forty years of public service, largely abroad, and always there has been in the back of his mind this neighborly little town, set on the flat prairie, as representing the verities of America.

It is good for a political correspondent to visit Abilene, for it explains much. General Eisenhower's social ideas may be forty years out of date, his dream of returning America to the friendly simplicities of Abilene may be hopeless (and under certain circumstances perhaps even tragic), but of its meaning the daily tableaux of the homecoming celebration left no doubt. On that last morning, when only the candidate's own special train was left of the village of Pullman cars that had housed press and dignitaries, the general and "Mamie" finally appeared. He held in his hand a tender little bunch of flowers, the type of bouquet that a sentimental valentine would show a young man holding, and without any embarrassment he took them to his car. They were flowers from his mother's garden. Then for twenty minutes he and Mamie stood on the Pullman steps signing autographs for Abilene children—so fresh at the political work that he gave a full signature, "Dwight D. Eisenhower," while his wife with her bangs cheerfully wrote "Mamie Doud Eisenhower." Another homegrown bouquet was passed up to her; "Gee, there's nothing smells sweeter than a garden rose!" she observed. That's Mamie.

It was a tender scene, too, when Ike dedicated the foundation to his parents' memory. He spoke without a note, and he is a superb extemporaneous speaker in his simple sincerity. His parents' religion was "live and lusty," he said—there was "nothing sad about it." He added: "And they were frugal, possibly of necessity, because I have found out in later years we were very poor—but the glory of America is that we didn't know it then."

That is his memory of Abilene. European correspondents were startled by his constant public reference to the Deity. They were told that it was frequent in American politics—look at Truman. But was it sincere; was it in good taste? The question of taste was optional, American colleagues replied; but as to sincerity there seemed little doubt. Eisenhower and his five brothers were raised on the Bible in a devout Mennonite sect. At the dedication ceremony he recalled that just eight years before, to the day, he had postponed the D-Day landing because of the weather—the most agonizing decision of his life. He pointed out—reverently—that the storm abated just enough to allow a landing but not enough to undeceive the enemy, who were consequently taken by complete surprise. This column does not wish to be irreverent. But the weather in Abilene on homecoming day seemed almost in control of Eisenhower, too. Rain stopped just long enough for the dedication, began again but cleared briefly an hour later for the big parade, poured like water from a faucet thenceforward till nearly 5:00 P.M. CST when Ike had an appointment from an unsheltered stand in the fairgrounds with 10 million radio and television fans, stopped on the dot of five, and then started punctually again as he finished.

The Eisenhower speech was a shock to correspondents. It was devout, platitudinous, and dull. It probably lost him a million votes.

Far more revealing was the question-and-answer press conference next day. It occurred in the local movie house, with TV cameras winning their battle to be present against the angry protest of reporters. The floor writhed with radio and TV cables, and the murals on the walls were garish fairy-tale landscapes drawn by a house painter. It was a mad setting. Ike was master of the ordeal every minute. He was natural, sincere, warmhearted. He qualified almost every answer, or spoke in generalities. He could not be pushed beyond the line he set for himself. He has an effective little trick of non sequitur in which he begins, "I do not think this," and after developing at length what he does not think, says suddenly and positively as though in a burst of confidence, "But I *do* think this," and comes out with the answer to quite another question. There could be no doubt who won the Eisenhower-reporter duel. He charmed his audience and left it still uncertain. In a very important sense Eisenhower since his return to America has never had a press conference at all. What he has done so far is to appear on television shows where reporters asked questions, as captive performers, without being paid for it.

Even with this kind of mechanical protection, however, the Eisenhower replies outline a conservative man. Most revealing was the disclosure that Ike accepted the Republican Congressional Declaration of Policy of February 1950, written for the midterm campaign. Ike accepted this, with unspecified reservations, as representing his "political philosophy." Liberal Republicans who are now foremost in supporting Ike against Taft—Lodge, Margaret Chase Smith, Ives, and Governor Dewey—either criticized this declaration or rejected weasel-worded phrases on labor or foreign policy, which Taft, on the contrary, eagerly accepted. Friends who chatted with Ike later got the impression that he had not known that his close supporters found fault with the declaration; as he explained, it sounded all right to him. The circumstance is significant. Eisenhower is a shrewd man. But he knows little of politics and almost nothing of many modern social and economic issues. He does not know his own political handlers. He is in a terribly exposed position. It is charming to hear him say boldly, "I don't know the answer." But once this present honeymoon period ends, he must know the answers.

Nobody could doubt the well-meaning nature of the candidate's philosophy—a little to the right of Taft here, a little to the left there, and always couched in generous, modest, patriotic terms. He is exposed to pressures by vested interests whose slogans of "free enterprise" and "antibureaucracy" appeal tremendously to him. Indeed some of this appeared later in informal talks with friends. He spoke approvingly of an effort by self-constituted representatives from nineteen states to work out a farm plan. He frankly admitted he did not understand it perfectly, but what delighted him was that each and every one condemned the "Brannan Plan," the epithet-phrase in agriculture which symbolizes for him the hated "centralization."

Was Eisenhower asked by Truman to accept the Democratic presidential nomination? President Truman has denied it. The categorical assertion was written by Arthur Krock, head of the *New York Times* Washington bureau, and the report led the good, gray paper with three-column headlines. The American press has generally taken the position that it would believe Krock any day in preference to Truman. The only difficulty is that Eisenhower tells intimates the story is untrue. His version of the famous Truman interview does credit to both men. Truman began the discussion by saying that there was one subject, politics, he would not raise in order that there should be no constraint between them. At the end of the conference Truman praised Ike's service and observed that he would always have confidence in him. That was all. If the Krock story is right and both men are lying, he has the scoop of the century; if Krock is wrong, as seems likely, then it only shows that the reliable *New York Times* is human after all.

When you take the Army uniform off Gen. Douglas MacArthur his whole personality seems to collapse. But General Eisenhower, on the contrary, seems little changed. He is the same honorable, affable, impressive figure. He introduces his wife as "Mamie," and he and Mamie seem to share a sort of middle-aged exuberance in getting out of the army at last and in seeing the Kansas landscape around them.

Eisenhower's technical equipment as politician must be described as superb. He was the man picked out of all the army to run the European command because he was able to get on with everybody. After years of dealing with Monty and other Allied commanders, domestic politics seem like child's play. We watched Ike handle a trainload of delegates, and there was a verve and gusto in his technique that sublimated the ancient business of backslapping into something higher than art.

Underneath this charm there is steel. This was the man who made the 1944 decision to postpone D-Day. Reporters watched him at Abilene as the rain threatened to spoil the whole great outdoor TV setup. Technicians at last said there was still just time to move the whole thing under the grandstand if they worked fast. It was raining hard, but there was light in the west. Everything was at sixes and sevens. Suddenly Ike took command; he spoke crisply. They were going to hold the show outside as planned, he said. Everything fell into order. He walked to the exposed stand. A big market umbrella had been set up for him. "Take that thing away," he said briefly. There was no doubt about it—this was An Order. There was no loss of temper, or even geniality.

Add to this, finally, that Ike is one of the best informal extemporaneous speakers living, and then ask whether he can win the nomination by the tactics he is following. It is still an even-money bet whether the Old Guard regulars will prefer to take Ike or commit probable suicide with Taft. ("After all, aren't a lot of Democrats for Ike—doesn't that show he's unsafe?") Actually, Ike strikes us, with his turn-of-the-century Abilene idealism, as just about as conservative as Taft. He is, of course, infinitely wiser on foreign affairs. But his road is spread with pitfalls, carefully baited by designing men with Ike's pet prejudices. They will all tell him, again and again, that he can stretch a point for political advantage. Will he be smiling at the end of the campaign as he is today?

Stevenson

SEPTEMBER 22, 1952 Cynical newsmen covering candidates have the habit of opposing the politician they are with. Perhaps that accounts for the overwhelming preference for Stevenson in the traveling Eisenhower party. A recent poll showed 24 favored Stevenson, 7 Eisenhower, and 6 undecided. But a poll on the Stevenson plane also showed Stevenson ahead—19 for him, 9 for Eisenhower, 7 undecided or not participating. Totaling them, that is 43 to 16. We can't recall such an overwhelming reporters' preference in a quarter-century campaign experience.

Meanwhile, back home, publishers are doggedly for Eisenhower.

Editor and Publisher reports 80 percent of the press for Ike on the basis of circulation. This is an old story, of course. Publishing is business and the publisher is business-minded. The unfortunate editorial writers ghosting for the publishers are regarded by most reporters as more to be pitied than censured. It is a little discouraging, however, to note as we did on last week's trip with Stevenson how bad the normal newspaper is. This is accompanied by a pathetic feeling among readers that their particular town is unlucky and that other communities are more fortunate. The fact is the whole average is pretty low. It was amusing to run into the same editorial snarl against Adlai's good-natured Portland, Oregon, speech in which he twitted the newspapers all across the continent. With a good deal of witty sugarcoating Adlai told some homely truths about American newspapers. There was no factual answer possible—so many papers just snarled. What good is it to have schools of journalism in America if you don't have schools for publishers?

Stevenson is a reporter's dream because he is polished, urbane, consistently entertaining, and writes his own speeches. He is a Woodrow Wilson with a sense of humor. He has an aristocratic contempt for the ignoble compromises that the unfortunate Ike is making. These have reached a point where they are indeed pretty dreadful. Taft ignored Ike's plaintive telegrams for nine weeks. Meanwhile Ike anxiously told the press that Taft would be one of the "greatest figures" in his administration, and to the dismay of Paul Hoffman and the uncomfortable *New York Times* had a political necking party with the loathesome Senator Jenner, and winked meaningfully at "red light Liz" McCarthy. In his Canadian retreat, meanwhile, Taft coldly told interviewers that the general would have to meet certain conditions for his support.

What, then, of Adlai Stevenson? This western trip was our first close contact with him. He is an extraordinarily gifted man. His knack of felicitous improvisation, when he responds to the chairman's introduction, is remarkable. He wins almost any audience. His San Francisco speech, in which he outlined a generous "New Deal" for Asiatics, showed him far abler than Truman to explain world affairs to perplexed Americans. His Town Hall speech in Los Angeles on the responsibility of business and the citizen for corruption in government was one of the most enthralling we ever heard. It was a largely GOP, businessman audience and there could be no question of his effectiveness. The nation has not seen as sensitive and articulate a presidential aspirant since Wilson. So much for the credit side.

Let us put the debit side in two parts. The first relates merely to his effectiveness as a campaigner. Aside from certain technical and elementary mistakes on TV that could be easily remedied, Stevenson often fails to rouse an audience emotionally. The crowd leaves smiling rather than gritting its teeth. It is their intelligence, not their heart, that has been touched. The practical problem in an apathetic democracy where only 50 percent of the citizens vote is to get the indifferent (largely the lower-income group who are predominantly Democrats) to come to the polls. After the raw pigments of Truman, Stevenson seems like a pastel candidate. And this raises the second question.

Like Roosevelt, Stevenson's family background is aristocratic. He is a reformer but chiefly in the sense that he is a humanitarian of integrity who couldn't stand the corrupt Republican Illinois machine. Roosevelt suffered a paralytic stroke that changed his outlook and above all he had Mrs. Roosevelt; he saw the need of sweeping social reform and promptly became a "traitor to his class." By contrast, it is revealing to see Governor Stevenson's North Shore Chicago friends and those in Springfield. He has been the pet of wealthy Republicans as governor. He values their friendship. He is alone and wifeless in the echoing governor's mansion.

Stevenson is a worrier who will be dead two years after he enters the White House prison if he doesn't remarry. Stevenson has had no emotional experience with poverty, and he does not arouse emotional response when he deals with the problems of the underdog. His alarmingly well balanced Seattle speech on public vs. private power must have sent a chill down the spines of Roosevelt-Truman supporters. A later speech on social legislation only skimmed the surface. Even his answers on Tidelands and Taft-Hartley have been carefully qualified.

We are all for Adlai for president for what he is, for what he may become, and for those against him. But sooner or later he must make a heartbreaking decision—whether or not he will be a traitor to his class.

Will Ike Beat Ike?

S E P T E M B E R   2 9 ,   1 9 5 2   It rather looks to us as though Eisenhower were going to be licked, and in a way it is too bad. There is evidence that the public would really like a change of party in Washington after twenty years, and in some respects this might be a good thing. A respectable school of thought holds that if the GOP isn't given a term of responsibility quickly it will go mad, with a case of galloping McCarthyism. This may now happen. We think Governor Stevenson is a remarkable figure—possibly one of the really great politicians of this century. But if Eisenhower is defeated, it won't be Stevenson who did it: Ike will have knocked out Ike.

Some of Stevenson's speeches have been magnificent. But the crowds have flocked to Ike, while Stevenson's crowds are disappointing. To us this indicates something pretty significant: the public by now knows the Democratic line pretty well; what it wants to see is the great war hero and whether there is actually going to be a rational, competitive political brand put on the market. It is the old story. The polls of public opinion every four years put the Republicans way out ahead at first: then the big, disappointed American audience turns away.

Of course this is all premature. If the public has really made up its mind it wants a change, nothing that Stevenson says, no matter how splendid, can alter its will. But we have a premonition. Ike is an earnest, sincere man, but his speeches are still dull.

And Ike has done these things: (a) announced he would support "all" GOP candidates (no matter how bad); (b) greeted despicable Senator Jenner, the vilifier of Ike's own beloved General Marshall; (c) embraced the Dulles "liberation" program for satellite countries, scaring half Europe until he lamely retreated; (d) refused to disown Joe McCarthy (who, according to Ike's adviser, Senator Carlson, will campaign for the ticket); (e) capitulated to isolationist Bob Taft; (f) picked Richard Nixon for his running mate. There are supposed to be

15 million "independents" and more Democrats than Republicans in the electorate. Much as the public yearns for a change from Truman philistinism, it looks to us now as though Ike has pretty well knocked himself out.

We never had an easier time writing this column. All we have to do is put in what other periodicals leave out. There never was more material. The handicap of having 80 percent of the newspaper circulation on your side (as Ike does) was never more evident. Take the case of Poor Richard. The *New York Post* in a copyrighted piece from Leo Katcher, its Los Angeles correspondent, Thursday, September 18, gave a full, detailed story of the $16,000 millionaires' club fund for Nixon. It created hardly any stir at first in a press 8 to 1 against the Democrats. On the eighteen-car Eisenhower Special, riding exultantly to lash at crime and corruption at Kansas City, Ike was not told of the story. His press secretary told the United Press correspondent, "We don't comment on any *New York Post* story." Asked by *Post* reporter Max Lerner why, the answer came, "You know that just as well as I do."

The story only became a rumor slowly on the press cars. Bundles of the *Des Moines Register* were thrown aboard, but these carried a secondhand report; later that night the *Omaha World-Herald* came aboard—the murderous story was over on page 57 with the funnies. Editorial pages, of course, support Ike, although the news staff of most papers is for Adlai 3 to 1. Significantly, the full impact of the Nixon revelation came to the Ike train from a bit of doggerel on the front page of the *St. Joseph* (Missouri) *News-Press* entitled, "They're Fixin' Mr. Nixon." The paper apologetically pointed out that it was for Ike but that "someone in the composing room" had turned out the item. The voice from the composing room asked how the reformers were going to clean up Washington "when millionaires are slipping them the dough?"

The secret has to be divulged that enthusiasm for ambitious young Mr. Nixon is not always at the boiling point. In an inspired comment in the Stevenson press party, George Hall of the *St. Louis Post-Dispatch* observed, "I wouldn't have wanted it to happen to a nicer guy." Nixon, the Subversives' Nemesis, was just finishing a whistle-stop denunciation of Washington's low ethical standards at Marysville, California, when some oaf yelled, "Tell them about the $16,000." Drawing himself to full height, eyes flashing and fist clenched, our man Richard told the conductor to hold the train until he had met the dastardly innuendo. The crowd cheered the noble fellow as he revealed that communists had promised to "smear" him if he ran for the vice-presidency, adding dramatically, "They started it yesterday." The crowd cheered again—and next day two influential Republican papers, the *New York Herald-Tribune* and *Washington Post*, told him to withdraw. But not Ike. He handpicked Nixon to get better personnel in Washington and now said he had full faith in his honesty. Poor Ike: he was busy knocking himself out.

Notes Attorney General McGranery isn't missing any tricks: he has just arrested a new batch of Commies and announced that British subject Charlie Chaplin, the comedian, may be kept out of the country if he applies for readmission. . . . Everybody hopes McGranery's supply of Commies will last through the election. . . .

THE EISENHOWER YEARS
[*1952-1960*]

The President-Elect Meets
with Taft

DECEMBER 1, 1952 It seemed natural, squatting there on the green carpet of the Commodore Hotel in New York. It was the sixth floor where Ike's headquarters were. Seventy people at least jammed the twelve-foot-wide passage—the corridor to the new White House. From the protective instinct of long habit, this correspondent slid down under the oil-derrick tripod of a movie camera. "It's like the Resolutions Committee at the Chicago convention—remember?" said another reporter down there.

We looked out at legs and feet. An earnest man down the aisle told the woman beside him she looked "like a woman of prayer" and explained that he had come to enlist Ike's help for a "Christian inspiration training school." The woman said she was looking for a job. Other reporters crouched beside us.

The "up" and "down" lights of the ten elevators blinked and the red-coated elevator man at number two stopped and watched with arm up to hold back the sliding brass door. A rush of white, like birds, swooped down the glass mail chute recurrently. Joe Martin, the next House Speaker, got off and was instantly blocked. If it had been a year ago, the carpet would have been ankle-deep with spent flashbulbs when he left, but technical progress has taken care of that—now cameramen strap batteries on themselves and use permanent bulbs. Things quieted for a moment; Taft was due in fifteen minutes.

"Seems like old times!" repeated the reporter. Indeed it did. The transition turmoil was tapering off. You could tell it in the good nature of the correspondents. Too much traveling on campaign trips sours people. One reporter morosely put it, "I've crossed the Great Divide so often I feel like a hemstitching machine!" Cramped on a pounding Campaign Special, trying to hit portable typewriters on the upbeat, everybody gets to hate everybody else.

"Well, how was Augusta?" we asked.

The veterans chimed in with impressions. "Ike can't read, of course," said a man whose knees were all we could see. Others nodded understandingly. "Gets everything by ear. They leave an important paper on Ike's desk, and a day later his managers find he's not looked at it. He's been getting things by briefing for forty years. What we're going to have at the White House now is a general staff system."

"Yes, and lots of commissions. All with the best brains," said another.

When we asked what kind of brains there would be, there was a snort. "You ought to see the Augusta National Golf Club—that would tell you a lot!" came one answer. "All millionaires—see? It's limited to two hundred members. Ike fits right in there. He has a natural affinity for millionaires. Imagine little Harry Truman in a place like that." Everybody laughed at the image.

"He learns quick," interposed another defensively. "You got to admit he absorbs things. You wait; he may turn out a lot better than those speeches. You see, Ike just doesn't understand the legislative process. Yes—I think he believed everything he said in his speeches; yes, even the self-contradictory things. It was all so general, anyway. He was saying what the staff wrote out for him and, of course, supplying his own moral sermons, too. Augusta showed one thing. He's got Dewey men now salted up and down his staff. They're shifting from Dewey's payroll to his."

"How about Taft?"

"That's what Bob's coming for today. He's just notifying Ike that he's going to take over Congress. Sure, there's bound to be a break there, but maybe not for a while. One thing Ike does understand—defense and foreign affairs. He's bound to be firm on them whatever the Taft Congress does."

It was good there, talking to the old gang again. The ministerial man down the way was telling about the efficacy of prayer. He had prayed in that Nixon incident, he said, and see how it had come out. As for the reporters, of course they all worked for Republican papers. They reported the ban on anything even hinting of criticism of Ike was even stronger now than during the campaign. It was "good sportsmanship" and consisted of blocking realistic stories about

Dulles, Stassen, and other best brains. Everything had to be lauda-
tory. It was good to have the tension removed, everybody agreed, and
the honeymoon would not last.

"One thing the public doesn't understand yet," said a reporter, "is
the sensation Mamie is going to be. Every week she gets younger.
The country has no idea yet what's ahead of it there."

"Boy! Morningside Heights is changed," contributed a press association man. "Yeah, I was up there this morning; the Secret Service
has moved in. Muscular young men rocking on their heels everywhere. Funny how they always put the biggest dick on the grand-
children. He's getting that harassed look already; he comes out of the
airplane carrying a teddy bear and a balloon."

"They're about the only thing Ike cares for," put in my friend.
"That, and fishing and golf. Everybody begins by asking Ike his
score, which is a mistake. He tells them—shot by shot."

Reporters groaned. "Press conferences will be something," said
one. "Do you realize he's never faced a hostile press conference yet?
Not a press conference during the campaign, and before that the
TV cameras always present so you couldn't needle him."

"Aw, the papers will protect him!" said somebody. But a chorus
denied this. "Wait till the honeymoon is over," they said. A minute
later Taft stepped off the elevator, bland, paunchy, and benevolent,
and it was over.

The 80-Percent Press

DECEMBER 15, 1952 America has an "8o-Percent Press." It
was 8o-percent Republican in the presidential campaign; it is 8o percent
now. It is one of America's greatest dangers. For who is going to tell
what goes on in Washington in the next four years in a press that has
relegated Adlai Stevenson to page 13 in the past four months?

Eisenhower deserves every bit of cooperation possible in Korea. Yet who will point out, in the 80-Percent Press, that peace is harder to get today because Ike was willing to throw Korea into campaign politics? This was the one partisan attack Stevenson could not forgive. It made votes for Ike, lots of votes, and it also upped the Communists' asking price for peace, with every Republican speech on America's war weariness and every GOP example of national division whipped up in the monolithic attack.

Now Ike returns triumphantly from the Korean visit. This is the trip the ex-*Life* writer thought up for him. Having visited Korea and held his conferences, Ike says it is a tough problem, not susceptible to panaceas. Yes, we seem to remember that is what Adlai said, on page 13, in the campaign. The three-day visit to Korea has made the 80-Percent Press oh so happy, and left nothing more to be done—nothing, that is, except to solve the bloody stalemate.

The next four years may see the biggest lobby drive since Grant's day to loot the public domain, reverse history, and crown big business. Ike has picked a cabinet of eight millionaires and one plumber. Who is going to tell the continuing story of Washington in the 80-Percent Press? When they hand the Capitol dome, or offshore oil, over to the corporations, will your local paper tell the story? We hate to ring in a commercial at this point, folks, but if you really want to know what gives in Washington in the next 12 months, a subscription to a *Certain Magazine* is always handy.

We like Ike. A lot of things about him are attractive. But he keeps worrying us. For instance he gave a "press conference" in Korea. It was one where no questions were allowed reporters; he just did all the talking. The monologue sounded like one of Ike's agreeable little rear-platform campaign talks. Will he do this as president? Ike has been protected from reporters all his life. He is the first president in modern times to take office without ever facing the ordeal of a full-scale White House-type press conference. Ike already has the editorial pages on his side; won't reporters even be allowed to ask questions?

The Taft explosion against Ike's secretary of labor last week shook commentators like David Lawrence and Fulton Lewis but they reacted manfully; chins up. Lawrence, who has made himself the all-but-official expositor of what's in the minds of Ike and Houndstooth Nixon, came through hastily on December 3 with a column which the Washington *Star* significantly labeled "There's No Taft-Eisenhower Rift." After thinking it over 24 hours Lawrence however decided next day that "General Fumbled Appointments." Our man Fulton reacted faster. In his commentary, December 2, he found the Durkin choice "frightening to say the least." Saddest thing was that he hadn't known about it in advance. Chagrin showed all through his report that he had talked to "innumerable Republican leaders" and that, like him, they were all "completely surprised." We fear Lewis has lost touch with the Dewey wing of the party. After making the astonishing pronouncement that "Taft's version of what labor law should be was a major factor in the landslide victory of November 4," Lewis demanded why Ike had "openly offended and flouted Senator Taft?" Stormy weather ahead, Ike; stormy weather!

The Senate Still Fears
Joe McCarthy

JANUARY 12, 1953   On December 21, 1945, Senator Joseph McCarthy's debt to the Appleton (Wisconsin) State Bank was $169,540 and his Washington checking account was overdrawn. His financial condition was "quite desperate," says the unanimous three-man Senate subcommittee report just published. His Wisconsin bank debt was "in flagrant disregard for the state banking laws." What did he do?

McCarthy was a member of the Senate Banking Committee, the supervisor of RFC loans—among others to the floundering Lustron Corporation, makers of prefabricated houses. Lustron suddenly paid McCarthy $10,000 for a manuscript on housing which, says the report, "was neither finished nor in publishable form." The acceptance of "this $10,000 fee," says the report, "would appear to have been highly improper, to say the least."

Did he use the $10,000 to reduce his loan? No. A senator, it appears, has access to tips, hot tips that can be turned to cash. The Seaboard Airline Railroad was also indebted to RFC—for more than $15 million. From his place on the Banking Committee, asks the report, did McCarthy have "confidential information relating to the stock?" The stock was then a drug on the market at $21 a share. But McCarthy was on the inside; not only did he invest the Lustron "fee" in Seaboard stock but advised friends to get in. Everything depended on the RFC. Ultimately the RFC disposed of Seaboard holdings, and the value jumped. McCarthy got 1,700 shares under his control; in September 1951, he sold 1,000 with a profit of $35,614.

In 1947 McCarthy's financial position was still precarious. Where could he turn? McCarthy was also on a banking subcommittee on sugar. It seemed providential! The Department of Agriculture advocated continued controls on sugar; the big makers of sweetened soft drinks fought controls. For example, there was Pepsi-Cola—it denounced the army's purchase of Cuban sugar. So on December 5 or 6, 1947, McCarthy "hurriedly consulted with Russell M. Arundel," Pepsi-Cola's Washington representative (lobbyist), telling him of his "financial predicament." What a friend! Arundel indorsed a $20,000 six-months' note, and the day after the note was signed McCarthy made a "special appearance to interrogate the Army Secretary" on this very purchase of Cuban sugar which Pepsi-Cola denounced.

Did McCarthy have a tip on the soybean market? Between October 1950, and January 1951, McCarthy plunged heavily. The Commodity Exchange Authority, Department of Agriculture, had just conducted an investigation of alleged soybean market manipulation, involving, among others, a number of Chinese traders. The subcommittee asks, "Did Senator McCarthy have confidential information with respect to the trend of the soybean future market?" He cleared $17,354 up to January 2, 1951.

The Senate gave a 60-to-0 vote of confidence to the Hennings subcommittee. The latter asked McCarthy six times to come before it and explain these and a dozen other sinister-sounding episodes. McCarthy said no. He "deliberately set out to thwart investigation of him" by charges of "smear" and "Communist-inspired persecution," the subcommittee says. Now the committee passes the buck to the Senate. It is a matter, it declares, "which goes to the very core of the Senate body's authority, integrity, and the respect in which it is held by the people of this country."

The subcommittee report was issued late Friday afternoon, January 2. Next day the Senate reassembled. On the basis of this extraordinary compilation would the newly elected McCarthy be seated? McCarthy was present everywhere on the floor, laughing and backslapping. When his name was called to take the oath, there was a hush. Nothing happened. The cowed Senate sat mute. Nobody uttered the words, "I object."

In the movie *High Noon* Gary Cooper acts the sheriff who vainly appeals for help to meet a returned killer. He appealed to the church —in vain. Well, if the Hennings subcommittee report had been an official Afghanistan text on milkweed the sacrosanct *New York Times* would have printed it in full. It only printed a column of the Hennings report, however, as reporters complained that it was "400 pages" long. Actually, it was 52 pages—plus a documented index. The *Herald-Tribune* printed a story twice as long as the *Times*. Little help here.

Gary Cooper didn't get help from the community, either. And how can the US press attack McCarthy now when it backed Ike 80 percent and Ike backed McCarthy? It is true—Ike deplored McCarthy's methods. This is rather funny. The methods are the man; it is like backing Hitler but deploring Hitler's gassing the Jews.

Many and many a time we have reassured apprehensive visiting European journalists not to worry over America's "hysteria." But when the Marine Corps, that proud and magnificent institution, granted McCarthy combat medals last week, it was at that moment that we had a real shudder of fear. Now McCarthy is aiming at the colleges. Harvard, Smith, California—the long list is ready, alumni will be roused, education authorities bulldozed. It is militant anti-intellectualism, the professor substituted as target for the diplomat. Who will rally to stop the killer? Not Congress! McCarthy has knocked off LaFollette, Tydings, Benton; the rest will hide under the bar. Some will lift their voices; this magazine will. But who else will aid the sheriff? Stop a bit; instead of fearing the sheriff, McCarthy *is* the sheriff. Republican victory makes him head of the top Senate police committee. What killings lie ahead for McCarthy, to be sure, in the colleges—and the stock market!

Millionaire Cabinet

JANUARY 26, 1953   Everybody hoped and expected that Ike's Inaugural Address would be a fine one. But everybody knew by now, too, that Ike in his appointments was off to an appalling start. Ike had correlated "best brains" with business tycoons as the army does. What this meant was shown in horrible caricature as General Motors chief Charles E. Wilson sought Senate confirmation as Secretary of Defense. The senators' reactions were not ones of antagonism but simple wonder.

How could the press tell the story? They were for Ike—80 percent; they were for GM advertising—1,000 percent. But everyone in Washington knew Wilson had talked to the interrogating committee on his first appearance like one conferring a favor. Wilson made senators think of their own $12,500 salaries compared to the one he was giving up—$566,000. True, GM was continuing a retirement bonus that would total by 1957 $635,000 in cash and 1,800 shares of stock. As to the $2 million worth of GM stock Wilson already held, how could he sell it? It would involve heavy tax losses. There are some sacrifices a man can not make for his country.

Real bewilderment settled on Washington. Was this a cruel parody of government by millionaires? With Wilson were three other business tycoons. In the new, topsy-turvy world, Ike was everywhere acclaimed for picking the boss of the company with the biggest of all defense contracts to slash contracts; but wasn't it a bit, well, odd, for that boss to do this and still keep his GM connections? The law had been all right for Democrats—maybe it could be changed. The trouble was that the incident had dramatized the whole issue no matter what happened. As this column, almost alone, has pointed out, these able US business chiefs swarming into the new administration seem innocent as children of the climate of political opinion and the atmosphere of American government.

Dulles, also, gave a foretaste of policy in answering senators. David Lawrence, a friendly columnist, quoted him as promising Cold War policies "strong but not reckless" that will "end the peril without provoking a dying spasm of total violence." (It was this promise to "end the peril" that gave Ike millions of votes.) Dulles impatiently continued that those who argue that little can be done to liberate enslaved peoples "just don't know what they're talking about."

Here is the new dynamic policy that scares Europe and rejoices Henry Luce and the Scripps-Howard and Hearst press. The contrasting Acheson policy of patience and strength is denounced as "negative." One more warning about the "liberation" policy came on Inaugural Eve from George Kennan, America's outgoing top Russian expert. Its prospects of success are small, he said, and its danger great. But Dulles knows better: he leaves for Europe at once with Harold Stassen.

Moscow's growing attack on the Jews, meanwhile, of which the "doctors' plot" is the latest incredible, nightmarish example, makes many here wonder if the Soviet dictatorship is hurrying now to some terrifying climax. Persecution of the Jews is a landmark in the historic pattern of many European dictatorships which, when reached, shows insecurity at home and a possible willingness to menace all civilization.

McCarthy's Week: (a) Wrote menacing letter to Navy air official at Pentagon telling him not to discuss matter of McCarthy's Marine Corps medals; (b) saw an old enemy, Edward P. Morgan, former counsel of the Tydings subcommittee that investigated McCarthy, involved in an inquiry before the Senate committee which he (McCarthy) now heads; (c) warned Senator Hendrickson (R, N.J.), who signed the recent report attacking McCarthy, that he would campaign against him in 1954 when Hendrickson runs for reelection; (d) called George Kennan's farewell warning, directed against witch-hunts that might wreck the State Department, "a typical Acheson-type tirade against those who have been exposing traitors"; (e) prepared to ask the cowed Senate to double funds for his investigating committee.

We keep thinking about Eisenhower. We are all in the same boat with him now. There is the temptation to make partisan attacks, but what for, when we all stand or fall with him. There can be no doubt of his warmth, patriotism, and good intentions. We followed Ike over America in the campaign. We heard him make that lovely, extemporaneous speech about his parents at Abilene, Kansas, and thought we recognized him as the wistful exponent of a simpler and lost America. Then we heard him make campaign speeches filled with amazing clichés, contradictions, and platitudes. They alienated many reporters. But for the life of us (and this is the thing that keeps striking us as funny), we aren't really sure about Ike. Is he a leader—of the kind we need so badly—or is he just a front? We have watched him and heard him, and honestly we don't know. It would have been of immense help if we could have had press conferences with Ike, under White House rules; he is the first president of modern times to take office without the precaution of this searching probing. Ike has never faced a hostile press conference in his life, so far as we know. Does he really know the score—or is he a well-meaning man entirely surrounded by people who know exactly what they want? Well, the whistle blows, the game starts, and we don't know.

Dulles Sees Pink Elephants

FEBRUARY 23, 1953 "If a man tells you he sees pink elephants, you don't help any by telling him he is crazy. You take a gun and go out and shoot and then say the elephants are dead. Then the man is happy."

That is the philosophy some Republicans have been trying to adopt in Washington. It is no longer possible to tell the public Washington isn't honeycombed with subversives, they say, so the newcomers are making great to-do about clearing everybody with the FBI. Secretary Dulles, too, has been stressing the "pink elephant" approach in foreign affairs. Embassies here say he has been reasonably mild and placatory in private dealing with their governments, but for the sake of voters back home he has been allowing the impression to spread of a new "toughness" in foreign dealings and is stressing "seventy-five-day ultimatums" to our allies. Actually, in most particulars he has been following the Truman-Acheson foreign policy. He has been prodding allies, it is true, but he has also been firing off blasting caps at pink elephants for the home folks—pink elephants which he himself helped materialize in the 1952 campaign.

The Dulles approach is bold, and doubly dangerous. As Adlai Stevenson said over the weekend: "We will frighten no Russians by threatening our allies." The second danger is in Congress. Something bordering on hysteria gripped excitable Republican senators last week. They thought they had got the administration signal to shoot real elephants. Foreign Relations Chairman Alexander Wiley was on the point of bombing the Chinese mainland; Knowland and half a dozen others were ready to blockade the coast. Ultimately Dulles and good old sober Omar Bradley had to go up and soothe the fury the administration had created. Deneutralizing Formosa isn't going to end the war right away, it appears—in part it is "psychological warfare."

As Eisenhower learns how vastly more complicated everything is in Washington than he saw it in the campaign, things should get easier for him. He probably did not foresee the row over the confirmation of Charlie Wilson; the chances of tax reduction and Korean peace probably seem more distant now than they did in the campaign. He could not have understood the bad timing of Secretary Benson's lecture on self-reliance to farmers at St. Paul last week, just when farm prices are slipping. There is evidence also that Ike is shocked by the way everything leaks from Congress, such as his decision on Formosa—it certainly makes it harder to practice psychological warfare. He is not getting much help yet from his green cabinet, with the possible exception of Treasury Secretary Humphrey. There, if this column is any judge, is a tower of strength. It is a bit early to say, but we guess this Cleveland industrialist may be to Ike what Ogden Mills was to Hoover—the Treasury strong man of the administration.

As a military man, psychological warfare appeals vastly to Ike. With all our heart we hope it works. But what confuses Moscow is certainly, we see, going to confuse Washington; this devious policy is going to be vastly harder for a democracy to implement than for Russia. Perhaps, after all, the best psychological warfare of all for

America is not military but domestic effort at social betterment at home, fair racial dealing, a world reputation for tolerance to minority views—idealism, democracy, and Point Four diplomacy rather than "dollar" diplomacy. Somehow we keep coming back to Adlai Stevenson and what he said Saturday night: "If we win men's hearts throughout the world, it will not be because we are a big country but because we are a great country. Bigness is imposing. But greatness is enduring." We wish we could write like that. . . . "Only a people who can achieve moral mastery of themselves can hope to win the moral leadership of others."

The Rosenbergs got a fair trial; they were rightfully condemned; the president rejected their appeal for clemency and they must die. And now we must all be harrowed by watching Communists turn them into "martyrs." Somehow, it seems to us, Ike missed the point in rejecting their appeal for mercy. In the course of this very business of psychological warfare Moscow is using the miserable couple for its own ends; it would, of course, much rather have the Rosenbergs dead than alive. A mild sentence like that which the British gave the traitor Fuchs, or to Alan Nunn May—or even life imprisonment—would have made it harder for the obscene Communist propaganda. But who can even suggest such a sensible point any longer without fear of being attacked as "weak to Communists"?

We can't somehow get worked up over falling meat prices. The cattlemen organized the strike against Truman in 1946 by withholding meat, and the hubbub over prices, scarce steaks, and "federal mismanagement" gave the GOP the congressional election. Now if the GOP declines to help the unhappy cattle industry when there is a glut, it's fine by us. The Republicans are being admirably consistent, and we like it.

GOP Dream World Collapses

MARCH 2, 1953   The Eisenhower administration hasn't reached manhood's stature yet, but it is out of its crib. On a dozen fronts reality is breaking through the opium haze of GOP campaign promises. The sooner this happens the better for everybody, for obviously Ike can't shoulder his heartbreaking job otherwise—the job that is so much harder than election speeches indicated.

Let's put down some praise for Ike first. We thought he did a good job at his first press conference. It was a terribly hard ordeal—breaking the ice. He put on a cool, brisk, split-second show. The commercial was too long and the time for reporters' questions too short, but a filibuster was natural in the circumstances. Ike was an attractive, commanding figure who had done his homework. There will be trouble later if reporters don't get more scope, but it was a good beginning.

In our judgment, anyway, Ike is right in taking off most controls. Truman's Council of Economic Advisers in its last report indicated it was about time they came off, for the threat of inflation is almost over. Again in farm prices: the farm lobby is the biggest, most bipartisan and arrogant in Washington. If Ike disregards it, so much the better. Personally we are glad Ike is letting cattle prices sag, and if farmers get a taste of decontrol, that is what they ordered in the election.

Having said all this, let us put down a list of developments so far in which reality has broken through the Republican dream world of the 1952 campaign.

1. Ike came back from his election-inspired trip to Korea saying it was a tough problem; this is what Stevenson said all along.

2. The "best brains" turned out to mean millionaire businessmen. They have a lot to learn as politicians, as the Charlie Wilson explosion emphasized.

3. The GOP hinted it could cut taxes right away, found it couldn't without unbalancing the budget. The GOP split on taxes has begun.

4. The GOP thought it could balance the budget right away but found it couldn't without slashing either defense or foreign aid. A GOP split on this looms.

5. GOP congressional leaders came away from the White House last week chagrined over tax cuts—they had just discovered that the world situation is "grim." Democrats tactfully remained silent—they had known it for years.

6. Dulles, in a series of off-the-record chats, is emphasizing the extreme gravity of the global situation. The question: Is it really any worse or is Dulles just finding out what responsibility is like?

7. After scaring Europe over proposals to blockade China, the administration is quickly retreating. In the same way, it turns out that the deneutralization of Formosa is little more than what Truman had already countenanced.

8. Rearming Korean divisions to replace US divisions also continues Truman policies. It will cost lots of money (like the proposed aid to French Indochina) which is something GOP tax-cutters haven't realized yet.

9. Ike has so watered down the GOP plank to "repudiate" Yalta and Potsdam (and his own campaign speeches and State of the Union address) that Democrats actually hail his proposed condemnation of Russia. It is the die-hard Republicans who threaten revolt.

10. The GOP majority in the House Ways and Means Committee has pigeonholed for this session Ike's proposal for greatly expanded social security.

11. Agriculture Secretary Benson's admonitions to farmers against "give-away government programs" which are "steadily and surely" undermining "moral and spiritual values" are in laughable contrast to the tone of Ike's farm campaign speeches supporting the goal not merely of 90-percent parity but "full parity."

12. The dream-promise that Ike would curb McCarthy has, of course, proved absurd. Ike's victory put McCarthy in power. Now the State Department is fawning on him. If Dulles capitulates to McCarthy in the test case of John Carter Vincent, it will be hard to sustain Department morale.

Are the foregoing points put down in malice? Not at all. Only five weeks after Ike took office reality is breaking in as it had to do if this country were to be safe. Ike is carrying forward the Truman-

Acheson foreign policy in basic particulars. We prayerfully hope the ruffles and flourishes he is adding won't bring war; maybe they are wise, but it would be absurd to deny they add to the risk.

As to Ike himself, we expect to support him with everything we have on a lot of issues, issues on which we expect his die-hard opponents will be Republicans—men who, in many cases, put him up as a campaign front for their own purposes. We will support Ike on tariff cutting, foreign aid, above all on the continued need for national sacrifice. We will back him against the newly restated (and cardinal) heresy of Taft that the cost of domestic defense is a greater danger to America than Russia. And we expect to support Ike when he finally ends his disgusting alliance with McCarthy, a break that we deem inevitable and that, when it comes, will mark puberty for the slowly maturing Eisenhower administration.

The Vice-President

SEPTEMBER 21, 1953   When a nation has a vacationing president, it is wise, perhaps, to look at its vice-president. Richard Nixon has been busy recently. He met the president's airplane the other day to report on possibilities for the Supreme Court vacancy. He returned to Denver to canvass the choice of Secretary Martin Durkin's successor. He is here and everywhere. No one should underestimate our Dicky—or his ambitions.

The crucial point in the Durkin-Eisenhower talks on changes in the Taft-Hartley Act came when some opponent "leaked" the Durkin version to the press. It is particularly satisfying, we think, that a big business administration should pick the *Wall Street Journal* as the vehicle. The story appeared August 3. It is widely believed that the undercover maneuvers and the leak were engineered by Nixon, "always a strong T-H supporter," and that he had volunteered "to throw his weight at Cabinet meetings on the side of Mr. Weeks against Mr. Durkin."

It is Nixon everywhere. The *Los Angeles Times* revealed that at the request of Representative John Phillips (R, Cal.), spokesman for big Mexican-employing Imperial Valley planters, Nixon agreed to intervene with Attorney General Herbert Brownell to "temper" the drive against wetbacks—the illegal Mexican immigrants who cut American wages by working for next to nothing. Nixon, you see, was made White House lieutenant for the absentee president, to the discomfiture of fellow Californian Knowland. Mr. Knowland, the Senate majority leader, is another energetic young man with soaring ambitions. And, now that Adlai Stevenson is back home the GOP talks about sending Nixon round the world to cover approximately the same itinerary. As somebody put it, this would be sending a boy to undo a man's job.

Durkin's resignation was a jolt for the administration. Ike has unwisely allowed himself to be identified with big business. Now the millionaires have thrown out the plumber. What is happening to Ike may well turn out to be a tragedy to a national hero and a nice man. If Ike had been Taft, the nineteen amendments to T-H, worked out by Durkin and the White House staff (supposedly with Ike's approval), might well have been adopted. Taft knew that T-H had to be ameliorated, he had the power in Congress to do it and the iron will to deal with the Sinclair Weeks type of businessman whose mind is as absorbent of new ideas as a shower bath curtain. Without Taft, Ike followed Weeks and Nixon, and the flirtation of 15 million trade unionists with the GOP seems about over.

Even the *Chicago Tribune* urged McCarthy last week to call off his silly accusations of subversion in connection with a US Army report on life in Soviet Siberia. The fact is Joe desperately needs new ideas. With Democrats out of power his attacks inevitably have to be against Republicans, the overseas libraries, the Government Printing Office, Allen Dulles of the Central Intelligence Agency, and now the army. Joe doesn't mind breaking with Ike, he expects to, but the time hasn't come yet. Meanwhile he has been taking some bad buffets. Our estimate is that McCarthy's impetus is temporarily halted but he has not been knocked out. There is an equilibrium of forces pro and con McCarthyism. Our guess is that McCarthy will turn increasingly to jingo imperialism as a substitute for domestic Red-baiting if he can't find enough of the latter, with increasing attacks on the UN. Perhaps his upcoming investigation of alleged subversives in the UN indicates the course.

It seems a strange thing that a congressional committee should dump out into the public prints, without any particular effort at verification, and without any formal judgment of its own, the hearsay charges of ex-Communists that "600" US ministers are subversive. If a city council should dump its garbage truck on Main Street and say, "We are only exhibiting this noisome offal because we think it might be a good idea to consider the subject," the irresponsible act would be equivalent to dumping a truckload of rumors like this by a crew granted advance immunity. This is part of the Attack on Intellectualism. It is going on all over the country. It is the revolt of the yahoos against rationality. The teachers have had it, the diplomats, the liberals, and now the ministers of the gospel. The pattern is standardized. If charges are proved correct, or partly correct, against one individual, then all become suspect; find one Hiss in the lot and the Protestant clergy is condemned.

This yahoo process was exemplified at the recent American Legion convention. Without any roll call, without discussion, by a standing vote it demanded an investigation of the American Civil Liberties Union. The attack brought immediate condemnation from conservative newspapers like the *New York Times* over the country. It was a repetition of last year's resolution and will probably be duplicated next year. The ACLU doesn't need any defense. But what is the process by which this Heil Hitler unanimity is achieved? The Legion passed another resolution—"we are unalterably opposed to Consumers' Union and to its publication, *Consumers Report.*" Again unanimity. CU sells 200,000 copies each month analyzing advertising claims; it is a good deal like condemning *Reader's Digest* because it is un-American in not printing any advertising at all. We have a vague notion, perhaps overoptimistic, that the fever of American anti-intellectualism is burning itself out. But let there be no doubt about it, the diagnosis is correct, the disease is the scourge of democracies, America has an authentic case of a deadly plague.

Herbert Brownell

NOVEMBER 30, 1953   Herbert Brownell wants to fight espionage by legalizing wiretapping and watering down the Fifth Amendment. He will demand legislation when Congress meets. Let there be
no doubt where this column stands on the Brownell proposals, weak
though they are: we're for them. We have long felt that subversives
were sheltering in the Constitution, traitors hiding in the Flag. We
back the Brownell proposals (timid though they be); we also advocate revival of torture in espionage (and related) trials, to facilitate
confessions. How else can the FBI complete its job? Indeed, Brownell's halfway measures strike us as suspicious; is he, too, coddling
Communism? Let's put our heart into this Crusade! Let's install
thumbscrews at police stations, put lead wires from all home telephones to Washington, and declare a five-year holiday on the Bill of
Rights. Then we'll really get those damn Reds.

When Brownell presented his testimony in the Harry Dexter
White case to the Senate subcommittee he knew that he was doing
two things. He was omitting two crucial sentences from the February
1, 1946, FBI report on White that put Truman's action in quite a
different light, and he was also breaking confidence with a friendly
foreign nation, Canada, by publishing a secret FBI letter dragging
Canada into the mess. These were reckless things to do but the political need was great. Truman's ferocious speech had to be answered
and crushed. Brownell was willing to set a precedent of making *ex
parte* use of secret police files for his purpose. His unparalleled action
shocked the democratic world but temporarily strengthened his case.

The FBI sentences Brownell omitted were a frank admission by
J. Edgar Hoover in his twenty-eight-page report to Truman on White
of February 1, 1946, that he didn't have the evidence to convict White
and that he couldn't get such evidence insofar as past offenses went.
In other words, the only hope of trapping White was to keep on
watching him. Mr. Truman may have been wrong in 1946 in continu-

ing White in office under surveillance, but it was these sentences, written by J. Edgar Hoover, that did it.

Those sentences have never been published. Brownell has them. He was aware of them when he declared under oath he was giving all "the essential facts." He was aware of them when he implied—to a question of Senator John McClellan (D, Ark.)—that the failure to convict White was due to inadmissibility of wiretap evidence, whereas actually the Hoover sentences raised broader problems. Washington newsmen have appealed to Eisenhower to arrange a press conference with Brownell, but the latter is strangely shy.

The Canadian matter, coupled with Senate committee efforts to summon Igor Gouzenko, ex-Soviet cipher clerk in Ottawa who tipped off atomic espionage in 1945, naturally strain relations with our neighbor. The orthodox feeling is to deplore this. We cannot agree. When frock-coated statesmen slap their chests over the absence of forts on the international border we always enter a private dissent. The nature of nations being what it is, friendly countries never learn much from each other. The country that is influencing America's culture and thinking least today for its size is Canada.

By contrast, enemy lands cannot study each other enough. In Britain, the greatest civilizing influence for three centuries was hostile France. By contrast today, no American gives two hoots what Canada thinks about anything.

We live beside and ignore a country that doesn't have nightmares over "socialism," has a responsible party system with parliamentary government, prefers to check espionage with a royal commission rather than McCarthy, holds the balance between decency and commercialism on radio, balances its budget, and maintains its global dignity. All these lessons are lost for the US, because we take Canadian cordiality for granted and look south, east, and west but never north. By all means, let's have some forts on the border.

When Brownell and Hoover testified last week we counted thirteen motion picture and television cameras on tripods, plus two other tripods for still shots. It was an oil derrick forest in miniature. There were six tall iron stands for blazing sunlamps. On the table before the witnesses were fifteen separate microphones and two separate glasses of ice water.

Attorney General Brownell is a short, oddly insignificant figure with sparse sandy hair.

J. Edgar Hoover is a different type. He is thick and burly, broad-shouldered, and wears the dark-blue business suit that is the unofficial FBI uniform. His wavy black hair was sleeked down with glistening dressing, and there was the beginning of a fleshy roll at the back of his neck.

The Senate committee showed deference amounting to awe. The senators were afraid of the cop. And Hoover, head of the internal security police, was taking part for the first time in a partisan political quarrel. The kid-gloved claque applauded. It was not a cool, neutral, dispassionate account from an objective civil servant but one that hinted at deep emotional resentment at Democratic years. Repeatedly Hoover said that the FBI "did not evaluate," and again and again he evaluated. He convicted White without hesitation and denied that the FBI in 1946 had approved keeping White in office, which President ·Truman had not charged. He departed amidst an ovation.

Poor old Ike is the forgotten man in all this—breathing pious hopes that Communism won't be an election issue. He left it to the 179 reporters at his press conference last week whether his administration had embraced "McCarthyism." The *New York Times* polled 80 of them afterwards. Their verdict: Ike hadn't, but his administration had.

What's the difference between Brownellism and McCarthyism? The first is cellophane-wrapped; the second is scooped out loose. McCarthy is the wild dog leading the pack, Brownell is the Master of Hounds, blowing his horn. In short, the results are the same, but Brownellism is McCarthyism from a Madison Avenue church pew.

Eisenhower's Program

JANUARY 18, 1954   The president came smiling down the center aisle. Everyone rose and applauded. Ike wore a light television-blue shirt. He may have had on a touch of makeup. He delivered a fifty-five-minute, moderate speech that was in many parts a mild continuation of the New Deal. It was not reactionary or counterrevolutionary. The style was dull and uninspired. Applause came from Republican conservatives at all the wrong times. The only genuine burst greeted the one really false note, Ike's proposal for "decitizenizing" Communists. Puzzled congressmen didn't know what it meant but were glad to show they hated Reds. There were forty-five other interruptions of handclapping by two or more people and five more by single endeavorers who didn't get off the ground. There was universal sour silence when Ike asked for a higher debt limit.

It is not possible any longer to say Ike doesn't have a program. He has. It is precisely twelve months late, and he offers it to an election-year session instead of to the victory-charged first session when chances would have been better. In his own phrase, Ike has set out to be "progressive and dynamic" just at a time when Walter Lippmann, his anxious sponsor, warns him that his true role is not this at all but to "quiet its [the nation's] frayed nerves." This conception of Ike as a sort of national sedative is novel and has possibilities. But there is nothing much in Ike's to-be-continued-in-our-next program (except the Red citizenship item) to fray the nerves of anybody except conservatives. Conservatives dominate Congress, however, and they are now ganging up to see how much of the pseudo–New Deal parts of the program they will block.

Our guess is that about a third of the Ike program will pass, that he may win some marginal victories on another third, and that the rest will fail. This Congress is hell-bent on tax reduction, and we see the Treasury red-ink figure becoming a lot higher than Ike forecasts. This will be particularly true if the Truman Boom recedes further into the Eisenhower Recession.

The administration's continuing efforts to saddle McCarthy are amusing, if you find that kind of thing funny. Vice-President Nixon went down to Miami to talk to Joe. He was accompanied by William Rogers, deputy attorney general. Nixon, incidentally, is the real administration leader in the Senate, not Knowland (R, Calif.).

"Be good, Joe!" pleaded Nixon. He urged these reasons: (a) Ike has awarded the US license to hunt Reds to Senator Jenner (R, Ind.); (b) other senators are getting sore at Joe's trespassing; (c) if Joe will stick to general, non-Red investigating, the Justice and Internal Revenue officials will feed him good leads; (d) for his own reputation Joe can't afford further flops like the Fort Monmouth "espionage" hunt; (e) to further his political ambitions (i.e., to be president) he should start acting "constructive" and make a speech, maybe, on the farm or tax program (written by the best ghosts money can materialize). McCarthy listened attentively and Nixon came back hopeful. He made the mistake of voicing his hopes, and McCarthy promptly repudiated the whole thing as a plot probably Red-inspired. Our tentative judgment is that other senators are now just about sore enough to give McCarthy real pause; he may very well stop hitting the Red bottle for a while anyway—until the administration takes him off the wagon next fall to try to get rid of Democratic liberals like Senators Humphrey, Douglas, Murray, and others.

The climate of official opinion is changing quite fast on Red China. Or rather what the State Department is now beginning to think it is safe to say. If war doesn't break out again, it will be possible to look at things realistically before long. The point is that China is here to stay; that our real enemy is Russia, not China; that Chiang in Formosa (though our friend) hasn't a chance of invading the mainland; that our real interest is to split China from Russia, and that our allies, notably Japan, have to trade with China sooner or later. If things quiet down for a year or so, it will be possible to come right out in public with the things which high diplomats are already noting privately.

One of the real phonies of the Eisenhower administration is the charge that 1,456 "security risks" have been fired since it took office. The purpose of this ambiguous phrase is to imply that Communists are still being found and purged. We are sorry that Ike has joined in this hypocrisy. At a press conference he awkwardly stumbled around in refusing to give a breakdown of the figure, and in addressing Congress he raised it to "2,200." McCarthy, Brownell, and administration spokesmen constantly use "security risk" interchangeably with subversives, thereby seeming to substantiate the charges of Communists in government. Now conservative Congresswoman Katherine St. George (R, N.Y.) comes forward, in the conservative *Washington Star*, to say she is informed that only "10 percent or less" of the security-risk cases involve the question of loyalty. Others are drunks, crooks, or bar-mouths who would be fired anyway, by any administration. The security-risk figure is one of the palpable and transparent hoaxes seen here for some years. It is being kept alive for political purposes, and it is too bad to see Ike helping.

Indochina

APRIL 26, 1954   We got in late as Nixon was talking to the editors in the big Statler Hotel banquet room last week, ate our dessert first, tipped the waiter half a dollar to bring us back some excellent shad, and learned to our amazement that what the vice-president was saying was "off the record." And what he was saying was sensational. It was, in brief, that the Eisenhower administration thinks the loss of Indochina would be so disastrous that the USA should fight alone—if necessary—to save it.

Nixon spoke gravely, carefully, in great detail for more than an hour, and the 1,000 or more editors and reporters sat enthralled as the young man, in his double-breasted dark suit, outlined the situation. France and Britain want to quit; the US is absolutely convinced this means Communist control, and that we can't afford it. There wasn't a doubt that Nixon was giving a calculated disclosure of administration policy. The real stake in Indochina, (as in Korea) Nixon said, is Japan. Japan has half the industrial potential of Russia herself. We can't afford to let Russia get Japan or to retreat further; we must send US troops, if necessary, to hold Indochina. With startling frankness Nixon told a questioner in the audience that yes, maybe we had come away from Korea too soon; that "in hindsight" it might have been better to fight that war out to a victory rather than let Red China escape to mobilize its forces against Indochina. (There was no reference to this answer in the *New York Times*' account of the story next day.) Nixon wound up by telling another questioner he thought Oppenheimer loyal though there was a *prima facie* security risk under existing law.

We haven't a doubt that the administration knew Nixon's name would soon be connected to this Indochinese trial balloon. What we read in the affair is that the administration is now deeply concerned, and is trying to tell the country so. Incidentally, it is telling London, Paris, and Moscow that it means business. It is a tough task because it is one of the greatest political reversals in a lifetime. Ike won election on the "no more Koreas" issue; his administration has spent fifteen months pompously trying to argue it has a different foreign policy from that of Truman-Acheson; it has cut army strength and pretended that A-bomb "instant retaliation" would end little wars. As recently as March 15, Nixon himself, in a pretentious answer to Adlai Stevenson, accused Democrats of falling into the Communist trap "to destroy us by drawing us into little wars all over the world with their satellites, where they themselves were not involved."

Nixon (who now says we left Korea too soon) challenged Stevenson, March 15—"Does he think the Korean War should not have been stopped?"

The administration's reversal is breathtaking. Only a very grave danger, we think, could cause politicians to eat words like this. The political implications are incalculable. Ike built his 1952 campaign on the charge Democrats "blundered" into Korea, that he would end Korea, and, as president, "would eliminate the chances of a new Korea" (Joliet, 9/15/52). . . . Ike deserves patriotic support if the situation is as bad as this, but what a way to get it! The public has been lulled by huckster sloganeering, and Democratic legislators—who now as always will be the backbone of internationalist support—have been snubbed, misrepresented, and reviled with charges of "Twenty Years of Treason." In the old days under FDR and Truman there were Republicans in the government's top defense echelons—Stimson, Knox, and Dulles himself. Ike doesn't let a Democrat get near his team.

Ike ordered a "blank wall" for Dr. Robert Oppenheimer on atomic secrets—which is about like telling Einstein he can't have a physics book. Oppenheimer admittedly knew Communists in the mid-thirties, repented, and then more than any one man was responsible for giving the US the conquering A-bomb. Under the Truman security program Oppenheimer was okay; but under the Eisenhower program of May 27, 1953, he must be tested as a security risk in order to head off McCarthy. Oppenheimer in 1947—unanimously supported by the General Advisory Committee and a majority of the Atomic Energy

Commission—opposed the "crash program" of making the H-bomb. When Truman said "Go ahead," evidence indicates Oppenheimer loyally carried out the order. One of the minority of two who favored the crash program was Lewis L. Strauss. Strauss was delegated to tell Oppenheimer that he must face security charges—or resign quietly. If he had resigned, he would have been a sitting duck for McCarthy's later attack on grounds that silence indicated guilt. To us the Oppenheimer case is the ultimate insanity of the nightmare Eisenhower security order. Under the logic of hundreds of earlier cruel dismissals, how can the administration keep Oppenheimer? It's just as Defense Secretary Wilson told a press conference. He wouldn't use Oppenheimer now, he says, regardless of the outcome; maybe Oppenheimer has reformed, but he once played with Commies, didn't he? Somehow our outrage at this affair gets confused with our admiration for the hideous logic of the plot in the drama. . . . At the Nuremberg trials Reich Minister Albert Speer told prosecutor Robert Jackson that Germany suffered irreparable delay in atomic development "because unfortunately our best experts had gone to America."

"The policy of driving people out who didn't agree with Germany," said Jackson, "hasn't produced very good dividends, has it?"

"That, as far as we were concerned, had a very decisive disadvantage particularly in this sector," answered Speer.

"Drive them out!" says Wilson.

Some Praise for Eisenhower

DECEMBER 6, 1954 Big news does not always hit the headlines. Sometime in the past six months occurred the biggest news in Washington. It was Ike's decision that we have reached atomic stalemate, that he will not risk a military solution of the Cold War, that competitive coexistence must continue for a long time with emphasis on economic factors, particularly in Asia. These decisions are crucial. To this column they seem intelligent. But they mark a foreign policy reversal. They threaten to split Ike's party. The question is, can he implement them? That requires a bit of background.

Congress threatens usurpation of Ike's foreign policy control. Such a drive has followed most wars; strong presidents defeat it. Ike has weakened himself by inconsistency, and by a certain political dilettantism. As to the first, note the reversal of these 1952 campaign positions: A balanced budget was implied; but now Ike has indefinitely postponed it (wisely, we think). Ike promised, or made farmers think he promised, 100-percent parity; this is dropped. He promised full support of TVA; now comes Dixon-Yates. He tried to appease McCarthy and more than any other man made himself responsible for not slapping McCarthy down when it would have hurt Eisenhower and his party least; now he wants McCarthy disciplined. Ike started his presidency with a hands-off notion about Congress, reversed himself when he found it didn't work, and fought the Bricker Amendment in self-defense. But even so he weakly dropped his tariff program. All these switches have confused his party and increased his problems.

As to "political dilettantism," Ike has to run the presidency and have his golf and fishing, too. He has cut press conferences. He is the first president in modern times who doesn't read the papers. As the *Milwaukee Journal* says, "No modern president has such a record of absenteeism." In his first year he was out of Washington almost one third of the time; the 1954 score will be about the same. The sympathetic press does not criticize the president. But anxious reporters ask themselves privately how strongly he holds the reins of government in his own hands.

Now comes the biggest policy reversal of all, in foreign affairs. The Republicans took office pooh-poohing economic Point Four and attacking Acheson "containment" as too weak. The Dulles-Eisenhower policy was aggressive, and started with thunders of slogans. Now Ike has swung around; it is an about-face. We are delighted at the change. As Ike learned the meaning of H-bomb warfare, he got religion. He has twice already in six months rejected the Take-a-Chance-on-War Party, at Dien Bien Phu, and at Formosa. Now in the past fortnight everybody in Washington knows the administration has briefed the press on the new thesis: the necessity to boost noncommunist Asian countries with long-range economic assistance. Former Budget Director Joseph Dodge has been called back to mobilize the policy.

To this column Ike's new avowed moderation seems splendid. We do not mean to carp in pointing out three difficulties. First is GOP Senate leader Knowland & Co. Knowland followed Ike-Dulles in their "tough" phase, but he is now left out on a limb. We size up Knowland as wrongheaded but immensely sincere and earnest. He is also formidable. Second difficulty is McCarthy: Ike tried to appease him and now Joe is catalyzing all the crackpot conservatives and patrioteers in what, fundamentally, is an attack on Ike. And finally there are The Economy Boys. How they have laughed in the past at "Point Four Globaloney"! Now Ike calls back banker Joe Dodge, of all people—the man who was ready for any suicidal economy to balance the budget—to mobilize economic aid for Asia! It has its funny side, like sending strong-jawed George Humphrey, Secretary of the Treasury, down to the Rio Economic Conference to infuriate all the Latins by his sound businessman's approach. We would as soon have thought of Messrs. Dodge-Humphrey organizing a big program for have-not nations as we would of Messrs. Dixon-Yates playing Santa Claus to TVA.

In summary, however, Ike has definitely adopted the moderate policy. It may split the Republican Party, but in spite of Red China's provocations, we think most Democrats, and the American people, will go along.

The McCarthy battle starts up all over again, every day deepening the split in the Republican Party. Extreme right-wing and isolationist groups rally around Joe; as Eric Sevareid says, these divergent groups "have at least a basic emotional condition in common and that is anger—anger at the whole course of American domestic and foreign affairs over the last twenty-five years . . . they seem to feel that their opponents are not quite patriotic. . . ." Was McCarthy really sick? His ardent supporter, John Fox, publisher of the *Boston Post*, says that was all "a lot of nonsense." There were strategic reasons for interrupting the Senate performance. Mr. Fox continues: "So Senator McCarthy got a 'shattered' elbow. It wasn't shattered at all, of course. As a matter of fact, there wasn't much wrong with it at all. But they had to stop the show somehow." Nice to be frank about it, anyway.

"The Most Electrifying Words in the English Language"

DECEMBER 13, 1954   Vice-President Nixon hit the desk with his ivory gavel and said the most electrifying words in the English language. "The clerk will call the roll." "Mrs. Abel," said the clerk. . . .

The bells began ringing. They are softer than fire bells, milder than church bells, less terrible than doorbells rung at night in totalitarian countries, but they are the most compelling bells on earth. Once sounded, nothing can stop a Senate vote, and they symbolize majority rule and all the things in democracy which McCarthyism leaves out.

". . . Aye," said Mrs. Abel (R, Neb.). "Mr. Aiken," continued the clerk. "Nay," said a Vermont voice.

It was the first test vote—the Dirksen substitute resolution—a last, desperate attempt to whitewash McCarthy. Down below in the great railway station of a chamber the bald heads and foreshortened bodies seemed to swim among the desks, splashed with their white papers. Reporters' eyes smarted with the long vigil. Yet the atmosphere was somehow cozy and intimate, even with several thousand spectators crouching over the rails. A kind of hypnotic fog filled the air—not a palpable vapor but the ghostly exhalation of millions of words uttered here by generations of politicians.

Hearts pounding, reporters marked long sheets of ninety-six names, Republicans inked large, Democrats small, "yeas" on left, "nays" on right. As the tally proceeded the experts added a cumulative number on either side; they could tell at each second how the record stood.

"Mr. Anderson," said the clerk. "Mr. Barrett. . . ."

The suspense equaled the start of the first ballot at a presidential nominating convention. All week the senators had played their favorite roles—being themselves, Brahmin Saltonstall, saccharine Dirksen, vibrant Mrs. Smith (R, Me.)—whose conscience spoke first in 1950. Now they answered their names, Republicans wildly floundering, Democrats united after giving McCarthy the silent treatment—the treatment he will get hereafter. The press knew them well, the men down below.

There was fragile Watkins (R, Utah), revealing the terrible wrath of a Puritan once roused; Case (R, S.Dak.), a member of the committee—the little man who almost broke under pressure; Flanders, the Yankee mystic, who consulted his God and came up with the censure resolution. There was Langer, last heir of prairie populists, erratic as an unroped steer, chewing a cigar through cellophane and voting against censure; aged Hayden (D, Ariz.), beaked and bald as an amiable buzzard, who saw Bingham censured 25 years before; judicial Ervin (D, N.C.), the new Democratic hero, whose tic sends his eyebrows up and down like awnings; Alexander Smith (R), that strange old man from the state of New Jersey who meets every call of principle by trying to compromise it.

Then the party leaders: A sigh rises as barrel-chested Knowland votes for McCarthy and repudiates the men whom he put on the Watkins committee. Supple, gum-chewing Lyndon Johnson has miraculously brought the Democrats through united; every man below knows that when Knowland defected Johnson jumped to his feet to uphold the Watkins committee.

There are the McCarthyites: Hickenlooper who prowls as he talks and can't deliver a speech without ten feet of carpet. There is McCarthy himself, lumpish and slump-shouldered, looking more Napoleonic than ever with his arm slung to chest by a theatrically big bandage, and coat thrown over shoulders like a *maréchal*'s cape. And there are the Men of Hate, Jenner and Welker—the passionate men. All over the world there are men like these; there is one in every mob—who gives the scream or fires the pistol that precipitates the holocaust.

Jenner is the jerky one, he has been angry from the nipple on—Eisenhower insured his election in the same 1952 campaign in which he backed McCarthy. Reporters could hear his yells in this debate back in the press room behind the swinging glass doors. McCarthy, Welker, and Jenner have this in common, contempt for the anachronistic Senate and the silly old duffers who sit in it and who like to tell each other comfortingly that it is "the greatest deliberative body in the world." McCarthy never showed his contempt more than in the very form of his so-called apology.

Of all the great drama, that and the sequel—Dirksen's speech—

were the two strangest scenes: Dirksen, the curly-haired, syrup-voiced Liberace of the Senate, urging nauseated members to remember the season and show forebearance in the month (he said) when men sang "O Little Town of Bethlehem" and "Hark, the Herald Angels Sing."

Reporters dash for telephones. The vote is overwhelming—the Dirksen whitewash substitute defeated, 66 to 21. Next day the Senate votes condemnation, 67 to 22. In the final vote six of the eight Catholic senators present vote against McCarthy—an important point in the background story (that everyone whispers and nobody writes) of the rise of the new bigotry fanned by McCarthy.

The Senate has dropped the Zwicker count. This means that the smug old body condemns browbeating senators but not private citizens; that it still hates the executive and anybody connected with it, even officers. Well, that's like the Senate. All those specific questions of Joe's finances are dropped, too—did he play the market with money contributed to fight Communism? But there it is, McCarthy has run true to form—censured by fellow lawyers as a Wisconsin lawyer, by fellow judges as a Wisconsin judge, now by fellow senators as a United States senator.

From now on Joe is the man with the Scarlet Letter. He has C written on his coat, put there by men who know him best. . . . Well, well; a good week! McCarthy censured by the Senate—and in the White House, on foreign affairs, Dwight Eisenhower acting like the President of the United States!

Midterm Serenity

FEBRUARY 28, 1955 The time has come to report that there has been a substantial and encouraging improvement in Washington climate. People are talking more rationally about subversives, atom bombs, China, and Russia. We are frequently startled by the comment of a friend that would have been ranked as heresy a year ago. It may be too early to say it, but America seems to be slowly returning to reality after the binge of the century.

Let's look at the evidence. McCarthy has been censured, paid informers are recanting, people are not merely suspicious—they are bored—over charges of Communists under the bed, demagogues are regretfully hunting out new rackets.

Now take Ike and Dulles. Two years ago they were grandiloquently "unleashing" Chiang, substituting "rollback" for containment, and frightening Europe out of its wits with "massive retaliation." That era, with its loudmouthed slogans, is about over, thank heaven. At that time the administration was competing with McCarthy and simultaneously snubbing Truman. Now signals are reversed. Most of our present trouble comes from our silly past talk. But anyway, the deification of Chiang is about over, we acknowledge that the idea of invading the mainland is (and was) a myth, and it is possible to say right out that the reason we remain fuzzy and hesitant about Quemoy and Matsu is not some noble, moralistic reason but because we are afraid the morale of Chiang's aging troops will be irretrievably lost if the islands are abandoned.

Two years ago Taft was calling Truman and Acheson "traitors" for setting a limited goal on war in Korea; today that is the goal Ike sets on war if it comes in Formosa. Signs of sanity are seeping back. We learn that the administration is actually sounding out allies about swapping surplus butter and grain with Moscow—an idea greeted with horror last year. The whole boundary of what is "patriotic" is being pushed back. Last week Dulles referred to "historic friendship" with Russia (not, mind you, the Soviet Union)—a phrase we haven't heard around here in years. Just below the official level it is now admitted that "two Chinas" have come to stay and that Peking ultimately must enter the UN and be recognized.

And now the administration has spunked up courage to tell the awful truth about the fallout from the H-bomb blanket. One bomb may poison 7,000 square miles. Not cheerful, eh? Yes, but how much better for national morale than the panicky belief that national morale couldn't stand it! We don't mean to be premature, but we live in the Washington sickroom and we can report definite improvement. Any day now they may let the patient out of his straitjacket.

We don't really see what the Republicans will do at their San Francisco convention next year. Everything was decided here in advance at last week's GOP meeting. It will be Ike and, alas, probably Nixon. (Ike will be seventy at the end of his hypothetical second term—the oldest of any president in history—and we do hope his health is good if reelected.) The campaign program will be "peace, prosperity, and lower taxes." Chairman Leonard Hall's confidence is such that he feels safe to berate the ultraconservative GOP wing. Ike has obligingly coined one of his sparkling aphorisms: the goal is going to be "dynamic conservatism" (née "moderate progressivism"). The Gallup Poll indicates Ike would beat Adlai by a bigger margin now than in 1952. Most Washington reporters agree.

What is Ike's secret? Well, he is an attractive personality and national war hero. He comes when the nation yearns for normalcy. Instead of making enemies by strong stands on social issues, he shoots quail. When he should have been on the telephone last week rallying bolting House Republicans to pass his tariff bill, he was playing golf. It was left to Rayburn and the Democrats to save him. On the issues where Ike does take a strong stand, he is sincere; he feels almost religiously that "private enterprise" must be guarded, that TVA threatens "creeping socialism," that local initiative (always foggily defined) is the way to salvation.

Coupled with these devout bromides is a fiscal pattern that is actually quite modern, unorthodox, and Keynesian. For example, Ike has gracefully dropped the pledges to balance the budget; it is hard for supporters to face the fact that he has deliberately chosen not to balance the budget and probably won't balance it for all four years. It is hard to face it, so they don't face it. (Economists generally applaud his big financial switch.)

Ike believes in progress. He has not tried to repeal the New Deal. Indeed a kind of yearning ameliorism for the masses runs through his awe of business tycoons. He offers palliatives in health, education, and social welfare. He is a baker of half loaves. Most of these viands he proposes to buy by strangely unorthodox fiscal devices, devices which would make his followers scream with alarm if a simple fellow like Truman offered them: he would set up Ponzi-like intermediary private authorities, financed through Wall Street, to float billions in loans that would not show up as "debt" on the unbalanced budget. This is most particularly true of the odd installment-purchase proposals Ike is really interested in—Dixon-Yates power plants and vast new highways.

Is this the whole Eisenhower secret? No, in fairness, it isn't. If we are correct, besides all this Ike has recently tuned himself in to the deep, pacific mood of America and is expressing the national will in his restraint of generals and admirals. He is not consistent here, either, of course, for these are the same military men he himself appointed; nevertheless it is he who is vetoing war and dampening down the atom rattling of the Radfords and Nixons. This total combination is formidable. Perhaps, in the present national temper, it is politically unbeatable.

A Visit with Lincoln

APRIL 25, 1955   We came away from the Supreme Court's hearing on the segregation cases last week in a philosophic mood. Spring has seeped up to the Capitol now, and everything is a-bud and a-twitter. There were sixteen buses for out-of-town high school kids parked one behind the other on the Capitol Plaza (where the over-coated crowd shivers every four years to watch the new president sworn in). The languid spring breeze rocked the little green bomb-shells of maple sprays, and the sightseeing youngsters complained of how their feet hurt. It was dull in Congress, they said. Well, a century ago they would have heard demagogues inside steaming up for the Civil War.

There is so much that is tawdry and commonplace in Washington that a cynical reporter can spend a lifetime here finding fault. Yet now and then he catches a sense of greatness. It was so, last week, in Cass Gilbert's glittering marble Supreme Court building. There the government still has dignity. You go into the courtroom where every architectural trick has been bent to awe you, and you see the nine justices in black robes asking courteous, perceptive, searching questions. There is no hurry; there is no delay. Originally the justices were supposed to sit in elaborately carved chairs, but they preferred to bring over their own comfortable ones, in all sizes, and you can practically see the Nine stamped out in the leather after they have left. There's a new ceiling to improve acoustics, and now a big, temporary loudspeaker with a crude mosquito net over it sticks up twenty feet or so over the chief justice's head, and you can finally hear in the place. These housekeeping arrangements are curiously comforting: they show judicial flexibility and common sense, and a capacity to make even a Greek temple work.

Eleven months ago the Supreme Court decided—unanimously—that segregated schools in America won't do. The Court is now working out judicial procedure to put its decision into effect, a process that seemed to us very much like legislation. It is quiet here in the court, but the attentive ear can hear emotions and passions roaring round the place. Not today nor tomorrow, but ultimately, segregation will end.

We got to thinking about it as we dropped in on Abe Lincoln in his Memorial at the other end of the Mall. They have put him in a Greek temple, too. We pay a call now and then, and have never yet failed to come away feeling better. He looks out through the open colonnades, brooding and whimsical, toward the Capitol and the Court, and the nation behind. "Golly!" said a schoolgirl from Nyack looking up at him. She said everything we felt. We were envious of her gift of literary compression.

Well, ninety years have passed and the Negro in America still endures injustice and humiliation. On the other hand, what other nation, faced with a social problem like this, has ever come so far? The pace is now accelerating. Competition with the communists doubtless is a stimulant. But anyway, there it is. Negro voting rights are accumulating, lynching is over, accretion of purchasing power attests higher living standards and brings with it greater respect. Now schools must improve. We often think the United States is a hard place to figure out. There is much that is tawdry and ignoble, and there are bigots and demagogues. On the other hand, Abe still sits in his marble temple and there are nine black-robed justices who speak quietly but firmly. There is splendor in Washington, too.

Stevenson No Match for Prosperity

J u l y   4 ,   1 9 5 5   One thing Adlai Stevenson's candidacy should give is a real opposition to Eisenhower. The Democratic op- position to Ike in Congress today is largely make-believe. A strong, articulate voice analyzing Ike and his administration in a presidential campaign may do America profound good. It is not too much to say that a man might lose the presidency itself and still by his campaign change the course of history.

To be brutal about it, we think Stevenson's chances of winning are not too bright. He is a match for Ike, but perhaps not for prosperity. It looks as though the GOP would have both in '56. One thing is cer- tain, Stevenson can't win by pussyfooting. In an uphill fight the chal- lenger must be bold. Ike is the conservative, and if Stevenson doesn't take the full liberal line he might as well not try.

The indictment of Ike is in three parts: He doesn't work hard enough at being president. He is also letting the presidential func- tion revert back to the weak role it held for thirty years after the Civil War, and again under Harding-Coolidge-Hoover. And, finally, he looks at life through big business eyes.

No Republican can win without Democratic votes, and in vote after vote in the states since 1952 the Democrats have been getting stronger. It is Stevenson's job, if he gets the nomination, to push that liberal movement ahead.

That is not being done by Democrats today in Congress, as we see it, and no clear-cut choice is being created for the voters between the parties. The Democrats are running out on the Dixon-Yates bill, and it looks as though they would do the same thing in the natural gas fight. Like the offshore oil giveaway this natural gas fight is Texas vs. the Nation, and Sam Rayburn and Lyndon Johnson both come from Texas. It is a fight of city dwellers against the oil-producing states; consumer vs. producers. The oil companies want federal regulation killed to boost gas prices. There is no question where Democratic interest lies in this battle. Party strength is in the city dwellers. Yet Speaker Rayburn has ignobly appealed to Eisenhower to help scrap federal regulation. If Adlai Stevenson wants to start the 1956 campaign right away, on a real issue, he can jump into this fight now.

The Hoover Commission report on water resources and power comes out shortly. It would turn the clock back twenty years, while the report of its task force under Ben Moreell, chairman of Jones & Laughlin Steel, would turn it back half a century. From that viewpoint alone the Hoover report is relatively mild. We doubt, however, if any single expression more clearly shows the real direction of Republican thinking on power policies than this Hoover report. Its frankness may embarrass the GOP, and cause them to try to disown it, but Ike's own prejudices follow the same direction. He is now opening the way to straitjacket TVA through Dixon-Yates, to undercut Hell's Canyon dam, and to end the federal "yardsticks" over the big private utilities. In most legislative fields Ike has followed a sort of watered-down New Dealism, but in the field of power it is different. Here he is backing the reactionaries' counterrevolution.

Notes Signs of abating national hysteria on the loyalty front continued last week: the Senate draw a noose around McCarthy's throat on a resolution dealing with the Big Four and jerked it tight in a vote of confidence in Ike and lack of confidence in Joe, 77 to 4; Secretary Benson reluctantly admitted maybe soil expert Ladejinsky is not a "security" risk; and a distinguished panel of the US Court of Appeals here unanimously forbade the State Department to withhold passports by "arbitrary" procedure. On the other hand the Defense Department reportedly suspended the security clearances of California Tech's Swiss guided-missile expert, Fritz Zwicky; chiefly, it seemed, because he was Swiss. . . . Harry Truman got a rousing demonstration at the UN tenth anniversary celebration at San Francisco—the man whose implementation of UN pledges in the Korean invasion made this the single most important act in the UN's life to date.

Kick-off Dinner

APRIL 30, 1956   Oh, what a rollicking time we had with Ike and the Republicans last week at the kick-off dinner for the 1956 campaign. Silverware and napery were of the finest, tables were heaped with "I Like Ike" flags and clusters of colored balloons and state standards, and ennobling speeches everywhere. A Georgia delegate promised that Ike was going to break the vicious one-party system this year in Georgia, and the lady lieutenant governor of Vermont promised that Vermont would keep right on voting Republican this year as it always has. The crowd cheered both statements. The organ played "I-ow-ay," and the state delegation rose and showed what good sports they were by joining in the fun. A Negro member from New Jersey told how much he liked Republicans, and Nixon gazed shyly down into his plate and looked modest and noble while the crowd gave him a standing ovation—sparked by an ironic demonstration from the press tables which spread like slow wildfire to the diners.

And then the climax, waiters coming down the darkened aisles with Fourth of July sparklers scintillating from ice cream trays . . . the release of the colored balloons . . . the organ playing "Hail to the Chief" . . . the arrival of Ike and Mamie. Well, we just can't do it justice.

The presidential speech that followed was right off the top— standardized Eisenhower Inspirational. Good, sound, old-fashioned morality, nothing highbrow about it but serious, and high-toned, too, with arresting statements like "The individual is of supreme importance"; "The spirit of our people is the strength of our nation"; "America does not prosper unless all Americans prosper." Splendid things like that.

The 800 GOP leaders looked, listened, and pinched themselves to believe their own good fortune. What a product to merchandise! Estimates are that $100 million will go into it. There was Ike, ruddy and jolly, having the time of his life—standing up with his arms way over his head and a big victory grin; then a minute later there was the earnest, serious Leader preaching a sermonette and telling the crowd that "To stay free we must stay strong"; and "The purpose of government is to serve, never to dominate." Warren Harding couldn't have done better.

Reporters looked at each other, miserably, it is true, but after a while even their interest grew; after all it is a professional challenge to try to find a news lead in an effusion of that sort. This particular columnist idly began underlining certain high-powered words; in the four-and-a-half-page text he found "God" mentioned five times, two "Divines" and two "Crusades"; "Spirit" or "Spiritual," eight times; and "Principle" (either singular or plural), sixteen times. It took us back nostalgically to the 1952 campaign—and you know how the American public loved *that*.

Well, we came away realizing that we had heard a little classic. And just to confess the limitations of human nature, do you know that the thing that stuck in our mind was not any of the terse Eisenhower epigrams, like "Government must have a heart as well as a head," but the irrelevant detail of how the hotel gets those colored gas balloons down from the ceiling after they are liberated. There they hung, each trailing a long piece of string. An air rifle, maybe? Curiosity got the better of us, and we called up. Seems the gas comes out of the balloons after a while, when the people have gone and the place grows dark, and they quietly sink down. They can be used again and again. The sparklers are safe, too, we learned, because they are just for show; no heat in them. There was no hint of political irony in our unknown informant's voice.

Notes A whole lot of disagreeable information on the subject of Red China is about ready to fall on Americans—most of it probably not till after the election. The next president (whoever he is) will have to begin the disagreeable job of educating citizens to the fact that the USA is almost alone now in trying to keep Red China out of the UN and of pretending that it is appropriate that the island of Formosa should be a member of the eleven-member UN Council—with its veto power and all.

Stevenson vs. Kefauver

JUNE 4, 1956   The Stevenson-Kefauver primary battle
reaches its climax next week in California following this week's bitter
round in Florida. We have been down on the Spanish-moss circuit and
herewith offer some random notes.

Kefauver gives his public simple short words in simple short sentences delivered with an air of diffident understatement in a calm,
level voice. As, for example, on top of a fruit truck-trailer before the
Touchton drugstore (Rexall) in Sanford, Florida, at 8:30 P.M. last
week, with a palm tree stuck up on the street like a theatrical prop.
(The newcomer keeps pinching himself and saying, "How like Florida!" and remembering it *is* Florida.) The trailer top is enormously
long; seven tubular aluminum seats have been stuck on it; the local
Kefauver leaders have been hauled on board; there's a full moon in
the sky, temperature about eighty degrees, and below a miserably
small crowd of about 100 registering indifference.

Just what makes Kefauver tick still baffles reporters. He seems to
have a feeling of destiny that buoys him over obstacles, the chief of
which now is apathy. Florida has already held the gubernatorial primary in which it was really interested: moderate Governor LeRoy
Collins beat a field of rabid racists; 800,000 votes were cast. Florida
tends to be Democratic in local elections and Republican in national
elections, which is the way the two-party system is emerging in the
South. Of forty daily Florida newspapers only four supported Stevenson in 1952. The same ratio applies today. Ike won in '52.

Well, the lanky figure on the fruit trailer is now telling his Sanford
audience that it is a shame the US doesn't have nuclear reactors, and
he will push the idea if he gets to the White House. There is something in his talk for about every local interest. Then he opens up on
Stevenson. It is hard not to feel that this is demagoguery. The Kefauver bus carries circulars printed by a California old-age outfit,

offshoot of the Townsend Plan, charging that Stevenson vetoed a 10-percent increase in "old-age and blind pensions." It neglects to say that Stevenson actually boosted pensions in Illinois and vetoed this particular bill because it was a make-believe, passed by the GOP legislature without any accompanying appropriation. The GOP legislature passed many similar phonies, and Stevenson exposed them by vetoes. A reporter who admires Kefauver's liberal record in Congress is disheartened by this kind of attack. There is no way to verify the charges at the time (Stevenson, of course, immediately brands them as "scurrilous"), but the reporter reflects that not even Nixon used them in '52. Here on the street of Sanford is a gloomy moment for progressives.

We had some fear that we should find a "new" Stevenson. Nothing of the sort. He is still enormously entertaining. "You can't teach an underdog new tricks," he said of Kefauver. He is still merry and deeply serious. He doesn't like the political handshaking but is doing it rather well. Stevenson wants to talk to the nation on national issues and is caught in primary battles on parochial issues. It is a process of running for the presidency in terms of the county sheriff. The man who could say in Chicago recently, "I agree that moderation is the spirit of the times, but we must take care lest we confuse moderation with mediocrity, or settle for half answers to hard problems," spends part of his sixteen-hour day in a Jacksonville department store shaking hands with surprised customers. On the other hand, at a Lake City rally—under live oak trees cobwebbed with Spanish moss—we heard him make an unexpected plea for racial moderation that moved the southern audience almost in spite of itself.

Stevenson's delivery is uneven—sometimes ideas crowd too fast or he shows a kind of breathlessness, as in the joint TV appearance of the candidates at Miami. But at his best, we think, Stevenson is about as good as they come.

Travel is broadening. It was instructive to be here to see how the newspapers played Eisenhower's Texas speech. Big, happy headlines everywhere proclaimed "Communism a Gigantic Failure." Practically nothing else was quoted from the speech. But what more was wanted? Once more Ike (or Dulles) has cried all's well, communism is slipping, we are winning, go back to sleep again, it's ten o'clock by the village clock and the Great White Father has the world in hand! This is government by sedative. Stevenson tries to suggest that the Soviet Union is more of a threat now in its new phase than ever, but thirty-six of Florida's forty daily papers scoff at him. The funny thing is that Ike himself seems surprised when he gets back to Washington that Congress cuts foreign aid after he and Dulles have been implying that the game is already won. If communism is a "gigantic failure," why worry?

Deep in Florida we heard some amazing stories about the supposed horrors of school desegregation in Washington. The yarns were preposterous but it suddenly burst upon us that the District of Columbia is from now on a deadly challenge to the whole South. The ratio of Negroes in the District is 35 percent (schoolchildren, 50 percent) compared to only 22 percent in Florida. Yet integration has been put through smoothly and quietly.

The truth is integration hasn't actually changed things much in Washington because white communities still have almost all-white schools and Negro communities almost all-Negro. Integration has forced the city to face the fact that Negro schools have been neglected. An idealist would like to pretend that desegregation came by popular demand; acually there was no nonsense about voting on the question in defranchised Washington: it was imposed autocratically from above. It would have been harder if the District had had the vote. And who has blocked the vote? Why, the southern congressmen, to be sure, hating desegregation! They are the ones who forced it to come so swiftly when it came.

The Republican Convention

SEPTEMBER 3, 1956 As the crowd roared its welcome to the president at the San Francisco Cow Palace, attendants tugged at the ropes of two great fishnets hung under the rafters of the cavernous hall, and colored toy balloons came cascading slowly down in a pretty shower. The balloons landed in the press section, and for minutes thereafter it sounded like corn popping in a skillet as reporters applied cigarettes. Then the noise of the great multitude rose again, higher than the band, higher than the organ, in a tremendous shout that made the spine tingle. So a medieval army hailed its chief. It was the climax of a convention that was otherwise infernally dull.

The president read his acceptance speech. He told them that the Republican Party was the "Party of the future." Nobody smiled. Tens of millions of Americans watched him on TV; ask them the next day what he said and they couldn't tell you, but they remember the image of the good, patriotic fatherly man explaining that things are in good shape, the country in good hands, and the GOP modernized and re-built. Relax, folks, and on Election Day let independents and Democrats come forward to aid the party of the future.

As the president talked under dazzling lights, around the hall or on the platform were Old-Guard senators like Styles Bridges of New Hampshire, Everett Dirksen of Illinois, William Jenner and Homer Capehart of Indiana, John Bricker of Ohio, Bourke Hickenlooper of Iowa, Labor-hating Barry Goldwater of Arizona, Herman Welker of Idaho, and such worthies as Sinclair Weeks, Herbert Hoover, Jr., and Douglas McKay. They rubbed their hands. With Ike the election is, they believe, in the bag. They try to spend five minutes a day before a mirror saying "don't be overconfident," but their voices lack conviction.

Rows of people diminished away in perspective before the president. As he spoke they looked like bee clusters at the far corners. Attendants crowded in from cement corridors outside to jam the side entrances; snack bars and soft drink booths were deserted. In far-off press cubicles and bars the same earnest face appeared on TV screens saying the same thing.

Reporters watched from pine benches. The president looked pink and confident. The day before at his big press conference (which washed out Stassen) Ike showed verve and bounce. He has made great physical improvement since his last conferences in Washington.

We noticed from our seat a certain gauntness in his figure, which has shrunk considerably under doctors' orders. He has been ill or convalescent or hospitalized for eleven months. There is a little stoop in his shoulders and neck now which was not there before. We thought his delivery flagged a bit toward the end, but it was a long speech, forty minutes.

If the president has changed little, the change in forty-three-year-old Nixon is spectacular indeed. He is universally called the "new Nixon." For his speech immediately preceding Ike's, he wore a dark, conservative suit, but not too conservative. He threw bouquets to everybody, was the model of propriety, modest and charming by turns and favoring all the right things: young people, better schools, peace, military strength at home, allies abroad, and above all spiritual strength. Oh yes, above all spiritual strength. The convention glowed. Women cooed. How could anybody distrust the dear young man?

We thought we heard a chuckle as we came out into the night air from the Cow Palace, but it was only a couple of ghosts left over from the GOP Chicago convention of 1952. Remember who delivered the keynote address four years ago? Why, General Douglas MacArthur. And who delivered another main address? Why, Joe McCarthy, whose speech was then described as moderate, right down the middle of the gutter. McCarthy tactfully withdrew to the hospital this year instead of coming to San Francisco.

"They've forgotten us," said the military figure wistfully. "Yes," replied the heavyset man with the blue-black jowls, "but I think we've got something in there, Doug, that looks promising, maybe smarter than us too." Another chuckle, and the two figures were lost in the crowd.

But let us go back a bit. Before the Cow Palace show started we did a little research among our files and particularly looked up the second Eisenhower State of the Union speech in 1954. This was the time (according to the Donovan book, which was prepared with official permission) when Eisenhower was so disillusioned and disheartened with the Republican Congress that he considered starting a new party. Did his address at the time show his disillusionment? No, indeed. It was a proud recapitulation of the progress of his administration, a happy suggestion that the GOP was the party of the future.

And so again the president at the Cow Palace told the nation that the party is finally modernized, streamlined, and reformed. The ghosting was done by Arthur Larson, former Dean of the University of Pittsburgh Law School, now Undersecretary of Labor and author of

A Republican Looks at His Party. Mr. Larson, too, argues that moderates have taken over the GOP, that the great civil war is won.

Look at the conservatives and reactionaries waiting in the wings, eager to troop on once the election is won. The Old Guard controls the party in Congress and the machinery in most of the states.

Looking back over the two conventions, one sees that at Chicago the Democrats decided the control of their party, with Stevenson winning against Truman, that at San Francisco the Republicans left it all undecided. An uneasy truce prevails with Eisenhower the regent and the new Nixon the heir apparent. The GOP convention was not merely dull: it was dynamically boring. The difference is the same as between mere sleeplessness at night and sleeplessness plus your wife's snoring. Television wouldn't let it slumber alone. Millions of dollars worth of equipment had been flown in, and the unfortunate announcers had to fill the unforgiving minutes with excitement that wasn't there. Even now with the whole thing a memory their eyes glaze over as they recall the ordeal, the complicated apparatus, two-way communication ballots printed for possible contests, the lip-reader imported to read the secrets of distant caucuses (who reported that nothing was being said but dirty stories and most of them old at that), and the frantic effort to sustain the Stassen house of cards. Well, they did get the "Joe Smith" episode, and that was funny for a minute or two.

Most people left San Francisco with the feeling that the full Stassen story hadn't been told. What really happened? It is known that Stassen went to the president just before the latter's trip to Panama and told him what he proposed to do. A word from the president would have stopped him. Why wasn't it given?

Stassen is an experienced, knowledgeable fellow, aware of the rules of the game. How could he have continued without encouragement? To be fair, it should be said that once he committed himself this massive, courteous, politician with the curiously large head walked his tightrope superbly, refusing to be drawn into personal criticism of Nixon and keeping his balance while reporters tried to knock him off. There is an almost universal feeling that top members of the administration, probably the president himself, would have been glad at the end to ditch Nixon.

The new Nixon had outmaneuvered them with the help of Chairman Len Hall. Together they equated attacks on Nixon with attacks on the president's health. Ike's ambiguous failure to endorse Nixon specifically angered the young man, but he wisely kept his peace and depended on Hall. The latter knows his own mind and how to make up Eisenhower's. It was he who created the atmosphere in which it seemed natural for the president to run again; this time he created the atmosphere that virtually predetermined the action on Nixon.

The president likes to postpone hard decisions, and when he thought it was time to act, the decision was already made. As the convention started, Stassen presented his long-awaited poll. It was made by competent people and indicated Nixon would cut the president's support 8 percent. This would be serious for congressional candidates in close districts but Senator Bridges, the canny Old-Guard leader who arranged the remarkable "spontaneous" write-in for Nixon in the New Hampshire primary, came up with his own poll. Why, Nixon was as popular as, maybe more so than, the president. Who could doubt the poll's accuracy when it employed for collectors "only former FBI agents in each and every state of the Union"?

Well, we know the result: Stassen was foredoomed. Without direct White House aid he quit in the kind of atmosphere you wish you could forget but can't. Stassen went in to see the president (who flew into San Francisco a day early) and had his big renunciation scene taken away when the president himself hurried down into the cluttered, disorderly hotel pressroom and, before live TV cameras and anxious Secret Service men, broke the story. Nixon got out a magnanimous statement. Stassen asked for a chance to abase himself before the convention by making one of nine seconding speeches for Nixon. The delegates got ready to boo, but Len Hall quietly sent a message to heads of delegations requesting self-control. Stassen was unctuous and oily and reminded one strangely of self-accusers at a Russian trial. At this point, for the first time a batch of reporters suddenly realized that the new Nixon is the leading power in the Republican Party. He is on the inside track, actively sponsored by the Old-Guard wing of the party, which Eisenhower says no longer exists. The president, in his speech, obviously tried to rub off some of his popularity on his party. He painted a pleasant today and a happy tomorrow, urged cultural interchange with communist countries (while refusing to let reporters enter Red China) and told questing youth to cheer up, things are still not quite perfect: "There are still enough injustices to be erased, still enough needless sufferings to be cured, to provide careers for all the young crusaders we can find." Stevenson in his own acceptance speech grimly remarked, "Thirty million Americans live today in families trying to make ends meet on less than $2,000 a year," a fifth of the nation ill-fed, ill-housed, ill-clothed, and the comfortable Ike promises young reformers that the world is still not a Utopia.

Well, Eisenhower finished. The crowd applauded. Some hasty resolutions were passed, and the final stage of the 1956 campaign began.

On their way out reporters popped the last of the pretty balloons with their cigarettes.

Stevenson Disappoints

OCTOBER 15, 1956   Adlai Stevenson has made the mild suggestion that we ought to have another go with Russia at trying to limit H-bombs. It seems a reasonable idea to a lot of people. But statements by Nixon ("catastrophic nonsense") and Eisenhower ("wicked nonsense") make it appear that it is somehow unpatriotic even to discuss an arms race that may shrivel up Man like a blast of DDT on an anthill.

We honestly don't know whether it is a practical proposal or not, but for the life of us we can't see why it shouldn't be tried. Oddly enough this is about the one new idea of the campaign. We are confident that when the election is over, whoever wins, the Stevenson proposal will still be a live issue.

America originally urged Russia to discuss atomic disarmament under conditions which Moscow rejected. Then Moscow said it would accept these conditions, but things had changed and the USA imposed rigid new preconditions, including mutual inspection. Again Moscow balked. Today neither Nixon nor Eisenhower really is talking about what Stevenson proposes when they assume their pose of shocked surprise. If the argument could be joined on the real issue, this column might be won over to the Eisenhower "inspection-first" school. We don't know. But we do know that rigidity, lack of imagination, and self-righteousness are features of the Eisenhower administration repeatedly displayed in foreign affairs. Today all these characteristics are evident in rejecting what appears to be, in essence, a simple proposal to try to get off dead center, and to get the auto off the track before the express hits it.

Atomic Energy Commissioner Tom Murray has always seemed to us a sensible man. He says we now have all the big H-bombs we need. By "big" bombs he means the mass-decimation, multimegaton weapon capable of rubbing out Long Island. Who is going to set these off anyway, when it means contaminating the earth's atmosphere? Murray is against further tests of this type of weapon, at any rate, as unnecessary. Surely there is room here for prayerful discussion. Surely this administration displays its essential smugness when it slams the door on argument, shouts "peace," and equates any new idea with "wicked nonsense."

Nixon has been offering another interesting campaign argument. He doesn't like to have Stevenson mention "distress areas" and economic hardships in his speeches because this plays into the hands of the Soviet. Such talk, Nixon said at Philadelphia the other day, is "grist for the propaganda mills of those who are trying to tell the uncommitted peoples of the world that their best hope for a better way of life lies in turning toward communism rather than freedom." Put in plain English, Nixon means that anybody who complains aids the enemy, exactly the argument Moscow Communists use in exiling malcontents to Siberia.

The campaign is developing according to schedule. From now on Eisenhower will be making speeches all over the place. We forecast this months ago, and of course almost everybody expected it, except maybe the president himself. When he was ill they persuaded him that he could get reelected without a fight; now that he is committed they are urgently calling for his help.

Stevenson's speeches continue to be disappointing. We have had some interesting correspondence about this from readers. Generally the feeling is that he fails to project himself or to strike sparks from an audience. The speeches themselves are all right—often brilliant; the trouble seems to be with his delivery. Stevenson often appears to be self-conscious and mike-shy. Is it lack of resonance, is it poor breathing control that gives him difficulty with his beautifully balanced sentences? We have heard him make some of the best speeches we ever got from a political figure, but they have been few in this campaign. What we always hope for is that Adlai will lose his temper, throw away his text, and then express for us better than we can for ourselves the passionate distaste for a business-oriented, pietistic donothing administration. Commentator Eric Sevareid put down this vague dissatisfaction with Stevenson speeches the other night: "He gives us the words but not the music. This is one great element lacking in his public image, the missing key that would unlock his personality for real public understanding. All else is there—wit, intelligence, integrity; anger is missing."

The result of the foregoing is that, in state after state, the Democratic Party seems stronger than its candidate—that the party is carrying Stevenson, not he the party. This is just the opposite, of course, from the Republican situation. Translated into election terms the result could be a Democratic Congress, a Republican president, and four more years of dead-center government—with young Mr. Nixon coming up.

First Lame-Duck President

NOVEMBER 12, 1956   Dwight Eisenhower now becomes America's first lame-duck president, forbidden by a Republican-devised constitutional amendment to succeed himself. His age and health would not permit him to run for a third term anyway.

In the moment of his triumph in the early hours of November 7 he implied that he was no longer bound by the Republican right wing and he attempted to prove that "America" (in his words) "has approved of modern Republicanism." Nonsense. America has approved of the Father Image and repudiated the party which created it. Not for 108 years, not since 1848, not since another military hero, Zachary Taylor, has a president been elected while seeing his party rejected by the voters in the sense that it failed to carry either house of Congress. Republicans may capture the Senate, but as this is written it seems unlikely. Any voter last Tuesday who tried to split his ticket realizes the difficulty of doing it, and yet in this election millions achieved the feat that produced a Democratic Congress.

Comforting voices will now be raised saying that this odd political balance is all for the best, that the American people want moderation, want things as they are, want a legislature of the center to cooperate with a president of the center. But will Congress cooperate? Why should the isolationist GOP Old Guard cooperate with a president who openly repudiates them? They have nothing to gain from him anymore; their man is Nixon. If Eisenhower tries to push through a substantial legislative program, he must look, we guess, more than ever to the Democrats. And now, thanks primarily to the direct, blunt criticism of Adlai Stevenson, the Democrats are not likely any longer to stand in awe of the president or to follow him uncritically. We expect a striking change in the congressional atmosphere in the next four years. Maybe that is Stevenson's chief legacy.

We hope for a period of constructive cooperation. This is not partisanship anymore, this is a matter of desperate national concern. It is not that Eisenhower may do the wrong things in the next term but that he may do nothing at all. The world is moving at a frightful pace. Is there enough energy and imagination in an elderly and tired administration to meet the crisis, and how about issues at home? America is having a tremendous love affair with an economic boom, but it is the kind of situation where firm guidance is necessary.

This election in its final weeks had one extraordinary feature. An administration was profiting politically by its own mistakes. Reporters watched the process in awe. The Dulles foreign policy collapsed, and yet in the danger of this debacle the voters instinctively felt the need of unity and rallied behind the president whose shortsightedness allowed the Dulles collapse to occur!

In vain Stevenson in a series of powerful last-minute speeches pointed to the fantastically optimistic statements made just before the collapse by Dulles, Nixon, and Eisenhower. Rarely have public figures been so exposed by their own words as utterly ignorant of what was transpiring. In fact, for four years the administration has lulled America into a false sense of security by continuing unrealistic statements of world events. But when the collapse came in the final minutes of the long campaign, Stevenson had, we believe, lost the ear of the public. It seems to be agreed that the British-French invasion of Egypt and events in Hungary helped Eisenhower.

The administration's first reaction to the discovery that it had been duped by London and Paris was anger that was almost hysterical. As often happens, it was Nixon who expressed it. Note the timing of events. It was on the Friday before election (November 2) that Nixon made his speech at Hershey, Pennsylvania. Speaking for the administration, he tried to put a reverse twist on the situation, to show that we had broken from our allies, not the other way about: "For the first time in history," he declared happily, "we have shown independence of Anglo-French policies toward Asia and Africa which seemed to us to reflect the colonial tradition. That declaration of independence has had an electrifying effect throughout the world."

Even for Nixon this was a remarkable statement. He was seeking to extract political benefit from a cataclysm. The crassness of the invention is revealing and stupefying. Maybe it is true that the US has emerged from the sorry business looking better than England and France, but the weakness of our alliance has been exposed—a revelation which probably helped Moscow decide that it could put Hungary back again on the rack. And it showed what a house of cards Dulles and Eisenhower have erected.

Inaugural Parade

FEBRUARY 4, 1957 Dominating the Inaugural parade were the missiles. The massed stands were built out into the street of be-flagged Pennsylvania Avenue, and the long, winding procession of bands and floats and rolling politicians had the intimacy of a Roman triumph. Silence settled as the missiles trundled by on their futuristic mounts.

They are sleek, beautiful, lethal things with the fearful symmetry of a coiled rattlesnake, capable of crisping cities 1,000 miles off and given affectionate, humorous nicknames by their crews, like "Corporal" and "Honest John," in man's ancient instinctive determination to hide from himself the unbearable horror of what he is doing.

The desire to see them discharged is irresistible. We kept thinking of our grandfather's farm—the summer we got our first rifle—a single-shot .22 Stevens made in Portland, Maine. The itch to pull the trigger was beyond us. Before we knew it, plunk—a neat hole in the ingoing and outgoing side of the galvanized RFD mailbox, right between the initials of "B. F. Lang, So. Lee, N.H." (We had fired from the barn gate, above, so the passage was at a slant.)

Well, we wonder what fingers are going to yearn over the controls of "the Snarks," "Matador," "Sidewinder," and fight the compulsive urge to push the buttons? Who can restrain the temptation—are these superb weapons to be achieved and not used? What a great pop there will be, to be sure, when they go off!

Here are notes jotted on our wet pine plank before the Capitol, where we sat in the press tier.

Stands damp; heavy drifting clouds with rare blue patches; rotten snow in corners . . . better weather than expected, raw day, one's breath faintly visible, not sun but aura of sun in clouds. . . . Stage built out on stairs of gray ancient Capitol whose dome rises behind, covered with pigeons disturbed by the crowd. . . . Near at hand the tommy-hawking sculptures that show up in Brady's blurred photographs of Lincoln's Inaugural, from what Mark Twain called the "delirium tremens school of art." . . . Reporters in earmuffs hitting portables with numbed fingers, and Morse code telegraphers (almost extinct breed) transmitting "color" stories. . . . Silver-gray US Navy dirigible drifts like darker fish against gray clouds. . . . Plaza crowded like kind of saucer filled with humanity. . . . Gaily clad Marine Band in red and blue uniforms plays cheerfully, leader wearing sword. . . . 11:50: the Supreme Court, black-robed, bareheaded comes on platform above us; the benevolent chief justice moves to podium. . . . Sky lightens. . . . Awed reporter whispers, "He's not merely going to

make the sun come out; he's going to make cherry blossoms bloom!"
. . . Noon: band gives opening bars of "Hail to the Chief" for Nixon,
stiffly cut off at point protocol permits for vice-president. . . . Four
flourishes and "Hail to the Chief" as Ike arrives: sun dodges out. . . .
Friendly applause, subdued compared to 1952. . . . Styles Bridges and
"Stars and Stripes Forever." . . . Ike wears formal black overcoat with
velvet collar, looks well but thin, face lines deep, sunk. . . . Army-tank
Knowland administers oath to probable 1960-rival sly-fox Nixon, adds
"Congratulations, Mr. Nixon!" . . . Band plays "America the Beautiful"; brings applause; glad to see it creeping up on "Star-Spangled
Banner." . . . Everybody up and down for third prayer, then "Amer-
ica"–nobody rises; sun plays dramatic peekaboo. . . . 12:23: band
gives four flourishes. Ike doffs overcoat, steps forward, repeats after
Warren in firm, full voice–tremendous oath, tremendous scene. . . .
Inaugural Address: reads with conviction, fervor, yearning–man fully
convinced of what he says, lofty internationalist commitments, like
sermon. . . . Lofty generalities; what does it mean? Don't know. . . .

Things are changing pretty fast in Washington; it pays now to watch
closely. Eisenhower has been reelected and can't run again, so in a sense
he's a has-been and the politicians' interest is turning to next-man
possibilities. Just at the time when the president is a little less sacrosanct
the inflation problem bursts its seams and hard-money man George
Humphrey shows evident signs of distress and possible mutiny. The
changed tone toward Eisenhower by the conservative financial press
like the *Wall Street Journal, New York Times* financial writer Edward
H. Collins, and fiscal tories Raymond Moley and Henry Hazlitt of
Newsweek is fascinating; they are now becoming vicious in their
soured love affair.

Simultaneously the Democrats have now, finally, boiled over in
resentment at Dulles. "Eden has gone in London, why can't Dulles go
here?" they say. The administration wanted Congress to pass a resolution to show national unity in the Middle East crisis, in itself a
natural and desirable thing. But it finally goaded the Democrats too
far. They don't object to the resolution–will pass it when the time
comes. But they see it as a device to share responsibility for Dulles's
failure in Suez and to give the appearance that this Congress is giving
the administration a vote of confidence.

The last thing the Democratic group has is confidence in Dulles.

They know they are over a barrel—if they delay the resolution, they will be denounced as aiding Moscow. Nevertheless they have delayed it long enough to let their real feelings appear. These run deep; they believe Dulles has not merely been inept but has shown an actual lack of good faith.

They charge him with following a political line, minimizing world troubles for political purposes and then callously exposing them after the election. We listened last week to Senator William Fulbright (D, Ark.) in the vast marble Senate Caucus Room read his indictment slowly and dispassionately while Dulles's face slowly crimsoned. It was on January 24, and it marked the end of a chapter. The administration had an opposition at last.

Regulatory Agencies

MARCH 4, 1957   We have ached for months to devote a whole column to the federal regulatory commissions. These are the seemingly dull, faceless agencies that protect the consumer. They are the anonymous fourth branch of government which regulates your life and mine in ways past imagining—the kind of radio program you get, the kind of protection you get on the stock market, the degree of monopoly permitted to the men who sell you goods.

As Voltaire did *not* say, "I care not who makes the law so long as I pick the regulatory commission that enforces it!" The type of man selected is likely to have more to do with the result than any legislation Congress passes.

There is a sullen feeling now in the business community that Eisenhower is too "radical"—that he has gone over to the New Deal! It shows how naive American business really is. These commissions in Washington have been carefully, steadily, and methodically stacked against the consumer interest and for the business interest since Eisenhower took office. The result sets the tone of Washington as much as any other one thing. We doubt if Eisenhower knows how far the process has gone. His subordinates pick the men, he names them, the conservative coalition in Congress confirms them, and that is that.

There are eight main regulatory commissions with fifty members and a dozen minor cases. Regarding the Big Eight the *Congressional Quarterly* made an interesting discovery a year ago. The tradition of reappointing commissioners whose terms expire, it announced, had been "broken." Not one single commissioner first named by a prior administration had Eisenhower reappointed! At that time he had filled twenty-seven of the fifty posts. In the Big Eight we can find only one reappointment—Chairman William Martin of the Federal Reserve Board, leading exponent of the tight money policy.

At his press conference January 30, Eisenhower said he knew nothing about the forthcoming vacancy on the three-man TVA. Commissioner Curtis's term expires May 18. "You have given me my first intimation of it," the innocent president said. Yet on a desk in the White House is a dossier an inch thick of possible replacements to this crucial post. Eisenhower named General Herbert Vogel to replace Gordon Clapp in 1954 after consumers' champion Clapp opposed the Dixon-Yates grab. But Vogel has been constantly outvoted by colleagues Curtis and Paty. Now he will boss the show after May 18 if and when Curtis leaves. The whole direction of future TVA policy hinges on it.

Almost certainly the president does not bother about these things. That was Harry Cain's experience when he tried to take his fight from the Subversive Activities Control Board to the White House. He never got past Sherman Adams until he made a national outcry and then, of course, was dropped.

Take another pending vacancy. Thomas Murray's term on the Atomic Energy Commission expires June 30. He is the sole Truman dissenter left. The AEC has been dragged into politics, involved in the Dixon-Yates case, and made the exponent of private industry control of atomic energy by Admiral Strauss, the chairman. You will see Murray's head roll soon.

It would take too long to list all the cases—but the fact is, Eisenhower has shown a genius for naming men to regulatory commissions whose antecedents indicated their hostility to the goals professed. The steady process of purging liberals and the consumer-minded has never stopped. Some appointments are shocking.

Albert Cole as a Kansas congressman was an archfoe of public housing; he was made administrator of the housing agency.

Ex-Congressman Joseph Talbot was a Taft Republican who voted against the Reciprocal Trade Agreements Act; he was put on the Tariff Commission.

For twenty years Edward Howrey was a leading lobbyist before the Federal Trade Commission for clients accused of antitrust violations. He was made chairman of the FTC. (He has since resigned; his work, as he said, "completed.")

And so on . . .Chairman Jerome Kuykendall of the Federal Power Commission was originally a lawyer for gas utilities in rate cases; ex-Chairman Guy Farmer of the Labor Relations Board previously was an advisor of management; Chairman George McConnaughey of the FCC (whose authority includes long-distance telephone rates) was a Bell System lawyer.

Your eye will not pick out a single distinguished advocate of the consumers' interest on the list of Eisenhower commission appointees. Roosevelt at one time or another had William O. Douglas, Ferdinand Pecora, Joseph Kennedy, Jerome Frank, James Landis, Sumner Pike, and Leon Henderson on the crucial Securities and Exchange Commission. Who is there now? Senator Lehman protested in 1955 that Eisenhower had replaced all five sitting members of the SEC with men representing the industry they were supposed to regulate.

Some of these commissions are required by law to be bipartisan. Eisenhower has taken to picking "Eisenhower Democrats" to meet this condition. The Republican National Committee admittedly cleared Harold Patterson picked to fill a Democratic vacancy on the SEC. Again, Miami corporation lawyer Louis Hector, a registered "Democrat" who voted for Eisenhower in 1952 and 1956, last month went on the Civil Aeronautics Board. (He replaced Joseph Adams, an outstanding liberal, who made a spectacular fight for consumers.)

These individual appointments are too inconspicuous for the public to sense their meaning. Now and then one creates something of a stir —like the failure to reappoint Gordon Clapp, ex-Senator James Mead (FTC), Frieda Hennock (FCC), or the like—but only rarely. Yet nothing like this mass exodus and subsequent upheaval has occurred in a generation. Now Representative Oren Harris (D, Ark.), chairman of the House Commerce Committee, plans an investigation. We can tell him right now that it is here—here—that the foxes are being let in to guard the chickens.

Civil Rights

J u l y   2 9 ,   1 9 5 7   Most thrilling words to a Washington reporter are, "The secretary will call the roll." Nixon uttered them. "Mister Aiken," intoned the clerk. "Aye!" came the dry answer.

Would the Senate take up the civil rights bill to safeguard Negroes' votes? A queue a block long waited outside. Reporters strained over their name lists. The chamber itself, seen from above, changes color with the seasons, dark and dignified in winter—now (with summer suits) a lighter, mottled tone of dacron and linen on this July 16 at 5:00 P.M.

"Mister Byrd—?" "Nay!" . . . Reporters checked names, hearts pounding. Revolutions never come at moments of greatest grievance, whether bloody or peaceful; they wait till the wheels start turning a little the other way, then they explode. So in the South today many Negroes already can and do vote; this is the time to widen the breach. Forcing the social revolution now are twin imponderables, the Negroes' own slow, inexorable economic improvement and the Cold War competition between democracy and totalitarianism.

Checking a Senate vote accurately is a frantic job. This correspondent had only a second to glance across at the Diplomatic Gallery on the other side of the chamber. It is just a little too far for accurate observation but I wanted to see if They were there. I imagined I saw them—Nikita Khrushchev and Mao Tse-tung of Peking—watching the United States debating civil rights. All the Communist propagandists and all the enemies of democracy around the world, who have declared for generations that the US Senate is powerless to function because of the filibuster and that America preaches democracy abroad but prevents Negro voting at home—they were all there looking down, relishing the spectacle. I could imagine Khrushchev bouncing with glee as Russell (D, Ga.) tried to panic the Senate with his inflammatory speech and Mao rubbing his hands with enjoyment as Byrd (D, Va.) denounced Chief Justice Warren.

But then the vote came—only the first vote in the great struggle—but a smashing victory, 71 to 18. I looked across at the Gallery. They were gone.

Eisenhower issued a statement interpreted as advocating a "hard" civil rights bill the evening of the preliminary vote; made replies indicating he favored a "soft" bill at his press conference next day. Ah, Eisenhower! Everybody loves him; but nobody knows where he stands. It recalls the story going round of a man defending the purchase of the new helicopters for the White House. Why, he exclaimed, they wouldn't cost so much and they would save the president's time—two minutes here, five minutes there—twenty-five minutes in all. "And a splendid investment," he added, "for that will double Eisenhower's working day!"

Under the Senate's Rule 22 it takes 64 votes to apply cloture and end a filibuster, an almost impossible task in a present chamber of ninety-five members. But what isn't understood is how sentiment against Rule 22 itself is rising. A move to end it in 1953 was defeated 21–70, but another attempt this January was closer, 38–55 (with three absentees favoring the motion). That is the trump card of civil rights advocates now. True, a minority filibuster might kill civil rights, but it would almost certainly kill Rule 22 too, when it comes up again in January 1959. Vice-President Nixon has already ruled against the archaic conception of the Senate as a "continuing body" which can't change its rules; just seven more votes and the rules will be changed and the ancient bugbear killed. The last-ditch southerners know this, of course; they are bargaining from weakness, not strength.

Little Rock

OCTOBER 7, 1957   What happened at Little Rock diminished us all. Though we protest, we are made smaller. Least concerned of any, it may be, are the Little Rock Central High students themselves—the few Negroes, stoically heroic; the many whites (so far as one can judge), largely indifferent. It is the adults who breathe the poison.

Eisenhower in his first broadcast missed the point. He said he intervened because of "anarchy" and "mob rule" when of course he intervened because a state governor used troops first—to defy judicial power. It was Faubus who created the mob, not the mob, Faubus. Eisenhower fogged the issue, at least until he made his reply to Senator Russell. Presumably he will stress the real point with the southern governors here. He left many in the South thinking it was he who precipitated the crisis when, of course, it was Faubus who first picked up the sword and would have repealed Appomattox.

Eisenhower didn't mention Faubus by name on TV because he will not deal with "personalities." He once angrily said he would "not get into the gutter" with McCarthy. Faubus is a slick southern McCarthy in whose mind, we imagine, Freud would be interested, judging by his preoccupation with reports of alleged (and false) molestation of "teenage schoolgirls" by wicked troops.

We sighed with relief when Eisenhower finally spoke. Honestly, we had feared he would not act at all! Is it moral flabbiness, or does Eisenhower lack, as somebody has said, an adequate consciousness of the existence of evil? He assumed the good faith of the Communist leaders at Geneva. Now at Newport, he has assumed the good faith of Faubus's half-promises to abide by the court's orders.

Nixon would have done better. He lacks convictions but can see the point. He knew instantly (unlike Eisenhower) that it was Faubus who had created the issue, and he said so publicly (drawing always a little further away from the diminishing president).

A good many political forecasts are now being made on the basis of Little Rock but we think it is too early. There is talk of a southern "third party." Maybe. But wait a while. What is happening is a steadily weakening position of the South. Under FDR the South lost its two-thirds veto rule over the nominee of Democratic presidential conventions. In recent years the South lacked the votes to block a civil rights bill. Its strength now is centered in two Washington institutions: Senate seniority, which gives Dixie members key committee chairmanships (i.e., Eastland in Judiciary), and Rule 22—the rule which makes the filibuster possible. A bolt by the South—? Southern senators would lose their powerful chairmanships immediately, and

Rule 22 would probably go down the drain, too (it may anyway in 1958). Senator Douglas (D, Ill.) put the whole thing in a nutshell when asked if he thought the South would now bolt. "I hope so," he replied sensibly.

Space Age

O C T O B E R   1 4 ,   1 9 5 7   We got our news of the Soviet earth satellite courtesy of Pepto-Bismol. Attuned to the new Space Age we kept our radio on with feelings as mixed as the programs. Brrp-brrp-brrp went the basketball-sized beep-bug hurtling through space, flashing round the globe in one hour, thirty-six minutes, and two seconds (as somebody calculated). We heard the excitement in the broadcasting stations, the astonishment of American scientists, and the greater awe of the purveyor of Pepto-Bismol—"gentle massaging action in the lower digestive tracts. . . ."

President Eisenhower took the historic Communist triumph calmly at his Gettysburg farm and played golf as usual. There was a note of cool reserve. Mr. Eisenhower appeared prepared to treat the satellite as though it were Adlai Stevenson. No, said Jim Hagerty, the US will *not* speed up its efforts. The US program, he said, "is geared to the International Geophysical Year." It sounded as though the Russians had been rather unsporting about the IGY in some obscure way. "Winston tastes good like a cigarette should," said the new sponsor.

Another word from Jim Hagerty: "It does not come as a surprise." (The Hungarian revolt found key American ambassadors absent from their posts but Central Intelligence Agency head Allen Dulles said, "It did not come as a surprise." When the Soviet jet transport recently swooped into Washington, officials explained reassuringly, "It did not come as a surprise.") Pepto-Bismol for relief of upset stomachs.

Well, the Space Age began October 4, 1957. We confess it rather frightens us for we are not as young as we were, but the children take it lightly. They are way past basketball-sized rockets; they are out on interstellar spaceships already. "Why didn't we beat the Russians to it, Pop?" they ask idly. Yes, why?

Perhaps it is because the United States never lost a war. Perhaps it is because we have Pepto-Bismol. Americans cannot believe that they do not have a corner on technological knowledge. The thing to do is to take it easy, trust Ike, and cut taxes!

Air Force Research Secretary Trevor Gardner resigned in February 1956, charging the Soviet was beating us in intercontinental missiles. Result? Committees were set up.

Eisenhower pooh-poohed Stevenson's election charges that we are losing the peaceful atomic-power race. But England actually has such a commercial project operating; we don't.

The Soviet lead time (drawing board to finished project) was about five years on their Bison (intercontinental jet bomber); it took us about eight years to produce our B-52.

And now the little beep-bug, whizzing around the globe. "Where's my mashie?" says the president. "It did not come as a surprise," says Hagerty. "Tastes as good as the syrup put on ice cream," says Super Anahist Cough Syrup.

1957–Incredible Year

DECEMBER 30, 1957 When Harry Truman was playing the piano one time in the White House the piano leg went through the floor. Investigation showed the hallowed edifice eaten by termites and spongy with dry rot. The place had to be torn down, rebuilt. That's what A.D. 1957 did to some of America's most hallowed illusions. It was the year the piano went through the floor.

Any way you look at it, 1957 was extraordinary. It began with an election result unparalleled in a century—one party winning the White House, the other the legislature. Party labels meant less than ever; new forces were at work. A transition was under way.

Congress met—and a second thing happened: a civil rights bill passed for the first time in eighty years. As a law it left a lot to be desired. But it passed. No filibuster. Why? Because new conditions existed, only partly understood but beginning to show themselves.

The ancient filibuster rule—the Senate's historic Rule 22—was threatened. That grew evident in 1957. As the Senate met, a drive to repeal began. It failed. But contrast the votes: in 1953 the attempt collapsed 70–22; in 1957 it was defeated by only 55–38, with three absentees (all for changing the rule) so the real sentiment was 55–41. In four years repeal strength had doubled. The South did not filibuster the civil rights bill after that because it dared not; it knew it would be the last filibuster. Look ahead twenty years and see where 1957 points here.

It was, too, the year the old Dixiecrat-GOP coalition stalled. This is the coalition which in one way or another has dominated Congress for years—at least in things that interested it.

The old Farm Bloc also weakened in 1957. This is another ancient juggernaut of a lobby; in its heyday the strongest lobby in Washington. But it couldn't oust the obstinate, self-righteous Mormon Apostle Benson, who met it head on, though it could bloody his head and hold him to a tie. Why was the bloc weakening? Not because of Ezra Taft Benson. It was because of other intricate developments, because of time and changing attitudes: fewer farmers, more city consumers, the technical explosion of agriculture, the anger of taxpayers made to support the price of things they had to buy, the final division and conflict within the bloc itself between cattlemen, dairymen, cotton and grain growers. The great Farm Bloc still looked impressive but the veneer was coming unglued.

That wasn't all, either. A.D. 1957 saw northern Democrats telling the South more loudly than before to go jump off the roof if it wanted to. Inviting them to jump. The new Advisory Council of the Democratic Party spoke clearly, whatever its congressional leaders did. Here again the finger pointing to the future. Jump off the roof? What, said Dixie senators aghast, and lose seniority rights in Congress, committee chairmanships, and all the other appurtenances of power! Truman had won without the South. Many northern Democrats ardently wanted the South to jump. Significantly southern leaders began changing tune. Could they go to the Supreme Court? Not with the unanimous segregation decision. To the Republicans? Not after Little Rock. The year 1957 didn't settle anything, but it laid bare the problem.

It was the first year, too, that the Twenty-second Amendment had political effect. For the first time in 180 years America had a constitutional lame-duck president. It showed itself in small, subtle ways: the role of Nixon, the decline of Eisenhower. Back in 1953 Eisenhower was applauded enthusiastically fifty-five times in his first State of the Union speech; in 1957 only five times, tepidly. His blown-up image began to take smaller and more realistic proportions now that the forces of business, conservatism, and the status quo, which operate through the communications media and to whom he had given two splendid victories, found the old soldier of diminishing value. The old soldier, who had preached the homely platitudes of Abilene with fervor and conviction, who epitomized the national wish for security, prosperity, and sanctity—who hated the political drudgery of the White House and reduced the presidency to baby-sitting, fumbled awkwardly over his budget with angry George Humphrey and could not understand what was happening.

Well, you know what I am going to say next. Yes, the year 1957 ended this other era, too.

Herbert Hoover in 1929 said, "Prosperity is just around the corner." Dwight Eisenhower in 1957 said, "The satellite . . . does not raise my apprehension one iota." End two eras. The great drama sweeps on—the dawn of the space age led by Russia, not the United States. . . . What is that odd slant to the piano, Mamie?

The story moves ahead, the administration attempt to make it seem nothing had happened, the gathering anxiety over the country, the hasty call for a NATO conference, the second satellite, the decision to make the chins-up speeches, the first speech of reassurance with dummy props of nose cone and MIT president Killian, the second speech—now in graver, duller tones with recognition of dangers not admitted before—the "chill" at the airport, the stroke, the gallant trip to Paris, the attempt to pump up the minuscule results there into another press triumph like that which hailed the "Geneva Spirit" of 1954.

But it was not 1954. It was 1957, the year of transition, the year when new political forces stirred beneath the surface, old coalitions were toppling, when Americans were stunned, chastened, and confused into a mood of salutary humiliation after five years of un-paralleled complacency—and began searching subconsciously for a different kind of leadership, a rail-splitter, maybe, or a man with uptilted cigarette.

Yes, that was 1957 folks. The year the piano leg went through the floor.

Sherman Adams

JUNE 30, 1958   We watched Sherman Adams last week sit ramrod-stiff for his public humiliation in the great cream-yellow barn of a House caucus room as big as an airplane hangar. Here was the mysterious, rarely seen Adams—small, white-haired, ascetic; muscular proud face, a gnomelike man with a square jaw. He came prepared to admit that he had been "a little imprudent" and he was prepared to die, apparently, before he would go an inch beyond that. We are inclined to believe he is sincere in this attitude, too, for it is his extraordinary insensitivity rather than his deeds that tell the story.

Curiously enough the mood of the affair was sad, poignant, transcending politics, transcending Sherman Adams even. For who can see pride humbled without a tear or watch mistakes exposed without being himself in the dock? There was an odd kindness about the committee—the kindness of the death call. The great moment came when Representative John Moss (D, Cal.)—not tauntingly and almost as though it were driven out of him unwillingly—recalled to Adams the "whiplash" of the Republicans' smug charges in the 1952 campaign against the Democrats.

Adams sounded crisp and cool and almost plausible. But consider these additional facts. (1) Adams professed to tell the whole story in his public statement June 12, and Press Secretary Hagerty next day announced that he had given "all the facts"—subsequent to which came word of the $2,400 oriental rug, the vicuna coat, and, even in the very committee room, of hospitality at the Waldorf-Astoria! (2) Adams said the rug was a "loan" from Goldfine; an interview in the *Washington Star*, December 28, 1954, with Mrs. Adams, told of the "immense" oriental rug she had "just purchased." (3) Adams's explanation that he thought the shifting Boston hotel suites were rented permanently by Goldfine became ridiculous when the New York hotel suite was added. (4) And how can anyone believe—or believe Adams believes—that his telephone calls to regulatory agencies (many of whose members he selected) would not have "influence," or that his securing of information (in violation of rules) would not benefit his client (Hagerty says Goldfine already "had" the information; in that case, why ask Adams to get it?).

The scene shifts to the Eisenhower press conference and the heartfelt comment, "I need him." When all else is forgotten of this administration that poignant cry may be remembered. It summarizes all the desolate story of delegated powers, lack of leadership, and inadequacy.

Administration defenders are raising the *tu quoque* red herring that congressmen also exert pressure and take junkets. Obviously congressmen should mend their ways, but the analogy falls on its face. Congressmen are elected; Adams is not. They don't appoint regulatory commissioners; Adams does. They don't throw moral thunderbolts from Eisenhower's elbow; Adams does. They don't take sanctuary from the press in the White House; Adams does.

What is happening now is the slow, dreadful realization of the public that the Adams affair isn't merely a lively Washington drama which doesn't affect it, but something that concerns us all. The longer Eisenhower clings to Adams and condones him, the more his own moral authority oozes out. This moral authority is Eisenhower's great gift. None of us benefits to see an administration collapse. For all his faults Eisenhower has urged valuable bills: his three pending "imperatives"—Pentagon reorganization, foreign aid, and reciprocal trade extension—are all strongly backed by the White House. On those occasions when Eisenhower exerts a positive authority and when he makes his appeal bipartisan and when it concerns world affairs or defense, he (or any president) commands enormous influence. The Sherman Adams case strikes at this precious influence because it develops cynicism, and it is alarming now because the world situation is deteriorating. As we write this we know of no single reporter who believes Adams will stay.

Quemoy and Matsu

SEPTEMBER 8, 1958 Eisenhower fights Governor Faubus and at the same time gives him support. The courts must be obeyed, he says, but he allows a suspicion to circulate that he questions the wisdom of the courts. Isn't integration being pushed too fast?

Thus America's preachingest president has never, in four years, taken a stand on the moral issue of the unanimous Supreme Court decision ordering the beginning of the end of school desegregation. Now the Court is ruling on the latest Little Rock developments, but Eisenhower's ambiguous position is at the heart of the enforcement problem. The president's public stand is that he supports the Court out of compulsion, not necessarily conviction.

This really is a dreadful situation. Mr. Eisenhower's personal conviction is to be a hands-off (technically, "weak") president. He wants to be above the battle, the president of "all" the people. It's too late now to do anything about that. But he probably has a specific argument. He withheld condemnation of McCarthy, but let's see what happened to *him*! And in this instance doesn't he strengthen his hand with wavering southerners by putting his contest with Faubus on the broad, unemotional issue of law-enforcement rather than on the angry ground of racial equality? Didn't Lincoln (he might ask) withhold attacking slavery at the outset for the broader target of supporting the Union?

The fallacy of this argument is: first, that the Court has already spoken; it cannot back down without a greater loss to our institutions than anything the president apprehends; and second, that this is first and last a moral issue. It is impossible and absurd to try to separate the moral from the enforcement issue. Southern segregationists already know in their hearts that they are fighting a losing battle. The question isn't "whether" anymore, but "how long." Unless Eisenhower plainly and unequivocally supports the Court's decision on *moral* grounds, the use of force against force in Little Rock is self-defeating. This is an issue in which jurisprudence and morals cannot be separated. By abdicating his chief presidential functions—the creation and guidance of public opinion—Eisenhower isolates the Court, isolates dismayed liberals in the South, and aids the man he is supposed to be fighting.

Tension shifts quickly from the Middle East to the Far East as developments recall the three unstable elements of our foreign policy: 1) we decline to reduce our ambitious commitments around the world although technical changes make these increasingly difficult to fulfill; 2) we solidify the Peking-Moscow axis by airily pretending that a nation with a quarter of the world's population does not exist and decline to recognize Red China or make any concessions that might serve to detach her from Moscow, thereby leaving the initiative entirely with Moscow to try to detach us from our Allies. And 3) we refrain—or decline—as a nation to make the sacrifices necessary to keep us ahead of Moscow in missile warfare, though our lag has been solemnly and repeatedly spelled out.

Any one of these questionable policies may, perhaps, be justified by itself, but the three together are radically contradictory.

Few people realize the provocative nature of our support of Nationalist China in Quemoy and Matsu. These are not geographical parts of the island of Formosa, they are 100 or so miles away, lying right off the Red mainland like stationary aircraft carriers, blocking use of the two big harbors of Amoy and Foochow. Quemoy occupies the relative role of Sandy Hook, say, to New York City.

Whether or not the Chinese really feel the presence of the Nationalists so nearby puts them in danger, as some believe, one can't say, but it's an anomaly indeed—a nation of 10 million on the front porch of one of 625 million and our policy is frozen to the little one. When Senators Kennedy and Fulbright at the last of Congress pointed to such commitments as this, and our weakening military position, the administration sent in good, gray Saltonstall to warn that if we worried too much we might fall into a mood of "psycho-surrender." There is nothing so reassuring as a Madison Avenue phrase.

Nixon Moves In

OCTOBER 13, 1958   What you are seeing now is a transfer of Republican Party leadership from Eisenhower to Nixon. True, Eisenhower will campaign extensively, earnestly delivering his ghosted speeches on peace, prosperity, and free enterprise. They will attract attention, do the GOP some good. Everybody likes Ike—will continue to. But nearly everybody now knows his leadership is flabby.

Eisenhower told the press last week that he was surprised at reports of "apathy" and "complacency" among Republicans. The White House has not always been disturbed by apathy and complacency, but the president set about curing it in this instance. What could have caused it? Well, the president's intimates probably won't tell him. There is this business of part-time incumbency, being above the battle and all that.

Added to this now is a purely mechanical handicap. Eisenhower is maimed by the GOP-passed Twenty-second Amendment that made a lame duck of him at a time when most of his predecessors were making believe (however silly it sounded) that they might seek third terms. Silly? Well, yes, but the kind of thing that would keep Nixon under control.

Instead Nixon has stepped out, front and center. The old Nixon. All through the '56 campaign, Bill Blair, *New York Times*man, tracked Nixon with a miniature German-built recording machine to catch, beyond peradventure, any charge Nixon hurled. Nixon didn't hurl. He confused the press by being the "new Nixon." Victory was sure and he wore company manners.

But in the first kickoff of the uphill '58 battle Nixon quickly spread charges Blair vainly sought two years before. Somebody in the State Department, he cried, was knifing Dulles. His opponents favored "labor racketeering" and talked "rotgut." He established a character-istic sinister target; the new menace—"the radical ADA Democratic left wing."

Why did Nixon pull off his '56 disguise? Here is an attempted answer: First of all, Nixon's rousing campaigning ingratiates him with every local Republican he aids; it helps lay the basis for that over-whelming nomination in '60. Next, the election gamble. If the GOP makes an unexpectedly strong showing next month, Nixon's tireless campaign will give him a lot of credit. If the GOP takes its expected licking, however, who is to blame—Nixon, who didn't make the policies but loyally defended them, or Eisenhower, the amiable, part-time golfing president? The answer is obvious.

Then again, Nixon is reestablishing the old GOP party identity before Eisenhower introduced "modern Republicanism," and identi-fying himself with its conservatism, (cf. his Boston tax speech and his no-retreat Formosa line). Finally (and perhaps most important), Nixon is drawing a tacit contrast between the flaccid White House and himself as a young, positive, energetic leader. Nixon's keen politi-cal intuition tells him the country aches for leadership. Well, he has it. If it is a little sharp and blunt, all the better. He is tough—he can march right up and use the word "rotgut"; he is positive—he lashes out at disloyalty in the State Department without shilly-shallying.

Nixon's personality is complex, fascinating. He has a first-rate in-tellectual equipment under iron control. Every move is charted, every effect planned. He has little humor and does nothing on impulse. At home he is gracious, deferential, a model head of family. He has an eager Eagle Scout look and a responsive smile under that Bob Hope ski-slope nose.

In politics this quiet young man is a killer. He has an instinct for the jugular. Many people cannot credit this. This young man, the in-ventor of McCarthyism in his attack on Jerry Voorhis, Helen Gaha-gan Douglas, Dr. Condon, and the like? Impossible! "That was the 'old Nixon,'" they declare. "Why, he's no worse than Truman in his charges."

But there is a difference. Wild as some of Truman's whirling words are, any audience can see there is nothing cruel in the man. Truman would not impugn an opponent's patriotism for victory. Republicans are misguided but not traitors! Certain charges are not made; there are unwritten rules in the great game of politics. But the lethal young Nixon does not accept these rules. He is out for the kill and the scalp at any cost.

Two weeks ago we likened the Formosa moves and countermoves to a kind of waltz—a waltz on the brink. Now Dulles has made a formalized step to relax tension, and the Reds have responded with an appropriate counterstep. For the minute, war is further off.

Both sides retreat a little. Dulles in particular is carrying on a brilliant withdrawal operation camouflaged by double-talk. If you don't believe a man can go in two directions at once, watch this delicate job of extrication. On one hand it permits poor Nixon, who was caught out on a limb at Los Angeles proclaiming support for the administration's supposed "no retreat" line, to assert that there has been no basic change in US policy. But at the same time Chiang Kai-shek, who of course knows the score, denounces the US "retreat."

The Chinese Reds throw in a temporary sop. A situation may be developing for a mutual saving of face. What the State Department has quietly dropped overboard is a myth—that Chiang can someday reconquer the mainland and that Quemoy and Matsu are necessary to Formosa's defense. Only myths, but important, too. For it is myths that keep rulers in power, hold nations together, cause wars.

A final word to hail the anonymous teachers of Norfolk, Virginia. Too often the underpaid US teacher is forgotten and ignored. But when the Virginia segregationists tried to set up a "private" school system in Norfolk, the plan collapsed. Why? The teachers balked. Odd, isn't it? It hadn't occurred to anybody that you can't have school without teachers.

Something But the Truth

DECEMBER 1, 1958 The nation wants to back Eisenhower. It yearns to. In the new crisis over Berlin the cry is, "Be calm and firm and support the White House!" Fine.

Meanwhile the White House moves to cut 70,000 from the armed forces and the Pentagon orders an economy slowdown in the intermediate-range ballistic missile program. The cuts are just a start—"we must balance the budget." The nation shudders. Maybe the cuts are justified. Can we trust the administration?

Well, when Eisenhower took office he promptly cut Truman's inadequate budget of $1.6 billion for research and development to $1.3 billion; then in June ordered a further 25-percent slash. Humphrey, Wilson, and Dodge, the insular innocents, were at work.

On Eisenhower's desk, January 1953, were holdover reports showing the impending loss of America's defense lead and the ghoulish danger of the new H-bomb. They led to a bold White House proposal. Why shouldn't the president frankly tell the nation the concealed story; urge it to tighten its belt, unite behind his leadership? Again—fine! Robert Donovan in his official book *Eisenhower: The Inside Story* tells how the secret project was born and nicknamed Operation Candor. But the president never made the speech. The idea whimpered out. The president did not wish to dwell on "the single, gruesome theme of human destruction." Donovan tells how Operation Candor was supplanted after months of vacillation by another one, this one called oddly Operation Wheaties.

Robert Cutler, secretary of the Security Council, later said of Operation Candor, "the thesis was that the American public could take bad news; officially apprised of the facts. . . . But other and, I think, wiser counsels prevailed." So Sputnik told the bad news after all. Even then the administration (with the notable exception of Nixon) tried to minimize it.

Eisenhower's former top economist, Arthur F. Burns, in a poorly reported speech in Washington last week, said the administration had bungled the job of meeting the 1957–1958 recession. It is exactly the point made by the liberal Democrats. Burns did not say it straight out to the Joint Conference on Economic Education but it was there, between the lines. Burns, you remember, advocated a tax cut—the remedy Eisenhower and Nixon denounced as "radical" and "socialistic" in the election just finished. Burns politely noted that instead of a tax cut the government launched random spending projects, the sum total of which "came to a much larger total than had been planned or advocated." Most of these projects were too late to affect the recession; ironically he said they are just now coming into force, when the crisis is over and all the government's endeavor is to cut down spending! "This is precisely the condition that responsible advocates of a general tax cut sought to prevent," says Burns drily.

What licked the recession? As much as anything a group of "built-in stabilizers," says Burns; these kept national income high when employment and profits slumped; one example: unemployment insurance, which gave workers a buffer in their spending. What should be done now? Burns advocates, among other things, something from which Eisenhower and Anderson recoil: blanket unemployment insurance extended to workers on a much more generous scale. At the moment he calls this "the most useful step."

Agreeable, Lyndon Johnson-loving William S. White, who tries to be fair-minded about civil rights in spite of his Texas upbringing, fears the forthcoming Senate fight to end the filibuster will split the Democratic Party. White is a sincere Democrat and he hates the thought. Paul Douglas and Hubert Humphrey, it appears, are "advanced liberals" (presumably Lyndon Johnson is just a "liberal") and they are demanding an alteration in Senate cloture rule, says columnist White, "so extreme that its adoption would end the Senate as a unique deliberative body." Can you guess what their proposal is? Why, to let *majority* rule prevail in ending debates!

In his remarkably frank and honest discussion White really gets to the heart, we think, of the pro-filibuster argument. Boiled down it is in his words that "the Senate is fundamentally a nonmajority institution." He doesn't say so but what he means is that it is our House of Lords.

End the right of filibuster, White says, and you "would make the Senate only a somewhat slower House of Representatives." We think White has cut through a lot of twaddle and candidly put his finger on the real issue. He has done a service thereby. Our own response is easy enough. We don't like a House of Lords in this country. Even in Britain they have curbed the Lords' veto power. It has become a picturesque but impotent anachronism. The fight to preserve the Senate as an American House of Lords is going to be fierce. There is a better chance of a reform bill passing next year than at any previous time in history. If majority rule splits the Democratic Party, well—too bad.

Johnson & Martin & Halleck

JANUARY 19, 1959   The Chattahoochee River could flow right into the Sahara Desert and disappear. The arid sands would swallow it up without a trace. The big liberal victory last November looked important at the time. It looked like a flowing river. In the history of elections never before did one party win so many seats as the Democrats won. The victory flowed right into the desert of institutionalized political Washington—and disappeared. The thirsty Sahara swallowed it up.

Lyndon Johnson is still running the Senate, offering phony anti-filibuster resolutions. Sam Rayburn is over in the House, blocking any change in the autocratic Rules Committee. The House Un-American Activities Committee is right there, too. Eastland is chairman of the Senate Judiciary Committee and Byrd is chairman of the Finance Committee. These men are made stronger than ever by the election; their seniority is greater. Liberals who voted Democratic actually strengthened the grip of the conservative southern chairmen.

Of course, the Chattahoochee River doesn't pass out of existence completely. Like the newcomers in political Washington, it is diffused.

Scientists would say that the African water table had risen somewhat. We mustn't get cynical about Washington: the liberal water table has risen here, too; there will be a few more oases because of the election, and they will be greener; a surprising palm tree may sprout up suddenly where you hadn't expected it. The disappointment lies in the tremendous effort it takes under the American governmental system to get such seemingly petty results.

We were outside when the House Republican caucus that defeated Joe Martin 74–70 broke up. The white movie spotlights were on in the marble corridor and the elderly bachelor came out like somebody who has stepped out of an auto wreck, dazed and crumpled. He had been knifed by regretful friends; they considered him too old, and since they can't afford the luxury of disregarding the election mandate as the victorious Democratic hierarchy has, they dropped him. His political career was over. Charlie Halleck had finally beaten him.

It was grimly fascinating to see how fifty years of political experience led him to make his automatic responses; he was doing it without thinking, making the game jokes that were expected of him—like the man in the wrecked car giving his name automatically to the policemen. In sheer pity the reporters blunted their questions to the tortured old man, but not the photographers. "Hold Mr. Halleck's arm," they said, "come closer—closer. Now smile!" It was one of those obscene sights you can never quite rub out.

The last word on the unhappy fight against the filibuster isn't said as this is written. The hope is that at some point in trying to amend the Johnson resolution the liberal opponents of the filibuster will get a maximum vote somewhat above the thirty-eight they mustered in 1957. If they do, even though they lose the immediate battle they will have gained momentum and warned the segregationists not to go too far against the new civil rights legislation that is surely coming before this Congress. In 1957 liberals had thirty-eight votes, plus three more absentees pledged to their side.

There was an unforgettable scene here, too. It was when Lyndon Johnson, the amazingly supple majority leader, could not forego the exquisite pleasure of taunting the defeated liberals. At the heart of Johnson's character there is a raw lust for power, though it is concealed pretty well under his genius for manipulating votes. Few men have ever been more adept in this. In this instance he played circles round the liberals. But at one point they laughed at him. He had made a tiny slip. He had overstressed his case. He was arguing that the Senate can operate by majority rule, which, theoretically, it can; the only difficulty is that the point never comes when a simple majority rules: opponents of civil rights will filibuster the preliminary motion "to take up." Johnson cried that any senator can amend the rules, "if he can get a majority . . . and can get a vote."

Laughter swept the whole chamber at this last phrase and galled Johnson. He is proud and hot-tempered and not one who brooks laughter at himself. A minute later he was telling the Democratic liberals to "laugh that one off, if you please," and from there on his attitude hardened. "My!" he cried, "where are your parliamentarians?" It is not wise for a majority leader thus to alienate a score or so of his followers. Hubert Humphrey (D, Minn.), who has his own reserve of power (perhaps deeper than Johnson's), rose to urge him "to be a little tolerant in this, his moment of triumph." A little scene, perhaps, as Johnson's inner personality peeped through, but not one that can be easily forgotten.

"Imagine Him as President Kennedy"

M A Y   4 ,   1 9 5 9   With deep interest we watched the performance of Jack Kennedy in the thrilling Senate battle over the labor reform bill. We came without preconceptions and must report Kennedy's performance was impressive. Against the old-fashioned emotional oratory of John McClellan (D, Ark.) Kennedy stood like the calm voice of reason. Under particularly trying parliamentary conditions he remained articulate, lucid, unruffled.

Many must have watched him, as we did, trying to imagine him as President Kennedy. He looked like a popular young college professor. There is a mystique about the American president that assumes he must resemble Michelangelo's God, or at least Warren G. Harding. Kennedy, at almost forty-two with his shock of hair and boyish smile, looks younger. More than his religion, we think his age is a handicap. We imagine many who opposed Kennedy's Catholicism in an election would hide their real motives by attacking his age. It is the case of a man who might be president if he had a bald spot. At any rate, giving this column's firsthand impression, we thought he made an unusually attractive and impressive figure on the Senate floor last week.

Friends of the late Senator Joseph McCarthy will dedicate a bust this Saturday at Appleton, Wisconsin. It will be of heroic proportions, rising with its pedestal eight and one half feet in the two-story courthouse lobby. Presentation will be by Senator Styles Bridges (R, N.H.), a happy choice, for he was one of the eleven who supported McCarthy in trying to block Ambassador Bohlen's appointment to Moscow in 1953. (Of that little group, that band of brothers, Malone, Welker, McCarran, and Bricker are no longer in the Senate; Mundt, Goldwater, and Schoeppel remain to keep McCarthy's memory green; and Dirksen is minority leader.)

We would like to nominate attendants at the Appleton rites. There would be the five supporters and advisers of Stevenson in the 1952 campaign whom McCarthy called disloyal, and who supported the Democrats ("the party of treason"). There would be Owen Lattimore and the group on the Far East desk of the paralyzed State Department, hounded and harried as a preface to our present frozen nonrecognition policy.

There would be eggheads and scientists, Harold Urey, and Nathan Pusey of Harvard (Harvard is a "sanctuary of Communists"). There would be the nineteen unlucky employees of the Army's research center at Fort Monmouth, New Jersey, suspended without pay in a reign of terror—one of them because his mother enrolled him in the Young Pioneers at twelve. There would be a large group: America's entire body of "Protestant clergymen" whom McCarthy's assistant, J. B. Matthews, declared in the *American Mercury* were "the largest single group supporting the Communist apparatus in the United States today."

For low comedy there would be Roy Cohn and Dave Schine romping about the ceremony as they did on their celebrated purge through trembling US embassies in Europe, when Schine chased Cohn round a hotel lobby swatting him with a rolled-up magazine.

There would be grave military men on hand: combat-decorated

General Ralph Zwicker, told by McCarthy that he was "not fit to wear the uniform," and General Marshall ("steeped in falsehood"). And then for background I would nominate certain others, those who aided McCarthy out of self-interest or timidity, a presidential candidate who expunged praise of General Marshall from a campaign speech, a vice-president adept in McCarthy tactics on his own, GOP Chairman Leonard Hall who called McCarthy a Republican "asset"; Senator Robert Taft who egged McCarthy on (Ah me! Taft's memorial bell tower now serves as a precedent for similar Capitol monuments on what may ultimately be called Mortuary Hill).

It is not really McCarthy, nor even his victims, however, who should come first at these obscene Appleton rites. It is the crowd of frightened respectables who, in the McCarthy era, knew the truth and would not testify. Who could have guessed how many and how easily terrified! Surely it is easy to make a revolution! Publishers who looked the other way, boards of regents who let faculty members be lynched, businessmen who paled at boycotts, an administration that tried to go along. McCarthy showed the way. Not this time; no, not this time! But the haunting doubt remains.

The Khrushchev Visit

OCTOBER 5, 1959   He's left, but it won't ever be quite the same again and who will ever forget those thirteen incredible days? I can see him now, acting out in pantomime the cancan dance he saw at Hollywood, giving his heavy posterior a wriggling imitation and roaring with laughter. Or holding the squawking duck against his paunch at the Beltsville Agricultural Station, chuckling with glee. Or solicitously inquiring of the unfortunate Henry Cabot Lodge— whom he used as a straight man for his jokes (after deflating him almost overnight from a Truth Squad into a cloying guidebook)— "How is my Capitalist holding up?"

Or I can see those little fat eyes narrowed to angry slits and looking out ruthlessly on us—a competitor nation that might be laughing
at him and his peasant origin (you could never be sure!)—or worse
still, laughing at Little Mother Russia.

There are other memories of that amazing trip, with 350 reporters
and cameramen, twice across the United States; the hurried, perfunctory visit to Roosevelt's grave at Hyde Park where he had no time
to eat but came out waving a seeded roll, shouting in gleeful English,
"One for the road; one for the road!" (And Mrs. Roosevelt's quiet remark: "No, he was not interested in me. That gentleman is interested
only in power.") Or I can see him coming, with Lodge and body-
guards and cameramen, down the aisle of the rolling fourteen-car
special train that carried him up between the blue Pacific and velvet
mountains on a spectacular trip from Los Angeles to San Francisco;
coming up in his queer walk (halfway between an amble and a wad-
dle) in a floating press conference and shaking hands with each news-
man . . . and the strong grip of those short, iron fingers.

Oh, well, there is only one story like that in a century I suppose,
and we won't have another like it until Chou En-lai comes over.
Television and radio coverage reached saturation, and the enormous
accompanying press party included gray flannel English correspondents ("Well done, old boy!"), toothy Japanese cameramen (in
Tokyo everyone carries a ladder), agile representatives of Paris *Match*
and German *Quick*, rough-hewn Russians with a suspicious look, who
knew English but wouldn't talk it, and everyone else down to the
Syracuse Herald-Journal.

When this typewriter is rusted and the writer forgotten, stories
will still be told in the National Press Club of the Khrushchev party
swinging into the supermarket in San Francisco like a California flash
flood that brought a near riot and scenes which even yet I don't believe, though I saw them happen. I watched a cameraman scale a
mound of glass coffee jars ("special for the day") which collapsed
noisily after a shot or two, with fragments and grounds all over the
place. An attendant came up and fussily tried to clean them up with
two pieces of cardboard, oblivious of the pandemonium around him.
One cameraman rolled on the floor with a butcher, with few to interfere or care. "What did he fight you for?" we asked at the hotel later.
"Nothing, nothing at all!" he explained—"I was just standing in his
meat."

And whether apochryphal or not, another story expressed the grim humor of the affair—two cameramen stepping over a recumbent woman on the supermarket floor! "She's fainted," said one. "Either that or she's on sale," said the other cameraman.

Nikita Khrushchev stands five feet five and weighs more than 200 pounds, and at San Francisco the hotel got out a special news release quoting the chef as saying he was on a salt-free diet. That means high blood pressure and certain temperamental characteristics of interest to diplomats, just as Mr. K's overweight is presumably of interest to his physicians. He eats with gusto, putting his head down close to the plate. And just when you think of him as a comical clown with his peasant origin written all over him, he rises to his feet for a speech which, even through the translator, is moving and menacing and compelling. It may be sacrilege to some but I found his frank acknowledgment, as an atheist, of the knowledge of the precepts of Christ, and of his identification of some of them with his own visions for Russia, of deep interest. This man, and do not doubt it, believes in his own propaganda.

At his press conference, August 12, Eisenhower told rhapsodically of the good things in America he hoped Mr. K would see. He wanted him to see "a free people, doing exactly as they choose." Well, perhaps that is what he saw in the substation of American culture, the Twentieth Century-Fox studios at Hollywood where they danced the cancan with its laughable climax, tearing off the little girl's panties. He was to see "our great industrial plants": that was Pearl Mesta's mile-long, nonunion Mesta Machine Works in Pittsburgh, busily working while the great Jones & Laughlin and US Steel companies were silent and somber on strike.

Eisenhower wanted him to see "our farmers, each one operating on his own, not regimented." He saw banker-farmer Bob Garst's mile-square corn patch, at Coon Rapids, Iowa, rented to tenant farmers, mechanized into a kind of factory in the field, and turning out subsidized surplus for government storage in the most socialistic example of control the nation offers.

In addition to that, Khrushchev saw Americans, shirt-sleeved ranks of them, standing with sober friendliness, neither hostile nor enthusiastic but curiously taking his measure, as he took theirs. It was good, I think, that he saw them; good that they saw him. He did not beguile them. But at the same time they saw that he did not wear horns. It will never be the same again.

Eisenhower held a press conference after Khrushchev left. He seemed ill at ease. In the vague communiqué there was no evidence of Soviet concessions. But Eisenhower announced that the conditions that had previously blocked a summit meeting were now met. Reporters could only wonder if Khrushchev's threats had once more succeeded.

The Upper-class Accent

JANUARY 25, 1960 A slight, boyish, patrician figure stood at the podium of the National Press Club last week and said things we have waited a long time to hear. It was Democratic candidate John Kennedy, and in a clear upper-class accent that oddly recalled FDR he told what the office of the presidency should be and how Eisenhower has debased it. It was an eloquent, stinging indictment, comparing Eisenhower with Coolidge, and bringing a shudder in reminding how Coolidge departed in a blaze of plaudits and unsolved problems. The problems Eisenhower leaves are terrifyingly bigger, Kennedy observed.

We watched Kennedy appraisingly. Nobody these days, of course, has the flailing power, the slow rise and awful sledgehammer fall that Bill Borah achieved, or that titanic scorn of Churchill's. Kennedy is good and getting better, but it is still hard for him, we think, to let himself go.

Eisenhower's budget is about what you would expect. If he gets his small surplus next June and the big one he hopes for in 1961, he will have had four years in the red, four in the black with an overall deficit balance of $15 billion. Eisenhower has somehow argued himself into the position that money spent for space missiles isn't "defense," and he has to insist on this every time, presumably to reassure Americans that Moscow's moon shots and huge rocket boosters don't really threaten us a bit. We are doing fine, the president said; we shall be "ready to attempt actual manned spaceflights within the next two years." We hope Russia will wait.

Newspapers told last week that Egypt has begun the first stage of the great Aswan Dam with Soviet help. Asked about it at his press conference, Eisenhower said that the US, Britain, and the World Bank might help in the next stage. He said it so casually that you almost forgot the background. Only three and a half years ago, with studied insult, Dulles—the man Eisenhower called the greatest secretary of state in history—publicly withdrew the offer to help build the dam. "Why did Dulles turn down Nasser so brutally, without a chance to save face?" asked *Time* correspondent John Beal in his eulogistic biography, *John Foster Dulles*, published in 1957. Why, he explains, it was a wonderful gambit, part of Dulles's brinkmanship, "a calculated risk . . . on a grand scale, comparable . . . to Korea and Formosa." Dulles, you see, was out to "expose the shallow character of Russia's foreign economic pretensions," believing that Moscow really wouldn't help with the dam.

A week after the Dulles step Nasser seized the Suez Canal. Dulles was in and out of that, too, finally convincing France and poor Anthony Eden that he was a slippery double-crosser they couldn't trust, so they made their own ill-fated attack on the canal without telling us. It is amusing to read Beal's final chapter—"the Peacemaker." Well, Dulles is gone, Nasser has the canal, and Moscow is helping to build the dam.

About once a year we try to explain what the GOP-Dixiecrat collaboration really means. This is a good time in connection with the civil rights bill. This mild Eisenhower version is now deadlocked in the twelve-man House Rules Committee. The committee won't act, and there are not enough signatures available to bring it to the floor by petition. The reason is, of course, that the GOP and Dixiecrats swap favors: the sanctimonious GOP helps the South keep the blacks in place, and the South helps kill liberal spending measures. On the Rules Committee there are four northern Democrats, four southern Democrats, and four Republicans. The Republicans won't help the northerners, so the bill is stalled. Again, it takes 219 House signatures to discharge the committee. Northern Democrats don't have that number and need about 50 or 60 GOP signatures for the job. Republicans won't sign. One telephone call from Eisenhower and the GOP would fall into line. He doesn't call.

This doesn't mean there won't be a bill. We expect one. But not until the GOP has squeezed out the last drop of advantage by demonstrating the Democratic split. Or wait—another possibility! This is a perfect setup for young Lochinvar Nixon; he settled the steel strike and befriended labor, didn't he? We think the GOP would love to cultivate the Negro vote for Vice-President Nixon by letting him dramatically settle the civil rights case.

A year ago Eisenhower proposed setting up a Committee on National Goals, privately financed, that would tell America what it really is aiming for. Every now and then some reporter needles the White House by asking what's become of this grandiose scheme, but nobody knows. Not a word about it in the State of the Union Message.

On the other hand the president did get together a first-rate, blue-ribbon Commission on Civil Rights. Last September it brought out its long-awaited report. Its chief proposal, approved 5 to 1, was to establish federal registrars in southern communities if the local officials refused to list Negro voters. Eisenhower gave the proposal a frosty reception at last week's press conference; he didn't even know if the idea was constitutional, he said; much better stick to his current civil rights bill (i.e., the one stalled in committee by GOP votes). It is reported that some of the commissioners will hand back their blue ribbons if they don't get White House support. It's no fun doing a nasty job if the boss won't back you up.

U-2

MAY 30, 1960   This reporter watched the collapse of the summit conference from the remote turmoil of the Oregon primary, snatching nightmare bulletins out of the air by pocket radio and desperately searching regional newspapers for scraps of background information. Kennedy beat Morse here in Oregon—making seven straight primary victories—and it now rather looks as though America would have a Catholic presidential nominee for the second time in history. Simultaneously Hagerty defeated the hopes of East-West accommodation. Hagerty—? Why, to be sure!

Faced with the alternative of saying the president didn't know what was going on in the U-2 flights (the escape exit eagerly offered by Khrushchev) or of pretending that he knew about and hence approved them, Hagerty firmly chose the latter. It is Hagerty dogma, supported by a cooperative press, that Eisenhower is master of his administration. So Hagerty, at a press conference May 9, specifically denied a *New York Times* report that the president had ordered U-2 flights stopped. Christian Herter cautiously reaffirmed this, and the president backed it up at his May 11 news conference. That doomed Paris.

The military seems to be running things. Returning from Paris, Defense Secretary Gates frankly acknowledged that it was he who ordered the terrifying worldwide US armed service alert, May 16, right on the eve of the summit. While Eisenhower tried to talk peace, Gates rattled the saber. Asked if the president ordered the alert, Gates replied, "It was on my own. I advised him."

A front-page picture in the *Seattle Spokesman-Review* last Saturday showed Eisenhower welcomed home with a banner across Pennsylvania Avenue, "THANK YOU, MR. PRESIDENT." It is simply too cruel to ridicule this scene. Eisenhower is a tragic figure. Yet in all kindness it is not safe for a nation to pretend that a debacle is a triumph even though some nervous people now think that is the patriotic thing to do. The truth has to be faced, palatable or not. Somewhere on the golf course Eisenhower lost civilian control of his espionage agency and the military

It was something to watch, the stunning effect of this on remote American cities—and it is still reflected on their editorial pages. Most of them simply blasted away at Khrushchev and then dropped the subject as too dangerous to explore. In scanning a dozen or more local papers each day for a week, I do not remember a single one criticizing the president.

The frustrating effect of local journals on eastern journalists was comic. The serious interpretation of the crisis, as well as the spot news, really came from television and radio; local papers had a great deal of advertising and very little news other than the desiccated press associations. We fell back on the San Francisco edition of the *Wall Street Journal*, America's first national newspaper, and also on a strange source, a Hearst paper, the *Seattle Post-Intelligencer*, which began printing gobs of *New York Times* news service reports. Surprisingly the *Oregonian* reprinted the electrifying column by Walter Lippmann which coolly put responsibility on Eisenhower. With scraps and strays from Reston, Alsop, Drew Pearson, and Peter Lisagor, it was possible to piece the news together. The climax, of course, came in Adlai Stevenson's "crowbar and sledgehammer" speech at Chicago, to which West Coast papers gave a few paragraphs on inside pages.

The primary was rather fun. Wayne Morse, who used to be a political fireball himself, assumed a posture of pained moral superiority before audiences that rarely filled the hall. We have always been fond of Morse's heavy black eyebrows, as nicely arched as a couple of croquet wickets. He belongs to that great tradition of Senate rebels and eccentrics without which the chamber would be a very dull place.

Kennedy, on the other hand, the young, patrician Harvard overseer, hedgehopped the state in his quarter-million-dollar private political flying carpet (a converted twin-engine Convair) and blocked traffic with his street-corner rallies. Aside from his novelty and glamor, Kennedy does make people feel that he is sincere and honest; the outcome was plain from the start.

Kennedy's religion, in our judgment, helped him a lot in the primaries. Relatively few votes are cast in a primary, and any candidate with a hard core of ardent supporters is benefited out of all proportion. In private, Kennedy sometimes refers to the hierarchy of his church as though it were another political opponent; the timing of some of its announcements, like the bishops' on birth control, and the latest assertion of the Church's right to interfere in political matters by the *Osservatore Romano*, seem almost calculated to injure him.

The real test of prejudice will come if and when Kennedy is nominated. He has all but silenced audience heckling on the subject, but we suspect it is not buried very far beneath the surface. The multitudinous Southern Baptists, including Billy Graham, have just adopted a no-Catholic-for-president resolution. And a breakdown of the latest Gallup Nixon-Kennedy poll by religion shows Protestants dividing 64 percent for Nixon to 36 percent for Kennedy and Catholics supporting 79 percent to 21 percent for Nixon.

It was Adlai Stevenson, not Kennedy, who finally threw the brick into the post-summit make-believe. Somebody had to say that Eisenhower had lost his clothes at Paris; Stevenson did it. Republicans gave a knee-kick reaction: Democrats were unpatriotic! Nixon, too, seemed reverting to type. In his upstate New York trip he suddenly revealed two mysterious, hitherto secret Red spy attempts; and after producing the right creepy-crawly atmosphere, looked reproachfully at any Democrat (presumably Kennedy) who would have Eisenhower "apologize" to Khrushchev. This soft-on-Communism theme, laced with spies, has promising possibilities.

Johnson-Kennedy Confrontation

JULY 25, 1960   The first big moment at the Democratic Convention was the Johnson-Kennedy confrontation scene in the crystal-chandeliered grand ballroom of the Biltmore Hotel. It was conducted with the surface politeness of a court duel and the underlying emotions of a West Side rumble. Johnson challenged Kennedy to public debate, apparently expecting to blast the young man right out of the water, and Kennedy surprisingly took the dare although he had everything to lose. What followed was a raw test of nerve of two of the fastest men on the draw in American politics. Nobody who jammed into that immense gilt and mirrored room (with TV cameras poking out like machine guns from every curve in the undulating gallery) will ever forget it. Kennedy combined a vigorous appeal with a light evasiveness and some who had not seen the young man before came away mildly surprised.

Another memorable scene was on the grass in the gloaming in the Memorial Coliseum as the day's heat turned into cool night. With

Californian abruptness, Kennedy made his terse acceptance speech. Kennedy must still learn to talk slower, to improve his timing for applause; and he fluffed one fine line, "I appeal to their pride, not their pocketbook." But for all that, it was stirring.

But here in the gathering darkness, as one battery after another of night baseball lights came on and as finally even the hovering photographer's helicopter went away, was a young man offering positive leadership and presidential power used to the uttermost.

A third scene was anticlimax, perhaps, but we found it fascinating: it was the ancient kiss-and-make-up rite of victor and vanquished performed at a semiprivate breakfast before well-heeled Democratic contributors. Adlai was there, always with his suave quip ("TR said, 'talk softly and carry a big stick' " but today the phrase is, 'don't talk while I'm putting' "). Lyndon was there, trying to put a smile over a heartbreak as he offered leftover "LBJ" campaign buttons with a new motto, "Let's back Jack." (We would have sworn his voice broke as he said it.) Lyndon's backer, Sam Rayburn, touched the grim joviality of the affair most perfectly when he asked where Jack had been keeping his father. (For the whole convention multimillionaire Kennedy was kept tactfully out of sight.) "Where's old Joe?" demanded old Sam. "Well, I don't know, but he's around here in the bushes somewhere—we felt his power, we who backed another candidate."

Like half-suspicious clans that have united to attack a third, many a chuckle came at the irony of the warriors' love feast. Kennedy himself touched on it, but even here he was only briefly diverted from his major theme of vigorous, all-out attack. We trust we take a properly reserved view of the young man, but here again he seemed to us to strike deftly the right note.

This reconciliation breakfast and Johnson's selection for second place really go to the heart of things. Was this convention just another hoax on gullible liberals? Do the radical professions in the Democratic platform really mean nothing?

Well, it comes down to an interpretation of Kennedy's character. Platforms, however liberal, mean little; vice-presidents, however conservative, mean little, compared to the importance of the all-powerful American president. Johnson's selection was an opportunistic—"cynical" if you like—example of an American political tradition. This balance is supposed to strengthen the party. It must be said in fairness that the catchall American political coalitions that are called parties, whose purpose is to channel power, do by their very amorphousness help to prevent class, sectional, and racial schisms. Famous political scientists say that sharper party differences would split the country.

Yet when this is all said, we think the northern Democrats pay too high a price for their alliance with the South. Johnson has been the symbol of this association in the bitterly disappointing Eighty-sixth Congress. (Maybe he will become more active in his new role, in the three-week August "rump" session.)

Those of us who swallow hard at Johnson's selection are called ultraliberals; even James Reston refers to the "extreme Democratic liberals" who wanted to try to win the election "without the South." Well, we are an ultraliberal if it means thinking that 100 years is too long to wait to give Negroes the vote, or that a minority in Congress should not tyrannize a majority. Things are relative. Of course Johnson wants a faster rate of progress than the South; we want a faster rate of progress than Johnson. But his nomination fogs the issue. Of one thing we are certain anyway; constant and unremitting pressure on the South is essential. There is some evidence that it is already pushing the stubborn clock ahead a little.

Why Johnson took the role is hard to figure; if he thinks he can run the Senate from the presiding officer's chair, we believe he is mistaken. The choice puts nearly irresistible pressure on Rockefeller to take second place.

Democrats have now endorsed what Nixon sneeringly called "growthmanship," a clear-cut economic issue that could last a generation. It will be a fierce campaign, we believe, with the new Nixon starting lofty and aloof and gradually reverting to old Nick.

Are Nixon and Kennedy Two Peas in a Pod?

AUGUST 8, 1960   Who will win in November? At this stage we won't guess. It will be hard for Nixon to attract all the independents and Democrats he needs to get a majority. But others factors are involved also. Two of them, we suspect, won't be discussed widely and could be decisive. One is Kennedy's Catholicism. The other is the deep-seated and (we are persuaded) widespread distrust of Nixon. How can you compute and balance off such emotions that defy logic and analysis?

Whatever you think of Kennedy's choice of Lyndon Johnson, you have to admit its galvanic effect on Nixon. He had expected to take the South; when Kennedy picked Johnson, Nixon wrote that off. He acted with boldness and decisiveness. He changed all his plans. He made his surprise pilgrimage to Rockefeller, pressed a strong civil rights plank, sought in every way to pin a liberal label on the GOP, and fatalistically accepted that he must somehow win the big industrial states and the restive farm belt. Ezra Taft Benson was doomed anyway, but Nixon chucked him earlier than expected. Then he picked handsome, lightweight Lodge as running mate to build up what he considers his trump suit—toughness to Moscow.

We watched the political old pros at Chicago nod their heads approvingly. For the moment at any rate the big thing there seemed to us to be to get rid of Eisenhower. Whoever wins in November, we shall have change—moderate change with Nixon, a great deal of change with Kennedy. Maybe the real issue in this campaign is how much change you want.

Eisenhower's big farewell day at Chicago was a recapitulation of his dreary eight-year themes—tranquility, serenity, complacency. He implied that it is unpatriotic to criticize or point out that the West's overall position in the Cold War has declined during his incumbency. Yet every student knows it. Next day Eisenhower made his silly attack on the Swedes ("A fairly friendly European country," he extemporized). They have "a tremendous record for socialistic operation," he said, and hence their drunkenness and suicide rates have gone up! It was unbelievable, unless you saw his earnest, eager face, that a man with notions like that should be guiding our country in time of peril. Few recalled he made just another such attack on the French in 1952—as a doubtful ally because of their loose home life.

We always invite trouble when we praise Nixon. Yet we can think of no GOP nominee in our time who compares with him in political skills. At Chicago, after his nomination, he put on an unrehearsed midnight TV tableau with mother, wife, and girls that was far more sophisticated than his Checkers broadcast. It was a perfect thing of its kind, we thought, as he registered humility and responsibility. Then his acceptance speech was one of the most impressively effective political fifty minutes we ever witnessed. He rang every bell. We think Nixon is better equipped to do this sort of thing than any man the GOP has nominated in half a century, and young Mr. Kennedy had better realize it.

On the evening of the day last month when Kennedy made his Khrushchev "apology-regret" statement to an Oregon street rally, this reporter—in an hour's relaxed end-of-campaign discussion with twenty other newsmen—rather paternally suggested to the candidate that he had, perhaps, made a slip of the tongue. It was in the U-2 crisis and all the State Department chickens were coming home to roost. Kennedy dismissed our comment lightly, but with a little undercurrent of uneasiness.

His meaning had been plain enough, as the transcript shows. Khrushchev demanded not merely an apology but that the US should "try those responsible," an impossible demand. Unfortunately, in explaining this to a curbside questioner, Kennedy repeated the word "apologize," coupling it with his own word "regret" and half-assented to it in order to repudiate more strongly Khrushchev's demand for a public trial. "If he [Khrushchev] had merely asked that the US should express regret, then that would have been a reasonable term," Kennedy said.

Many writers assert Nixon and Kennedy are alike as two peas—cool, calculating automatons. We disagree. Nixon would never have made this slip. We doubt if he makes any slip in the campaign. By contrast, it was Kennedy's candid responsiveness that produced this incident. He is an attractive figure as he answers questions; he is unemotional and hates histrionics, but he does give the audience the impression of saying what he thinks, of speaking his mind.

There is one clear-cut, astonishing party difference this year: Democrats have come out unequivocally for federal responsibility for speeding up national growth, and base their whole expansion program upon it. Any way you look at it, this is radical—though based on a coherent modern economic philosophy. The Eisenhower economy has been repressive; his advisers in their hearts oppose full employment as inflationary. But have they carried this too far; is a new recession coming? Note that the day Nixon was nominated the Reserve Board threw a lifeline to the laboring stock market by reducing margin requirements. (We smiled to discover Merrill Lynch, Pierce, Fenner & Smith had tickers at GOP amphitheater!)

The one economic sin is to keep a democracy's industry idling; that is the situation in the US today with 5 percent unemployed (4.5 million), and steel production only 55 percent. Idle men, idle plants! The administration can't learn. Fearing a deficit the Treasury drastically cut defense orders in July 1957, triggering the 1957–58 recession with its incredible $12.5-billion deficit. Fortuitous government spending, answering the Soviet Sputnik, cured the recession, though the administration has never seemed to realize it.

The Catholic Issue

SEPTEMBER 26, 1960 The candidate's voice bounces off the limestone front of the Lebanon Bank all around Penn Square. They have stuck the bannered speaker's stand in front of the Elks' Club, across from the Wiemer Hotel; one policeman guesses 4,000, another thinks it's maybe more—all agree that it's the biggest crowd assembled in political history.

The "Walk–Don't Walk" sign flashes at the corner of South Ninth and Cumberland but the problem isn't walking, it's breathing. Kennedy crowds have been unusual all week; bigger than expected; bigger than Stevenson got at this stage in 1956.

This is Pennsylvania Dutch country, the home of Lutherans, United Brethren, and Evangelicals; there's a report that 300 Mennonites have registered and the Democrats know what that means: the "plain people" normally eschew voting. It's Republican territory, too: 2½ to 1 at the last registration. But this is also a gay, shirt-sleeved American crowd, eager to hear the band, to see the show, eager to see this controversial figure.

They see a slim young man with broad shoulders, tanned face, brown hair, white teeth, dressed in a well-cut, gray, pinstripe suit. Before he says anything they avidly watch greetings and introductions on the platform—a sudden attractive smile on a sober face that makes him look like—who is it now?—well, maybe young Lindbergh.

Adlai Stevenson needs a jet runway to launch him into the high altitudes of his eloquence; this one seems to need no takeoff at all for a less lofty flight; in fact he seems, sometimes, almost tone-deaf to the rounded, rhythmic period. He stands there for a second, half diffident and shy, and then it bursts out of him, an earnest, urgent stream with a single rigid, up-and-down gesture of his right arm. What he is saying is, essentially, that America has been standing still when it ought to be moving, that its relative strength and prestige are slipping, that to be strong with Khrushchev it must be strong at home. Rarely has America been offered such different appeals in the election process where normally all appeals ultimately blend into a kind of indistinguishable sludge; Kennedy is saying, "Awake, America!" Nixon is saying "Relax!"

He has not learned some of the basic platform tricks. He does not wait out laughter or applause; he does not use ruffles and flourishes; habitually he looks only at the right-hand side of the crowd. Photographers scramble to his right—"When he looks left," one said, "he's only doing it because he's been told to and his expression is no good!"

He is an advance-text skipper. Twice he has offered prepared explanations of his position on the crucial economic matter of "growth," once at Cadillac Square, Detroit, again last week at the Shrine Temple at Harrisburg, and each time some reporter who trusted the release wired out quotations ahead of time that he never gave. "Very well," you say, "so what? He moved the crowd in each case with his extemporary remarks!" True, but what weight does a candidate attach to a "five-point program to meet unemployment" which he forgets to deliver? It is disconcerting for Harvard's Archy Cox, who is trying to coordinate his talks.

There is a subdued air of hope in the Kennedy entourage. Crowds have been good—better than expected; they also think Kennedy scored on the "religious issue," particularly that television show from the blue-draped crystal ballroom of Houston's Rice Hotel, September 12, when the nation watched the lonely young man keep his temper before an unctuous inquisition. (We have a hunch Democrats before long will offer evidence that conservative economic interests are financing some of these church groups.) But the real test is yet to come. How will Kennedy do in his joint TV appearance with Nixon? And above all—what is the mood of the nation—does it want to be soothed, or is it dissatisfied enough to want to march forward again? That probably will decide the election.

Kennedy stops speaking and the motorcade storms on. It is interesting to watch the complicated young man try to preserve his dignity. At York Fair they tried to photograph him with a donkey, no go; when he "bought a brick" for a dollar for the new Salvation Army home he didn't seem to hear photographers urge him to "hold the brick up." He was even more self-conscious in explaining his wife wasn't along because she was going to have a baby. There is something patrician in this pinstripe radical.

Is "radical" the word? We think Kennedy is saying things every day that would be called socialistic if Hubert Humphrey said them. Maybe we are wrong. Kennedy's lifeline seems to us moving steadily left. His basic economic thesis is that America can have fast growth and full employment and finance it by its own expansion. That is one of the most sweeping conceptions any candidate ever advanced.

Says *New York Herald-Tribune*'s Robert Donovan, "not even Adlai Stevenson went so far in his campaigns of 1952 and 1956." Broadcaster Edward P. Morgan says, "Kennedy has already taken positions on such controversial issues as public power and civil rights sharply to the left of Stevenson's." Syndicated columnist William S. White, who is close to Lyndon Johnson, warns Kennedy not to go so far "to please the left wing of his party"; his campaign is "in trouble" because of it, White cries. And finally John A. Grimes in the *Wall Street Journal* says Kennedy's "all-out liberal line . . . (is) as hard as the jut of his jaw." Well, maybe America isn't ready for it. But that's the way it looks.

Meanwhile, back at his old tricks, Nixon at the Machinists' Convention at St. Louis offered what he called a direct quotation from Kennedy to make him say "what labor wants, I want." This was a neat twist from the actual statement, "I know labor wants what I want." And the campaign is young yet.

By 300,000 Votes Out of 67 Million

NOVEMBER 21, 1960 A few days more and Republicans will convince themselves they won the election. No doubt about it, Kennedy would be in stronger position if he had won by a 1932 landslide. He didn't, and it's worth analyzing the result.

This was a wonderfully close election, a difference of some 300,000 popular votes out of 67 million. A couple of Republicans named Hayes and Harrison back in 1876 and 1888 won the presidency on electoral votes alone and overcame the handicap. Republicans see the situation hopefully. It will be, they say, like the 1958 Democratic victory that turned out to be a terrible dud.

How much substance is there in this? Some, we think, but not too much. A huge majority seemed developing on that strange, unforgettable election night but it melted away like a snowbank after 12:00. Now the GOP would like to discredit the new administration entirely and argue it has no mandate at all.

This is silly. To begin with, this isn't 1958. The problem there was Eisenhower's veto, requiring an unobtainable two-thirds vote in the Congress. That is gone for keeps. Next, though the Democrats have lost two seats in the Senate and twenty-two or more in the House, their previous majority was so top-heavy that they could hardly go anywhere but down. One can predict even now with reasonable certainty further losses two years hence. They will still run Congress.

A point to remember, we think, is that the religious issue is deflated. The wonder is not that a Catholic was elected by a close vote, but that he was elected at all. The skip-jump quality of the result is fascinating; Kennedy's religion apparently helped him in the concentrated big-city vote of populous states; damaged him in rural Protestant areas outside the South. But now the precedent is shattered. Conservatives say nothing should ever be done for the first time: but once something is done the argument collapses. We know Kennedy is going to lean backward in an attitude that we have previously described as "anticlericalism." When he runs for reelection in 1964 we suspect the religious issue will be forgotten.

We also suspect the Republicans don't know even yet what hit them. In spite of exhortations from the most popular president in history, in spite of the religious issue, in spite of Kennedy's youth, the American people chose the man who was telling them bad news instead of the one telling them good news. We find this enormously encouraging.

It is argued that Lyndon Johnson and the South have a mortgage on Kennedy and will revive the old GOP-Dixie coalition. Maybe. We admit we don't see much chance of abolishing the 27½-percent oil depletion tax loophole that has made so many Texas millionaires.

But whatever Johnson may think, he accepted the leftish Democratic platform in toto in the campaign and there are rumors he got religion at the last in Texas when the GOP Neanderthalers called him Judas and roughed up him and his wife. More important, we think, is that you are going to see crackling leadership by Kennedy with a powerful legislative team—Johnson, Sam Rayburn, Mansfield, McCormack, and others—and no veto to fear. We predict now, for example, that the House Rules Committee nuisance will be abated. It was the power of this committee under Chairman Howard W. Smith (D, Va.) that more than anything ruined the rump session of Congress. Sam Rayburn says little about this committee, but a certain look comes into his eye. There are several ways of curbing it. Put this down; it will be curbed.

There is one more thing. It is our estimate of Kennedy. We have hardly dared to mention it, it is so high. Maybe we are wrong, but we think you may be seeing the beginning of an important political personality. Certainly, at forty-three he should be around for a good while.

This feeling grew at his first press conference last week at Hyannis Port. The week's excitement brought $50,000 in business to the little community and before the tiny "port" lapsed back to normal late-autumn population of a few dozen (after Kennedy flew off in the *Caroline*), the small Hyannis Western Union office had received 13,000 congratulatory telegrams and the post office was knee deep in mail sacks.

The friendly but businesslike press offered Kennedy every opportunity to stub his toe, every chance to fall into a pit. Reporters are not hostile, they like him, but it is their job to spread bait for the unwary. For example, did he consider the election a "repudiation" of Eisenhower? Quite skillfully and with poise and dignity Kennedy refused the bait. "Repudiation"? Certainly not that word. And he sent a tactful message to the hero-president.

What happens now to Nixon? If Republicans want to run him in 1964 as some backers hope, it will be all right by us. We still think Rockefeller could have beat Kennedy in 1960, but four years hence nobody will beat him.

Ho-hum, we must come back from politics. We are in a recession, Eisenhower's third in eight years. The bad news on unemployment was held back till after the election. Jobs declined when they normally go up, unemployment rose when it normally sinks. Total unemployment is 3,388,000. This isn't too bad by itself but comes to 6.4 percent seasonally adjusted, with a brutal winter ahead unless things improve fast. Eisenhower has actually started to pump out government contracts and the interest rate has been brought down. Just possibly the psychological lift of electing Kennedy will bridge the gap; if it doesn't he will take strong action two months hence.

Summing it up, it is our judgment that Kennedy and the Democrats have the momentum to put through the program that stalled in the special session. We expect education, health, housing, and minimum wage bills to go through, and probably a lot more.

THE KENNEDY YEARS
[*1961-1963*]

Ring Up the Curtain

JANUARY 9, 1961   The cabinet is chosen, Congress has met, the show begins. How do the first high scenes of drama compare with the other performance—the great one—FDR in 1933? Well, there are a few similarities. Once more there is a bewildered outgoing president who obviously doesn't know what it's all about. To friends Eisenhower still uses the phrase "young geniuses" in reference to the newcomers. He uses it derisively, defensively. . . . Poor, tragic Hoover didn't understand either; never did.

Banks were closed in 1932, some smelled revolution. Nothing like that today, and it makes Kennedy's task much harder. People in 1932 were lean, hungry, scared; today many are fat, complacent, tranquilized. FDR had a palpable crisis and a huge mandate; Kennedy has a half-mandate and a crisis half the nation won't acknowledge. That is why Kennedy's crucial task is to establish rapport with the people; he must do that before anything, he can't give leadership without followship.

FDR had to hold the people; Kennedy must reach them. FDR invented the radio "fireside chat" (six in 1933 and 1934), and also employed the twice-weekly press conferences. (I can see him now as we trooped in, sitting behind a desk cluttered with dolls and totems, cigarette holder atilt, grinning like a cat in anticipation of the contest to which he came like a skilled player!)

Kennedy knows about publicity too; he is using his outdoor conferences to strengthen the impression of informality, alertness, competence. Soon he will try some live evening press conferences over TV; a wise move, no doubt, from his point of view, though a little irritating to reporters who become unpaid performers in what essentially sounds like a combination "fireside chat" and TV quiz show.

215

One searches for further resemblances. Kennedy was only fifteen when FDR came to Washington. Each had an upper-class education, found a life of public service more attractive than money-grabbing, and each had a respect for the decencies. At heart, too, each had a kind of patrician reticence, an impervious private dignity.

But no, 1961 isn't 1933! The New Dealers who poured into Washington to take over government were as gaudy a bunch of amateurs, intellectuals, and crackpots as this experienced capital has ever seen —men whom FDR set against each other with sometimes unkind virtuosity, catching the sparks in a net.

What a gang!—Hopkins, Wallace, Ickes, Fanny Perkins, Tommy the Cork, Henry the Morgue, Ben Cohen, Adlai Stevenson, General Johnson, Ray Moley, Abe Fortas, Alger Hiss—the list goes on and on.

The Kennedy cabinet is competent—enormously, reassuringly competent, but nothing like this. It begins with *cum laudes* and works up to Rhodes Scholars. One instinctively compares it with the Eisenhower crowd and shouts hosannas; good-bye stuffed shirts, businessmen, and pietists! The president-elect has made a swell selection, no doubt about it.

But note that it is all under control or seems to be. It is disciplined. Compared to the wild men FDR cheerfully threw at each other this bunch looks like a troop of Eagle Scouts. Some FDR advisers came like mystics to a shrine; some were Frankfurter's finds who began fertilizing ideas before they reached Union Station.

Oh well, we can't have fun like that again, I suppose . . . those gorgeous, disorderly far-off days when anything was possible! In no time at all the whole upper-class elite hated FDR with a psychotic hatred; chiefly, it seemed, because he had reopened their banks and saved their bacon. Kennedy wouldn't want a team of players like that. It wouldn't really be appropriate. He is a different type.

Kennedy, I guess, will not commit the errors FDR did. He is both more surefooted in some ways, and reserved. Furthermore, he dare not take the other's risks. FDR could take risks because he had the emergency and a majority and also because he had imposed his personality on the public: the gay, confident champion of the little man, the image of human warmth. People forgave him because of that. Under the onionskin layers of his complex and contradictory personality you peeled down to a man who deeply cared, who was capable of brilliant dramatization because he was fervently committed.

That is the problem now for Kennedy as the new Congress opens the show—the youngest man ever elected. He has picked a fine cast and offered a good prologue; the *New York Times* likes him; he has shown personal force and dignity. But there is a certain coolness and grayness in his very orderliness. His one true objective is to create a new mood in the American people, everything else is secondary. He must capture the country's imagination—but this needs evangelism, not intellectualism.

It is not fair to ask Kennedy to be FDR. All the same his success turns on showing he cares, cares passionately, and doing it before the elite turn against him and begin to hate him for saving them.

Perhaps I have omitted one other similarity between the two, in most ways so utterly different, men. They both wanted to advance. They profoundly felt the need for getting off dead center and loathed complacency in the face of danger. The one in a wheelchair and the other with his touch football, were apostles of change. Action.

Whether Kennedy can swing it nobody knows. It is enormously important for all of us. But his motto January 20 when he takes the oath might well be like FDR's, twenty-eight years ago, on a bleak Saturday in March—"The nation asks for action, and action now. . . . We must act, and act quickly."

Yes, that's it.

Wake Up, America

FEBRUARY 6, 1961   The moment everybody had waited for came suddenly. The Kennedy cold wave crossed the Eisenhower tepid front. The young president took the rostrum and told Congress, "Wake up—it is later than you think!" His actual words were, "Every day we draw nearer the hour of maximum danger." Just a fortnight earlier Eisenhower sent the same Congress three lullabies.

Kennedy found America tranquil; he left it—not roused, maybe—but disturbed. A nation was waking.

At 12:15 the senators marched in, two by two. It was the great oblong hall of the House of Representatives and each addition to the audience was announced by a little man in civilian clothes looking sheepish. We do these things very poorly—nothing like the costumed ceremony of Parliament; but this scene had irresistible drama of its own even if the staging was drab. There was applause suddenly as Jacqueline Kennedy took her place in the gallery. She hesitated like a schoolgirl, not certain it was for her, then gave a little bow that was somehow appealing.

Next—ambassadors. They came and came and came—through the swinging glass doorways in the rear; I have never seen so many; in fact some had to stand behind the guardrail. "The Chief Justice of the United States and the Associate Justices of the Supreme Court!" cried the sheeplike usher trying to roar like a lion. Next, the cabinet, and the big audience craned to see the new faces. All wore white carnations from the FDR memorial services. They looked younger than in their pictures. And finally the president. He spoke slowly and seemed at last to have mastered the art of reading a prepared text.

Could Kennedy be describing the same nation that Eisenhower described? It seemed incredible. Most newsmen I talked to felt stirred. Kennedy has a big asset in the friendly Washington press corps; they deplored Eisenhower and disliked Nixon.

As to the speech itself, Kennedy used shock treatment; you do not gentle a drugged man whose life is threatened. On the economic side most readers of this column have heard the story told again and again. On the military side we are in poor position to judge. On foreign affairs we particularly liked his comment on Cuba that we favor social and economic reform; it is the communist intrusion that we oppose.

All told it was a tingling, exhilarating start. By standing and stretching forward we could see the brown head below, as he shuffled the small sheets with the large type, and tapped the lectern with the three fingers of the right hand. Kennedy gains in confidence.

Sail On

MARCH 27, 1961   Who can describe the new Washington? Washington is crackling, rocking, jumping! It is a kite zigging in a breeze, it is a city released from a heat wave. At first reporters glanced at each other in wild surmise, later they asked, "Do we really know this man Kennedy?" Now they gasp and hold on.

Just three months, yet it is hard to remember the fogged outlines of Eisenhower, or Christian Herter, or the Secretary of Commerce—let's see, what *was* his name? Forgotten already! Now there is a sixteen-point priority list of legislation, messages every other day, a try at better relations with Peking (no luck); with Moscow (uncertain); with Latin America (the new ingredient of social reform added to foreign aid). Seven press conferences, a dozen follow-up statements, television every other night, a firm stand on parochial schools (the current quip—"I wish the Catholics would quit picking on my president"). . . . All this and Caroline, too!

It is like a ship that Richard Henry Dana sailed on, a proud Cape Horner or stately Indiaman, that is long becalmed. Suddenly the vacant winds flap, the crew comes up speculative, the breeze rises. "Sail!" cries the captain; the great vessel comes around, gains headway; the spars begin to talk, water ripples under the keel, she begins to fling foam from her bows. What a moment! Now under a pyramid of canvas the erstwhile listless vessel has come alive, clouds swaying overhead, the whack and rhythm alongside as she moves gloriously through the water—dignity restored, bound for great destinies.

Last month's descriptions date quickly in this movement: the *Manchester Guardian* reporter caught the flair and élan of new Washington but wrote, "The most forlorn figure in the United States today is Adlai Stevenson" forgotten amidst America's "notorious fickleness." Absurd! Adlai Stevenson is having the time of his life, doing his most important service at the UN. "He has taken on Valerin Zorin, the

Soviet delegate, in public debate and quietly plucked him naked," commented *New York Times*man Reston last week.

Incidents tell the mood of the new Washington. Tall, handsome, dark-haired Ribicoff testifies in the barracklike House caucus room for the new school bill, in desperate danger. All the old traps are sprung by polite Republicans. "Do you favor federal aid to parochial schools?" Ribicoff pauses. "I am absolutely opposed to it in any form," he says grimly. "I think it would be most tragic to include it."

Or Edward R. Murrow. He has given up $200,000 at CBS for a $21,000 job under Kennedy to head the US Information Agency. Now he is being interrogated by senators at confirmation hearings. He slumps in his seat, sad-faced, dark, intense but controlled as Hickenlooper probes. Weren't those scenes in your celebrated documentary on migrant labor faked, Mr. Murrow? Murrow quietly says no. Senator Capehart (R, Ind.) fussily backs Hickenlooper's view that USIA should tell only the nice things about America; it's like . . . well, it's like selling a Cadillac, isn't it? Murrow could say yes. But in a level voice he says, "We cannot conceal our difficulties or our controversies even if we would. We live in an open, pluralistic society. If we don't report them responsibly and accurately, somebody else will report them worse." They are doubtful but they vote for him.

Then again, the Justice Department. Lights burn late in the windows. Part of it seems silly, boyish; "Bobby" sends notes of commendation to staff members whose license plates show they were present on Washington's Birthday (some of them had merely parked their cars while they shopped). There is a touch of Big Brother in Younger Brother. Even so, there is enthusiasm, here; commitment, energy. The Department's antitrust division throws the book at General Electric and Westinghouse in the rigged bids case.

Is Kennedy having an effect on politicians abroad? Berlin's Mayor Willy Brandt comes to town, sees the president, makes talks. Broad-shouldered and powerful, he speaks colloquial English. As a talker he shifts weight from foot to foot in a movement which would creep him forward into the audience if not blocked by the podium. Brandt's scalp lock is still a peninsula but it is in more danger of encirclement than West Berlin. But as to politics! It is unfair perhaps to compare Adenauer to Eisenhower, but here is another ambitious young man waiting to push out the older generation. The Washington wind is blowing in other countries.

And now a little comedy relief: it is the big new TV weekly, the "Ev & Charlie" show. Senator Dirksen and Representative Halleck, the two minority leaders, stand before a battery of microphones in the dignified old Supreme Court chamber in the Capitol once a week while TV lights glitter on the chrome ice pitcher and they take potshots at the administration in their individual styles. Honey-voiced Dirksen mellowly mourns; Halleck, looking like a barkeep in a tough district, uses the bungstarter. It is a wonderful team, they change places at the mike like Huntley and Brinkley. If you want something laughable, try Ev; if you prefer the somber and horrendous, there's Charlie! The one thing that is lacking is the voice of Modern Republicans. But anyway, the recession is better, they say (i.e., things are getting worse slower). "What we have to fear today about the recession is some of the proposals to cure it."

Yes sir, that's Washington! Something doing every minute. Kennedy moves so fast reporters lose track; this writer discovered to his surprise he had been out unreported four miles to a local TV station; making shots and practicing Spanish ardently. (He mispronounced "Bolivar" with accent on first rather than second syllable.)

What all this sounds like out there where you are, folks, I don't know. It's fun here!

The Worst and the Best

MAY 1, 1961   We watched Kennedy, fascinated. Thursday the editors; Friday the reporters. Here was a president in trouble, taking a licking on Cuba, tempted to turn a fiasco into a disaster. Would he panic?

The band gave four ruffles and flourishes, then broke into the first bars of "Hail to the Chief" as he strode up behind the long speakers' table in the big Statler ballroom for the editors' annual meeting. Every eye searched his demeanor. It was a good speech for what he did not say. He did not bluster nor pound the lectern; he did not make excuses, he did not mawkishly invoke God. On the other hand, he did not say very much. There wasn't much to say. He was grim and cool and collected, still using understatement. One thought of his youth particularly. Here was a young man who had made a bad mistake of judgment but who seemed capable of learning. The audience, I think, was deeply impressed.

Next day, the press conference. Now the furnace was hotter. The secret was out now. All pretense was over—we had mounted the invasion, planned it, drilled it, financed it, delivered it: it was invasion by proxy. It made the public anti-intervention qualifications by Kennedy and Adlai Stevenson look cheap. The scheme was inherited from Eisenhower but was adopted by Kennedy. It had been intended as a skirmish with only about 1,200 men involved, but it had been Madisonavenuized until the whole world knew of it in advance with the CBS broadcaster in Miami seeming to have a copyright on it with a blow-by-blow account of the "thousands" who were to be hurled in.

These revelations were in Friday morning papers. But there was still an off chance they weren't true. Kennedy came in, always at a brisk athletic pace, blue pinstripe suit, reddish necktie, handkerchief triangled in breast pocket, and moved to the lectern. Four hundred and two correspondents present. Then he chilled us. He would say nothing more on Cuba. So—it was true.

This was the worst day of his presidency, and the best. It was his day of success in Congress. He won four big victories all together: minimum wage, depressed areas, aid to dependent children of the unemployed, and House extension of Social Security Act benefits. None of the votes final but each pointing to ultimate victory. Yes, the ice jam seemed cracking; it was an historic moment—Kennedy's public popularity finally rubbing off on Congress. Almost certainly it means he will get the major part of his legislative program.

And Cuba came at just this minute! Unless you knew Kennedy, there wasn't much change in him. He was courteous, reserved, and controlled. "I'm the responsible officer of the government," he said quietly of the Cuban fiasco. But there were no smiling interchanges and I thought he seemed quieter and more gentle than usual, perhaps "chastened" is the right word.

That Kennedy is just as politically tough as ever showed in the way he brought Nixon in for a Cuba briefing followed by the Camp David chat with Eisenhower. All quite patriotic and inspiring, of course! . . . but just in case the GOP *had* intended to play politics Kennedy coolly reminded them that it was originally an Eisenhower invasion, with Nixon inferentially committed.

That was the big news last week till the bigger news of Algiers topped it. The Cuban invasion was giving French journalists a good laugh —"Budapest managed by choirboys"—until, alas, disaster put de Gaulle against the wall. No nation can be smug very long, it appears, save the Russians!

So much for the Cuban fiasco. But how about the future? The thing to remember, I think, is that we can heave Castro out of Cuba anytime we want to with a wave of the hand. We have the regiments all right, and most Americans ache for the excuse. But if we do it we might as well pull our ambassadors out of every country in Latin America; they will be no good to us anymore. The terrifying thing is the amount Americans have got to learn in a hurry; I still rather think young Mr. Kennedy may learn it.

Maybe last week's invasion was botched. But the fact is that the Cuban people did *not* rise. Fidelismo is allied closely with communism, may turn into communism, and is past peradventure a dictatorship; but it has gained a hold on the masses (maybe temporarily) because it has given them reforms.

That is what we have got to learn. This reporter suspects social revolution is inescapable throughout Latin America and he doubts if we have the time or our bankers the wit (Export-Import, International Monetary Fund, and the like) to steer it through gradualist channels. We want a nice democratic social revolution in which United Fruit Co. property rights are respected. Our conservatives want to fight communism the cheap way: jail liberals at home and cut down foreign aid. Well, we are sorry; we don't think it will wash. We can appeal for "liberty" and "democracy," but what do those words mean to empty bellies? How can you be free if you are landless and starving? The peasants of Cuba have got the promise of land, or think they have, and they and the plundered continent of Latin America now have the new image of Fidelismo. We can knock out Castro anytime we want by force but that, we think, will only make the real problem harder.

"A Major Risk of War"

JULY 3, 1961   It was Khrushchev who pressed the crisis button; it is well to remember that. Even after Vienna, and the bogged disarmament talks, Washington could not be sure. Then Mr. K, in bemedaled army uniform, announced flatly in Moscow he would sign a peace treaty with East Germany "at the end of this year . . . and those who try to threaten us with war . . . bear the entire responsibility. . . ." The end of this year—six months! The two big ships are on a collision course.

There were three things to do: consult allies, fix contingency plans, alert the public. Without quite knowing how it came about the public suddenly discovered the crisis. The Washington press was alerted first. This came when background talks took on ominous overtones that could not be ignored—"a major risk of war"; "nearly the certainty of some form of military action" if Mr. K continues.

Critics can, of course, argue the crisis was made in Washington. We don't think so. A crisis is the last thing the West wants. Why then is Mr. K running this risk—the worst risk of nuclear war so far? The frank answer here is that he thinks time is running on his side. He underrates the West. Put more brutally, he doesn't think the West can unite or that the US would fight. So there will be a hair-raising test of nerve on the brink.

Kennedy's problem is to lead the nation—and control it. He must convince Moscow of our toughness yet not slam the door. He must do this while GOP critics from Nixon down scream "timidity" and "no appeasement!" Mild proposals of Senators Mansfield (D, Mont.) and Cooper (R, Ky.) to reexamine our Berlin position are denounced as softness. The pressure from the political right is toward nonmaneuverability.

Now after six months in office Kennedy has no alternative, we believe, but to speak direct to the nation in the educational process which has been the one big lack of his administration so far. His press conference this week is the first since May 5.

Friendly critics have increasingly complained that Kennedy is not using his pulpit sufficiently. In part this is understandable. Problems are complex and the pace backbreaking (or back-straining, anyway). Kennedy has created a viable coalition in Congress which seems likely to achieve a fairly good record of legislation. He probably does not want to disrupt it with too much ideology. This year, it is argued, is an Eisenhower retread; next year there will be time to change to all-Kennedy whitewalls.

There is something to be said for this policy of expediency which has watered down the "urgency" slogan of the campaign. But it also shows lack of boldness and confidence. Kennedy has taken a defensive attitude toward the postrecession deficit, for example, when he should if anything boast of it. (By contrast Treasury Secretary Dillon, a Republican, told Congress cheerfully, "There is a deficit—so what?"). Walter Lippmann pointed out another example of this defensiveness, when Kennedy half-apologized for the "burden" of foreign aid. The fact is this burden should be a lot bigger.

We all want the president to educate the people for us and each fresh problem—civil rights, the Massachusetts road scandals, economic needs, foreign affairs—inevitably brings hope that the White House will mount the pulpit. Of course it is impossible to take on all these jobs at once. But there is a personal aspect of this too: Kennedy tends to understate things, he dislikes melodrama and theatrics; the kind of colorful exaggeration of Al Smith, Mayor LaGuardia, FDR, does not come naturally to him. He has his own way of achieving effects. The very restraint of his somber report to the nation after meeting Khrushchev in Vienna was impressive. In the same way during the campaign when he confronted the Protestant ministers on the issue of his religion he spoke quietly, without heroics, and was all the more effective because of it.

Yet part of the president's job, maybe the big part, is to crash the cymbals and bang the drum. Things still are "urgent" in the United States. The eight years' false indoctrination that all federal spending is necessarily a bad thing must somehow be eradicated.

No matter what is said about current business recovery, dangerous unemployment continues and there is every indication that taxes will once more balance the budget at too low a point for full recovery.

The administration, we guess, has about two good business years ahead of it in the normal course of the economic cycle. Unless something of a basic nature is done meanwhile to reduce unemployment, that timing will bring the customary "Eisenhower dip" just when Kennedy least wants it, in 1963–4, as the presidential campaign warms up. Economic need and political expediency both point the same way—bold new Kennedy programs rather than current Eisenhower retreads.

The Big Four

JANUARY 22, 1962   When will the Message be ready? "Not before eight at least," the White House tells reporters; so we know it won't be till after midnight and go off to the Women's National Press Club banquet for congressmen where Walter Lippmann stills the great Mayflower ballroom with a level, quiet voice, listened to almost reverentially. It is a noble speech dealing with an apocalyptic world where the two great rivals are caught between "a war that cannot be fought and a peace that cannot be achieved" and where, accordingly, "frustration, confusion, and compromise" reign. Uncomfortable certainly, but, says Lippmann, we must know there is something worse; neither US nor USSR must push the other beyond "the tolerable limit of provocation and humiliation," for even the sanest nation "can be provoked and exasperated to the point of lunacy where its nervous system cannot endure inaction—where only violence can relieve its feelings." That is Lippmann's lesson; it is the business of governments "to find where that line is—and to stay well back of it."

So now it is 2:00 A.M. in zero cold, and muffled secretaries are just leaving the floodlit White House where bare trees cast black shadows on the snow. Streetlamps drop frozen cones on empty Pennsylvania Avenue and the steam-plumed car parks without fear of a ticket. High up on ledges the line of birds twitter all night, and now and then a frozen starling falls to the ground as stronger ones take its place. The reporter seeks his warm, silent office and works and meditates till five. Has he appraised the speech aright, caught its mood and nuances—a few hours of fitful sleep raise these doubts.

. . . Now it is noon in the great hall of Congress, filled with representatives and senators—cabinet sitting in front—every gallery jammed, clerks bawling announcements, ambassadors and ministers trooping down the center aisle two by two; and then the whole crowd rises and applauds and gawks at a pretty girl who sits in the president's gallery. Yes, it's Jackie.

Kennedy strides smiling down the aisle, young and vigorous, making his welcoming committee look old as Druids; then he begins and the nation listens. The state of the nation—the state of the world. . . . He speaks confidently, resonantly, and the speech that seemed tired last night comes partly to life (though Kennedy cannot make a phrase give off hot sparks as FDR did). It sounds better than it read, though, and it sounds better over TV than in the straining chamber itself where routine Democratic applause wars with routine Republican silences.

Kennedy speaks. It is the apocalyptic moment Lippmann noted last night. The Common Market Six are throwing down their historic challenge; the American economy still dawdles at halfspeed; Soviet Russia is training annually three times as many engineers as the US; France may plunge bloodily over the brink at any minute—and once more an American president comes to plead with this antique Congress for speed on a field covered with parliamentary flypaper.

Consider the House Big Four Democratic leadership—Boston Irishman Speaker McCormack opposes federal school aid; Oklahoma Majority Leader Albert opposes civil rights bills; Arkansas Ways and Means chairman Wilbur Mills opposes medical aid under Social Security; and Virginia primitive Howard Smith, Rules Committee chairman, opposes Progress.

These men, and chairmen like them, are not picked because they are wise but because they are old; seniority, not the voters, gives them key chairmanships in semi-autonomous committees; party responsibility does not exist in the American system. This is a rural legislature though 70 percent of America is urban; it knows timidly that it can do nothing without danger and forgets that to do nothing is most dangerous of all. It is a sound Congress if the world would only wait, and it is prepared to make a sound record by every standard except what must be done.

Kennedy's relation to his Congress is a puzzle. He will still use Eisenhower kindness to a legislature that swings to conservatism. Does he know his own strength? He has a grocerylist of proposals, many of which can't pass. Is this make-believe necessary? The theory is that maybe next year's Congress will be more "pro-Kennedy," but how can that be if he doesn't educate voters now? This week's press conference was the first in forty-seven days.

Kennedy is driving for one great goal—Common Market unity—and one supposes he is shucking off lesser objectives for this. Indeed, achievement of this goal could redeem a drab session, and its coming seems more and more inevitable. Even as Congress prepares to debate the issue the "if" becomes a "must." For the European Six have now agreed on a common farm tariff. The US annually sells $1 billion in farm products to The Six. If the European tariff gate clangs down, farmers will yell from Sacramento to Dixie.

A year ago this reporter sat in a snowdrift listening to Cardinal Cushing lecturing God and hearing the young new president preach urgency in the face of national danger. It was inspiring and the motto was, "We must move."

Now the first annual report shows much that is valuable and some that is splendid, and the word is, "Look, we are moving!" Fine, if only it is fast enough.

The Congressional Cycle

FEBRUARY 26, 1962   If you don't understand the congressional cycle you don't understand what's happening in Washington. The political year begins with a bang. The president sends three big messages to Congress, delivering one in person. Then more messages and reports. The purpose is to tell Congress what he wants, to try to grab the initiative, to outline a program. In a time of world crisis there is an awful lot to do. The president endeavors to whip up a sense of urgency.

This is the stage we have just come through. Mr. Kennedy has flooded Capitol Hill with messages and reports. He's held five consecutive weekly televised press conferences in succession. No doubt about it, he's had a big effect on the public. The press is full of it. Reading the stories you get a sense of activity in Washington.

Nonsense. What you read is the activity of the White House. A sluggish Congress is just looking down Pennsylvania Avenue with vacant indifference blended with mild distaste. It knows this preliminary phase. It knows that when all the White House shouting is over it will be its turn. It will climb into the old stagecoach that the Founding Fathers fashioned, with a Conestoga ox-team ambling behind. Hurry—? Why?

What happens after the president's appeals for haste? Well, first Republicans toddle off home and spend a leisurely week making Lincoln Day speeches. Then they return (this week), and everybody pitches in for a desultory four working days interrupted by Washington's Birthday. (The Senate has agreed this week, however, to vote on the Department of Urban Affairs.) On the third week Democrats desert Washington and go home and make speeches about Jackson and Jefferson. Party leaders agree to have few if any roll calls in these sacred intervals.

The beautiful thing about this system is that it insulates Congress from the pressure of all this urgency from the White House. Some of the more excitable might have been influenced by executive exhortations. Having a comfortable three-week cooling-off period restores balance. Like a Berlin wall, it divides the first phase of the annual cycle, the phase of White House entreaty, from the second phase, when dawdling Congress takes over and begins its long, random, reluctant consideration of distasteful proposals for Change, looking at them with the annoyed glance of a man who has found some foreign substance in his soup.

There is a third phase in the congressional cycle. But we won't reach that for months yet. That is the brief hysterical, hot-weather, last-minute rush stage when everything is jammed together before

Congress stampedes home. Action on civil rights? The hostile Judiciary Committee, to which a batch of such bills has just been assigned, will suddenly report them out—too late for action of course. Shrewd congressmen will strike pork-barrel bargains to let "must" bills through, knowing their power is greatest when a single vote can block unanimous consent. Lights will burn late, Congress will work all night, newspapers will suddenly discover the dramatic story of Congress racing for adjournment. It will be exciting, I tell you!—and they will set the clock back, and the temperature will hit 102, and Congress will suddenly adjourn. And everyone will smile indulgently, explaining that for all its faults we have the oldest democracy in the world, and what if the education bill didn't pass—we can't hope to be as efficient as the communists can we?

If Mr. GOP went to a psychiatrist he would find he had a bad case of muddled mystique. He favors *local* controls but at the same time dislikes the cities. If Mr. GOP could only straighten out this kink he would look as carefree and happy again as the man on TV who has just taken somebody's liver pills.

The GOP confusion goes far back. Conservatives always hated federal controls because they were efficient. Any great vested interest—railroads, life insurance companies, banks—always wanted state control because it was weak. Over the generations some Republicans forgot why they really favored states' rights—their reaction to federal social security, medical aid, slum clearance, banking laws, and the like was compulsively hostile to "controlization" and the like.

But if the GOP likes "local" control, as stated, why aren't they pals with the cities? Because the great farm-to-city migration which has put 70 percent of us in urban areas has made the cities the prime advocates of change. The cities aren't "progressive" in the immediate sense; they just have social problems which require bold action—quick. The cities appeal to their local state governments and find them gerrymandered in favor of farm areas. So the cities leapfrog the statehouse crowd and come to sympathetic Washington. Republicans haven't adapted themselves to the change. They may end up by becoming a kind of rural party.

Republicans regard the necessity of voting on the new Department of Urban Affairs bill as a dastardly plot. If they join southern Democrats against it and the proposed secretary, Robert Weaver, they put their necks in a noose. This is particularly true of House members.

They beseech the Senate to veto the measure this week to spare them later on.

Notes   Last week Navy Judge Advocate General, Rear Admiral Mott, told the Senate drily that "we have no need for space-age witch-hunters: amateur anti-Communists are as useful as amateur brain surgeons." Another official wrote, "Today far too many self-styled 'experts' on communism are plying the highways giving erroneous and distorted information. This causes hysteria, false alarms, and misplaced apprehension among our citizens." His name? J. Edgar Hoover, of all people.

The Rules Committee

APRIL 2, 1962   About the time you read this the House should be passing the Kennedy tax bill, first of the administration's big three. We dropped in at the Rules Committee last week to watch the final stage of preparation.

Long ago Kennedy proposed the measure—but what is time to Congress? Congress is the vat where urgency evaporates. Worried by slow economic growth Kennedy in 1961 noted that America's plants and machinery are disgracefully outdated in competition with other countries. Most of these give tax concessions for modernization and the administration thinks we should do the same. The idea isn't new; a good many economists back it though some aren't sure.

As concocted by Secretary Dillon and the House Ways and Means Committee the bill carried a $1.75 billion corporate relief package; this Treasury loss of revenue to be made up by closing loopholes elsewhere (including extension of the withholding tax to stock dividends and interest payments).

So now here we are in the cozy Rules Committee hideaway to which perhaps 100 of the million sightseers who come annually to Washington will ever penetrate. The room is small but opulent, it is about the size of the boardroom of a third-rate city. Seven blue leather chairs face seven others down the center table; a chandelier with ropes of prisms glitters above, and three small windows let in light through four feet of Capitol masonry. By actual count there are thirty-two seats for press and public, yet here is a seat of naked power in Congress, the bottleneck of progress—where haughty chairmen of other House committees quail and grow obsequious.

Stocky, red-faced Wilbur Mills (D, Ark.), chairman of the Ways and Means Committee, considered by many to have the best technical brain in Congress, is explaining his committee's bill. He is a doodler with a difference: he first draws a picture, then erases it, talking all the time. Mills is cautious, timid, and conservative so, by the mad incongruity of American government, he becomes spokesman for all the urgent, quivering Kennedy "must" bills—tax, trade, and medical aid. He is chairman, of course, not because he has brains but because he has seniority; seniority is the medium of exchange in Congress.

Mills explains the huge bill without notes for an hour. And he makes plain that his committee has granted the fat cats the concessions Kennedy recommended but has only partly met the cost with new revenue-producing measures. There is a big deficit.

Mills is a big shot in Congress. As a token of this, the committee room where he presides is so huge you could hold a basketball game in it. But here Mills is only an archbishop in a consistory of cardinals, with the pope at the far end. The "pope"?—Representative Howard W. Smith, 79, of Virginia—House Rules Committee chairman.

"Judge" Smith is tall and stooped with shaggy hair and an ancient codfish face. His tufted eyebrows, if waxed, would be as long as Salvador Dali's mustache. A sad, Grant Wood–American Gothic type, he looks like a judge of a municipal court which, in fact, he was.

With Smith's secretary leaning over his shoulder to find the place for him, and the glass of turbid water in front (which seems to have been left over from last week) you might think the judge an extinguished ember. But a coal burns inside him, a dedication—a Hooverian passion—for a balanced budget, come war, come pestilence. He fondles his long cigar with delicate relish. "We'll curry that horse later," he observes ominously at one point.

Mills draws his final doodle, tidily erases it, and stops. Then comes a memorable moment. In a grating voice Smith throws ten months' hearings out of the window. The bill doesn't balance, he says in effect, and so to hell with it.

Arbitrary? Maybe. But he speaks for the conservative coalition in Congress, the power that controls. And Mills doesn't seem too downcast. One imagines he anticipated this. It is up to him to go back and tell his committee now that they must meet Smith's wishes. Unless they do the bill won't get an exit visa from Rules and can't reach the House floor. (You are probably going to see the same process repeated on the trade bill, and particularly on the health bill.)

And so, forty-eight hours later, here we are again! Same place, same people, but changed bill. Mills succinctly tells what has been done that morning in the Ways and Means Committee to meet the Smith ultimatum.

Reporters' jaws gape as he briskly drops tens of millions here, hundreds of millions there. Instead of adding new revenue to balance the bill, the Kennedy program has been lopped back all along the line. In other words, it has been balanced down, not up.

Smith was right, it was a bad bill. In some ways it still is. Against Kennedy's wishes the utility boys have jumped aboard to get a free ride with their own 3-percent tax subsidy. (This is outrageous because utility rates are already adjusted to pay for plant modernization.) Yet this was not the reason Smith vetoed it. He applied his simple rule of a balance and when he got that let the watered-down measure through regardless of any other defects.

So now with the Rules Committee's nod the tax bill comes to the House floor. It has a "closed rule," i.e., the House must take it or leave it without change and with limited debate. Very little of this procedure gets into the papers. Few people understand it. Yet in one way or another it affects everything, sometimes merely exacting conservative tribute, sometimes killing a bill dead, like school aid. That's how it's done in Washington. We thought you'd like to know. ·

The Lobbies

JULY 30, 1962   In the second year of Roosevelt's New Deal the Supreme Court intervened. It killed NRA [National Recovery Administration], declared agriculture a local problem, outlawed a compulsory railway pension law, rejected a minimum wage for women, and knocked off other measures. It created a constitutional crisis.

And now here we are again. Once more the essence of the crisis is that government lacks the power to govern. Better schools are desperately needed: they are blocked by one or two votes in the House Rules Committee; city dwellers comprise 70 percent of the population; they can't get a Department of Urban Affairs because rural legislators won't let them; Congress rejects a proposal to deal with the farm surplus, whose storage costs a billion dollars a year, but is incapable of producing its alternative controls. Senator Kefauver writes a 35-page consumer bill after a two-year drive to get safer, cheaper drugs but the Eastland committee leaves only fifty-five lines of the original. The House rejects, 232–164, the proposal to harness the free by-product steam at the Hanford, Washington, plutonium plant which would produce 800,000 kw of electricity; why?—the coal lobby objects.

And this is only the start. Lobbies are in control. A lobby has given the oil-gas industry a 27.5-percent tax rake-off in the oil depletion allowance; modify it?—not with the veto power of the oil congressmen. Another lobby has made us subsidize sugar in half of Latin America in order to get prices high enough so we can grow sugar in the USA (which is like subsidizing banana-growing on Mount Rainier). The rest of the industrialized West has had health insurance since Bismarck but America can't have it because the medical trade union says no.

Perhaps most serious of all, at least immediately—the government can't get the legislative tools to deal with the business cycle. Our personal guess is that we are heading smack into another recession (if it isn't here already). Congress has ignored Kennedy's pleas to give him flexible tools and left him only the alternative of a one-shot tax cut which, even if adopted, is very likely to be too small and too slow.

It is the essence of the two-phase American political system that periods of advance follow periods of consolidation, operating like a two-cylinder reciprocating engine. But what if the advance phase gets blocked? It did for FDR in 1935–36; it is happening again now. If it continues it produces a constitutional crisis.

Kennedy's election represented the breakthrough of the New American—the new ethnic, religious immigrant stock, the big-city man. So what happened? Electing a Boston Irishman president automatically puts Eastland and Byrd in charge of Congress! Either one of a score of reactionary, segregationist moguls with seniority chairmanships in Congress can delay or kill a bill. They are the Supreme Court obstructionists of today. In the Medicare bill vote, for example, the Democratic chairmen of ten Senate committees voted against Kennedy.

Our curious government has two gears: normally it limps along aggravatingly in "low"; then in an emergency it leaps into "high" and works effectively. In an emergency the president takes semidictatorial powers. (We think this is an awfully dangerous system; it continually dangles temptation before strong leaders. Someday it is going to cause trouble.) The present constitutional crisis may have to reach the emergency stage, it seems, before it gets any better.

What should Kennedy do? He has got to go out and educate the public, we think, as he should have from the first. Kennedy's goals are good but he has tried to "sell" Congress instead of the nation. There is danger, too, in his middle-road approach. In the Cuban crisis one group told him to go in, another to stay out, and Kennedy took the middle course, which was the worst possible one to take.

So in the economic choice: conservatives a year ago told Kennedy to leave the economy alone; liberals urged him to act vigorously. Kennedy took a middle course and here we are with a recession ahead.

A president trying to get action must guide public opinion, that is his first job. Kennedy could have spent some of his immense 1961 Gallup Poll popularity telling the nation unpopular things about the sluggish economy; he didn't, and as the recovery slowed down Kennedy's popularity ebbed anyway.

Maybe we are crazy. But we think the cardinal thing the nation must realize is that it cannot allow 5 million unemployed workers to sit much longer on one side of an invisible line looking at 10 percent of America's factory capacity unemployed on the other. As somebody said—who was it?—we have got to get the country moving again.

A jury awarded former CBS performer John Henry Falk $3.5 million libel damage the other day from a nasty witch-hunting crew called Aware that got him boycotted in the 1950s, and before we forget about it we want to make an observation. We think the jury punished the wrong party. They should have assessed the damage against Frank Stanton, head of CBS. Why did CBS let Falk go? Because it welshed in its moral responsibility to the nation; one of its men became "controversial," so they threw the innocent to the wolves, the way industrialists did Jews to Hitler. If Stanton has any reply, we should like to hear it; in fact the public deserves it. How about a nice CBS documentary labeled, say, "How CBS Yields to Anti-Communist Blackmail"? . . . We were impressed and moved by Martin Luther King, who talked here last week. He speaks quietly, patiently, firmly, quotes Victor Hugo and Herbert Spencer, and follows Gandhi's nonviolent civil disobedience technique. One of the most important living Americans, we should say.

The Kennedy Technique

APRIL 13, 1963   The mood in Washington is subtly depressing, with Mr. Kennedy conspicuously avoiding showdowns with Congress, and Congress taking a ten-day Easter rest from the burden of not having done anything for three months. It is a recess within a recess. John F. Kennedy maintains a cool, confident demeanor and sticks to the legislative "rhythm" theory that Congress, left to itself, will ultimately act. It probably will, one way or other, in time. The penalty is, however, that issues are not dramatized, the country is listless and bored, and the president is increasingly on the defensive.

Mr. Kennedy's technique is now familiar—to talk a strong line and then compromise. The quickness of these compromises is startling and lowers supporters' morale. Sometimes they just form ranks when the battle is called off. Mr. Kennedy seems backing away from his tax bill (dangerously inadequate to begin with); he immediately cut half a billion from foreign aid after getting the right-wing Clay Report (a report with just enough good in it to be described as a mitigated disaster), and he threw in the sponge this week on the $2.7 billion general college aid bill, in return for House Rules Committee clearance of the $237 million medical school aid bill. It is assumed that the committee released the one as the price for dropping the other, or a settlement of about ten cents on the dollar.

It is often argued that this is the only way to operate "in view of the mood of the country." But how do you change the mood if you don't fight and occasionally charge the barricades? If Governor Rockefeller is the GOP nominee next year as expected (with a possible try in 1968), it is distressing to think how alike the two candidates will be. Seemingly there will be less difference than in 1960.

It is interesting to compare the UK and the US today on the economic front. Their problems are strikingly alike: sluggish economy and severe unemployment. But in Britain the unemployed riot; in the US they wouldn't think of such a thing though the rate is twice as high.

Leaders in the UK and the US propose the same remedy, planned deficits and tax cuts. The Tories offer this as a matter of course and give most benefit to low brackets; the US regards it with moralistic suspicion and President Kennedy finds it necessary to give the rich a bigger cut.

Finally, in Britain Parliament ratifies the cut at once and the medicine takes effect immediately; here, the House committee stage alone will take to June when hearings start all over again in the Senate. Will the US patiently wait, suspending disagreeable symptoms till doctors agree? Unemployment is down somewhat this month, but we still have grave doubts.

Wall Street, however, has few doubts. It is in fine fettle and everyone is getting rich. Normally the average yield from stocks is higher than bonds, to compensate for their greater risk. For over half a century the yield on stocks has averaged 5 percent, whereas today the Dow-Jones industrial average is down to 3.3 percent, a danger signal to some. Stocks have been climbing back to their '62 peak, when they sold to yield well below bonds. This is described as the most unfavorable relationship in sixty years, with the single exception of 1929.

Why don't the US unemployed riot? "I am surprised there is not more of an outcry," Labor Secretary Wirtz admitted to columnist Jack Herling the other day. "Unemployed are scattered; many are in isolated pockets. The group most seriously affected, the unskilled, the youth, the Negroes, the older people, are the least articulate politically." Then too, it seems to me, the long New York newspaper strike has strengthened misapprehensions about trade unions. The old labor ogre is trotted out again as a snarling Jimmy Hoffa. The fact is, time lost by strikes was only 0.16 percent of total working time last year, compared to a 0.27-percent average for the past five years: the figure is going down. It generally does when there is heavy unemployment. America lost more time by unemployment last year than it has from thirty-five years of strikes.

Is the trade union movement growing? We can't see it. Only about a quarter of American workers are organized, and the rate is declining. Well then, are workers' wage demands pricing them out of jobs? Not according to statistics.

Unit labor costs have risen 29 percent in West Germany, according to the National Industrial Conference Board, and 37 percent in France, but in the US only 6 percent since 1954, with a slight decline since 1958. In the US, in short, productivity has outstripped wage gains.

In the UK unemployment brings a riot; in the US it seems to be a more subtle poison. It is making it unsafe to walk in cities after dark because of idle gangs and juvenile delinquency; it is slowing down the economy as idle families retrench on purchases; it is costing the states more and more as unemployment drains insurance funds and tempts them to retrench on schools and hospitals. In the long run society might be better off with a riot.

Unemployment

APRIL 27, 1963   America's unemployment rate has been 5 percent, or above, for sixty-four out of the past sixty-five months. There is a continuing gap between actual and potential GNP of over $30 billion a year. Temporarily there is a business pickup, but almost nobody believes it will get to the heart of the problem of America's sluggish economy.

Once more President Kennedy goes to the country, this time through the forum of the American Society of Newspaper Editors, to explain patiently the facts of life. And once more the wailing counterchorus begins, warnings about the budget, the deficit, inflation, and the need for offsetting slices in Federal expenditures.

How long can this thing go on? We saw Eisenhower produce recession after recession and all the time scare the country with the inflation bogeyman. Now we see Kennedy compromising and limiting what has to be done to placate the ancient shibboleths. We have, in fact, been buying price stability at the cost of unemployment and business stagnation, and this, in effect, is what we shall continue to do without drastic action.

In the UK, Reginald Maudling has just budgeted for a bigger deficit, relatively, than Kennedy's, and a bigger tax cut and a bigger spending increase. Nobody in London cries "fiscal irresponsibility," or demands offsetting appropriation cuts, and the revered *Economist* asks why the tax cut wasn't two-thirds larger?

What is the difference between the two countries? It is, we think, that America is in the grip of economic infantilism. It is governed by ancient terrors of things under the beds. Kennedy gives the facts but the public can't believe them, though it can't deny them. Is the debt burden dangerous? How silly can you get!—its weight in relation to GNP has been cut in half since 1947. Is federal debt skyrocketing? The idea is preposterous! It has increased 15 percent in fifteen years while corporate debt has increased 200 percent. Is inflation here, or threatened? Nonsense! The US has had a more stable price level than any other big country; wholesale prices are actually now below five years ago.

We-ell, maybe these statistics are so, doubters say, but surely the president ought to make *some* concessions to ancient prejudices when he offers a tax cut on top of a deficit; he can at least balance it off by cutting federal expenditures by an equal amount.

This is enough to make a highstrung economist jump up and down. To begin with, Kennedy has been making concessions; his two years in office sometimes seem like one long concession. He came to the White House underestimating the economic problem and has only belatedly made it central to his legislative program. He has offered a tax cut that amounts to less than $3 billion the first year ($10–$15 billion would be better) and that pays obeisance to fiscal orthodoxy by freezing budget expenditures other than space, defense, and debt servicing. He distributes the proposed tax cut in large part to business or people with higher incomes (the UK tax cut will go almost entirely to smaller consumers).

As to the suggestion that a tax cut must be "offset" by budget reductions, that is a final example of economic infantilism. A tax cut stimulates the economy by giving people more money to spend; if the government simultaneously cuts its spending, it cancels out and negates the very thing it is trying to do. Yet this self-evident fallacy goes on and on.

Americans keep on paying attention to Cuba when the real problem in Latin America is Latin America. Nearly all countries are involved. Hubert Humphrey said recently: "We are asking for a peaceful democratic revolution. We ought to understand that such a development is unique in history." To put it another way, a revolution is inevitable in Latin America; the question now is only whether it will be a peaceful democratic one or a bloody communist one. This pessimistic reporter has always rather suspected it would be the latter.

Latin America recalls Karl Marx, a revolutionary who, by the way, never recommended violence. He merely looked at cruel European laissez-faire capitalism 100 years ago and decided that the rich would get richer, the poor, poorer, and the whole edifice would collapse of its own weight. Well, Marx was wrong. In most modern states the rich-poor gap has narrowed enormously, for reasons which Marx never foresaw. But the gap between rich and poor *nations* is widening all the time. A 524-page UN report last week had startling corroboration: lands with incomes below $200 a year had a 1950–1960 growth rate of only 2 percent; countries with incomes $700–$2,000 averaged about 3-percent growth a year. Marx may be vindicated in a way he never expected.

Limitations of the Office

MAY 18, 1963   Washington under Kennedy, somehow, isn't the way we thought it would be. A good many people are trying to decide why. It is worthwhile to pause and consider the matter.

The odd thing is that Mr. Kennedy seems disturbed and disappointed, too. He told the editors here, recently, about the limitations of his office. Last week he told the Machinists that he was "astonished" as president to see how "difficult" it is to pass reasonable, progressive legislation. It seems to preoccupy him. Mr. Kennedy campaigned in 1960 as a crisis candidate, who would make full use of presidential power. He would bring a sense of urgency to Washington. So far as we can see the country has little more sense of urgency now than in 1960.

Not a terrible lot has been accomplished, either. The president got extensive tariff-writing authority, but this is a tool, not a finished product. He will also ultimately get a tax cut. More important, perhaps, he has accepted, once and for all, the idea of a planned deficit when needed to boost the economy; a conception which, we guess, no later president can ever reverse.

But these accomplishments are much less than we hoped; in fact, the Kennedy administration is puzzling. Everybody begins to note it; it is finally symbolized in a Herblock cartoon showing 1960 Candidate

Kennedy reminding 1963 President Kennedy of what he said about using "presidential power." What happened? Whose fault is it? Let us marshal some commentators.

Cornell professor Andrew Hacker, writing in the *New York Times*, says there has been a diminution within the public of a sense of indignation, of idealism, of involvement. Not much use, he says, "in exhorting a self-satisfied public to a state of mind it does not care to embrace."

Apathy. That is the word. It constantly comes up. Richard Rovere in one of his admirable *New Yorker* "Letters From Washington," refers to "the immense political presence of public apathy. It deadens the air, and muffles and muddles controversy." Even the fixation over Cuba, Mr. Rovere suggests, is less because of public indignation (the Gallup Poll indicates that the public is not overly roused) than because Cuba is about the only issue the GOP has. America is fat and bored, in short, and, says Mr. Rovere, "there is evidence on every hand that the country fails to share Mr. Kennedy's alarm over the disorders he would like to remedy."

For eight years this writer thought the national apathy was due to General Eisenhower, the great human tranquilizer. But in all candor, we must readjust our thinking. Ike didn't want to get the country moving again; Kennedy seems unable to.

Is it because we are prosperous, or is it something in Mr. Kennedy? Critics of the president wonder aloud. Columnist Doris Fleeson sees "a creeping conservatism," and argues that the Kennedy view of the presidency is "undergoing radical change." He now frequently refers to the limitations of his office, she notes, whereas the "great" occupants of the White House have dwelt on its powers and expansibility.

Walter Lippmann talked about the president in his Olympian TV interview the other day: Mr. Kennedy is right, he felt, "not to get into a deadly fight" over issues he can't win. But he added, "he's sometimes too cautious. I think that a public leader, at times . . . has got to get into struggles where somebody gets a bloody nose."

This is at least the most specific charge, and we believe there is something in it. There are qualifying circumstances, of course. Mr. Kennedy can't win in the House without conservative southern votes. He must operate under America's incoherent political system, and deal with a legislature that is only efficient in a major disaster. Then again, the president, we guess, is preoccupied with world affairs: he speaks solemnly and responsibly of the nightmare of proliferating atomic weapons. Civilization is like a rat, trapped in a maze; there seems no way out.

In fairness, these difficulties and awful responsibilities must be cited. Yet, somehow, we felt Mr. Kennedy would do more. He is aware of urgent, even desperate, domestic issues yet he has not communicated his feelings. Political leaders, we believe, must create a certain commotion and tension; they must show passion, they must be involved; the public likes a scrap. Andrew Jackson did, and Wilson, and the two Roosevelts and, of course, revolutionaries always trot out some bogey or other, often spurious.

We thought Mr. Kennedy was taking matters into his own hands a year ago in the lusty row with Roger Blough over steel prices; he was right, he was irresistible and, we thought, splendid.

But the administration recoiled. Why, it said, it *loved* big business! It was almost abject in its professions. Today business begins to think the president maybe isn't too bad after all. This, to us, is a bad sign. Big business in the modern world is the natural antagonist of big government; the other pole of the power structure. Safety depends on the two keeping a wary eye on each other; the time to watch out is when they climb into bed together. Big business, experience shows, is desperately shortsighted on nearly every subject: when an administration breeds with big business you get a Clay Report.

Notes In 1952 Richard Nixon brought a lump to our throat with his TV account of Pat's cloth coat, the $80-a-month apartment, and the "house in Washington which cost $41,000, and on which we owe $20,000." Last week our Dick bought a $135,000, twelve-room, "luxurious" cooperative apartment (five baths) on Fifth Avenue in New York, with $10,000-a-year maintenance. Our hero has Made Good.

The Political Risks

J U L Y 1 3 , 1 9 6 3   This is a fascinating time in American politics. Take the Democrats first. President Kennedy has irrevocably committed himself to the civil rights cause. Maybe he came late, maybe he had to come, but here he is. Inevitable compromises lie ahead but there will be less of them if he has full liberal support. As Karl E. Meyer aptly described the Kennedy speech after the Governor Wallace episode in Alabama: "The succeeding words were those of an otherwise prudent politician who has crossed a moral divide."

There is a real political risk for the president. Southern segregationists despised Truman but seem to hate Kennedy. He quietly told Negro leaders at an off-the-record conference at the White House, June 22, that a forthcoming poll would show his popularity had dropped, for the first time, "below 50 percent." There was ambiguity over which poll he meant. The Gallup and Louis Harris polls both show a plunge since he took his civil rights stand, particularly in the South, but his overall popularity is still around 55–60 percent.

Mr. Kennedy may have referred to a particular question put by Harris, did the public like the way he was handling civil rights and race problems? The response was a toss-up: 49 percent favorable; 51 percent unfavorable. The South—75 percent unfavorable.

To sum this up, Kennedy might have postponed or temporized; he did neither; when the chips were finally down he acted decisively and swiftly with eyes open; he took big political risks.

The upheaval on the Republican side is still more interesting. It coincides with two other developments, the collapse of the Rockefeller boom (because of his remarriage) and the steady, nationwide infiltration of the GOP by the ultraconservatives and the Yahoo-right. The eastern internationalists (the "Eisenhower-moderates" as we might call them) have been thrown into confusion by the Rockefeller collapse and the Goldwater rush into the vacuum.

What is happening is a real fight for the Republican soul. The Yahoo-right is conservative first and Republican second; it seems incredible that it should denounce Eisenhower as too liberal, or that it should seriously threaten a great political party. But remember that a typical group, Lifeline Foundation, Inc., broadcasts over 300 radio and TV stations (in Washington you can hear it twice a day, seven days a week, over WFAX, a Virginia holy-roller-type station) and that the same kind of thing is being pumped out by other tax-exempt foundations over the country. They have captured a GOP salient, the National Federation of Young Republicans; they have seen Kennedy alienate the South; they have watched the liberal front-runner, Rockefeller, falter and all but eliminate himself, and they have their own leader of the far right, Goldwater.

As always, the perplexed General Eisenhower offers an element of humor. He doesn't like the Rockefeller type—too liberal, worries too much about unemployment, belongs to the twentieth century! On the other hand, when he took office Ike didn't turn the clock back. He accepted social reforms and merely called a holiday on new ones. What Ike can't understand is why the radical right hates *him* so. The quasi-fascist John Birch Society attacks presidents, the Supreme Court, and national leaders—Eisenhower is a "Communist stooge," Earl Warren should be "impeached." Ike doesn't know it yet but almost certainly, we guess, he will ultimately throw his weight to some moderate or compromise GOP candidate. It may come too late.

This brings us now to that dashing and attractive romantic, Goldwater. What does he stand for? The record is almost unbelievable. His foreign affairs approach: brandish the bomb, support banana dictators, withdraw recognition from Communist countries, invade Cuba, retreat from the UN, take a "strong" stand around the world, and save money by reducing military expenditures! The package of dogma symbolizes the myth of America's invulnerability and supremacy.

His primitivism in domestic belief is just as breathtaking. He would abolish the graduated income tax (substitute a fixed-rate income tax on all alike, rich and poor). He favors the compulsory open shop and calls the federal school program illegal until the Constitution is amended. He would make a tax cut conditional on a balanced budget. He believes unemployment can be solved only by private investment. The Birchites, he believes, are mostly fine people, though he thinks their founder, Robert Welch, is now a handicap and should retire. In general, Goldwater likes patriotism of the raw-meat variety; he considered the late Senator McCarthy a sincere man and was one of the few who voted against his censure by the Senate in 1954.

What is Goldwater? He is the poet of a romantic dream that is all over; he is the leader who evokes a mystic faith in ardent followers that somehow he can lead them back to the virile pioneer virtues to the sound of plunked banjos and of creaking Conestoga wagons. It is fortunate for the country that Goldwater has Jewish blood; it curbs the crypto-Nazi racism of some of his supporters. Goldwater is essentially decent; he is no racist. He believes discrimination is "morally wrong" though his remedies for it are doubtful.

Goldwater's formal education ended with high school. Would further study have made a difference? He told the National Interfraternity Conference at Los Angeles in 1960, for instance, that fraternities were a "bastion of American strength," that Harvard did not have them and was consequently radical. "Where fraternities are not allowed," he said, "Communism flourishes." The Radical Right sees a leader, a party, and an opportunity; can lily-white Republicanism reach the White House via the South?

Civil Rights

OCTOBER 26, 1963   The biggest single unknown factor in American politics today is the degree to which northern white workers and lower-middle-class voters are going to react against civil rights for Negroes. Nobody can predict this because it is a new situation.

In a competition for jobs the low-income white is often pitted against the unemployed, nonunionized Negro in big cities, just as the immigrant Irish were against slaves 100 years ago, in a bitterness that produced the draft riots and radical atrocities in New York City.

At the same time, the low-income family that has just taken a mortgage for a $15,000 house in the suburbs sullenly fears that its interest will be endangered by Negro infiltration. It produces a new phase of what Swedish economist Gunnar Myrdal called "An American Dilemma"—idealism vs. self-interest, guilt vs. greed, conscience vs. prejudice. This isn't a southern phenomenon but one in the big northern cities. "The Negroes are moving too fast" is the slogan. It is the counterrevolution against the Negro revolution.

The problem is not insuperable but it would be unwise to deny it. Mr. Kennedy has stated several times that he thinks civil rights is costing him votes. One or two mayoralty elections hint that the Negro upsurge—or Negro Mutiny, as it might be called, against second-class citizenship—is causing trouble to entrenched Democratic city machines from other minority groups. Particularly interesting will be Philadelphia, November 5, where Republicans are quietly using this election issue against Democratic Mayor Tate.

Analyst Louis Harris has come up with a poll on the subject for *Newsweek*. He thinks the administration has gained an additional million Negro votes since 1960 by its handling of this particular issue, and simultaneously lost 4.5 million white votes (particularly in the South). Even so, Harris thinks, the president would beat any GOP opponent by 4.5 million as of now.

(The latest Gallup Poll downgrades Mr. Kennedy with the lowest popularity rating since he took office, but still gives him a majority of 57 percent.)

Gunnar Myrdal in his new book (*Challenge to Affluence*, $3.95; Random House) is again looking at the United States, and is worrying about the recession after our next boom. Like nearly every other European he can't, for the life of him, understand why we distrust our government so. In Europe, the state helps ameliorate the problems of unemployment, sickness, and impoverished old age. Myrdal is a kind man, who loves America, but he sadly sees poverty hardening into a permanent "underclass" here; a tragic new caste of semitouchables. "There is an ugly smell rising from the basement of the stately American mansion," he says.

We thought it would be a bright idea to list the points on which Senator Goldwater switched position in his current Great Mutation from the extreme right to center, but we gave it up as too confusing. The

AP's Jack Bell offered some examples: Goldwater voted against the Kerr-Mills health-care bill, and after it was passed attacked the Kennedy administration for "sabotaging" it. Jerry Landauer in the *Wall Street Journal* had a try: Goldwater today, he reports, wouldn't call Chief Justice Warren a "Socialist," as he did in Jackson, Mississippi, in 1959, and he no longer believes that the Supreme Court's 1954 desegregation ruling "isn't necessarily the law of the land."

Benjamin Bradlee of *Newsweek* had the most amusing experience. Goldwater headed a national right-to-work committee in 1958 and introduced a "mandatory right-to-work law"; he now denies introducing such legislation. Bradlee recalls that Goldwater told *Congressional Quarterly* in August that the graduated income tax might be eliminated "if we had a budget of less than $50 billion." He now denies saying that (it was transcribed by a stenotypist). When asked by Bradlee why he had voted for the $6-billion farm appropriation bill last month in contradiction to earlier opposition, he denied that he had done so; when shown that he was paired for the bill, "he called the clerk of the Senate and had his vote changed to no." Defining Goldwater's position is like trying to nail Jell-O to a tree.

Sometimes it occurs to us that the country will ultimately just burst into a merry laugh over the candidacy of the man the Navahos christened "Barry Sundust." Of what other presidential candidate can it be said, as the *Wall Street Journal* seriously reports, that he is having a punch-card system installed so that he and his managers can find out what he has said on manifold subjects? At the moment they don't know.

Maybe we are wrong, but we doubt if Barry's views can stand examination. Rockefeller was mean to challenge him to debate. There is a tendency to forgive Barry as the victim of too many ghostwriters. But he has another enemy, too. His name is Mister Ad-Lib. Just on his recent trip to San Antonio, according to the AP, he told the Military Order of World Wars that Latin American military juntas "are almost entirely operated in the best interests of the countries." And reporter Ronnie Dugger reported to the *Washington Post*, October 3, of the same speech, that he said he didn't fear military men—"I say, fear the civilians—they're taking over." This is a long way from General Eisenhower's warning on the subject. The difficulty for the Republicans is that if Barry doesn't get the nomination his noisy far-right supporters are going to sulk, and sit on their pocketbooks.

And finally, a contributor sends a paragraph from the *Minneapolis Sunday Tribune* quoting Billy Graham: "If I'd stayed longer in England in 1954, I feel the Profumo scandal might not have happened. We had huge crowds and the whole nation was stirred, but I was tired and had lost twenty-five pounds. . . ."

How We Look

N O V E M B E R   1 6 ,   1 9 6 3   Suppose you could take a microslice of America today and put it under a slide 100 years from now, what would the historian note? The United States was the only industrial nation that did not have a comprehensive health insurance program for its people. The idea was still denounced as "Socialism," after that old creeping Socialist Emperor Franz Joseph, who introduced it in Austria in the '90s.

It was a nation with affluence and depression simultaneously. Three fifths of the prosperous public considered buying a second car; another fifth had poverty (families with income under $4,000), another fifth deprivation (income under $6,000), and there were 12½ million utterly destitute.

Unemployment over 5 percent had continued for six years, and the government was less and less hopeful of a cure; in 1961 the "interim" goal was 4 percent by 1963, but in 1963 the Council of Economic Advisers hoped for 5 percent, by 1965 or 1966.

The dial in the growth-rate meter pointed to "economic stagnation": only 2.8-percent growth in the 1953–1962 period. The growth rate of its rival, Russia, was at least twice that. However, this was not felt to be a threat because Russia suddenly had to use its gold to buy wheat, and this was interpreted as an economic "collapse," although the Soviet industrial splurge seemed to be continuing much as before. Russia has rammed its head again against the doctrinaire wall of collective farming where the cure seemed simple enough, anytime it cared to take it. America clutched the same fond hope in the space race; Khrushchev said he wouldn't be hurried to the moon, and Congress almost instantly cut space appropriations.

Who controlled this happy land? There were two great power centers, big government and big business. The former was shamefaced and apologetic for being so big, like an overgrown boy, and leading citizens denounced it severely for its fault. Population jumped 3 million a year (it was taboo or illegal in many states to offer birth control information), but Congress gasped at the government budget which increased with the people. Even the president bowed to this entertaining myth. In a groping way big government often defended the public, but the critics argued that affairs could much better be turned back to the states, i.e., that civil rights be turned back to Mississippi.

If big government was under attack, what was the position of big business? Two examples help give the answer.

The single biggest employer in the city of Birmingham, Alabama, was the gigantic US Steel Corporation, managed from Pittsburgh. Birmingham was filled with bombings against Negroes in the great racial upsurge which distinguished the period. (One bomb killed four fourteen-year-old Negro girls, dressed in their best at Baptist Sunday school, and J. Edgar Hoover's famous FBI couldn't find the culprits and made no report.) Would Roger Blough, head of US Steel, use the economic influence of his company on behalf of civil rights in Birmingham? At a press conference October 29, Mr. Blough recoiled from the idea as "repugnant to me personally." He said that to "attempt to exert any kind of economic compulsion to achieve a particular end in the social area seems to me quite beyond what a corporation should do."

Example No. 2 was similarly typical. Materialism and laissez-faire were elevated into patriotic symbols. Back in the '20s the new mass medium of radio offered itself for the first time for commercial exploitation. In 1922 a commerce secretary named Hoover called it unthinkable that these facilities should be "drowned in advertising chatter." Forty years later William Henry, chairman of the Federal Communications Commission, told a House subcommittee that commercial self-policing had failed; that the so-called industry "code" in 1948 proposed twelve minutes of commercial time an hour; that in

1963 it said eighteen minutes, and that stations habitually exceeded this, up to as much as thirty minutes. For thirty-five years of big government as policeman, FCC has been saying that "overcommercialization" was bad, but in all that time it had failed to say what overcommercialization was.

In the atmosphere of this quaint era, the House subcommittee chairman (Representative Rogers, D, Texas) denounced the FCC; not, interestingly enough, for failing to slap broadcasters down, but for presuming to think it could regulate them at all. Mr. Rogers proposed to amend the Communications Act to ban the FCC from prescribing standards for length or frequency of commercials. The public showed an amused interest in the matter.

This public detachment offers one of the most typical aspects and rewarding studies of the Affluent-Depression Era. The country elected a War Hero in 1952 and 1956, but from 1954 on gave him a Congress controlled by rivals. In 1960 it elected another president in a virtual tie vote, and left him with a Congress indifferent to his requests. No clear mandate came to Washington from the voters for a dozen years.

Emotions were occupied in this period with fears abroad; ambitions, with acquiring goods at home. Bemused between two rivals, big government and big business, an anxious, wealthy nation was content with the second-best. Chronic unemployment became accepted, and a kind of underclass seemed to be forming, composed of the invisible poor. Crime increased and churches thundered against it. Only in one sector was there pressure for reform, and this came from the Negroes.

THE JOHNSON YEARS
[*1963-1968*]

What About 1964?

DECEMBER 7, 1963   All we have to remember are some flashes of wit, the symbol of a rocking chair, and a phrase or two, "Ask not what your country can do for you—ask what you can do for your country." And, yes, a feeling that somehow we are guilty in some indefinable way, and let him down.

In the great hall of Congress where Lyndon Johnson addressed the joint session the audience tried awkwardly to identify itself with all this by applause. It was a good speech, movingly delivered on a great occasion—the kind of epilogue which Shakespeare lets a surviving character deliver over a stage strewn with hopes and corpses. Penciled at the bottom of one text are the words: "One of the most moving I have ever heard; they are applauding, I am weeping."

President Johnson's task so far is largely symbolic: to show the continuity of things; to make the ritual plea for prayers and help; to let the shrewd leaders of the world size him up; to demonstrate that a firm hand holds the wheel.

He did this; we thought he did it well. The stock market bounced back; the Senate killed the Mundt bill that would have blocked wheat sales to Russia; the president reaffirmed a policy abroad of power with restraint; at home he tried to pry Congress off dead center, suggested the civil rights bill as a memorial to a dead president and a tax cut to get the country moving again. It had style. Those who have heard his mumbling, side-of-the-mouth delivery in the Senate were pleased.

So, let's consider President Johnson's election chances. In the current wave of sympathy for him we think they are exaggerated. We guess his chances are fair but not good; risky but not hopeless.

The calendar is the first big hurdle. Mr. Truman had three years and six months after FDR to establish identity; Mr. Johnson only eleven months.

Almost worse than this, LBJ has no firm base of power. He is apt to fall between stools. He has just enough support from Negroes to alienate the South—and vice versa. Putting present evidence together, a case can be made that he is a liberal; also that he isn't.

Don't think the political truce will last, Republicans can't wait; we give it about a fortnight. The first primary comes in March and Republicans must get busy quick. The first missile at hand is the Bobby Baker case.

Baker carried out the Senate system of rewards and punishments with which the then majority leader ruled. It was against these punishments (for having fought for cloture) that Senator Clark (D, Pa.) started his continuing fight, with other liberals, against "The Establishment." Back on July 28, 1961, the *Wall Street Journal* noted: "LBJ's longtime lieutenant, Senate Democratic Secretary Bobby Baker, still consults him and keeps him informed, but is considerably less influential among Democratic senators than when Mr. Johnson was majority leader."

Two previous vice-presidents, Alben Barkley and Richard Nixon, decided that a majority of senators at the start of a session had the right to change the Senate rules to tighten cloture in a "rule" that could not itself be filibustered. But the new vice-president in 1961 supported the southerners.

Mr. Johnson has been growing increasingly liberal in Washington, but that has been less true back in Texas. He masterminded the nomination of Governor Connally in 1962, and snatched victory away from the liberal candidate, Don Yarborough (not related to the senator). His attitude toward Senator Ralph Yarborough, head of the Democratic liberal wing of the Texas party, is equivocal.

These points are not set down maliciously but with anxious concern. An arguable case can be made on the other side. President Johnson came to Washington as a young congressman who admired FDR. But that was a long time back. Recently he has been growing more liberal again and away from his background of oil depletion allowances and segregation. He got two, much-diluted, civil rights bills through Congress in 1957 and 1960, dealing mostly with guarantees of Negro voting rights. They set a precedent. He has worked energetically as vice-president to extend Negro job opportunities.

Last Memorial Day at Gettysburg he declared that 100 years after the battle "the Negro remains in bondage to the color of his skin," and that the Negro could no longer be satisfied with the command, "Patience." Strong stuff! Last month, too, he received a warm welcome from the Liberal Party in New York, and he stoutly condemned poverty and prejudice in America.

Take the evidence and weigh it yourself. We are not convinced either way. On the personal side the new president is a poor speaker, but with momentous power. He gets information by ear (like Al Smith); is suspicious of intellectuals (like Truman); his humor is earthy—the famous Johnson campaign train through the South in 1960 was satirically dubbed "The Cornpone Special."

When he was the majority leader, strangers found it an experience to visit his sumptuous Capitol office; dryads danced on the ceiling; there was a super-duper executive desk as large as a yacht, covered with electronic devices. He pushed buttons and spoke to unseen presences; paced the floor till the visitor felt he was watching a restless tiger; sprang up and down constantly; and with disarming vanity showed praise and citations to the embarrassed visitor.

Set against this, President Johnson is a man of ambition, courage, and decision, of ardent patriotism and of almost manic energy. He is thoroughly American—more so than Kennedy—in his mixture of tawdriness and splendor.

President Kennedy had three confrontations with Communism in three years, and the confrontations will continue. After Cuba, Europe decided that he was not trigger-happy; in fact a queer diplomatic minuet developed as JFK and Mr. K appreciated each other's difficulties and advanced or retreated accordingly. Can the new president do that? Nobody knows.

What should Mr. Johnson do in his election fix? Everybody is giving him advice—this isn't meant as advice, it's just an estimate of the problem. He ought to tie himself boldly, we think, to one side or another, and do it *quickly*. For a Democratic president, this would seem to mean the liberal side. We would guess a civil rights bill would be an absolute "must."

Taking a risky guess at a cloudy crystal ball we would expect a filibuster against civil rights . . . possibly another march on Washington . . . a compromise bill that throws out public accommodation, FEPC [Fair Employment Practices Commission], and other elements . . . and then an effort at a deal with Senator Russell: no filibuster, no cloture.

Would this satisfy Negroes? Would it enable Martin Luther King to control violence? Would it allow Johnson to carry big cities? We can't guess. We rather doubt it.

Hand It to Lyndon

FEBRUARY 15, 1964 Kennedy forged the nails of the legislation that Johnson is now hammering home. Bang, bang, bang, see them go in! There is the tax bill in the Senate, and the House is shortly going to pass the most sweeping civil rights bill of the century by a big majority that will isolate in advance the southern senators in their upcoming filibuster, and that will reflect the will of the nation.

Let's hand it to Lyndon. He is probably getting as much out of this Congress as anybody could get; more than Kennedy could have got, we suspect. He may even pull off Medicare.

Congress distrusted Kennedy. They had known him as an inconspicuous senator (i.e., not majority leader) and it was hard to forgive his success. He was an intellectual and in his speeches quoted foreigners the Centerville Senior Class never heard of. His views on economics increasingly challenged America's Victorian folklore.

In retrospect we see now that President Kennedy created the first White House court. Style, grace, elegance filled it with Mrs. Kennedy adding a touch of grandeur. Never forget there was a Camelot! Now as the eggheads quietly depart (Sorensen, Schlesinger) their place is filled by excellent Dr. Eric Goldman, Princeton historian, who will be Intellect-in-Residence (unpaid), ostentatiously picked, as the White House puts it, to draw "the nation's best thinking" into 1600 Pennsylvania Avenue. Judging by the lack of humor, what the administration needs even more is a court jester.

We may sigh for things gone, but the Kennedy bills are being passed. The business community distrusted Mr. Kennedy; they did it intuitively; now they are rallying behind President Johnson. Whether this love affair was made in heaven remains to be seen. Personally we hope not; it always gives us the heebie-jeebies to see big business and big government cooing in the same love nest. But the houri is being given a $12-billion tax cut and the union is being sanctified with a budget cut and so has the blessing of the Koran itself. Some economists may be aghast wondering whatever happened to tax reforms and whether the proposed stimulus isn't a bit rich for a steady diet, but when did economists ever understand these things? The Johnson program seems to guarantee a preelection boom, and if the Chamber of Commerce calls it holy, it must be all right.

You can see the political effect of this strategy from the sour speeches of Republicans. They make some attacks on Johnson fiscal "legerdemain," but then tend to drop the subject. He has stymied them. More and more they are turning to foreign affairs.

Here indeed gigantic changes are occurring irrespective of politics. We won't argue rights and wrongs; we just point them out. Before our eyes the great American postwar effort to isolate communism by nonrecognition and boycott is collapsing. Our friends and neighbors are scrambling to trade with Moscow, Peking, and Cuba. Even we are selling wheat to the Russians.

Secondly, we can beat our breast about Vietnam and General de Gaulle, yet the fact is that the situation is deteriorating and unless we are prepared to attack a privileged sanctuary and broaden the war we shall be lucky to escape even with a stalemate. And a stalemate (i.e., neutralization) looks like a good thing.

As far as trade with the Communists goes, this column generally favors it. We have earnest friends, whose opinions we respect, who abhor it. But we try to be honest and must say that we think the bonds of exchange and commerce, yes and man's cupidity, can aid peace as well as damage it.

Politically, however, this is a heaven-sent opportunity for Nixon, Goldwater, and Rockefeller too to beat their breasts and wail of failure. If President Johnson tries to work out an accommodation they can chant "soft on Communism." (The same thing is true of Panama;

Kennedy had achieved a technical skill after his Bay of Pigs debacle such that the crisis in Panama probably wouldn't even have happened.) It remains to be seen now whether Mr. Johnson can learn the diplomatic ropes fast enough to deal with a changing foreign policy, and whether he has the courage to face certain Republican attack. The alternative their "strong" policy offers in Vietnam is another Korean War.

There is just space left for two other observations. Looking down at the Senate tax battle, we see the white mane of Illinois' Paul Douglas wherever the fight for the little man is thickest. It is a complex debate but in a legislature of lawyers economist Douglas understands it. In a rich man's tax bill Paul Douglas is fighting for the common man. As we think over the great senators of the past, Webster and Clay, yes and Norris and LaFollette too, we believe we have one representative of the conscience-driven breed left, Quaker-crusader Douglas.

Does God need a memorial to be built to Him in Washington? President Johnson thinks He does. But then the president also thinks that the true image of Washington is not one of power, pomp, and plenty, but of a "prayerful capital of good and God-fearing people."

We mournfully suspect that Mr. Johnson is wrong on both counts. God doesn't need a material memorial, even one that is supported by all religious faiths, which is what the president suggested to International Christian Leadership when he spoke last week at its annual Presidential Prayer Breakfast. God does need pure and contrite hearts. And so does Washington, which could also do with fewer monuments.

TRB's Twentieth

MARCH 7, 1964   All this talk about the fiftieth anniversary of *The New Republic* caused us to look back at the dusty manila files of our own contributions. Good Lord, there were twenty of them! Yes, it was 1944 when we started making regular contributions to this space. We pulled out the crumbling pages uneasily, remembering the casual invitation of Bruce Bliven to take over from Ken Crawford, and wondering what monstrous blunders we should find.

January 3, 1944: "Mr. Roosevelt's implied criticism in his Christmas broadcast is interpreted by some here as the start of the fourth-term candidacy."

Ah, me! So that was it, was it? And next week FDR was re-capitulating New Deal accomplishments: "It was amusing to watch the president's face. He is a good actor and put on a look, whether real or studied, of self-deprecatory worth as he recited them, a good deal like a modest but excellent scholar compelled to read aloud the latest marks on his shining report card."

How it came back, the arch grimace, the cock of the cigarette holder, the self-enjoyment, the enemies that made us love him and the complete mastery of his medium—that was FDR.

In early 1944 there is talk of a man named Wendell Willkie; of "the forthcoming cross-channel invasion" (not "an" invasion, mind you, but "the" invasion) and a passing comment that "China is in a dreadfully difficult position" (just how difficult we were to discover soon enough).

TRB, we note, used the first person singular a good deal in those days, a journalistic problem not settled even today, though we always remember the man who told us that nobody should use "we" except royalty and people with tapeworms.

We got engrossed in our anniversary. Here we were needling the *Reader's Digest* for its article (August 1943) by Louis Bromfield: "We Aren't Going to Have Enough to Eat," grimly headlined by the editors: "What muddling in Washington has done to our food supply." Farmer Bromfield terrifyingly predicted, "The situation will grow worse this fall and reach its most desperate stage this winter, especially from February on. If it were possible, I would rather not think about next February. By then most of our people will be living on a diet well below the nutrition level."

Bromfield made his prediction of February famine in August, and now here it was February 1944, and it seemed legitimate to kid the magazine a bit. How young we were then. For twenty years *Reader's Digest* has had as dire a prediction of socialist calamity in nearly every issue, and its multimillion readership laps them up. The magazine was and is the only large-circulation periodical in the world that we know about (outside of Russia) that adamantly refuses to publish letters correcting mistakes, or giving the other side. (A letters-to-the-editor column is the Bill of Rights of responsible journalism.)

We find references to splendid newsmen of twenty years ago, Tom Stokes and Nate Robertson and Ray Clapper, who died that year on assignment. Suddenly, we discovered ourself, to our own horror, on shipboard off Normandy covering D-Day, the most scared correspondent of the war. Dawn found us on Hitler's doorstep like a milk bottle. We had a panoramic view of thirty miles of beachhead, and the only discomfort was the annoying jolt of our own eight-inch guns. War, you know. We remember how, suddenly, over from England thundered a line of glider-borne troops towed by transport planes, passing above us in soul-stirring formation, the twinkling spiderweb filament visibly connecting transport with glider; and even as the great endless host continued to roar past on one side of the ship, the first transports without gliders were returning on the other side.

It is a pleasure and a pain to read old columns. We never wrote one that couldn't have been better. A lot of our predictions look silly. We can't believe we ever influenced anybody very much, if at all, though it is nice to remember that JFK read us regularly; personally we deplore this staccato literary style which is an outgrowth of an effort, we suppose, to cram too many ideas into 800 words, like the coats bulging in a closet at a cocktail party.

Twenty years have brought TRB doubts about a lot of things but more certainty than ever about one, that private affluence can't continue beside public squalor, that "planning" has somehow got to emerge in America from being a dirty word, and that, probably, big government is going to get bigger, with the kind of social services in the US that all the other Western nations already supply.

We think these changes will come fairly quickly; yes, in another twenty years, and principally for this reason: Back in 1944 when this writer began here, the population was only 134 million; last week it rolled past the 191 million mark. The Census Bureau tells us that at the present rate it will be 252 million in 1980. Figure it out: just in a twenty-year eyewink America has added as many people as there are in the British Isles, and at the present rate of 3 million new arrivals a year it will add 61 million more in the next sixteen!

If you take an Olympian, twenty-year view like this, some things become simpler. Success in defeating reform by urging that things be "turned back to states" is about over, we think, because states are up to their neck in IOUs now. Washington's debt has been slowing down, so see what's happened to state and city debts!

In the same perspective, most of what the federal government is doing in social service is peanuts; the pending public-housing program of 60,000 units, for example, seems to us to be ridiculous tokenism.

Again, take public spending. If President Johnson feels he can win conservative votes by boasting of cutting down the budget, he is probably politically right; that is, till after the election. The old myths die hard. But population growth is implacable; selected public spending must increase. You doubt it? Wait twenty years and see.

The War on Poverty

MARCH 14, 1964   "There is an ugly smell rising from the basement of the stately American mansion," writes Gunnar Myrdal in *Challenge to Affluence*. The cause? Poverty. An "underclass" is trapped in affluent America. Poverty passes on from father to son.

Poverty is finally becoming visible because of the Negro revolt. President Johnson is launching a war on poverty. Good, so far as it goes. Quite independent of Mr. Johnson, the report of a three-year study, issued by the National Policy Committee on Pockets of Poverty, points out that "poverty is no longer a condition which strikes all kinds of individuals but rather tends to characterize the *great majority* of individuals in certain large 'poverty-linked' groups."

Only one in eight of America's families as a whole in 1960 had a cash income below the destitute level of $2,000, the report finds, but the proportion rose to one in three in the following poverty-linked groups: nonwhite families, families headed by a female, couples 65 years of age or over, some farming families, families whose heads had less than eight years' education, and families whose heads had at most only part-time work experience. Where a family had not merely one but two or more of those characteristics, the probability of poverty was overwhelming. It might rise to three in four.

President Johnson's war on poverty is fine—as a start. But it is not something that Sargent Shriver is going to overcome with a pilot project. Here we get to the heart of the maldistribution of opportunities and wealth in affluent America, and it will ultimately require collective action of a size which other big nations have widely accepted but which Congress has generally viewed with horror. Personally, we haven't the slightest doubt that the US will ultimately act appropriately, too, but it will mean the overturn of some of the nation's fondest myths. Medicare seems to be an opening wedge.

Tax cuts won't eliminate poverty—the destitute pay no income tax. Faster growth won't solve poverty—as Kenneth Galbraith says (in a recommended article in the current *Harper's*), "Growth is only for those who can take advantage of it."

What will help this increasing, debased subclass of poverty-prone families to climb out of their sandpit? Youth training corps and low-interest loans to industries will help, but in general we see no alternative to really large-scale, ameliorative federal social welfare action and payments. Just to put a tag on it, we mean something in the order of, say, $10 billion a year.

We aren't winning the war on poverty. Suppose you had to answer the question, "Are the rich getting richer, and the poor, poorer?" What would you guess? The answer is, we don't know for sure. The Council of Economic Advisers' 1964 report said one third of US families were below the arbitrary $3,000 poverty line in 1947, and about one fifth in 1956. Fine progress! But since then there has been little improvement if at all. "The progress made since World War II has not involved any major change in the distribution of incomes," the Council says. Indeed, the current rich man's tax cut may widen the gap.

The Pockets of Poverty Committee, whose roster includes Harry Truman, three Nobel Prize winners, and James G. Patton, head of the National Farmers' Union, as chairman, criticizes the CEA report as underestimating the number of impoverished families. It says the poverty gap is widening.

Modern society counteracts economic inequality by two approaches: the graduated income tax (which only a few extremists like Barry Goldwater oppose), and a whole complex of social services and · benefits (which most conservatives doubt, deplore, or decry). Schools, parks, old-age pensions, and school lunches superficially benefit everybody, but obviously the poorer you are the more they mean. They are like the graduated income tax. The conservative who cries "economy" against such measures is not hurting himself but the poor.

Recently TRB talked to some undergraduates in the Midwest and the discussion turned, as so often happens, to European experience, ignoring Canada. This rejection of Canada must be Freudian; we don't see something we don't wish to see. (Obvious solution: fortify the border; then we'd know Canada is there.)

Twenty years ago Canada passed the Family Allowance Act, under which the parents of every child under sixteen get a monthly allowance, rich or poor alike. Under ten it is $6; under sixteen, $8. It is the celebrated "baby bonus" and on the twentieth anniversary of its passage perhaps the most popular law in the Dominion. The flow of money stabilizes the economy; it has a connection with school which has improved attendance; it has meant better-fed and better-clothed children and, oddly enough, it has not apparently encouraged poor families to breed (as critics predicted); at any rate, the ratio of families with five or more children has declined. Parents haven't squandered the money on rum, either.

Annual cost to Canada: about half a billion dollars. US equivalent with ten times the population would be $5 billion a year.

Think what Canada's family allowances would mean to Negro families in Alabama and Mississippi! Can't they be annexed to Canada in some way? We are quite persuaded that US action of this magnitude is inevitable before long. Negro militancy has made American poverty as bothersome as a sore thumb. It won't go away; affluent America is not going to endure an impoverished hereditary underclass or that smell from the basement of its stately mansion.

Martin Luther King

APRIL 11, 1964   It would be more tactful perhaps if Martin Luther King, when asked about the civil rights bill, should smile blandly and say, "Pass the measure and I am sure all racial issues will vanish." More tactful, perhaps, but dishonest.

Social revolutions, alas, don't come to an end with a single bill. We have taken a long time to get this far and there are years of struggle ahead. Dr. King is a realist; in a gentle tone he tells reporters of three plans, each calculated to put opponents' teeth on edge. First, after a month's Senate debate he will conclude that a genuine filibuster is under way, and he will urge agitation all over the country. "Another march on Washington—?" He won't say.

Second, Dr. King says simply that the present bill is good but not good enough, and that shortly after it is passed (if it is) he will probably start working on another. And third: if the pending bill is passed, he and his friends will shortly thereafter stage a series of legal tests over the South to prove its efficacy and enforcement. It is hard to believe that such tests can occur without a battle.

In short, looking ahead, Dr. King in his mild way does not offer a very tranquil prospect. "If the bill doesn't end pressure," it might be asked, "what's the use of passing it?" The answer is, of course, that the pressure and probable violence will be vastly worse if no bill at all is passed.

Every great social revolution produces its inevitable counterrevolution. This has punctually appeared in the civil rights fight in what has come to be called the "whiplash effect." A number of northern white communities have been rejecting racial equalization proposals for residences and schools, and there are other portents of political reaction. How far they will go nobody can say, but it would be folly to ignore them. That is the spark Alabama's racist Governor Wallace is trying to fan, in entering presidential primaries in northern states.

The first of these comes immediately in Wisconsin. Nobody can guess how he will fare. It will be difficult to interpret the primary because Wisconsin allows Republicans to cross over and vote on the Democratic side and Birchites and Goldwater supporters will certainly do so. It is rather fortunate, on the whole, that the man who has made the challenge is Wallace. Shrewd Dixie politicians may be sorry that it is an all-out racist who is carrying the police-dog-electric-prodstick mentality into the South's appeal for northern support.

Every president is entitled to the kind of press conference he wants, but we think that something important has gone out of Washington if Mr. Johnson continues with the pattern of present Saturday gatherings. These are held, one would imagine, deliberately to keep coverage down. It is the worst time of the week for journalistic makeup with big Sunday editions going to press early and with many papers with no Sunday editions at all. Most of the bureau chiefs and columnists have closed up shop for the week, and the White House force is composed of "regulars"—the band of able and dedicated newsmen who are exclusively assigned to the executive offices and go with the president wherever he goes, from Texas to San Francisco. They can ask pointed questions but they are not apt to make an issue of things and still stay in the White House retinue.

There is nothing in the Constitution, of course, that says a president need hold any press conference at all; and yet in the absence of a parliamentary question period, the untrammeled conference has come to fill a place in American government. Press and president both benefit from it. The president can find out what the public is asking, and the press gets a chance to watch the man that they are writing about.

This reporter was never sympathetic to General Eisenhower's policies and yet time after time we came away from his press conference liking the man. The conference did much to reduce tension all around.

The Johnson press conference that seems to be emerging is a controlled affair. Notice is generally not given in advance; the time is arranged with a maximum degree of awkwardness for the reporter who normally has assignments elsewhere, and the limited group who attend are chiefly the spot news regulars who have a considerable interest in retaining passable White House relations. In short, it is the kind of limited conference that Mr. Johnson used to hold back when he was senator, informal but impatient, sometimes nonresponsive, and often brusque.

Mr. Johnson would be much more exposed, of course, if he submitted to the large-scale conferences of his predecessors. Not once, for example, has he been asked direct about the $1,200 TV advertising contract that came to the LBJ TV station at Austin, Texas, in conjunction with the $100,000 life insurance policy written by the then partner of Bobby Baker. It would be better for everybody if the awkward question were disposed of once and for all.

Lacking the old, air-cleaning give-and-take of large-scale press conferences we detect a larger than usual growth of rumors and "revelations" among the gossip columnists, and an enlargement of journalistic personality-sniping that often is associated with clogged news channels.

Johnson-Humphrey vs. Goldwater-Miller

SEPTEMBER 5, 1964   The two conventions are over now. We wrote this after midnight in the frantic, jam-packed pressroom after the nomination by acclamation of Johnson and Humphrey. And what did we think about? One thing: Are there enough zealots and bigots in America to elect a team like Goldwater and Miller? We hope not, we think not, and the polls say not, but just to have the possibility arise scares us. Who says Barry can't get elected? The very people who said he couldn't get nominated.

In daylight hours we aren't frightened. Barry seems to be floundering. His writings show him just next thing to a crackpot. Really, how can you take seriously a man who opposes the graduated income tax? Or one who would delegate the incinerating nuclear weapon to bomb-rattling generals? In wonder we ask about his trick of waggling his fingers through lensless glasses to a crowd; is there something symbolic here?

And his running mate. It's in dreams that we see Representative William Miller as vice-president. Goldwater picked him, this hack politician and graduate of the House Un-American Activities Committee, so near defeat in 1962 that he announced he would not seek reelection. In fourteen years, Mr. Miller never got a major bill named for him; he introduced the Eisenhower civil rights bill in 1956, and then changed positions and attacked it when it reached the floor. His bill for 1955 was to incorporate the "Moms of America"; in 1963 to repeal the prayer decision. Why was he chosen? Mr. Goldwater's explanation seems to fit the wildly improbable selection as well as anything; at San Francisco he told the GOP state chairmen, "one of the reasons I chose Miller is that he drives Johnson nuts."

That was San Francisco. The thing we remember best there was the convention crowd jeering Governor Rockefeller, and later on the stunned surprise of fellow newsmen at seeing the triumphant nominee rubbing the noses of Republican "moderates" in the mud even after he had beaten them. This broke all the rules of his own self-interest. Goldwater has thought better of it since; but his speech at Hershey wasn't the one he gave for his acceptance.

And now we have the sequel, the Atlantic City show. It would be nice to paint it heroically. We can't. Mostly it was a dreary wasteland of Lyndon-knows-best. Convention speakers like John McCormack kept saying unctuously that Providence guided JFK to pick LBJ in 1960. There was also a speech in favor of women. Yes, honest, just in favor of women. A woman made it, and said how important women are, particularly, we guess, Democratic women.

How does a reasonably modern political party react to a shuddering explosion of primitivism? The first discovery we made was that the anachronistic US convention system is so cumbersome that its passion drains out in clichés. It was like trying to slay a dragon with a stuffed club. Then the Mississippi Freedom Democrats arrived, and at first it seemed that this mostly Negro band of tattered heroes would be mangled in the convention system, too.

Just when we had given up in despair and decided that democracy couldn't be saved, if worth saving, we saw, with a kind of awed tingle, democracy climbing out of the pit. Yes, painfully, laboriously, ridiculously. The creaky convention system was actually functioning; in an organization as loose as a folk-moot, a consensus was forming; simple decency was defeating expediency.

If Alabama's Democratic committeeman, "Bull" Connor, who

started it all with his whips and police dogs, didn't like it, he could climb back into "Uncle Tom's Cabin," but the convention was going to, and did, seat a couple of these Freedom Democrats, with no discernible legal right at all, as delegates-at-large; and thank God for it. The astonishing precedent was set: the stuffed club had a flatiron in it.

Then there was the scene from which we came just before writing this, the anointment of Hubert Humphrey. Corny it was, to be sure, but for a couple of minutes it was a good theater.

The president has been trying to milk suspense out of his vice-presidential selection for weeks, and it reached the stage where it was just turning sour. If he hadn't named Hubert he would have disgusted the party. Well, he did it finally, we must say, in the grand manner. In his sudden appearance at Convention Hall he paused, waited, and then fairly yelled the name, "Senator Hubert Humphrey of Minnesota."

We lapped it up and so did the crowd. The White House these days is not a very emotion-stirring place, nor is it blessed with much humor. Hubert Humphrey can help in both respects. Again, Senator Humphrey's liberal record points the direction in which we hope the Johnson administration will go. Even more than the Democratic platform, Humphrey's mere selection underlines the contrast with the Goldwater party. Compare Miller's ex-membership in the HUAC with Humphrey's past and present membership in Americans for Democratic Action, of which he is a national vice chairman.

And finally Mr. Humphrey is about our favorite man in Washington. Amidst all the recent millionaires like Rocky, FDR, JFK, Barry, and Lyndon, it is nice to run into an old-fashioned, modest-income type once in a while. Humphrey still says he married his wife, Muriel, "for her money"; she had $600 and he was so broke he had left college to run the family drugstore at Huron, S.D.

Working heroically by his side, she helped him get back to college, and with shining eyes he ultimately paid her back with a degree *magna cum laude*.

"*Goldwater Will Be Badly Defeated*"

SEPTEMBER 26, 1964 A foreigner traveling with Barry Goldwater in the South wouldn't know there were any Negroes in it. They seem to have withdrawn from main streets; they don't appear at his political gatherings; they aren't asked to sit on the speakers' platform. Nor does Barry discuss civil rights. He tell reporters that "states' rights have superseded civil rights," so there's no use bothering with them. The issue is everywhere, it intrudes on everybody's thoughts, but it's like sex—it isn't mentioned.

Senator Goldwater preaches a moral revivalism with a mystic quality. "I don't like the way the country is drifting," he tells a breakfast at Winston-Salem. "I find it hard to put my finger on what's wrong. Something deep in your hearts tells you that something's wrong. . . ."

Again at Atlanta he says, "I believe you people have something on your minds, something in your hearts. I don't know just what it is. But I think that after another week or ten days I'll know what it is."

That was September 15, so by the time you read this the Republican nominee may have discovered what's worrying the country.

The senator baffles, frustrates, and ultimately infuriates many reporters traveling with him; curiously enough, he eludes many in his audiences, too. He is a striking, handsome, romantic figure as he comes before the microphones. When his interviews begin appearing in homes in the big TV program soon, his popularity ratings should jump. He has a dashing, sun-dusted, boyish attractiveness. He rarely uses oratorical flourishes. He says the most extraordinary things in a low-keyed, matter-of-fact way.

The audiences cheer, they applaud everything he says, but somehow he doesn't satisfy them. They want to be whipped up; he doesn't do it. They want a catharsis of emotionalism for their anxiety and frustration and hate but he doesn't give it to them. The lovers meet and neck and then go off to separate homes. The affair isn't consummated.

There's never been anything like the Goldwater campaign. He makes electrifying assertions and then wafts away; he offers programs but only leaves more questions. There is a dreamlike quality about it. Any one problem would take an hour to explain.

In October 1963, he suggested that the government sell the Tennessee Valley Authority. And so he comes to Knoxville, home of TVA, and explains that a president couldn't sell TVA anyway, and that what he said should be considered in the framework in which he said it, namely that "a power-mad group in Washington" is trying to get a "planned socialized economy." The important thing, he adds, is that "the people in an area should have access to adequate power at reasonable cost," and "that I stand by." The crowd applauds dutifully. What did he mean? Overhead an airplane tows a sign of masterful political compression: "Vote LBJ Keep TVA."

Mr. Goldwater wants a weaker central government but with a stronger foreign policy; he wants less federal spending but a larger military establishment; he would achieve economy by abolishing the draft and relying on voluntary enlistments (which would require higher soldier pay, and cost more), he wants the government to remove "bullies and marauders" from city streets but opposes a federal police force.

It goes on and on. He tells farmers that he would reduce or end price supports; Florida pensioners that he would not expand the Social Security system.

Most baffling perhaps is his 5-percent-a-year five-year tax cut plan for corporate and individual income taxes. He tells an audience at Birmingham that this is a "fair principle of equal treatment for all." He assails the "gimcracky" Johnson tax cut, which of course he voted against. Questions burst forth. How would a poor man benefit who pays no income tax at all? How is it "fair" to level off a purposely graduated tax so as to give far greater benefits to the big than the little? Mr. Goldwater doesn't say.

And endless debate goes on among the traveling observers as to whether he believes what he says. One correspondent recalls traveling with him and expostulating with him about his rash comments to reporters. Senator Goldwater disarmingly agreed. They arrived at Chicago and a group of newsmen were on hand; they put a microphone in front of him. "An American professor has just been arrested in Russia as a spy," they told him. "What do you have to say?"

"Maybe he is a spy," said Mr. Goldwater.

Senator Goldwater is going to be badly defeated. He is getting fair crowds but not enormous ones, and the South is his best hope. Doing better than Senator Strom Thurmond in Dixie isn't going to help him in New York. He is an amiable no-think, a man who shouldn't have been named by either political party, a failure of the convention process.

But Senator Goldwater is going to leave his impress on America. His nomination and campaign in the South come at a moment of historic party fluidity and realignment. The GOP will never be the same again. What he is achieving is a lily-white southern Republican Party that isn't likely to be effaced easily by party moderates in the North. Senator Goldwater will lose this year; but he's only fifty-five; he isn't going to pass and be forgotten like Senator Joseph McCarthy.

He is likely to leave a political legacy behind him.

Johnson Wins

NOVEMBER 14, 1964   Lyndon Johnson is the first man in history to be elected for defending the twentieth century. We have a stake in him, and hope he does well, and are going to watch him sharply. Normally we feel this is the Republicans' job, but there aren't too many of them left, and they are going to be busy for a while, anyway, moderates and Goldwaterites, blaming each other. We think each of them is right.

Why did moderates permit a patently unsuitable man like Barry to be nominated? He scared the whole world. It was a dereliction of responsibility. And why did even conservatives of the truculent type think they could elect a candidate whose clock goes tock-tick? But it is useless arguing with them.

Normally in America there are two parties, a party of Hope, and a party of Memory; a party of innovation, and a party of consolidation. And so in election year the Future debates the Present. But in this wasted year the Present debated the Past.

If there is one thing that the campaign proved to us it is that the old, motheaten Halloween bogey of "government bigness" doesn't really scare Americans anymore, if it ever did. You can see the candle through the pumpkin eyes too clearly. The American economy isn't going to drop "Capitalism," and it isn't going "Socialist"; it is going to be a Mixed Economy, as it is now and as most of the Western world is. It will continue to judge each proposal—whether TVA or Medicare—on its merits, and not by some scary (and often self-serving) label or epithet. In fact, we think the United States, by and large and most of the time, is mildly liberal—not enough so, perhaps, to satisfy us, but basically progressive for all that. It doesn't want the clock shoved ahead and it doesn't want it turned back; it does want the hands of the clock to keep moving forward.

Mr. Johnson, who is now president in his own right, strikes us as an intricate, complex figure; many men wrapped in one, layer on layer, like an onion. He is obsequious and imperious by turn, sensitive, garrulous, and gregarious. Sometimes he is hard to take. He indulges in shameless sentimentality and occasionally rises, if we may say so, above good taste. His mobile face and manner make him look like a kind of parody of the stage politician with Foxy Grandpa eyes. He is easy to denigrate and many Republicans do, who are now picking themselves up off the ground.

Mr. Johnson is also, we think, one of the supreme masters of the terribly difficult art of parliamentary control and consensus achievement. And what is an American political party anyway, but a collection of coalition minorities hunting for a consensus? The president has a capacity for finding common ground that is almost hypnotic. His versatility and repertoire are enormous. He can range from the noisy, hypothyroid "y'all come to the speakin'" appeal to outdoor masses, to the solemn, low-spoken earnestness of his final TV talk to the nation before the election, which we thought one of the most effective political talks we ever heard. Mr. Johnson, in short, seems to us after long and patient observation to have many qualities of greatness, and now it remains to be seen whether he has greatness itself.

One good thing in the election is how well the liberal Democratic senators of the class of 1958 and thereafter did. As pointed out by the National Committee for an Effective Congress, a lot of them were opposed by Goldwaterites. A year ago it was widely asserted that the whole batch was doomed. Instead, in the Johnson landslide they are mostly back again, starting second terms. They include men like Burdick, North Dakota; Yarborough, Texas; Moss, Utah; McGee, Wyoming; Hartke, Indiana; and others. It is in the second six-year service that committee seniority really starts. Give them a few more years and they will be a new power in the nation.

We don't want to carp. But the Goldwater campaign was, by all odds, the classic example of bungled politics in our lifetime. The press leaned backward, trying not to be judged unfair to Republicans, so that many points in the parade of errors went unemphasized. But consider: Barry praised brinkmanship to the German periodical *Der Spiegel* even before he was nominated; hailed extremism in his acceptance speech; picked unknown Representative Miller, N.Y., as running mate, who proved a disaster; demoted professionals in favor of amateurs in the national organization; denounced the Supreme Court; attacked TVA in Tennessee, pensions in Florida, and the antipoverty program in Appalachia; welcomed aboard that Jonah, Strom Thurmond; took the clergy to task; and—poor chap—even violated unwritten canons of good sportsmanship by delaying congratulations after he was defeated! This was either a man who actually courted defeat, or one with a tin ear to the tacit consents of American politics.

And now President Johnson has two years of power before the next election. He will probably enjoy more prestige and freedom to initiate now than at any other time in first or second terms. Will he use it? Ike wouldn't. Will he reconsider frozen policies toward Red China, Vietnam, de Gaulle? Will he push social amelioration measures in Congress? This is it, the now or never, the critical time.

New Deal II

MARCH 20, 1965   I don't think the public has grasped yet the social revolution going on now in Washington under Lyndon Johnson. Bills are passing, or being prepared, that would have seemed impossible two years ago. Some of us have dreamed about them for forty years. Popular attention, naturally enough, is centered on Vietnam and Selma, Alabama. But the social revolution is going on, anyway.

It can only be compared to the Roosevelt New Deal. In a sense it *is* the second half of the New Deal. The New Deal was interrupted by the Supreme Court, a balky Congress, and war. It was left unfinished for a quarter century. Now bills are becoming law, or are being readied (for almost certain passage) as important as the FDR programs.

Why isn't there more tumult and shouting? For one thing, their passage seems inevitable. The Supreme Court is favorable. Conservatives are impotent. They tied their hands when they nominated the preposterous Goldwater. They were crushed, and it served them right. They threw their veto power down the well.

Lyndon Johnson, a rather unlovable president, has a two-to-one majority in both houses, unusual manipulative skill, and a drive for greatness. It seems almost impossible now that anything can stop the Second New Deal, short of war.

Johnson is readying the greatest school bill since the Morrill Act (land grant colleges). The precedent-shattering Medicare bill can only be discussed in superlatives. Fantastically enough, there is a tendency to expand it in the House committee. Republicans and the American Medical Association complained that Medicare "did not go far enough." Trying to kill the bill they offered an alternative—a voluntary insurance plan covering doctors' fees, drugs, and similar services. What did the House Ways and Means Committee do? It added the AMA feature to its own bill. Will this pass? We don't know, but some bill will pass.

The Appalachia program became law last week. What the public doesn't understand is that this big measure creates the precedent for a new federal-state relationship. Almost certainly it will be applied to other areas. The federal government delegates its decision-making to the eleven state governors (working through a new regional commission), and the states and communities will do the planning and more or less run the show, subject to federal veto.

We can go right on. Bills are being prepared in orderly procession, like floats for a parade. The president sends up a housing and urban development proposal: true, the amount involved is relatively small, too small; but it contains a radical provision for direct federal rent payments to certain classes of disadvantaged citizens. FDR was denounced as a revolutionary, but we don't recall that he came up with that audacious plan. . . . A new civil rights bill is imminent; bills on crime, river and air pollution, high-speed rail transportation, and whatnot, are on the way.

The public just says ho-hum. With hardly a murmur it has accepted the technique of planned deficits. Who is that wailing out in the wings? Only a chap named Eisenhower; he seems to be all alone!

And now let us add another feature. Sums allotted to many of these Johnson programs are preposterously small for their ornate titles. The "War on Poverty" is a case in point. It suffers from acute malnutrition. But this must be said: the LBJ proposals will probably cost twice as much next year as this. They are precedents, a foot in the door, a camel's nose under the tent—in short, a first down payment on an installment purchase.

The Johnson Second New Deal is a "buy now, pay later" affair. We wondered at first that businessmen didn't object to it more. But after all, why should they? Buy now, pay later . . . they invented it.

In a spirit of nostalgia we went up to the Senate Foreign Relations Committee last week to see the launching of the latest $3.38-billion foreign aid bill. Such bills have been going up ever since 1946 or before. The annual wrangle is as typical of Washington as the cherry blossoms. Right away you could see that nobody loves foreign aid. It has no constituency.

It is a great big committee room with cork floors, waxed wood panels, dull bronze light sconces, elegant simplicity, and bad acoustics.

TV men have set up their lights. They reflect brilliantly from the curved crown of the secretary's head. He makes his pitch in a relaxed way. Don't turn back from "frustration or fatigue," he says.

It is a kind of alumni reunion. They all know Rusk; he knows them. Physically he is not imposing. But he sticks to his points. Nobody ever gets mad at Rusk. In the question period he makes no great effort to reply or respond. He gesticulates negligently with the stem of his glasses, or touches them to his mouth.

Facing him is a horseshoe dais of senators: old antagonists. Chairman Fulbright wears dark glasses against the blinding lights, and looks like a hood. Sparkman (D, Ala.), genial, putting on weight, takes up the questions. Then the ranking Republican, Hickenlooper, Iowa—who ought to be holding a pitchfork in Grant Wood's "American Gothic"—gives foreign aid a few isolationist kicks, but in the tone of one who knows the wrangle will probably go on for months, as it did last year.

The questioning wanders about. Clark (D, Pa.), wonders why we don't push birth control abroad. Lausche (D, Ohio), who has the pompadour of the elder LaFollette and the outlook of a Bricker, discusses tourists. Rusk keeps saying he will supply a memo on this or that.

From the sides of the lavishly inappropriate room, where reporters sit, Rusk's replies are often inaudible. Nobody knows how many hours, weeks, months Rusk will take on this, when he ought to be studying Vietnam.

TRB's Mother

OCTOBER 23, 1965 On May 22, 1894, James C. Emerson, the unofficial and unpublished chronicler of South Lee, New Hampshire, recorded in his journal, "Finished potatoes, planted 16 bushels." On

August 31 he wrote, "commenced digging potatoes"; on September 25, "Finished harvesting potatoes; no of bushels 172."

Not long ago TRB took the ashes of his mother back to South Lee to the family burial plot. From it you can see the farmhouse where she was born. She lived two years short of 100. Not many Americans, anymore, complete the cycle and come back at last to the place where they started.

The one-room school where Susie recited, with seven brothers and sisters, is now a shed, behind a crossroads store. It once stood on the Lang farm. A boy would take the pail across the road into the pines and dip into the ferned spring. Winter and summer everybody drove to the unheated Union meetinghouse where the minister spoke two hours, and the hooves boomed in the shed behind. A hundred years ago the township was mostly Congregational. (A hundred years before *that*, the descendants of the people who had cut off the King's head were Puritans and New England was pretty much a theocracy.) They still call it "the Mast Road" in Lee. That's where the King's men logged down the giant trees for fitting the Royal Navy; for all I know Lee timber helped Nelson win Aboukir.

They were Protestants; they were homogeneous; they were farmers. So, indeed, was most of America. There was the good feeling it would always be that way. They had come successfully through the Civil War. The race problem was settled; the Fourteenth Amendment fixed that. Susie's father paid the $300 bounty for a cousin to take his place in the war. The lad waved and laughed as he went down the dirt road. All her life Susie had the picture of what they told her—the gay boy going off. He never came back.

Susie and Edna boarded at Newmarket so they could go to high school, and Grammie Harvey kept house for them. The cocks woke them in the morning, but even before they got up they heard the French Canadians clattering down the street to the fortresslike textile mills. After sundown they came back. Once Susie found the French Canadian girl who lived above them sitting on the back stairway, weeping. Why was she crying?—she was making good money.

One Sunday afternoon Susie's father was signing five-dollar bills on the gingham tablecloth of the kitchen table. Yankee farmers did odd jobs and one of his was being bank president. (Nowadays, bank presidents don't harness up Old Zeno and carry dressed turkeys in the fall over to Portsmouth to sell!) Susie got bored and went up to the low, slant-ceilinged front bedroom and got absorbed in a book. She pored over it as the hens drawled and the light faded from over the Pawtuckaway Mountains—driving her nearer and nearer to the small-paned window that you propped up with a stick. She came down in a daze. The book was a Latin grammar. With that book you— anyone—could talk like the Romans. Yes, really, *anyone!* She decided to go to college.

She presented herself at Smith College in 1887. What, no Greek? . . . Tears, but not many. Setting a firm jaw, Susie went out to acquire three years of Greek in eight months at the New Hampton Literary Institute & Commercial College, at the other end of the state. Then she came back to Smith with a firm look. She sailed through four years at Smith, taking one year off to teach and help pay for it. (In 1961 she came back to her seventieth reunion and got a standing ovation as she told them the class motto: " '91 won't be outdone!" She was the only one left.)

America was changing, of course. But the real change wasn't the auto and the airplane and zoom-zoom things like that. Starting back there in the '80s, or earlier, it was becoming, really, a different America. Immigrants were pouring in, and later on the sons and grandsons emerged. Ribicoff in Connecticut, Goldwater in Arizona, Kennedy in Massachusetts. Good or bad—? How could anyone say! Of course things don't stop; there will be changes in the next 100 years, too—gigantic, no doubt. But will moon-travel alter the country as much as the quiet revolution in the American people of the past 100 years?

Suddenly, as it seemed, it wasn't wrong to enjoy the Sabbath. The railway came to Lee: they put a spur across the Lang farm. And then, seventy years later, they took it up again and made a highway. Boston & Maine stock sank to 10. (But at 2:45 on a dark night you can still hear the two longs and two shorts of the whistle for the Lee depot, and then the rumble of the Bar Harbor Express coming round the bend.)

What happened to the Yankees? The mills went south. Granite pastures couldn't compete with Iowa loam or California, for that matter. Lee township dropped from 800 to 350. But the change went deeper. The doors of the old Union meetinghouse swung rustily. There was a neat new white church—with thirty people in it. The expiring Puritan ember flickered once or twice: Prohibition; the quota law; Hoover beating Al Smith. . . . Maybe the Yankees had seeded the nation, as some said. But the new era had come.

It did not break Susie's heart. She wondered at some changes; she accepted some; some she loved. She loathed government debt; liked to clip government bonds. Girls wore skirts awfully high. Young people hugged and kissed in public. But there! Young ones had been silly before. She laughed at the way Will Plummer wouldn't sell rice for her marriage to the school principal; wasteful, he said. And the way George Swain on the buggy ride hurled the brandied chocolates into the sumac bushes. Alcoholic! . . . And her life Susie would recall George Swain, and how noble he was; and the chocolates, and regret them. Susie got older and older but she was always interested. She was not a mite afraid of dying, but she sighed a bit at not being around to see how things turned out. It was never half past the hour for her; it was always thirty minutes to something else.

Ninety-eight years is a long time for a person, and even for a young nation, too. But at last she is back on the farm again where she started. The shagbark hickory and the stone wall have hardly changed at all. It is quiet and serene and matter-of-fact. On a farm you put your potatoes in in the spring, and count them out again in the fall (a little wonderingly) when the harvest is ready.

Papa Knows Best

AUGUST 7, 1965   For a fortnight the nation waited in mounting tension. What next in Vietnam? Always the question, "What will the president do?" Never the question, "What should he do?" No debate in Congress; virtually no editorial advice in newspapers; a universal, overwhelming attitude of papa-knows-best. We don't ever recall seeing it quite so strong in the US before.

Then, finally, the press conference summoned for Wednesday, July 28. LBJ has decided. We are going to be told. Reporters hurry down past the White House; sightseeing buses are bumper to bumper across the way, along the entire side of Lafayette Park. Happy tourists snap pictures through the temporary mesh wire fence where the old iron rails are being renewed; they move in colorful, chatting, shirt-sleeved crowds in and out of the venerable executive mansion.

Reporters jam into the chilled East Room, its sacred precincts turned into a Hollywood set, gilt chairs, parquet floors, gold silk drapes, disapproving George and Martha Washington, scintillating sunburst chandeliers all tangled with snakelike cables. There is a new electronic gadget, a Polynesian-style ceremonial umbrella, crystal white, canted over the podium. A light glares up into its underside and apparently this reflects the beams down again, like a lens, on the speaker below. There is last-minute adjusting of two teleprompter one-way mirrors, and the huge TV machine, directly into which the president talks. It's a funny thing: he seems to be looking straight into the living room of 10 million homes reciting it all by heart, and what he's really doing is reading it from a one-way mirror, right through which the machine is taking his picture! It's all done with mirrors.

He speaks quietly and soberly. It is a kindly, patient, fatherly voice. Troops will be raised from 75,000 to 125,000; the draft doubled. We are "the guardians at the gate" (i.e., policeman of the world).

He finishes the Vietnam statement, then announces Abe Fortas's appointment to the "Jewish seat" on the Supreme Court. (And what a distinguished line it has been, Brandeis, Cardozo, Frankfurter, Goldberg!) Also, John Chancellor of NBC to head the Voice of America, the hardest job, some think, in Washington.

But what about Vietnam? Reporters ask questions. Answers tell little. In fact, after all this wait and buildup the president leaves the war much as before—not as escalated as some had expected and with new nuances, perhaps, for negotiation—but bigger, nevertheless. A ghost war in which every hope so far has been illusory, a land war in Asia against which all experts have warned. Gloomily and reluctantly the public moves further into a struggle where at best it can only hope for stalemate and at worst where demands will increase to bomb missile sites, factories, Hanoi, China, to use tactical nuclear weapons, to use H-bombs. And China rubs its hands at each new step.

Meanwhile a lot of odd things have been going on in Washington to which little attention is paid because of Vietnam. J. Edgar Hoover, for example, the septuagenarian super-cop, has erupted again. Attorney General Katzenbach, in a comment intended to defend the

FBI, was tactless enough to concede that sometimes law enforcement agencies "think they can make a good thing by going it alone." J. Edgar was back at him in a flash: There was "not a scintilla of truth in that," he said, "as it pertains to the FBI." Earlier, J. Edgar called the Reverend Martin Luther King, Jr., "the most notorious liar in the country." As for the Warren Commission, which had mildly urged closer FBI-Secret Service cooperation, Mr. Hoover denounced it for "Monday-morning quarterbacking."

Again, the American Medical Association seems to be recouping its strength. It is now fighting the Johnson proposal for a network of regional medical centers. Vainly it fought Medicare, now the law. Medicare has bumps ahead. There are not enough nurses, hospitals, doctors. The AMA will drag its heels. Well, we shall see. The AMA has proved one of the most inept political lobbies of all time. It derided the original mild Johnson health insurance bill as a fraud which left many uncovered. Then it unwisely backed a larger GOP substitute designed to kill the Johnson plan by reducing it to absurdity. Democrats quietly appropriated the GOP-AMA plan and wrote it into the omnibus law!

In the Vietnam blackout you probably haven't read of two big antitrust cases. Ten leading steel companies (US Steel, Bethlehem, and the rest) pleaded guilty to conspiring to fix prices in the $3.6-billion-a-year carbon sheet industry. Fines were preposterously low on the ground that the companies had not contested the case. Also, the government filed suit to recover double damages from six textile companies charged with fixing prices, holding secret meetings, using dummy codes in a conspiracy to rig prices of fiberglass fabrics. The patriotic companies want to win the war in Vietnam and get good prices for fabrics used in aerospace and missile programs while they are about it.

There are twenty-eight US astronauts and their pay varies from $11,000 to $22,500. Most people don't know it but they have been permitted by the Space Agency to sign a contract to do outside commercial writing, the only federal employees so permitted. Each one earns $16,250 a year above his regular salary, whether he or his wife or family write one or a dozen articles, or no articles at all. One astronaut, like Deke Slayton, is grounded; another walks in space, like Ed White, but they pool the literary take, up to $16,250 worth, and each gets exactly alike. It means that no favored astronaut makes a killing, but that each gets a nice tidy additional income. Space Administrator Webb argues that it protects the men from editorial pressure by giving them the magic formula, "Sorry, we're under contract."

The McCarran Act

NOVEMBER 27, 1965   We went back last week to hear the Supreme Court read decisions. Always impressive. Greek temple—with microphones. Same red carpet. Same red curtains. Same white marble floors, like interstate highway before traffic. Same feeling of awe. The nine chairs behind the bench look like the Chicago skyline: Byron White's tall oblong on far left; Abe Fortas's low one on far right.

They meet at 10:00 (with frugal half hour at noon for a sandwich). This morning, four minutes late by the two bronze clocks. Oyez, oyez, oyez! They trooped in through triangular furls in great red curtains, like Ivanhoe coming through an arras. The usher asked God to help this honorable court and a swatch of newly admitted lawyers swore to God to behave themselves. The tribunal got right to work.

The big news came soon. It was so calm, so casual, you hardly realized it. But it was the end of an era. A nod from the chief justice. Justice Brennan began to speak. He looks like a hard-as-nails Harvard Irishman. He eviscerated the 1950 McCarran Act (Communist registration). Short, terse sentences; no emotion, no purple passages. All citations, all learned logic omitted for the moment, though of course left in the printed opinion; Justice Brennan was just giving the verbal essence. Matter-of-fact. Calm. (There is little outward excitement in America's judicial Parthenon. It is the eye of the cyclone, as Holmes said. But if you hold your breath you hear the gale outside.) Brennan stopped talking. Any dissents? None. Unanimous. On the floor lay a mangled corpse, like Caesar. Next case.

We got to thinking. The year: 1948. *A Streetcar Named Desire* wins Pulitzer Prize. Berlin airlift. Draft starts. Truman reelected. Red scare accelerates. In Congress the great question: how to destroy the Communist Party without seeming to do it illegally? Two political unknowns, Representatives Mundt and Nixon, propose an answer: force it to register.

If you had your old gothic-arched Atwater Kent tuned in on May 17, you would have heard the Dewey-Stassen Oregon debate on the Mundt-Nixon bill; question, should we outlaw the Communists? Yes, said Stassen; No, said Dewey. Both, oddly enough, said they favored the pending bill. Everybody felt Dewey won the debate on points. The House whooped it through, but the Senate didn't act till 1950.

Next year the Soviet exploded the atom bomb. We were betrayed.

Probes, probes. Alger Hiss, Harry Dexter White. Owen Lattimore. The Protestant clergy. HUAC took on Hollywood. Senator McCarran took on teachers, trade unions, US employees at UN. All intellectuals were under suspicion; newer ethnic groups were out to show their patriotism. And on February 9, 1950, at Wheeling, West Virginia, a little-known senator said, "I have here in my hand a list of 205 . . ." (later 57). McCarthyism was off and away.

So now in 1950 the Mundt-Nixon bill came to the Senate and became the McCarran Act. Before the tumult had died, 13.5 million federal and civilian workers (one fifth of the total US labor force) would be exposed in one way or another to loyalty oaths or security tests. The Taft-Hartley Act would require a non-Communist affidavit (later rescinded). Richard Nixon would defeat Helen Gahagan Douglas on the Red issue. (Incidentally, he tried the same thing last month in New Jersey in the governorship race: same deprecatory smile; same modest patriotism; same Communist menace. New Jersey slapped him down.)

Well, that's when the McCarran Act was born. Truman vetoed it. The House overrode his veto, the same day, 286–48; the Senate, 57–10. Things got pretty wild after that. Unexpected people used "soft on Communism" and "twenty years of treason." Congressman Velde tried to subpoena Truman. McCarthy said the Truman administration had been "crawling with Communists" and that Ike wasn't so pure, either. The revered Taft still thought he could use "Old Joe." Herbert Brownell wanted to legalize wiretap evidence. He charged Truman had knowingly promoted "a Russian spy." Ike claimed he had ousted 2,200 security risks. And good old Nixon told a campaign audience, "We're kicking them out by the thousands."

Was everybody crazy? We went back to our office and got the

Truman veto message: seventeen pages, September 22, 1950, marked "Strict Confidence—Hold for Release" by Charlie Ross. We started and read it straight through. It was all Truman. He was against "the thought control business," he said. "In a free country, we punish men for the crimes they commit, but never for the opinions they have." Communists—? We had the FBI, didn't we? No president but Truman, perhaps, would have called the exalted work of Congress a "terrible mistake."

It all came back. What a funny little man. Always trying to knock a wall down by bumping it with his head. No subtlety. No tact. No consensus. And my, my, my, how refreshing!

"The idea of requiring Communist organizations to divulge information about themselves is a simple and attractive one," he wrote. "But it is about as practical as requiring thieves to register with the sheriff."

Predictions

DECEMBER 11, 1965   We got as far as our first "We predict," in a year-end political forecast, when we checked ourself. We fished out our folder marked "Predictions." It took us completely off the track.

"There is no cause for worry. The high tide of prosperity will continue." Andrew W. Mellon said that right before the 1929 smash.

"The economic condition of the world seems on the verge of a great forward movement," Bernard Baruch told Bruce Barton in an interview in the *American* magazine for June 1929.

Poor old Hoover. "I can observe little on the horizon today to give us undue or great concern," he said, as the bottom dropped out.

But that's old stuff. Let's look at the yellowed clippings of a later date, the FDR-Landon presidential race of 1936. You recall: Landon carried two states, Maine and Vermont. Our favorite predictor here was columnist David Lawrence: "Landon to win in Pennsylvania by 250,000," he wrote in the *Boston Transcript*, October 22. "New York for Landon," is another headline on a Lawrence column. Others were in there pitching, too: "California swings to Landon with rest of West Coast," said a correspondent of the *New York Sun*, October 31. "Kiplinger Sure President Vote Will Be Close," according to headline, October 22, in the *Boston Herald*. And the *New York Herald Tribune* published what it described as "a new type of presidential forecast" by Rogers C. Dunn, a voting research expert: "Landon To Win 33 States, New Forecast Shows."

Well, we were all younger then. We were, perhaps, more sure of ourselves. But a prediction that blows up in your face can be a humiliating matter. We know. Let's pass hurriedly over Dewey's "victory" against Truman in 1948. This column (we blush to say) was so confident of a Dewey win that we went to press on it. We still recall our conflicting emotions that Wednesday morning: exhilaration over Truman's victory and mortification over our forthcoming reference to President-elect Dewey. All we can say is that the public loves this kind of thing. Nothing rejoices a reader more than to point out with a smirk, to some hardworking columnist, a little slip he has made like naming the wrong president.

Hum, hum. Here's a nice column by Stewart Alsop, June 2, 1951, beginning: "Secretary of State Dean Acheson cannot conceivably remain in office very much longer." And here's the "Newsgram" page of the *US News & World Report*, February 13, 1953, "A Look Ahead": "Eisenhower will be a strong president, a leader." Even at that early hour of the new administration, something led us to file that away.

The *Boston Globe*, September 15, 1955, had a piece: "Why Ike Won't Run Again." Seems he had promised Mamie he wouldn't.

In 1957 the Soviets lofted Sputnik into space. In a way it resembled 1929. There was the same awful jolt to confidence and the same official rush to cover up. "The satellite is a nice scientific trick," said Charles Wilson, ex-Secretary of Defense. "Nobody is going to drop anything down on you from a satellite while you are asleep, so don't worry about it."

Senator Goldwater also refused to get excited "just because the Russians have lobbed a basketball into space that goes beep, beep, beep."

Clarence Randall, Ike's special adviser on foreign economic policy:

"The satellite is a silly bauble. I am personally very gratified that our nation was not first."

General Eisenhower mildly protested that it "does not raise my apprehensions, not one iota."

Our most notable modern prophet is Defense Secretary Mc-Namara. His field: Vietnam. "The corner has been definitely turned toward victory" (May 1963). "The major part of the US military task can be completed by the end of 1965" (October 1963). "We have every reason to believe that plans will be successful in 1964" (December 1963). "The US hopes to withdraw most of its troops from South Vietnam before the end of 1965" (February 1964). We read, with mixed feelings, his latest effort last week: "We have stopped losing the war."

So where were we when we got interrupted? Oh, we were just going to offer a few speculations, *not* predictions. Chief of these is that the dominant political issue next year will be Vietnam.

There certainly is a sour mood in this capital today. Draft calls and casualties are going up, and administration officials are beginning to educate the public to the idea that it's going to be a long war. The man in the street somehow can't understand it. How can a country as rich as the US, he asks, be thwarted in a silly little war? Surely there must be some easy way out.

This is what politicians call a "gut" issue. It affects everybody. It touches a naked nerve. The issue seems likely to grow—and it is eleven months to the midterm election. Republicans have been desperately looking for an issue: inflation—? centralized government—? Johnson the dictator? People don't get roused over such matters, not when the economy is booming. But a dirty war in Asia, with your boy in it, that is another matter.

House Minority Leader Gerald Ford of Michigan says he is resisting "increasing pressure" to break sharply with the administration. Senator Dirksen and Richard Nixon want to extend bombing. Many Democrats go along. Mr. Johnson is in a cleft stick. If he tries to negotiate it will be a sign of "softness." If casualties mount, it will be because he did not use air power, or The Bomb.

Republicans insist they will not make this a political issue. But we can't believe they will keep Vietnam out of politics any more than they kept Korea out of politics.

Of course we are better mannered and less excitable today. Leopards have changed their spots, and politicians are less anxious to get elected. Just the same we predict—but no, not this week.

Stuffed with Goodies

FEBRUARY 5, 1966   This is the week we put the fifth candle on the birthday cake; the fifth year of uninterrupted economic expansion, longest in peacetime history. What a boom! Every workday morning 10,000 more people go to jobs than left the night before. Unemployment is down to 4.1 percent now and will be 3.34 percent before the year is over, the Council of Economic Advisers says. Last year, GNP increased $47 billion and, as Mr. Johnson put it, italicizing as he went: "In only seven other countries of the world is *total* output in a year as large as the *increase* in our output last year."

Who can ask for more goodies? There is no statistical table of the quality of things, of course. There is no GNP of spiritual values. How about great plays, great paintings, great poems? We have the largest number of television sets, but the programs! It would be amusing sometime to compile an annual Report to the President on Intangibles, a little disheartening, maybe; patches of poverty in the artistic map; chronic recession in aesthetics; slum clearance needed in ethical standards.

To be fair to the president, he notes the other side: "degrading poverty, revolting slums, incredible traffic congestion, bitter racial tensions, physical decay and ugliness, political disorganization, and rising crime and delinquency."

It is an old cliché, however, to pretend to deplore wealth. We don't do that. National well-being does increase happiness, we have no doubt. Assistant Secretary of Commerce Andrew Brimmer, a Negro, has been studying current prosperity and finds that it has at last begun to slop over to the nonwhites. There have been five years of expansion: "Negroes have participated in a substantial way in only the last three," he says.

Negroes are the last hired, first fired. That is why it is so vital for them to keep this boom going. The delayed Negro participation in prosperity is taking hold. In 1964, Brimmer finds, the median family income of Negroes actually grew faster than the income of white families. Negroes are still way down the scale, of course. Their unemployment rate is twice that of whites; their income per head only a little more than half that of whites.

Just the same, there are surprising figures. Unemployment among married Negro men at year-end was less than 2 percent; the same as for white men of similar marital status. The nonwhite share of the nation's aggregate personal income is pathetically small. It was 6 percent in 1962. "But as more and more nonwhites were drawn into the gainfully employed," Brimmer reports, "the ratio rebounded sharply to 6.4 percent in 1963, and it made a further strong advance to 6.7 percent in 1964."

Putting statistics aside, what it means is that thousands of the American disadvantaged—whites and nonwhites alike—are just within finger reach of the first rung of the ladder. No, we won't sneer at prosperity! Keep economic expansion going another year, give it a sixth candle, and a whole new army of whites and Negroes will climb for the first time above the bare subsistence level.

There is a more discouraging figure in the same field, however. The Social Security Administration has been making studies of families on general relief and has discovered, naturally enough, that the number is way down in the boom. Unfortunately, this can't be said of another category, Aid to Dependent Children. It is found that numbers here are virtually unrelated to trends in the economy. The number of Negro children on ADC rolls is larger than their share of the population. Edwin Dale of the *New York Times* quotes an official: "The rise in the ADC rolls, as much as anything, reflects the tragedy of the urban Negro and, as some would say, the breakdown of the Negro family."

As Theodore White puts it in his *The Making of the President, 1964* —up to 1959, when unemployment dropped, so would the number of abandoned children. But in 1959, for the first time, then more sharply in 1962, 1963, and 1964, "this understandable correlation was uncoupled." We can now add 1965. Mr. Johnson is the first president to take note of this Negro tragedy, the absence of fathers in homes. The rate of illegitimacy is ten times larger than in white families.

White calls it "biological anarchy"; slum families living in "zoological tenements." No wonder Mr. Johnson feels there is urgent need to put the hand of the disadvantaged on the first rung of the ladder. One cannot ignore it. "Both Negro and white families are haunted," White notes, "by the biological potential of the despairing Negro for upsetting the entire course of American urban civilization."

Meanwhile, Senator Ernest Gruening (D, Alaska) is going ahead with his trailbreaking hearings on birth control. He had only six other senators with him last year, now he has five more cosponsors. Typical testimony by Philip Hauser, Director of Population Research, University of Chicago: By the time a child born today is thirty-five years old, world population will have more than doubled if the situation doesn't change—a population of 7.5 billion, mostly jammed into powder-keg have-not regions of Asia, Latin America, Africa. Can there be peace where there's famine?

Notes   Affluent Averell Harriman, seventy-five, buzzed back from a 35,000-mile peacemaking mission recently, remarking, "I feel like a million dollars"; an irreverent friend remarked, "He's sick." . . . Secretary Rusk gloomily observed the other day that the earth is round: "It means that only one third are asleep at any time; the other two thirds are up to some mischief." . . . Poor Ray Bliss, GOP national chairman, is still telling fellow Republicans that they must cultivate the big cities; meanwhile House GOP Leader Gerald Ford is attacking Mr. Johnson's city rehabilitation program. . . . The warhawks were happier last week, recovering from what somebody called "Joe Alsop's peace scare."

Capital Portraits

MAY 7, 1966   Five of the most interesting men in American public life have spoken here recently. We watched them, pondered them, and jotted down notes about them, mostly under blinding TV lights. Here they are.

Fulbright. Relaxed, low-keyed, tanned face. Wears Ben Franklin glasses; peers over them. Affable. Oxford. Has aristocratic loathing for demagogues, many of whom are colleagues. I remember meeting him outside the Senate Caucus Room years back when he first saw McCarthy in action. Voice shook. State of shock. Never forget the way he said it: "Why, the fellow's a *boor!*" He alone (repeat: alone) of all senators voted against continuing McCarthy's funds. Long ago decided it was better to vote Arkansas southern segregationism and be a senator than not vote it and not be a senator. Glad he so decided. Under mellow irony is passion. He is also lazy. Won't sully hands with influence-trading or political manipulation. Prefers college auditorium to Senate floor. Now is most effective, articulate, and temperate critic of LBJ foreign policy. Started national educational campaign. "In recent years Congress has not fully discharged its responsibilities in the field of foreign relations. . . . I conclude that when the president, for reasons with which we can all sympathize, does not invite us into his high policy councils, it is our duty to infiltrate our way in as best we can." More power to him.

McNamara testifying. Theoretically on foreign aid; actually, Vietnam. Strong man. Whiz kid. Power drive! Facts, facts, facts. They pour out. Likable. Rimless glasses. Bulldog face. Apolitical. What luck to have him in Defense Department. How awful to have him in White House! Focused like a laser beam. In controversy all the time. Why do men like this leave Ford salary to serve country? Patriotism? Yes—and *power*. People don't work for money, they work for power. He administers half US budget. He awes Johnson as he did Kennedy; same drive for efficient, united, cost-conscious, IBM management of armed forces. Get 'em there; give 'em bombs. He knows the answers; knows them before senators ask the questions. How Pentagon brass hates him. How pork-barrel congressmen hate him. He's won all arguments so far. Makes them hate him more. "Shocking mismanagement," GOP leader Jerry Ford says of his handling of war supplies. Nonsense. Ford not overbright. Some slips, sure, but actually it's been incredible what McNamara's done: a quarter million army, 10,000 miles away. McNamara smiles. "Next question?" he seems to say.

John Kenneth Galbraith: keynoter at ADA convention last week. Later he coiled his six-foot-six frame under table into hot seat before Fulbright committee cameras. Big, prominent features; scion of dour Scotch-Irish Canadian Covenanters; has a scalding irony, laced with wit. Wouldn't give a dime's worth of military aid to any country with per capita income under $200: "arming the indigent," he calls it. Says "we must face seriously the likelihood that there will not again be a government in Saigon which is seriously capable of prosecuting the war along with us." Funny how nice everybody is to LBJ; Galbraith disagrees with Vietnam policy, but it's those bad advisers who are to blame: "I'm among those who regard the president as a force for restraint." Well, maybe he is; maybe he is.

Hubert Horatio Humphrey: We love Hubert; everybody does. HH helped found ADA. In 1948 Democratic convention floor fight he forced through civil rights plank that separated party from Dixiecrats. Magnificent fight; will always remember it! Element of high drama when Hubert appeared last week to make banquet speech before anti-Vietnam ADA liberals, in behalf of administration which he must defend. TRB sat at table for ten; all watching and waiting. In basement dining room for 600. Distant thrum of dance orchestra came from above. Preliminary speakers surrounded Hubert with layers and layers of cotton wool against any confrontation, or "scene." Drama oozed out. Everybody terribly sweet and cordial; HH terribly sweet and cordial; made speech about peace and negotiation. Advocated an "Asian New Deal." What does that mean? Finished at 10:58 P.M. Applause forty-five seconds at end of speech. Still love Hubert. But where is the passion of yesteryear?

And finally—Dean Acheson. (What a galaxy of performers we get!) Always see Acheson with wig, cape, and sword, just stepped out of *Three Musketeers*. Aristocratic nose, splendid moustache, magnificent aplomb. However, present mood sad. He's not testifying on Vietnam but, for a change, the North Atlantic Treaty Organization. Expresses "gnawing concern" over NATO. All de Gaulle's fault. France like volunteer fireman, resigning in face of fire hazard "capable of being ignited by a spark." The hazard? Soviet Union, of course. Acheson puts on a brilliant show. Senators awed. Can remember when senators heckled him when he was Truman's secretary of state. Doesn't suffer fools gladly. Also had wondering, haughty look, implying, "How did you ever think up that silly question?" Acheson's mellowed; hair's grayed. Makes audience feel his sorrow now: like actor, every gesture, every quiet intonation counts. Living through very tragic era, he says. One of greatest opportunities since Roman Empire to win world peace. Europe plagued since Middle Ages by countries seeking hegemony; France for 150 years, till Waterloo; Germany, two world wars. Then hopes brightened. French statesmen, Robert Schumann and Monnet, caught the gleam. . . . But then, de Gaulle. General disintegration if NATO falls; Germany perhaps turning to Moscow. A situation highly dangerous to all of us. Acheson sighed. Held room spellbound. "This I find deeply depressing," he said.

"Fellow Amuricans"

M A Y   1 4 ,   1 9 6 6   Temperamental, difficult, crude . . . thin-skinned, quick-tempered, arrogant . . . I wake up some nights asking myself if I have been fair to him. So I write this.

It was "The Cornpone Special." The time fall; the year 1960. Thirty reporters started off from Culpeper, Virginia, slashing down through Dixie. Every meeting began and ended with cracked loudspeakers blaring "The Yellow Rose of Texas." And as they left Culpeper, the vice-presidential candidate with an expansive evangelical gesture shouted out to the largely nonexistent crowd the phrase that became the slogan: "What has Nixon ever done for Culpeper?" The trip split the South and won the election for Kennedy. (Everything won the election for JFK.)

It was April, two years ago. Most families in the eastern US were having supper. Those who had TV sets on heard sudden offstage voices, studio confusion, and then the appearance of the president's Great Seal. "The President of the United States," intoned a voice. And there he was, proud as a new father, his big ears fairly shaking with gratification, announcing settlement of the four-year rail dispute that would have shut down the carriers in forty-eight hours. He spoke with the same elemental naturalness that he had used on the disputants, one standing on either side—they praising him, he praising them. He made it seem that this was normal inside a happy America.

He had got to the TV station, sirens screaming: The five-mile ride normally takes thirty to sixty minutes. He had done it in nine minutes. His warmth exuded right out into the living room. He introduced the rival spokesmen like a Head Scout producing two troop members who had just won the rope-tying contest. They seemed to be moving in a mild daze, evidently pleased to be hailed as national benefactors. . . .

This time it is the annual, 1964, meeting of the US Chamber of Commerce. He is brought out onto the big stage of Constitution Hall and left there to sink or swim, like a pop bottle tossed into the ocean. The inimical crowd looks up at this stranger. He surveys them warily out of his small, hooded eyes. He begins gravely, long pauses between sentences, then quickens the pace, departing from text and, in effect, making a new speech—an hour long instead of half-hour. There is a murmur of laughter, a little applause. I have just reread the speech. There isn't a touch of word-luster or eloquence in it. But in five minutes he had them in his hand. It was man to man. They were eating it up, slapping their sides at corny jokes, identifying themselves with the man trying to save money by lightbulb switching, ultimately agreeing against their wills that "ignorance, illiteracy, poverty" at "Inez, Kentucky," is bad for profits; being told everything in specific, concrete terms. . . . The eighty-five-year-old penniless man in the hospital who "hadn't been permitted to put a dollar per month to match a dollar of his employer's in a fund which would take care of him, after he had worked forty years, to pay his hospital bill" [Medicare]. . . .

Then I have my notes, jotted in the press gallery, in March a year ago. He presented his revolutionary civil rights program in person. Window was "winder"; narrow was "narrer"; continue was "continyah." And he addressed, of course, "Fellow Amuricans." And I have marked applause forty times. It was solemn and dignified; simple and tremendous as a hammer hitting an anvil. "We shall overcome!" he quoted. I wrote three pages of notes. Halfway down through page two I find this comment, evidently addressed to myself for after-years: "I shall always like Lyndon Johnson better for his speech on civil rights." I must have been stirred.

Well, then, there is April 8, 1966. Here is the speech he gave at San Antonio: (You have to see Texas, particularly Johnson City, to understand LBJ.) He told about following his father barefooted, "squeezing the dirt up between my toes." The latter had once told him that to lead the people, "you must love them."

More than any speech that I know, this represents the populist side of the strange, protean, towering man: "Poor women, working all day for sixty cents picking pecans, eight cents an hour. . . . Seeing little Mexican children (1935) go up to the garbage can outside that cafeteria and take the grapefruit hulls out of that garbage can and try to get enough food in their body to sustain them by hulling the hulls. I saw that with my own eyes and I have not forgotten it."

That was the speech in which he promised to help finance dental services for children, in 1967.

And so now this crude Texan, who followed the urbanely proper Bostonian, has finally got the government's foot in the door with the rent subsidy program. And has followed this up with a tremendous new four-part civil rights bill of which the latter section would strike at racial discrimination in the sale or rental of housing all over the US. Rent subsidy came through more dangers than the Perils of Pauline and is but a shadow of itself. The germ of it, however, seems reasonably safe now.

The president didn't take his civil rights bill to Congress in person this time. His literary message to Congress has all the measured stateliness which the best ghostwriters can put into it. It can't pass without Republican support, which gives Everett Dirksen exactly the classical powerbroker veto authority which we have analyzed here for you before. We assume some sort of a compromise will be struck; the housing feature killed, likely, to get the first three parts passed.

Ignoble, no doubt; purists will lament, perhaps, that Lyndon has again "betrayed" them. Personally I don't believe any president in history could have done as much: not Adlai, not Hubert, not that splendid young prince, JFK. I wake up some nights with a gnawing sense that I have been unfair to him.

Three, Two, One . . . Ignition!

J U L Y   3 0 ,   1 9 6 6   The most compelling phrase in the English language after "I do" is, "three . . . two . . . one . . . ignition." Let's talk about both expressions.

We found ourself down at Cape Kennedy last week watching the Young-Collins space shot in a world wholly unfamiliar to us. People talked what sounded like English, but wasn't. It was like sending a Hottentot to cover Luci Johnson's wedding.

The shot itself, of course, was the main thing. We had never seen one before; television doesn't do it justice. There was that heart-stopping split second after "ignition." Then a burst of smoke across the meadow, a mile and a half away. Then a hot light. Seconds later a rumble of sound. This was the *Agena 10*—the target rabbit that *Gemini 10*, the hound of heaven, would chase and find. After 100 minutes' head start the countdown came for *Gemini* again. "Ignition."

This time the puff of smoke was bigger and the white light at the side intensely bright, like an acetylene flame. The noise, when it got across the meadow, might have passed for summer thunder but it had a rhythm in it, a kind of pulse. Then the great silver needle rose in slow splendor, carrying its forked flame behind it. It was unbelievable.

It was the Indian rope trick done with a freight car. What was most impressive was the *deliberateness* of the rise with a kind of regal assurance, straight up. Birds flapped wildly around over the Florida sandflats. There was a great cloud of condensation vapor as it hit the sky. In no time Messrs. Collins and Young were on their way like a couple of gnats riding a Roman candle.

Experts briefed the newsmen afterward with a vocabulary of angstroms, azimuths, burns, ions, and glitches. The whole space experiment would collapse if they couldn't use "umbilical." What impressed this aging reporter was the youth of these brilliant technicans, also their mood. It was unmistakable. They were dancing up and down with excitement; tests to measure the pressure of sunlight; finding out if a satellite carries an atmosphere of earth dust; peeking at stars outside the earth's curtain; testing whether microorganisms can live in space (maybe that's how life got to earth). The scientists are on the fringes of the universe; they are looking over the fence. Here is the great laboratory that is changing "don't know," into "dimly perceive."

As a young man TRB accompanied Orville Wright and an official party in top hats down the Potomac to commemorate the twenty-fifth anniversary of the first flight. The sand dunes at Kitty Hawk were unstable, but some local gaffers had agreed to take oath that such and such a sliding hill was the right one, and everyone made speeches about the amazing progress of aviation since the silly old days of 1903. They were still flying biplanes, then.

And shortly the US will be celebrating the fortieth anniversary of Lindbergh's flight. Well, you need landmarks like that to get perspective on Cape Kennedy. Today earth-orbiting is so routine that the public says ho-hum. It takes a sudden emergency like that of Collins and Young with the noxious fumes to recall the perils that brave men accept so matter-of-factly. Pursuit, rendezvous, and union are as natural now as the ascent of the water moth in its nuptial flight above a New England pond, till it meets its mate beyond the sight of men.

What awed us at Cape Kennedy even more than *Gemini*'s single flight was the production line of spacecraft that are now operating.

We had never got the hang before of the three stages in the $20-billion moon operation.

They all fit together. First were the one-man Mercurys. They are over now. Today the two-man Geminis are also almost phased out. They are being put up at six-week intervals with two more flights scheduled. Then comes stage three: Project Apollo.

This is simply stunning. The Cape doesn't wait to end Gemini to start Apollo. The hangar or "barn" for Apollo is all built, higher than the Statue of Liberty; in fact you could push the entire United Nations building into either door.

A stupendous mock-up Apollo points upward at its landing pad, speculatively eyeing the moon. It is as impressive as a pyramid. But this thing, or something like it, will make a lunar trip within the foreseeable future.

The cost is vast. Maybe unwise. Personally it makes us tingle. Man is a puny thing in a lot of ways but, let's face it, he is indomitable. What the Russians have up their sleeves we don't know, but since they launched their last manned spacecraft the US has put up half a dozen. At the Kennedy Space Center they are now running sight-seeing buses for the public to see the place. They charge $1.75, which seems outrageous, but at least it's public.

Earlier we mentioned "I do" as a phrase of equal potency with count-downs. Normally we don't read women's pages. But a chance dinner-table encounter with a society editor tore a veil from our eyes—the absolutely frenzied world of Luci Johnson's wedding, August 6. Where have we been? Every woman in the whole country is talking about it. Brides always have their backs to the public.

Ah, but the expression of this one, clad in a gown which *Women's Wear Daily* has already been penalized for prematurely revealing, will be reported. Something about a peephole through the banked Cathedral's flowers, we believe, from which a pool correspondent will scurry back to give eyewitness details to "the gals" (society reporters are always "the gals"). "She smiled softly"; "her lips trembled"; or—oh rapture—"she dropped a tear." Somehow we sympathize with Papa Lyndon till this ordeal is over.

Requiem for Liberals

SEPTEMBER 3, 1966   Two years ago the voters elected one of the most liberal Congresses in American history. It was one of the great landslides of this century. It was one of the few that resulted in a major shift of the balance of power in the House. With the aid of Goldwater, a House that had been closely divided on a backlog of basic liberal measures emerged with a clear majority for the president's program. Congress enacted a social revolution.

We shall look back to this Eighty-ninth Congress for a generation. For we are now sadly saying good-bye to it. We see no sign that it will be continued. We are going back to normal times: a shifting balance between liberals and a GOP-southern coalition.

Let us consider for a minute the last two years. Democrats won forty House seats, lost ten seats, made a net gain of thirty-eight. But this isn't the whole story. The new Democrats were liberals. The great majority of the defeated Republicans were conservatives. In all, forty Republicans with ratings by Americans for Democratic Action of under 20—i.e., ultraconservatives—were dropped. Even the scattered Democratic losses aided the liberals—four of the six seats lost in Alabama, for example, were conservatives. For one of the rare times in history a president had an absolute majority for liberal measures in Congress, making possible the enactment of a magnificent program. A study of twelve selected Great Society roll calls in 1965 showed that of all new Democrats, 89 percent supported Johnson; from the North alone the record was 95 percent.

Party labels are deceptive. In this instance the decisive factor was the *new* members. Take Medicare. Republicans made a motion to recommit (kill) it, April 8, 1965; it lost 191–236. Forty-six of the forty-eight Democrats who replaced Republicans in 1964 opposed the GOP resolution. They saved Medicare. And so on and on. Theoretically Mr. Johnson had a two-to-one majority. Actually his effective majority was thirty-five to forty-five seats.

We think a lovely era is passing. Here are some of the reasons:

Mr. Johnson in 1964 brought in a big coattail vote: Democrats won sixty-one House seats by less than 55 percent, including thirty-seven seats by an eyelash margin of less than 52.5 percent. The Democrats are extremely vulnerable.

Democrats, too, are bucking the traditional recovery of the "out" party at midterm. Here's the House record for the last seven midterm elections. In each case "outs" recovered seats at off years.

YEAR	"OUT"	GAIN
1938	R	80
1942	R	47
1946	R	56
1950	R	28
1954	D	19
1958	D	49
1962	R	4
AVE.		40+

The only exception to this in modern times was 1934. The FDR whirl-wind was still blowing and the "outs" (Republicans) lost fourteen seats. But for practical purposes, if the GOP doesn't regain around forty seats this year it will have suffered a technical defeat.

After the 1920 Harding landslide the Democrats regained seventy-five seats at midterm; after the 1936 FDR landslide the Republicans bounced back with eighty seats in 1938. In other words, the "outs" make a bigger than normal recovery after a landslide.

However, there is one other little point. There is a remarkably constant ratio of around 60–40 between Democratic and Republican partisans. People who identify themselves as "Democrats" outnumber "Republicans." Unfortunately for Mr. Johnson, Democrats aren't very good voters. They forget to register and so on. The effective majority has been closer to 54 percent. And at the off-year, midterm election the national vote is at least a quarter less than at the presidential election. Frightened conservatives keep on voting.

That's the statistical story. We expect on the day after election every columnist in the country to attribute Democratic defeats to a different cause: Vietnam, inflation, racial tension, whatnot. We think a lot of this will be bunk. Maybe we are wrong, but we see no one issue dominating the voters so far.

We see this election developing on localisms, with a little extra GOP bounceback now, because of their debacle two years ago. The sad thing is that the victim, we think, will be the liberal class of 1964 —a very wonderful group.

We find little realization among trade unionists and divided liberals in the country of the tremendous stake involved. This is a requiem for liberals.

We got out with Mr. Johnson in his weekend eastern swing. It was great fun at FDR's old home at Campobello Island, with Lester Pearson, Canadian police, a bagpipe band, sea gulls, lobster dories, Passamaquoddy, and the famous cottage. It was all right except we kept expecting the red-coated Mounties to march down, front and center, and burst into "Rose Marie, I Love You!"

Mr. Johnson, humiliated in turn by management, labor, and the banks, flung himself on the Buffalo and Syracuse crowds. He was a parolee out of the White House prison, grabbing hands over airport fences, going down the joyous lines with an overhand stroke arm over arm, something almost sensual in his satisfaction. On this trip, anyway, he controlled his jibes at Vietnam critics. Instead of being a "dictator" here was a man at the moment at least beset with rising prices and falling popularity ratings, needing reassurance. Before him loomed a prospective GOP midterm "victory." Bobby Kennedy was on the platform in New York and got the big cheer and the squeals; LBJ got moderate presidential applause.

It was an unexpected idea, the thought of Mr. Johnson as underdog! Mr. Johnson is trying to do something no president has done successfully so far in this century, intervene in an off-year election. Wilson, FDR, Truman, Ike, all tried it; none succeeded.

Robert Kennedy

NOVEMBER 12, 1966   Robert Kennedy looked like a man riding a surfboard down Jos Campau Avenue, Hamtramck, Michigan. He was standing up in an open car, Mennen Williams beside him, jiggling about in surging crowds that seemed like waves. Later on in the Upper Peninsula, Williams with his green polka-dot tie sat behind him on the platform of the Escanaba gym, and Kennedy mischievously said that everywhere he had gone in Africa he knew "Soapy" had been before him. The natives hurried up, he said, wearing a loincloth and a bow tie, and shouting "Vote Democratic."

There was a carefree boyishness about it, an exuberance. Bobby told that story about his brother (we heard it nine times in two days): getting a telegram: "President is in Asia; Vice-President is in Midwest; you are in Michigan. Have seized control." Signed "Teddy."

The Kennedy brothers do a fraternal act. Some time ago Teddy accepted a plaque for his brother, who was out of town. He said it was hard to keep up with Bobby, and told this story. Seems two brothers went fishing, one with expensive equipment, the other with an old pole, and of course the latter got all the fish. Next morning the one with no fish stole out early with his brother's crude pole, mystified by his bad luck. Still he caught no fish. He tried and tried. As he sadly got ready to depart, a fish stuck its head out of the water and asked, "Where's your brother?"

What is the charisma, magnetism, or whatever it is that makes the teenagers jump and mothers coo for Bobby? Partly it's the penitential American mood; if martyred Lincoln had had a younger brother he might have gone far politically, too—for a time. But it's more than this. Bobby can control a crowd, even with drunks in it, something Adlai Stevenson couldn't do. He can do something harder and stranger, he can quote highbrow poetry to a crowd and hold them. We don't recall many in that political league.

He climaxed his evocation of his brother's memory at the 1964 Atlantic City convention, you remember, with a poignant passage from *Romeo and Juliet*. And last week, before our two-day trip was over, he appeared at an upstairs balcony in the Park Plaza Hotel, Waterbury, Connecticut, under the frosty stars, and quoted Pericles and Dante to a flattered but incredulous crowd, and concluded with that passage from Frost that ends, "And I have promises to keep, / And miles to go before I sleep, / And miles to go before I sleep." Yes, it was thrilling, what with the harsh lights, the eerie sky, the hushed, hypnotized crowd.

But he also packs a mean punch. At Manchester, New Hampshire, in one sentence, he blasted Neanderthal H. L. Hunt, McCarthyite William Loeb ("the most unreliable newspaper publisher in the country"), and blimpish GOP senatorial candidate Harrison Thyng, a retired general, who wants to bomb Vietnam off the map.

President Johnson on November 3 called the press into the Cabinet Room. He looked sprightly and tanned, with the happy expression he has before a big surprise. We expected to hear of a four-day Johnson preelection "blitz." Calmly and casually, he said he was having a couple of small operations, a throat polyp removed and a hernia protrusion from his gallbladder operation. Time out: two or three weeks. He spoke with dignity and left, turning the affair over to five doctors. Reporters hopped up and down in agony to get out. Then the mob scene, the hysterical rush, the bulletins shouted into telephones.

This is written before the November 8 results, but it might be interesting to put down the preelection Washington thinking. It boiled down to a guess—that the GOP would win back around twenty-five seats, give or take perhaps five.

Actually, by any normal midterm average after a landslide, this is a poor showing. We had expected it to be sixty or seventy or more. The Republicans haven't done too well in the last two years. Their leader has been chameleon Dirksen, their record in Congress negative. The great hope was that the former GOP governors would somehow lift them off the ground. They did establish a Washington office but their leader, Governor Robert Smylie, was defeated for renomination by a Goldwater Republican. Maybe with a few more governors the party can begin rebuilding again. It looks as though they would control the big states.

Well, what will happen after the election? In Vietnam we expect escalation. Signs already appear. Our arms are smashing the North Vietnamese and this phase of the conflict may end. We think the job of pacifying the countryside and putting back the landlords will be turned over to General Ky, while we have the job of policing the place. This may be a dreadful, repressive period. Major General Moshe Dayan, the Israeli soldier who has been touring the battlefield and who is reasonable and objective, lays down two postulates in the *London Sunday Times:* "I do not believe that Hanoi can continue for very long to wage a regular war against the American forces." And, "If the Vietcong abandon regular warfare and go over to guerrilla operations, I do not think that the Americans will be able to subdue them. . . . I do not believe that Americans can bring pacification to Vietnam." So there you are.

How about the postelection home front? Our guess is that Mr. Johnson is about to lose effective control of Congress. He will retain a large nominal majority, of course, on paper. We hope we are wrong, for if it happens it will be good-bye to important social welfare legislation. Signs of retreat were already evident in the second part of the Eighty-ninth Congress. The crucial test in the Ninetieth will be right at the start, whether to continue to curb the House Rules Committee. The curb (the "twenty-one-day rule") may go.

Nuclear Balance of Terror

M ARCH 4 , 1 9 6 7   Buds are thickening on elms along Pennsylvania Avenue and snowdrops are carrying on their secret love life
under the mantle of the last snow. We take a deal of comfort out of
nature when we approach the distasteful subject of nuclear weapons.
But you ought to know how the debate stands over the antiballistic
missile (ABM) defense system in Washington. The immediate stake is
around $40 billion. The ultimate stake, of course, is your life.

We have got used to living under the nuclear balance of terror.
We rarely think about it because it's so disagreeable, but it's there
just the same; it hasn't gone away. America and Russia can annihilate
each other; could do it tomorrow if they wished. It's the supreme
accomplishment of our wonderful Scientific Age. From time to time
new nations join the Club. Mankind has never yet invented a weapon
it hasn't used. Despair?—of course we don't, but it's nice to have those
elm buds and snowdrops to think about after a session with the
weapon boys.

The new variant on the situation is the ABM. The US has good
intelligence behind the Iron Curtain. Some years back we learned that
a new defense system is being deployed. In a posture statement Secretary McNamara recently said that "it now appears" the Soviets are
placing Galosh antimissiles around Moscow; also that another type
of defense system is being deployed elsewhere. "But the weight of
the evidence at this time," he said, "suggests that this system is not
intended primarily for the ABM defense."

The US has been spending half a billion dollars a year for several
years to experiment with an ABM system (Nike-X) but has not deployed it. Here are McNamara's reasons: The weight of objective
scientific advice is that defense can't cope with offense in nuclear
weapons. It isn't a matter of intercontinental missiles. We could wipe
out Moscow tomorrow without firing a missile; one or two of our
intercontinental bombers would always get through.

Again, we have an extraordinary capacity for overkill. We have three or four times the ICBMs [intercontinental ballistic missiles], submarine missiles, and intercontinental bombers that Moscow has. This is probably far more than we need. It is terribly expensive, but of course it comforts the public. (And frightens the hell out of the Russians, too.) In brief, if Moscow attacked us we could destroy 90 percent of their industrial complex and 40–50 percent of their population in the return salvo.

But here comes the rub. How can we know for sure that some fantastic new scientific breakthrough hasn't neutralized our weaponry —laser-beam defense, for example? We can't. That's why we spend half a billion a year to experiment. And here comes another problem. If the Russians are deploying a defense system, shouldn't we do it, too? Candidly, US technicians think our technology is way ahead of theirs. But the diabolical part of an armaments race is that neither side can ever be sure.

Secretary McNamara stoutly opposes deployment. Forty billion would be just the first cost. So far he has been backed by the president. But a controversy like this is a three-front war: the military, the Russians, and the public. The Joint Chiefs of Staff unanimously favor deployment. Their job is to *spend* money; their profession is to defend the nation, and there is also a lot of "get McNamara" sentiment in the Pentagon.

As for the Russians, they have always been defense-minded; they shudder at US nuclear armament. Still, if they can get the US to spend $40 billion to little avail it will be no mean achievement.

Last week in Moscow, Deputy Defense Minister Batitsky and others boasted that they had achieved an infallible ABM defense. The Pentagon quailed and the US public quivered. "Nonsense!" said scientific observers here and Batitsky's boss Grechko withdrew the claim. But it had its effect all the same.

The third front is the public. Mr. Johnson sent Llewellyn Thompson to Moscow to try to talk Kosygin out of an ABM arms race. How it will come out, nobody knows. But Mr. Johnson's budget message already weakened his position by saying that if discussions with Russia "prove unsuccessful, we will reconsider our deployment system." That is a half-promise.

McNamara simply believes that no defense system, no shelter system, no present scientific knowledge can protect us against a coordinated attack by ICBMs. A few years ago there was terrible pressure on Kennedy to start the Nike-Zeus system, which he resisted. Now all sides agree he was right and that it is obsolete. But new efforts are beginning in Congress.

The Republican National Committee has just issued a "background report" which it calls objective, and not intended to influence policy. It is entitled in big letters "Is LBJ Right?" It carries frightening statements that the Russians "are years ahead of the US" in establishing a defense system.

Has Mr. Johnson permitted an antimissile gap? You will be hearing more of it. There will be talk at first of a compromise, of starting a "thin" defense costing, say, $4–$5 billion. (The Republican background report says shelters have improved to a point "where only a modest $2.5 billion" program would suffice. That's political miniskirt modesty, we suppose.)

Step Up or Escalate

MARCH 11, 1967   Secretary Rusk says one thing, Moscow says another. The issue is negotiations in Vietnam. The only way you can resolve the issue is to ask President Johnson at a press conference. But Mr. Johnson rarely holds regular formal press conferences. He holds sudden, informal gatherings attended by the thirty or so reporters regularly attached to the outer lobby of the White House.

The Washington press corps is a large, cohesive body. A few hours after Secretary Rusk holds an off-the-record briefing, as he did the other day, everybody in Washington knows what he said. He still takes the position that Hanoi has made no possible offer, and further, that Moscow is on our side to the degree that it wants Hanoi to make a better offer. (Maybe Moscow does want peace; on the other hand, however, some wonder if its interests aren't better served by war, and the possible diversion of China's paranoidal hatred at us.)

Last week, with no notification, Mr. Johnson called in the lobby reporters to put on the record an important and revealing conference. They are excellent correspondents, but there was no time for homework or specialized inquiries. Nobody pushed him on Moscow or the points of the Rusk briefing.

One good thing—no radio or TV was present. Those reporters fortunate enough to be there said Mr. Johnson was quiet and appealing. He seemed to have made a decision; there was an air of finality about it.

He had decided, he implied, to "step up" the war; not "escalate," step up. It would come moderately, he implied, little by little. Bombing North Vietnam, he said, keeps a communist military and labor force of 500,000 men off balance. "I do believe this is the best course," he said quietly.

He left so many questions unanswered. The formal press conference evolved here in Washington over forty years as a vehicle for gathering the press together, but Mr. Johnson has all but abolished it. As he left the position he will not destroy Hanoi, as the hawks want, nor will he halt bombing, as the doves (including Kennedy) want. The latest Gallup Poll, incidentally, says 67 percent of Americans favor continued bombing. If the Vietcong *should* capitulate, Mr. Johnson will be a hero. (We see no sign of it; they are using bigger Soviet weapons.) If they don't surrender, the war will drag through the election and will be the one issue. Republicans will charge the administration can't win the war or make peace. The issue will be Mr. Johnson's credibility, and his judgment.

The country and the world are uncertain but the president does not know how to gain their trust. He finds regular, candid communication with public opinion and its representatives distasteful. His alternative methods are only partly successful.

It must be said that the Republicans are mostly mired, too. They don't know which way to jump. This appeared in a revelation in Governor Romney's recent five-state tour. He did all right till he got to the subject of Vietnam. Then he lost his poise and refused to answer questions.

Another aspect is the sense of frustration in Congress. The latest $4.5-billion military authorization passed 89 to 2, but not before a vague, "sense-of-Congress" position paper was tacked on, 72 to 19, that meant anything you wanted it to mean: it backed presumed administration peace efforts and desires to prevent escalation. Nineteen suspicious hawks voted no. From the submerged restlessness came significant individual statements. Homespun, respected Senator Aiken (R, Vt.) said flatly the military policy had "failed." Senator Mansfield rather pathetically promised to remove US troops "six months" after peace.

Senator Javits came out against bombing. Robert Kennedy offered a three-step proposal. Halt the bombing and bombardment of North Vietnam and say we are ready to begin discussions within the week. As soon as bombing is halted, international teams under the United Nations or a strengthened International Control Commission would report any effort by either side to increase its strength while peace talks proceed. Under the direction of the UN, and with an international presence gradually replacing American forces, all the people of South Vietnam, communist and noncommunist, Buddhist and Christian, should be able to choose their leaders through free elections and re-solve the question of Vietnamese reunification.

Kennedy explained that his proposal would be a test of the sin-cerity of statements by Soviet Premier Kosygin and others, that if attacks on the North were halted, negotiations would begin.

A lesser tragedy of all this is that Mr. Johnson is sending up to Congress, message by message, one of the finest programs of liberal proposals ever compiled by a president. It is being obscured by Viet-nam. These have gone up in such a flock that we doubt whether you have grasped their significance. He has not interpreted the election as a call for retreat, he is outlining an agenda that will occupy Congress for years. His proposed 1967 civil rights bill, as we read it, is just about as stiff as the one Dirksen filibustered to death last year; the president calls for it urgently and eloquently. How can the nation let Negro GIs come back from Vietnam to find segregated housing? he asks. Politically, it might have been easier to drop the subject. He didn't. "I am proposing fair housing legislation again this year," he said, "because it is decent and right."

There is everything in this snowfall of messages: you name it, we have it. A start to federally aided educational TV. A pilot program for free meals for preschool children. An anticrime program that forecasts a floor under ghetto incomes to cut off poverty from crime. Also Paul Douglas's old truth-in-lending program. It's all there.

Jobs and Social Justice

SEPTEMBER 9, 1967   President Johnson recently has been see-ing groups of newsmen informally. He talks steadily and justifies himself. It apparently gives him relief. The country will judge him next year, he says, on whether he did enough in Vietnam and in civil disorders. He feels his policy is right and he is going ahead.

Our view is that if the war continues next year he will be defeated. There is factual evidence: nearly half of eighty-four senators polled by the Associated Press say they no longer endorse the Johnson war policy. George Romney is switching to the dove side. The Harris Poll reports a drop from 51 to 37 percent in six weeks among those willing to keep fighting "to get a negotiated truce." Gallup says Romney now leads Johnson (49 percent–41 percent) in a trial presidential heat. A state poll by the *Minneapolis Tribune* shows support for the president dropping from 47 percent to 38 percent—an all-time low.

But we trust personal observation as much as polls. No war songs! We thought Tin Pan Alley could glamorize anything. Is it just un-popular, this war? Again and again we hear people say that there must be some easy way to win. By machines. By bombs. By pushbuttons. They can't believe a little country can defy the mightiest.

That is why Secretary McNamara's testimony was vital; he cate-gorically denied that Hanoi can be bombed to the peace table. At first, we think, the man in Sanderson, Texas, won't believe it. Here comes General McConnell, Air Force Chief of Staff, who denies it! For a while the public may be more confused than ever. This journal has been saying for some years now that bombing wouldn't win, and it's nice to have Mr. McNamara's authoritative support. Millions of Americans haven't understood; they have only gone along with the war because they thought there was some quick, sanitary way to vic-tory. Remove that faith, and anger follows.

We assume Mr. Johnson knows the political score as well as anybody. We assume he will push efforts at settlement. The Saigon election opens an opportunity. If this doesn't work, there will be more escalation. There are signs that Mr. Johnson may be giving support to the McConnells at the Pentagon rather than to Secretary McNamara. Mr. Johnson argues that he is holding warhawks in check. The days do not look easy for Mr. McNamara.

The war takes $2 billion a month but the real price is different. The US can afford the war, and the moon shot, and the War on Poverty. Gross national product will increase by $55 billion this year. Yes, the cash is there. We see three other items, however.

Disillusionment from Vietnam is likely to cause a revulsion from all foreign action, useful or not. The UN drive to aid have-not nations has all but collapsed. In five or six years we are probably going to see the worst famine in history. But US foreign aid is being cut sharply: Vietnam is the excuse.

Secondly, there's a moral blight that falls particularly on youth. The draft is grossly unfair; it damages the young man evading service more than the one who fights. We are raising a generation of cynics.

Finally, there's poverty. Lippmann says no nation can carry on two crusades at the same time. There's money enough, we believe, for both, but the emotional reservoir runs dry. Mr. Johnson's mistake is thinking he can fight both simultaneously.

And that brings us to the racial issue. We keep thinking about those charred shells on Twelfth Street in Detroit, one of the most racially enlightened cities in the nation. If it could happen in Detroit, it could happen anywhere. Detroit was full of community action programs. Our observation in Detroit convinced us that the whole panoply of enlightened, ameliorative actions (while good in themselves) won't stop riots; the only things that will stop them are jobs and social justice. We think Whitey hasn't learned the lesson.

We would expect riots to continue next summer in the presidential race. If so, they will aid George Wallace's effort to throw the election into the House. It could be the bitterest contest in modern times.

Congress shows no disposition to meet the flickering racial mutiny. Many congressmen are aching for a showdown, with savage repression. They see "hoodlums" organized by communists causing the riots; i.e., a conspiracy. They vote down a rat control bill; advocate an antiriot bill; cut down poverty funds.

Yet these brief past two months look dangerously like a polarization of black-white antagonism. Even the tortured middle-class Negroes may be alienated. And to paint the full picture, all this time in Alabama and Mississippi, Negro mothers are taking biological revenge against society with an astonishing birthrate.

Ultimate polarization can be averted; we have probably not passed the point of no return. And yet the symptoms are there. Guns are purchasable at the nearest sporting-goods store. Ten-year-olds can make Molotov cocktails. Cities are flammable. Violence is depicted everywhere. (A movie about the St. Valentine's Day massacre followed us recently across America, and the film derives roguish pleasure from murder by social pariahs who "have nothing to lose.") In Detroit the jittery National Guard sprayed homes with machine guns; their performance was disgraceful. Newark's Mayor Addonizio told Congress it is a "cruel myth" that middle-class Americans want to save the cities. "Affluent Americans," he said, "are more gripped by the need to buy a vacation home, a sports car for their college-bound son, and a second color TV set than with sharing their affluence with the poor." ... That's Watts; that's Detroit.

"The Likability Gap"

OCTOBER 14, 1967 Thumping his desk, Senator Dirksen shook the famous locks that have been compared to the tangled kelp in the Sargasso Sea and bemoaned the charge of fellow-Republican Thruston Morton that the military establishment had brainwashed Mr. Johnson on Vietnam.

"Have you heard the British demean *their* king and queen?" he cried with a fierce thespian flourish. "No, you do not demean the ruler."

The president, he hastened to add, is not our ruler, "but you do not demean him in the eyes of people abroad."

Mr. Dirksen is a friend of Mr. Johnson who helped get him the $300-million atom smasher in Weston, Illinois, the other day, and he stoutly defends the Johnson war policy. Lose Vietnam, he warned the Senate, and "the whole Pacific coastline of this country will be exposed."

"What does the senator say is the objective of our war in Vietnam?" asked Senator Fulbright drily.

"I mentioned security," said Dirksen. "Did I not recite the right of those people to decide their destiny for themselves? . . . We undertook to fulfill a commitment under the SEATO treaty."

"That means we stay?" needled Fulbright.

"What does the *senator* want to do?" exploded Dirksen. "You have not heard *me* quarreling with what we have done. *You* have been quarreling for the last year about the conduct of the war!"

"What I would like to see happen," said Fulbright calmly, "is a reconvening of the Geneva Conference, and our agreeing to abide by the result. We did not agree the last time at the last minute. . . . I would like to see a negotiation under the cochairmanship of Great Britain and Russia: full and free elections throughout South Vietnam to create their government; and we would come home."

The question in Washington no longer is whether Mr. Johnson is liked—he isn't; but whether he can hold the country to its present course with polls running against him, with hawks turning into doves in Congress, with costs mounting and even the "victory" of Con Thien (brave though the defenders were) looking like another phase of the prolonged stalemate.

One must not underestimate Mr. Johnson's determination. There was little new in substance in his TV-radio defense of his policy, September 29, but the mood was significant. There is no reason to believe that the president is not sincere in thinking that the country will someday thank him for pursuing a momentarily unpopular course where more and more people feel with Fulbright that "the price we are paying for this is all out of proportion to anything we can gain."

There is a great drama going on in the White House. Mr. Johnson has taken to carrying around in his coat pocket statistics showing that the US is winning the war—figures on tonnage, bombage, defectors, and body count—just as in happier days he used to whisk out Gallup polls on his popularity and political invincibility. In conferences with his staff he allows discussion of the problem of his "likability gap," and bolder advisers deal with it coolly. He himself attributes the gap in part to (a) a snobbish bias against Texans; (b) a new isolationism; and (c) some odd but acknowledged inability to get his views over to press and public.

The president often uses off-the-record meetings with callers— foreigners or newsmen—for monologues in which he marshals his arguments. Some of these meetings are protracted and embarrass modest visitors who feel they are encroaching on his time. Mr. Johnson gets relief from the practice, however, and followed it long before he came to the White House.

It would be folly for opponents to underestimate the man; he is tough and determined and, quite apart from the validity of his arguments, well aware that Republican leaders would hurl themselves upon him if he substantially altered his position or exposed himself to the charge of inconsistency.

In my judgment, the winds and tides have turned against the president on this issue, though I may be mistaken, and the change may be only temporary. But a way out of the national impasse seems as far removed as ever. The public hates the war but it hates the idea of defeat even more. Before long it may be groping for a scapegoat for its frustration. The polls may indicate the process has already begun. Unlike Harry Truman, Mr. Johnson would not make a very attractive underdog.

Some blows he suffers must be harsh. For example, he felt assured by intermediaries that Governor Rockefeller would stoutly support his Vietnam policy. (Washington generally believes Rocky wants the GOP nomination avidly; and would probably be the party's strongest candidate.) Now comes the well-informed *New York Times* to declare that Rocky is "turning away" from the White House on the Vietnam issue. If so he is only the latest GOP leader to feel a change in the wind.

Last spring Dirksen taunted Democrats for not supporting the war with the same unity as Republicans; today the GOP is just as divided. Some liberal Republicans find Dirksen hard to take; they say he gives the party the image of a character out of Dickens, funny but dated. One group would like to replace him with Senator Morton (Ky.) who stepped in to put over the Consular Treaty with Russia when Dirksen led the fight against it. Morton is a former party national chairman. Dirksen has a cozy relationship with the president, often swapping favors and giving him occasionally valuable help, as in the 1965 civil rights bill. (He fought the 1966 bill because of the open housing provision.)

Dirksen vainly opposed the one-man, one-vote reapportionment decision. He nominated Goldwater and is now suspected of being a Reagan man. His eye is on the chairmanship of the Resolutions Committee at the GOP convention next year where he could supervise the Vietnam declaration. High time for a change, a number of middle-road Republicans say.

Cloudy Crystal Ball

J A N U A R Y   6 ,   1 9 6 8   Our New Year's crystal ball grows cloudy at one point. Yes, we expect the Democrats to pick LBJ. Yes, we think the GOP will pick Richard Nixon. Nixon will say he's for present Vietnam policy only he'll do it better. He'll get peace faster. It will be cheaper. He won't say how.

Faced with Tweedledum and Tweedledee, people will snicker at elections. They'll sneer at politicians. War opponents will shrug and go on to the streets. They may find the Negroes there already. (We don't see the new session of the Ninetieth doing much about civil rights except passing antiriot legislation.)

Democrats have normally dominated national politics since FDR put together his winning New Deal. We see LBJ occupying a much narrower base, a labor-industrial-military complex. Nixon will get business, farmers, large chunks of the frightened middle class.

We expect George Wallace to be formidable in the South, and in the blue collar-white backlash neighborhoods.

We see a fourth-party peace candidate, Senator McCarthy or whoever, probably not carrying a state but possibly tipping big states (California or New York) one way or the other.

A lot of voters may just go fishing.

As we say, our crystal ball goes cloudy at one point. It's at that moment when the tense GOP convention at Miami Beach next August finally nominates its man and delegates go wild in their traditional war dance round the aisles. It's an electric moment. But with Nixon? With that poor old tired face wigwagged on banners? No, somehow we can't visualize it. Not even though polls show county professionals for him.

When we were much younger we saw the glum convention re-nominate Hoover in 1932. We still have a mental image of Senator Simeon D. Fess with a silly look of pretended rapture on his face waving a great picture of puffy-faced Herbert in a high collar on the platform. Well, the GOP knew it was licked then; it had to go through with it. But this year it can practically smell victory. Nominate Nixon? The tortured crystal ball grows milky and rocks uncomfortably on its base.

President Johnson is running hard for reelection, spurred in part, perhaps, by Senator McCarthy's defection. Speeches, interviews, and a wild dash round the world from antipodes to pope—show what a tough campaigner he is. We have repeatedly expressed confidence in this column that the nation would ultimately adopt 1) national income support legislation (like a negative income tax), and 2) a system whereby the government would become the employer of last resort. Mr. Johnson virtually endorsed the second in his White House TV interview, December 19. (He has proposed a commission to examine the first.)

We note that even in such a staged TV interview as this, seen by an estimated 52 million in prime time, the president's bristling attitude toward questioners showed through: he was testy, aggressive, snappish, and just missed a quarrel with Frank Reynolds of ABC, of whom he demanded sarcastically four times what his own solution to the ghetto problem was. Harry Truman was cocky, it is true, but he scored his points in a kinder way.

We have been making a list of year-end comments from the press, about the feeling of South Vietnamese toward Americans. Hanson Baldwin, military editor of the *New York Times*, strong advocate of the war, notes "some latent anti-Americanism." *Newsweek*, summarizing the war, finds "a significant amount of anti-Americanism." A weekly report distributed among the US mission in South Vietnam on

December 5, quoted by the *Washington Post*, charges "that many of the natives (of South Vietnam) felt that the US is 'deliberately prolonging the war.'"

The respectable *National Observer* begins a Saigon dispatch, "A growing number of Vietnamese don't like Americans." It quotes an unnamed member of the new House of Representatives: "Why should Vietnamese boys be sent to die for the Americans?"

With the best will in the world, we conclude, there are obstacles to friendship. Suppose the situation were reversed. How would you like to have your town filled with smiling, aggressive, self-confident foreign soldiers, each apparently eight feet tall, with a handclasp that made you wince? The Vietnamese look like dolls to Americans; the Americans like giants to their hosts. Maybe cordiality is possible for a time, but the mere physical disparity makes the relationship uncomfortable after a while.

Two more thoughts about Vietnam: James Deakin of the *St. Louis Post-Dispatch* points out that there is disagreement among senior military men about the US role. Backing the war program are, of course, the Joint Chiefs and most of the military establishment, including General Eisenhower. Opposing it, however, are certain retired officers like former Marine Corps Commandant General David Shoup, Lieutenant General James M. Gavin, Brigadier General Samuel Griffith, Jr., (retired Marine and authority on China), Rear Admiral Arnold E. True, and three brigadier generals, Robert Hughes, William Ford, and Hugh B. Hester. In a radio interview General Shoup called some hawk arguments "unadulterated poppycock."

The other point is about the prestigious December 19 statement of fourteen leading scholars about Vietnam. *Newsweek, Time,* and other media fooled us. They played it up as though it gave blanket assent to the Johnson program. Nonsense! It stated that an absolute communist victory would be "equally ruinous" as escalation into a global war. "At this juncture," it says, "nothing would do more to strengthen American support" than judicious de-escalation. We "must also," it said, show a "capacity to go down as well as up." That's the last thing the US has done. The war is all "up."

Off the Track

M A R C H   2 3 ,   1 9 6 8   A strange world we live in. America, with all its wealth, finds its dollar endangered. America, with all its might, finds its troops stalemated. America, with all its cities, finds them unsafe. America, with all its pride, finds its president circumscribed in movement.

Mr. Johnson, in an election year, hesitates to travel openly for fear he may be embarrassed or injured by demonstrators. White House reporters are given a couple of hours' notice before a trip and told to pack, they don't know for how long or for what destination. The presidential party when it arrives at a city goes unheralded in unmarked cars through unsuspecting streets and arrives before surprised audiences.

Surely something is wrong. Surely the United States has gone somewhere off the track. But the secretive president holds the cards to his chest and offers a confident face as he makes the critical decision whether to send an additional one or two hundred thousand men to Vietnam. His press conferences have long since been discontinued; even the Senate Foreign Relations Committee can't get solid assurance that its opinion will be weighed before the decision is taken.

We watched Secretary Rusk before the Fulbright committee last week. Nobody won, everybody was unhappy.

Mr. Rusk returned the ball as hard as it was served. He showed steely certitude and kept his temper. Grant his postulate that Southeast Asia falls if Vietnam falls, and that America must live up to every line of every containment treaty spun by Dulles or have its faith questioned, and there is an arguable case. We were fascinated by the big, bald man patiently fixing his gaze at the glittering water pitcher and then answering stoutly. Most of the committee questioned or assailed his premises. A good man defending a bad case, because it is contrary to common sense to imply that we may have to destroy Vietnam to save it; or to think that any other small nation wants to be "protected" by the US at such cost. God save them from such protection.

One man who was sitting pretty at the hearings was Wayne Morse, one of the two who voted against the original Tonkin Gulf resolution (along with Ernest Gruening). "I don't have to explain or alibi my position!" he told the other sheepish senators. In England the government would have fallen that made such a disingenuous presentation as that on Tonkin.

We sense a great shift of public opinion on Vietnam going on, yet how can Mr. Johnson extricate himself from his fix? We are not arguing the morals of the thing but the politics. If he should try to backtrack now he would admit a mistake or defeat and the Republicans would spring on him like wolves; every nation loves a scapegoat. So we guess that the official Johnson policy will be "more of the same."

But you could feel the shift in public sentiment right there in the Senate committee. A couple of years ago they whooped through the Tonkin Gulf business; now there seemed to be only four or five convinced hawks left. Other evidence abounds: Gallup says 49 percent now think the war "a mistake," and 69 percent dream of replacing US soldiers with South Vietnamese.

Then there is the New Hampshire primary and the mouse that roared. Senator McCarthy glided about the state with an "excuse me" attitude at first, and ended up with 42 percent of the votes! That is about 21 percent more than TRB would have given him when he was up there three weeks before. All of a sudden the curious candidacy caught on. Mr. McCarthy is the pet of the reporters because he is everything that a presidential candidate is supposed not to be and so he is fun to watch: witty instead of shrill, composed instead of noisy, talking sense instead of nonsense.

Then, again, all these starry-eyed kids brought into his campaign are attractive, some of the hippies even making the supreme sacrifice of lowering hemlines, or shearing whiskers, for their stately, knightly leader whom they regard as presiding over a substation of Camelot. Ah well, it's an odd sight to see a gang of students suddenly wondering if maybe the machinery of the democratic process may be a substitute for withdrawal and pot.

There's a change of US sentiment on when Rocky prepares to enter the fray and when suddenly Bobby Kennedy kindly proposes to relieve Gene McCarthy of the burden of opposing Mr. Johnson. But perhaps what impressed TRB most as a journalist is the change in tone of some of our contemporaries.

That radical old organ, the *Wall Street Journal*, suddenly came through with an editorial about the mess in Vietnam that sounded like a leader in the *NR* about two years ago. We began looking about among other magazines. *Look* has an enormous circulation with no editorial policy, so there was no use looking *there*. But we noticed that *Time*, which puts its editorials in its expletives, has dropped all these snide adjectives with which it used to transfix the silly critics of Vietnam. And here was *Life* declaring under an editorial headed "Vietnam: Let's not have more of the same," that it's time to "reassess" strategy while "deescalating." For heaven's sake. What would Henry Luce have said, and the China Lobby? "The strategic bombing of North Vietnam, beyond the rear of the battleground, should be halted," it said. We are speechless.

Finally, *Newsweek*, which has fine columnists both for and against the war, took its own position of advocacy, March 18. All we can hope to achieve now is "stalemate," it said. America should stop large-scale search-and-destroy operations, "and withdraw its major forces from the sparsely populated borders." A former paratroop commander (evidently a craven) and executive officer of a big Massachusetts management consultant firm (evidently a pinko) once recommended that. Yes, Lieutenant General James M. Gavin; that's the man.

We must hunt up some other crusade. Our position is getting too popular.

Johnson Won't Run Again

A P R I L 1 3 , 1 9 6 8   Mr. Johnson, so far as we can figure it, is having a swell time. He kept a secret and he surprised people and there is nothing he likes more. He is being terribly noble, and there is nothing more fun than to be noble. He loves action, and he is dashing about at a great rate and has just gone to Hawaii. He had painted himself into a corner from which there seemed no exit. The polls showed him with only 36 percent backing his handling of the government, and only 26 percent the war. And he was stuck with the policy of bombing which the Pentagon and Little Sir Echo Rusk, and all the rest of them, loyally supported.

When he went before the nation on that climactic Sunday night, think of what he had to tell them before his big announcement: more budget red ink, more troops needed, more appeals to Congress for his tax bill (a House with 435 members all up for reelection, and he asks them for more taxes!). His neglect of the Democratic National Committee, while he tried to run politics (like everything else), had pretty well ruined it. We think he is a bumbling politician, whatever anybody else may say, and this was illustrated by his debacle in New Hampshire, and by the loss of the Massachusetts delegates to Gene McCarthy without a shot.

Mr. Johnson is a proud and patriotic man, and he knew as he faced the mike that he was so unpopular that he could not travel anywhere in the country without risk of insult or riot. The country that he had wanted to unite he had divided. Where had that will-o'-the-wisp, Consensus, gone?

Mr. Johnson had toyed with the idea of not seeking a second term a long time, and everybody we talk to here now, it turns out, knew about it all the while. We didn't. We watched him make that speech to the AFL-CIO construction workers a fortnight ago and we were confident that it was a campaign speech and that he meant to run if the prospects were good. But then he realized that it was no go.

We are not among those who think that Mr. Johnson wears horns. He has a splendid record of domestic social accomplishment. Because of Vietnam we couldn't have voted for him, but we have always had a sneaking fondness for him, fascinated by his convoluted deviousness, his evident need of affection and inability to inspire it readily, and his frequent pettiness wrestling with his idealistic populism.

But this sounds like pity. How absurd! Mr. Johnson humbled himself on the broadcast with stricken face and painful intensity, and the bombshell at the end quite obscured for most people that he was admitting, in effect, that his policy had really been a failure.

A minute after he finished, his wife, who had given him words of warm encouragement before the talk, ran to his desk and, disregarding the technicians, threw her arms around him. No camera caught that scene. Her face, visible over his shoulder, was radiant. Mr. Johnson had a relaxed buffet supper after that with the family, and after that, a long talk with reporters, and he has been seeing more of them since. And four hours after his broadcast American bombers were back again, battering a target 205 miles beyond the Demilitarized Zone, and a mile from a provincial capital, and the old Lyndon Johnson communications failure and credibility gap was back again in an intensely suspicious Senate. . . . And now he is off on the trip to Honolulu. To be continued next week.

Mr. Johnson is out of the corner into which he painted himself, by means of his renunciation. Or is that the right metaphor? Would a better one be that he has got back to Paris from Moscow in his imperial troika, while the Army that he led deeper and deeper into the snow tries to readjust itself? How about Field Marshal Rusk; how about General Clark Clifford; how about water boy Hubert Humphrey? Yes, and all those good people who slapped their chests and cried that America must never, never stop bombing? General Eisenhower says that he is "bewildered," and as he has passed a lifetime among civilian matters that bewildered him we have no doubt whatsoever that he is speaking the truth. Others are, too.

We assume that the Democratic race may now become three-cornered with Vice-President Hubert Humphrey's broad hint that he's "weighing" his decision and will let us know later—perhaps after Hawaii. He would have some support from trade union and Negro groups who, for one reason or another, don't like Bobby or Gene.

The vice-president would probably help McCarthy in a stop-Kennedy movement. It is hard to see, of course, how he could pull himself out of the Johnson shadow in time to establish his own identity and, who knows, Mr. Johnson may be drafted yet.

One thing interests us greatly. We traveled over America last summer—Atlantic to Pacific, Canada to Mexico—and everywhere we felt the dislike of the war. They were willing to go along with it, though, because they knew it would be cheap, and short, and the big nation would soon chastise the little one. Since then, of course, the dislike has steadily grown more and more passionate.

But what bewildered us was how this feeling was to find political expression. The machinery was not there. It seemed hopeless. However, it appears that there are new political tools, the polls and TV. They have outdated the old mechanism for mobilizing opinion, the local leader and the party organization. Gene McCarthy threw his hat into the ring and TV helped him. The polls took hold of Mr. Johnson and pulled him further and further down. It appears that public opinion has finally broken through.

Notes Martin Luther King, apostle of justice, Nobel Prize winner, a man of peace, is dead—victim of the madness and brutality against which he set himself. Yet he, not his enemies, will overcome.

What Happens to Our Most Cherished: Kennedy and King

A P R I L   2 0 ,   1 9 6 8   What does anarchy look like? It has a laughing face. It is a wavering crowd of teenagers on your side of the street ready to dart across and join a more daring band breaking the plate glass of an electronics store. Crash, goes the glass. The boys on this side catch the hysteria; they dash across, somebody puts his arm into the jagged hole and pulls out this . . . and this . . . and this . . . and, laughing with wild excitement, they scuttle off with unimaginable riches. A police car drives up; they run like boys who have been diving from a jetty above a "No Trespassing" sign, each daring the other to climb higher, and here comes the watchman and they all duck and run. But one or two are caught.

Yes, that's what anarchy looks like. And how thick splintered plate glass feels to your feet on city sidewalks; why, if it were ice the pond would hold your weight.

Or anarchy is where two sets of people share the same city but not the same community, the same house but not the same room, and where, like different animals in a forest, they watch each other warily until provoked by some intolerable slight. Only *this* forest is made of streets and buildings and plate glass crying to be smashed, and where (it now becomes vividly and unexpectedly apparent) a small minority can upset the whole intricate city balance without too much effort, like a bullet shot into a million-dollar computer or, for that matter, a few guerrillas in a jungle defying a bomber. Cities, one suddenly realizes, are built on confidence, and the more modern and intricate they are the more confidence is necessary. Here is another unsuspected vulnerability, we discover, in America's wealth and magnificence.

And for a final thought on the anarchy, it is an idiot nation that lets hucksters sell handguns in hardware stores and rifles in mail-order houses, knowing full well that psychotics and firearms come together as inevitably as male and female to coitus, and where the most cherished and admired—John F. Kennedy and Martin Luther King—are shot through the neck by white snipers in order that sportsmen can have their guns and businessmen their profits. Yes, that's anarchy. As for us, we'd rather be with the larking Negro boys smashing plate glass and grabbing loot than with the officers and members of the National Rifle Association lobbying against a simple firearms licensing law such as they have in every other civilized nation.

We flew in from Indianapolis in the Kennedy party last week and saw the pillars of smoke rising from the capital as we made an evening landing. In the big university auditorium at Muncie, Indiana, Kennedy finished his speech on civil rights, and a Negro in the balcony boldly rose and asked: "You are putting great faith in White America, Mr. Kennedy. Is that faith justified?" "Yes," answered the senator unhesitatingly, and went out to find King murdered.

Now that President Johnson has bowed out, many people seem to be transferring their hatred to Kennedy. It is quite surprising how passionate this distrust often is. Maybe in its emotional state, the country needs someone who does not polarize passion: witty, low-keyed Gene McCarthy doesn't. He moves to his fate in the Indiana primary, May 7. All the experts tell us that he will not do so well there. The experts, it may be added, have been wrong most of the time—in this extraordinary year.

Or there is Hubert Humphrey. He is sunny and likable and the natural heir of the Democratic Establishment. We take his unavowed candidacy very seriously. He has been mistaken on Vietnam from our point of view, and almost a flunky to President Johnson; but even so it is hard to hate Hubert. One irony is that the people who used to dislike him most—the southerners and businessmen—and who regarded him as a brash, gabby radical, now generally prefer him to Bobby. The two have changed roles. There is a kind of universal fondness for "poor" Hubert overshadowed by Mr. Johnson, and his enthusiastic loquacity is a national joke. He is an eloquent man, it is admitted, only nobody has found the button that turns him off.

At Indianapolis with Senator Kennedy we witnessed an odd scene. He was supposed to dedicate a new campaign headquarters in a Negro ward. The outdoor crowd was gathered, ready for high jinks and enthusiasm. Mr. Kennedy brought the crushing news that King had been murdered in Memphis. Without notes and speaking with restrained tension to a predominantly Negro crowd suddenly silent and huddled against the night cold, he made a moving talk. Maybe Willard Wirtz could have made it, and certainly Adlai Stevenson, but few others that we know of. "In this difficult day, and in this difficult time for the United States," he said, "it is perhaps well to ask what kind of nation we are and what direction we want to move in."

The hired campaign searchlight behind picked at the low-hanging clouds. He continued quietly that he struggled in his own heart against the same kind of feeling of hatred and injustice that Negroes must feel tonight. "I had a member of my family killed," he said, "but he was killed by a white man."

He quoted from Aeschylus (his favorite poet, he told the wondering crowd)—"Even in our sleep pain, which cannot forget, falls drop by drop upon the heart until, in our despair, against our will, comes wisdom through the awful grace of God."

It sounded like a prayer. A strange evening, not soon to be forgotten.

Notes Congress finally passed a watered-down, open housing civil rights bill whose rejection at this time would have been a disaster but whose enactment, we think, won't really change things very much in the ghetto. They need two things above all, *jobs* and *income*—the government as employer of last resort, and income maintenance through a family allowance or negative income tax.

Resurrection City

J U N E   1 ,   1 9 6 8   Resurrection City is doing what Coxey's
Army and the Bonus Marchers failed to do. They came at a time of
depression, everybody knew there was misery. Resurrection City
comes in a surging boom when nobody wants to be reminded of
poverty. Yet this is the deeper tragedy; poverty is here and has been
here all the time; it is not that America doesn't have the wealth but
that it lacks the will to distribute the wealth more fairly. Compared
to other nations the US is undertaxed; we could end poverty if we
wanted to.

Resurrection City is a good place to stop and consider things. It is
a city of plywood shacks—wooden tents—set down beside one of the
loveliest glades in the world, the Reflecting Pool picking up the
Monument at one end and the Memorial on the other. And the hungry, the poor, the dispossessed are in between.

It is the greatest publicity stunt, advertising thrust, propaganda
achievement of modern times: it has evoked a superb documentary
from CBS on poverty, and it has put poverty on the front cover of
Time. Martin Luther King thought it up and he goes marching on,
and through the trees the beneficent figure of Lincoln looks down,
and on those steps King told 200,000 marchers in 1963, "I have a
dream."

But most striking of all is that over the tops of the great avenue
of elms, diminishing in perspective, is the dome of the Capitol. That
is the confrontation—Capitol and Resurrection City; Congress and the
Poor. It is a stunning juxtaposition; nobody who has seen it can forget
it. They settle down at night on wooden floors four inches above the
ground in shack city, and if they look out, there far off above the
trees is the dome glowing in the night.

This is a strange time. Like France, the US achieved a political
overturn by nonpolitical means. Suddenly what the French students

had begun shook the whole de Gaulle system. And in America there seemed no way for multiplying discontent to find expression through normal political channels, and then a brave man entered the New Hampshire primaries, and the polls continued their telltale story, and suddenly Mr. Johnson decided not to run. It happened like that. It was equivalent to the fall of a parliamentary government, and all done by extraparliamentary means. The forces of democracy had broken through.

It opened the way for our present extraordinary struggle. We are climbing out of the ruins of the Vietnam disaster and trying to make plans for the new city. Congress has had little to do with it. Congress is embarrassed by Resurrection City—by poverty. The Ninetieth is the Irrelevant Congress. On the great issues of the day—Vietnam, riots, student revolt, poverty—it has stood and looked. Yes, it did pass the open housing bill, but that was because of Martin Luther King's assassination. (Kennedy's assassination shoved through the New Frontier.) Which is the more out of place in that strange axis in Washington today: Resurrection City at one end, or Congress at the other?

Gawking sightseers who walk around this extraordinary excrescence often fall into passionate debate. The obvious point is that it shouldn't be there. It jolts you. Ambiguous spokesmen of the march, filled with leadership rivalries, promise civil disobedience in one breath and peaceful discipline in the next. Who knows Act II?

There are two engines in America: the engine of discontent in advertising and TV; and the engine of fulfillment through industrial production. We have a wealth-machine to turn out $830 billion GNP a year; we have a demand-machine for making people dissatisfied. All very well when these engines are in phase but a roaring monster when they work against each other.

How badly they are working now is illustrated by that documentary by CBS last week, "Hunger in America," recited with conviction by Charles Kuralt. A nurse on a Navaho reservation pleading for just a little milk to save a wizened starving baby looking sixty years old; a pregnant woman in a Mississippi cabin devoid of proper food; the same woman two weeks later, the baby born and dead. Malnutrition.

Congress shifts from foot to foot uneasily. The Senate debates the toughest crime bill in history with accent on riots; the legislature proposes to cut spending $6 billion. Everywhere Nixon utters the old Hoover cry, we cannot afford to act in social crisis.

The great ploy at present is tax incentives; incentives to get industries into the ghettos: Nixon and Rockefeller and Kennedy urge it. Frankly, we don't trust it. Maybe, here and there, it will work: but where does it lead?—should we give tax incentives for space capsules or moon shots?

Tax incentives, warns Stanley Surrey, assistant secretary of the Treasury, "to cure social problems can dangerously weaken our ability both to control expenditures and make them efficient." He says it might be a bonanza for business to go into ghetto reconstruction; an opportunity to make "tax millionaires" out of "doctors, lawyers, and other investors," rescuing the poor.

We just think US poverty is too big a problem to be solved by new tax loopholes. Certainly industry can help. But the task requires social engineering for income maintenance, we believe, on a scale too large for private sources. And meantime what outrageous things are done; CBS showed babies so weak from hunger they had to be fed intravenously, who weighed less in one year than at their births, and yet the Department of Agriculture has turned $654 million back to the Treasury unspent in the past few years under the surplus food law, and plans to hand back another $227 million this year. The department is there, you see, to serve the commercial interest of the producers, not to feed the hungry. Government food programs at present reach only 18 percent of the poor. So let's give a fat bonus to General Motors for a plant in Harlem.

Gun Control and the Death of Bobby Kennedy

JUNE 15, 1968   Americans love to grovel. Now they can have a fine time groveling about the killing of Bobby Kennedy. Think of all the fat little editorial writers sitting down at their typewriters, putting themselves in a properly melancholy mood and then dashing off an inspired article on "the shame of America." It is a "day of national humiliation," they will write.

It is, all right. An English journalist, Henry Fairlie, said it drily a couple of years ago: "There is an element of violence in American society which the outsider has to learn to comprehend . . . However much I may love and admire America, its gun laws come near to ruling it out of civilized society."

So now we can wallow in sorrow as we did when Lee Harvey Oswald shot Jack Kennedy, and when Charles Whitman mowed down the crowd in Texas, and when the killer got Martin Luther King, and now Bobby. But do anything about it?—point out that the revolver is the virility symbol in the American subconscious, that its arcane temple is the ultrarespectable, three-and-a-half million dollar, nine-story National Rifle Association building in downtown Washington, and that its spokesmen are the frightened members of Congress? Certainly not; better froth at the mouth at the individual crank to whom we make deadly weapons accessible by mail or by purchase at the nearest hardware store. We can always restore our national self-respect by dropping a few more cans of napalm on those little yellow Vietcong commies.

The guilty party for Bobby's death is right there in Congress. Let's not duck the issue. Yes, you and I share the generalized guilt for the National Rifle Association, but the responsible party is Congress. Poll after poll shows the nation wants gun control laws. But our political institutions are not adequate to turn a widespread but not very passionate desire for reform into legislation against a lobby that can send a blizzard of a half a million protests into Congress at the touch of a button. The NRA has 850,000 sportsmen members who don't want to be inconvenienced by registering their rifles and shotguns. They live out in suburban areas and farms, mostly; what do they care about the murder rate in teeming cities where anybody can buy a gun? The NRA has $10 million in assets and an annual income of more than $5 million, two-thirds from dues and another 25 percent from arms manufacturers who advertise in its monthly magazine the *American Rifleman*.

One really has to look down from the press gallery at the Ninetieth Congress to get a proper feeling of anger at the way the public's will is thwarted over firearms control. The crime bill started out as a fairly simple program from the executive and it was so passed by the

House. Then senators got to work; they added sections to undercut Supreme Court decisions, and to permit every small-town detective to tap your telephone. It is such a mess now the president may veto it.

At one point, poignantly enough, Bobby Kennedy's brother, Edward, tried to insert in the Senate an amendment to include rifles and shotguns under federal regulation as well as revolvers. This young man whose brother was murdered as president and whose other brother would soon be gunned down in Los Angeles told the Senate, "We have it in our power to make this nation a little safer today and to keep guns out of the hands of those who should not have them—that 200 million Americans can sleep and walk and work and play with greater peace of mind."

Well, they *can't* sleep and walk and work and play with greater peace of mind. The Senate rejected his amendment, 29 to 53. The covert racist appeals of some of the NRA propaganda came out in the arguments: let's not disarm America when there are riots in the streets. A senator from a typical, sparsely settled western state, Bennett (R, Utah) told members darkly that "we must realize that control of the ownership of firearms carries with it the inherent future possibility of police-state controls." Furthermore, he said, there's an obligation on Congress "to protect the general public from those elements in society who perpetrate acts of violence against our citizenry." You know whom he means; yes, *those* people.

We have said once or twice in this correspondence that we sense a conservative undertow: the Senate's attack on the Supreme Court, supported by Nixon; the overwhelming rejection of the progressive new state constitution by frightened voters in Maryland. And now in Texas the populist eastern areas that formerly voted for liberal Ralph Yarborough gave majorities this year to archconservative Preston Smith in the Democratic primary for governor. (We should certainly vote Republican this year if we lived there.) Finally, Republicans in California have apparently nominated educator Max Rafferty, one of the most objectionable of conservatives, to replace Tom Kuchel, one of the best liberals, as senator. What a team that will be! B-movie star hero Reagan as governor, George Murphy, the hoofer, as one senator, and Rafferty as the other. Maybe there aren't enough California Birchites to elect Rafferty, however.

Has anybody seen Hubert Humphrey lately? Who is he? *What* is he? We used to know him; he used to be a nice man. Now the liberals think he is a liberal and the conservatives a conservative. He is supported by the employers on one side and by the trade unions on the other; the Negroes think he is a friend and so do the southern governors. How long can this go on? It looks more and more as though the Chicago convention would nominate the little man who isn't there.

And just to send you all home happy—you can rest secure in bed tonight—Everett McKinley Dirksen is writing the platform on which Richard Nixon will run.

Riots in Chicago

SEPTEMBER 14, 1968   Looking back on it all . . .

The buglelike voice over the amplifier tells the soldiers to throw down their guns. They are doing the work of the Nazis. Come over to our side, the voice says; the American side.

Once again I'm standing before the open window on the third floor of the Chicago Conrad Hilton where the TV cables, like black snakes, climb the wall and enter the building to the candidates' suites. Beyond the trees is limitless lake, then the park, then the rally of the sandaled ones, the bearded ones, the antiwar protesters, then a double line of helmeted National Guard in battle dress, then imperial Michigan Avenue, then, below us, jittery bystanders, police in blue riot helmets, and Cadillacs bringing VIPs to the splendid hotel.

Hubert Humphrey is a traitor, says the voice. All the crowd across the way raises its right fist and shouts. Richard Nixon is a traitor, the voice continues. Lyndon Johnson is a traitor. Always the same rhythmic, hypnotic response. Then a series of satirical songs, excellently done; and then again the taunting, provocative appeals to the soldiers to mutiny.

I cross the street. A well-dressed passerby suddenly loses his cool, shouts "you are dirty" and is wrestled to the ground by a powerful youngster. It is fast and furious for a minute but not a matter of fists. Six feet away the soldiers, no older than the youths in the park, look on impassively.

An attractive red-bearded fellow in sandals tells me he is a high school mathematics teacher from Kansas. The beard is shaved on the side round a fresh cut. Police club, he says. Idealism shines in his eager eyes. But why, I ask, do you say Humphrey is a *traitor?* I got pretty irritated, I say, when Nixon called the Democrats traitors in 1952.

Two girls in unconventional clothing join us in the milling crowd; underfoot, torn newspapers. Traitor, they repeat. They go into semantics. Traitor in the sense that he defies, well, the Constitution. No use arguing. We part with a laugh, liking each other. The man at the bullhorn is taunting the cops.

David Broder, top-rank reporter of the *Washington Post,* says the party is in wreckage, and implies that the real convention is in the young dissidents in the park. His paper editorially the same day, however, recalls Humphrey as a liberal legislator and engaging party leader. *New York Times*man Tom Wicker, like Broder one of the best men in the business, writes that Humphrey lacks intellectual discipline. His paper, editorially, however, sees in the turbulent convention a successful forum that has vindicated democracy.

There are stink bombs in all the big hotels. Refused the use of Soldier Field for a mass meeting, the dissidents defy orders to clear the park and not to march. There is clubbing, tear gas, almost constant violence.

I see few Negroes in the crowd. This is a white man's war. If there had been Negroes there would have been shooting; every night at Miami Beach somebody was shot in the ghetto, nobody paid much attention. But here white youngsters are being clubbed; worse, cameramen, reporters; worse even, sacred TV personnel. The superpundits, Walter Cronkite, Huntley-Brinkley, Eric Sevareid, are justifiably outraged, almost hysterical. In the ghettos, blacks chuckle a little. Now they'll believe us about police brutality, they say.

Through the crowds, organizing them, manipulating them, move familiar figures, Tom Hayden, Rennie Davis, and others; those who founded Students for a Democratic Society, who disrupted Columbia University, who planned the Convention Week demonstrations long ahead, and who will continue terroristic, anarchistic tactics through the election. The present political system must be changed, they say. They do not say changed to what.

Now look at the other side. Democrats brought their convention to Mayor Daley's Chicago because they were afraid of him. After all, he represents progress: progress that is from comic Mayor Big Bill Thompson, who promised to smack King George's snoot. . . . Chicago is a little older now.

The *Chicago Tribune* and Mayor Daley are one; they pretend to compete but they serve the same archconservative gods. Outside of the *Manchester* (New Hampshire) *Union* perhaps, the *Tribune* is the most provincial paper in the country. Mayor Daley could not exist in a city with a *Saint Louis Post-Dispatch*. The *Trib* imposes its "Little Orphan Annie" value judgments on the whole realm.

The convention hall is ringed with defenses. But that is not really the trouble. Every window, every hoarding, every fluttering banner in downtown Chicago welcomes delegates in the name of Mayor Daley and always his name is biggest. It is one great panegyric for the mayor. "You are entering Daley Land," delegates read as they approach the amphitheater. He sits directly below the podium, surrounded by Illinois delegates who will vote as he tells them, and he calls the parliamentary shots to faltering chairman Carl Albert.

It is something free men cannot endure. He cannot understand. He sits there angry, stony-faced, while the antagonism in the great hall mounts. It is his police, his city, his *Chicago Tribune*, his party; what if his troops have roughed up newsmen a little?; he cannot understand it at all. He is the stupid, repressive, rigid adversary any revolutionary would die to get. His presence taunts the restless delegates as the bullhorns downtown taunt the soldiers. TV floor interviewers dash about asking nervous delegates to comment on wild rumors, keeping the whole pot seething.

Gene McCarthy, like Henry A. Wallace before him, finds that some of his supporters have been using him, not following him. All night long Conrad Hilton residents on the lakefront hear songs, chants, obscenities. The police commit unforgivable acts. The shocked nation sees one TV incident—a woman driver, sheltering hippies, caught between troops and the dissidents, screaming for help. That was democracy, caught between anarchy and Mayor Daley.

Nixon Will Beat Humphrey

S EPTEMBER 28, 1968 We rather assume Nixon will win this election. Five polls came out last week all showing him way ahead. We guess Humphrey will narrow the lead from now on, but whether he can do a 1948-Truman act is doubtful. It has taken a good deal of the suspense out of the affair.

Maybe we are wrong, but we don't think who wins makes much difference on Vietnam. The war has been lost. We started the war essentially to show that a revolutionary national movement could be stopped by armor, and like it or not, events prove that it can't. Americans now desperately want a face-saving formula to get out. The tug between saving face and saving lives has produced a galloping case of national schizophrenia; we have never seen America so tormented. The angry uncertainty becomes violence in many other fields.

Unless Mr. Johnson halts bombing in the meantime, we see the next president, whoever he is, soon becoming as unpopular as the war itself, or making peace. We think Nixon or Humphrey will move to make peace shortly after taking office. Very likely it will be done obliquely. It took de Gaulle three years to get out of Algeria. American patience won't last that long. And since America wants peace but dislikes defeat, the man who actually gets peace is apt to be denounced and reviled, unless he shows amazing footwork. We don't envy him.

We can set down the above thoughts with pert coolness, but actually we don't feel that way. We are terribly gloomy. Making America face up to the humiliation that probably lies ahead is a ghastly business. Maybe it can be camouflaged. No nation save the British has our capacity for righteous self-deception. We were trounced in the War of 1812 (even more unpopular than this one) but fixed our eyes resolutely on the victory at New Orleans, which had no military significance and was fought after the Treaty of Ghent. The treaty said nothing about impressment, which caused the war. So what?—we won a fine battle, didn't we?

Well, who has a New Orleans up his sleeve now? What we fear is a hate-filled, prolonged, post-Vietnam witch-hunt, pinning blame, finding traitors, and raising every point but the right one about our embarrassment over the fact that, at first, virtually the whole nation went along in a mistaken policy, a land war in Asia.

As we say, concerning Vietnam we haven't been able to see, so far, that it makes much difference who wins, Nixon or Humphrey. But on domestic matters it is a different story. The Republican Party has been strongly, actively, steadily opposing nearly every major piece of social-progress legislation of the past four years. Perhaps civil rights is an exception. If so, there are hardly any others.

Nixon's whole experience and bias is toward social conservatism, and he goes out of his way to emphasize it; he glories in it. Poverty, he feels instinctively, is the fault of the poor. Crime is the fault of the courts. On crime, he considers Humphrey "tragically naive"; "I say that doubling the conviction rate in this country would do more to cure crime in America than quadrupling the funds for Mr. Humphrey's war on poverty," he declares glibly.

Nixon carries Edward Brooke on one shoulder, Strom Thurmond on the other. He's for school desegregation but not for the federal financial pressure necessary to enforce it. If elected, he will probably not get 10 percent of the Negro vote. It's a question whether he can govern a seething revolt under those circumstances.

If there's one thing that's certain in this country, present inequalities of income must somehow be moderated. That, or apartheid. It's not an agreeable thing to say, but our taxes, as a ratio of national income, are low compared to most other democracies. We do less for the poor; our inequalities are greater. This pretense that the ghetto problem and unemployment can be sublet to big corporations to solve in return for tax concessions is the Nixon approach; it won't work. We honor Humphrey for saying recently that whatever private business does for the city the government's role remains "crucial" and that any genuine drive to improve the situation "will cost money —a great deal of it." Of course it will. Like it or not, federal intervention, and taxes, are going to increase.

It may be argued that turning affairs over to Nixon and the Republicans (we guess he will have a Republican House; not the Senate) will do no great harm—look at Eisenhower. But the cases are not the same.

In 1952, when Ike took over, the country needed a rest, and he gave it. He boasted that he was not a politician and it was true; he thought that was an asset. He did not know that the crucial period for a president is the first two years when he has maximum prestige and a malleable Congress. Ike did not even have a program the first year, and lost his seedtime. He did not set the clock back; he never knew the time. And after the first two years he had a Democratic Congress.

Things are different today. Nixon knows the score, he's an activist. The next two years may produce disaster even if liberal reforms are pushed; but, instead of that, we fear, Nixon will institute moves in the opposite direction. He will save money, cut taxes, try to decentralize, subcontract relief of poverty to General Motors. The country is in a conservative mood. With George Wallace looking over Nixon's shoulder (and setting his sights on 1972), God knows what Nixon will do.

Wallace is the dynamic force in this campaign. A man who received World War II service-connected compensation for psychoneurotic disability is rousing the frightened white lower-middle class against the blacks. And he may put the election into the House yet.

Humphrey's Logorrhea

OCTOBER 12, 1968   It's funny, sitting in a big hall, waiting for a riot to start. In this ugly election Humphrey, the most liberal of the three candidates, carries a built-in riot with him wherever he goes.

The yelling rises as you sit there, your pulse starts pounding, you can feel atavistic angers rising in the crowd. Humphrey didn't plan this. He is a warmhearted, likable man. His black hair drawn like a wig over his bald, bulging forehead makes him look like an actor playing "The Mikado." He is witty, quick, and rises to eloquence. Nixon won't debate him; wise, too. Humphrey would chew him up. But Humphrey has the worst case of logorrhea of any modern public man. The relationship of what he says to prepared text is only coincidental. On a panel show in California he answered only three questions in forty-five minutes. Friends despair. Sometimes he wows audiences and then won't stop. Even after a moderator has thanked him he is likely to be up and off again. He is like a mad vending machine: insert a dime and you get your peanut bar, and then another, and another. There is no stopping it. It rains peanut bars. He lacks intellectual discipline.

And now we are sitting here waiting for the confrontation. Bobby Kennedy—Jack Kennedy—would have been incredulous at the lack of curbstone crowds; people like Humphrey but they don't turn out for him. His campaign is next to broke; he scrounges time from local TV stations, interspersed with advertising "messages."

And yet he says things on the domestic side that make a liberal throw his hat in the air. On the basic issue, using government resources to reduce poverty and paying for it out of the expanding economy, he is passionately committed. And Nixon, our next president, isn't. If Nixon applies the economic policies he pretends to favor he will stop the clock; if he and Strom Thurmond apply the advice of Spiro Agnew to forthcoming Resurrection Cities ("Employ the steps taken at Chicago") he will have insurrection.

Wallace, the hillbilly Hitler, makes Nixon look good. And yet Gallup sees Wallace strength mounting, Humphrey sinking, and the Nixon landslide lead remaining the same. Even so, Nixon will be a minority president in a three-way split.

So now we are back in the hall. Sometimes they interrupt, sometimes they jeer, sometimes they use a bullhorn, sometimes they walk out. It is the walkout tonight. Humphrey's face is tight and grim; they chant "End the war," and maybe one in ten leaves the civic auditorium. Not all go: one bawls from the gallery, "Why don't you end the bombing?" In the third and concluding Humphrey peroration, the speaker pretends not to notice.

This is not normal heckling. It is a mass effort to break up a democratic gathering. It is disciplined. The Nazi youth did it in Germany. It is directed (as always in history) at the least reactionary of the several candidates. A placard brandished before police at San Francisco reads REMEMBER CHICAGO—YOU SWINE. Outrageous, eh? Self-defeating, too, perhaps; all my taxi drivers seem to be for Wallace. Humphrey may get a sympathy vote, but consider the other side. Here is a sour campaign of two antiheroes and a spoiler. Many voters are unhappy with all the candidates. And one minority passionately alienated. Look at this crowd of chanting youngsters outside Humphrey's hotel after the speech. It is like Chicago—they stand on one side of the street, the police on the other. But this is better-natured. A few are hippies; mostly they aren't. High school and college age. Here is a school kid showing off. Here is an angry undergraduate. Here is the son of a rich papa who has got out of the draft by going to college, out for a lark. Here is a concerned Quaker. Here is an agitator known to the FBI. And here are mostly young people stirred to their depths at being commanded by their elders to fight in a war they hate.

Political speakers deserve fair play, don't they? But are young men getting fair play in the present draft? Democracy requires live and let live, doesn't it? Yes, but does the older generation have the right to conscript the younger one for something they both loathe? Balance it off—why, if they don't like Humphrey, don't the youngsters quietly vote for somebody else? Who else? On Vietnam there are three rivals but only one candidate.

So that's how it is, traveling with Humphrey. He says things you cheer for. He talks too much. He attracts doves like George Ball and Arthur Goldberg. He angers youth. The worried nation looks on uncertainly. It is not used to this.

When a big vested interest has a grievance it hires a lobbyist, pays a million dollars, and wraps Congress round its finger. But youth has no million, no lobbyist, no candidate; it is politically adrift, going leftward fast, the perfect flock for Judas-rams to lead. Protest methods are outrageous if you like, but what other methods are there?

All signs indicate the nation will vote next month for lawnorder. That should give Nixon and Agnew and reaction, recession, and repression. But unless Vietnam is ended, will it end youth's mutiny?

Notes Robert McNamara is a banker with a social conscience. But good banking takes notice of people, not just money. If the world's birthrate is not slowed, he said last week, a transfusion of money will not help. There's not enough of that plasma in McNamara's World Bank. After six months on the job, RM has a Five Year Plan. He'd double loans, concentrate them on education and agriculture *and* birth control. "The rapid growth of population is one of the greatest barriers to the economic and social well-being of our member states," he said in his debut speech before the Bank. "More than anything else it is the population explosion which, by holding back the advancement of the poor, is blowing apart the rich and the poor and widening the already dangerous gap between them."

THE NIXON YEARS
[*1968-1974*]

"Mr. Nixon Will Offer Bad Solutions"

NOVEMBER 16, 1968   Let us soberly consider the next four years under President Nixon. He will probably wind up Vietnam pretty quickly. Anyone can see that the country hates the war that destroyed Lyndon Johnson. It isn't Nixon's war and he can blame everything on the Democrats.

He will open up communications with the public; for reasons beyond understanding, secretive Mr. Johnson cut himself off and lost touch; hence the "credibility gap." Mr. Nixon's Herb Klein (who isn't a press secretary but a "communications coordinator") is a nice fellow and should help get things back on the track.

We must try to be fair to Mr. Nixon. But we think he is in for a hard time. As this is written, temporarily at least, Hubert Humphrey appears to have a slight edge in popular vote. Under direct election and under the system recommended by the American Bar Association, Mr. Humphrey would be president. Mr. Nixon is the first man in the century elected without winning Congress too.

The Democratic Ninety-first Congress will try to cut him up. Its dominant force will probably be a GOP-Dixiecrat-Wallace coalition. Though it is conservative it probably won't help Mr. Nixon much. The fact is that after thirty-six years, all but eight of them under Democrats, the nation has taken a confused turn to the right.

The chief trouble Mr. Nixon will have, we think, is that the solutions he offers are bad solutions. He is hipped on the idea that you can quiet the ghetto by subsidizing big business to tackle the problem. Congress will love that, and maybe the public will buy it too, for a time, but we are quite certain it won't work.

Nor do we think Mr. Nixon's basic philosophy to "restore" free enterprise, to curb inflation by increasing unemployment, to cut down federal activity by turning things back to states, to reduce the budget at a time when population is increasing 3,000,000 a year, to slash foreign aid still further—no, those things won't work either. We give Mr. Nixon credit, he's no fool. He's not naive like General Eisenhower. We don't mean to flatter him by saying he probably didn't mean a lot of the stuff he promised in the campaign. Just the same, the conservative approach, pressed at this particular moment of history, will, we are persuaded, give Mr. Nixon a hard time. In our modest way we may try to add to it.

It will be a grim confrontation when Earl Warren steps forward next January 20 to administer the presidential oath. Maybe the admirable chief justice will take sick that day. We should guess Mr. Nixon will name three or four new justices to the elderly Court. He can transform it. Furthermore, in this genteel repression labeled "law and order" we should expect some new legislation. Very likely it will take the form of mandatory penalties, bypassing discretionary power by the courts. This is nearly always a bad thing, like compulsory death sentences for certain crimes.

You can see what we mean by a little item passed by the Ninetieth Congress. Congress approved large research and similar grants for colleges and added riders withholding funds from student rioters. Universities that accept the funds lose the right to discipline students and hand it over, in effect, to some funding agency, often the Defense Department. That's one way of trying to get lawnorder.

We stayed up all night election night watching the quiet folk give verdict. We thought Hubert Humphrey, with the Gallup Poll tied around his leg, made a gallant fight the last fortnight. All of a sudden Gallup, who had Humphrey lagging fifteen points behind, had him neck and neck with Nixon; the contest "too close to call." Of course the earlier reading of the tea leaves dried up gifts to the Democrats. It dried up Mr. Nixon too. Why debate when he was going to win anyway? Campaigns can be educational sometimes, and stimulate interest in affairs, but in this one everybody discussed polls instead of issues. What eloquent phrase or sizzling epithet distinguishes 1968 from its fellow campaigns and will bring it back, years hence, like FDR's comment about "my little dog Fala"? We can think of only one, a grain of gold shining in the pebbles. Yes, of course: "Spiro who?" We'll remember that.

For several hours in the early morning of November 6, most of us really thought this contest, for the first time in 144 years, would be an unelection. The electoral college time bomb in the Constitution ticked loudly but didn't go off.

It was touch and go whether Wallace would take enough electoral votes in the South to prevent either Humphrey or Nixon from getting the requisite 270 majority under the quaint formula. Wallace would have won them, too, if the South had stayed with him as he expected. But Strom Thurmond, who is as much of a racist as Wallace, had got in before him on behalf of Nixon. Thurmond is pals with Nixon, you remember, and escorted him to the platform at Miami Beach for his acceptance speech.

Wallace actually did pretty poorly—he got only Alabama, Arkansas, Georgia, Louisiana, and Mississippi, with forty-five electors. Had he taken any more he would almost certainly have succeeded in his design of stalemating the election. At a time of great crisis at the Paris peace talks, of war in Vietnam, and of unsolved problems at home, the nation would have been shaken by a constitutional crisis. Yes, we probably owe our escape to Strom Thurmond. We are reduced to strange circumstances when we must be grateful to him.

The southern Democratic base was blasted in 1968. Democrats won only Texas. Yet one-party southern chairmen still control eight of the fourteen major Senate committees, and ten of the seventeen in the House. We think the southern power base is collapsing. Control of these committees is its final stronghold.

The Nixon Coalition

JANUARY 23, 1969 Richard Nixon, the Man without Magic, is now president. There is no Pedernales. There is no Camelot. He has picked a cabinet of Nixons; they are committed to respectability and the status quo. He has a Democratic Congress and is a minority winner. Who knows; he may make a good president.

As to politics we have little doubt which way Mr. Nixon will go; he will try to demolish the old FDR Democratic coalition and create one of his own. His wrecking ball in 1968 shook the FDR coalition but knocked out only one segment, the South. Of thirteen southern states Mr. Humphrey got only one, Texas, and that by only 39,000 votes. (Ironically, southern Democrats still control the major congressional committees by the troika of seniority, chairmanships, and the filibuster: the situation mocks democracy and defies reason. It can't last if the South ever gets a genuine two-party system.)

So Mr. Nixon on the political front will try to win two allies, we imagine. First—the South. He has already begun this by an alliance with Strom Thurmond, by picking Spiro Agnew, and by hinting that he will soften enforcement of the public-school desegregation guidelines. (Maybe he can woo a Negro to serve in a high administration post under these circumstances, but it will be difficult.)

The other Nixon ally would be the ten million people who voted for George Wallace. This is really sociology, not politics. There is a big segment in the US class structure that starts just above the poverty line and includes lower-middle-class incomes. It rises from the so-called near-poor to the median family income of around $8,000. This group is bitterly alienated. Federal billions go to the ghetto; not to it. It's the stepchild of relief, it feels, and it has genuine grievances.

This group is ready to bolt. It is looking around for a new leader, and this is true not only from the five southern states which Wallace carried but from the row-house suburbs round the country. It should be noted that Pat Moynihan, Mr. Nixon's new urbanologist, is well aware of the lower-middle-class problem. He ardently backs federal income maintenance through children's allowances, for example. The so-called baby bonus would be paid the near-poor as well as the poor. "Any serious effort at income redistribution on a national scale," Moynihan says, "has almost got to seek forms that will emphasize the unities of the problem rather than the disunities."

There you have it. A bold move or two by Mr. Nixon could wrap up a political coalition of southern whites, the status quo American middle class, and the pro-George Wallace, alienated near-poor. In one form or another we suspect that Mr. Nixon will try this; it would be a tough combination to beat.

No president in modern times has come to office with so little known about his views—a situation that Mr. Nixon will remedy shortly. We see one problem that will begin almost at once. It starts dramatically.

Out of nowhere one day the surprised residents of Lynnfield-Wakefield, Massachusetts, saw uniformed men with trucks breaking down fences and overrunning valuable property where children played. When they angrily protested, they were told that they were being guarded against China. China? Yes, the incredulous people were told, this was the first of sixteen double installations, to cost $5 billion over five years, to set up a "thin" antimissile screen to knock out any warheads Communists in China might aim at Boston. Most of the stunned local people had heard nothing about it. "The military came in the most clandestine manner," a native told an interviewer from PBL-TV (which recently put on a brilliant ninety-minute documentary on the expanding military-industrial complex).

Johnson and McNamara recommended the "thin" system and Congress voted it, without hearings. Inhabitants of Lynnfield had the helpless feeling of people unable to control their government or even to have a say.

Now the toe is in the door for a big ABM system that will cost anywhere from $50 to $200 billion. Many scientists think it will be worthless. Mr. McNamara opposed it. The brass, however, wants it. One thing it will be in any case, if Mr. Nixon can't work out an agreement with Russia: it will be the armaments race literally and actually to end all armaments races; that is, till we go back to stone axes.

It will take more money than the Vietnam War. It will send Nixon's finances, we guess, into a tailspin. It will come up in Congress fairly quickly; this time Senators Proxmire and Percy guarantee to have it argued out. Some think Mr. Johnson gave the go to the thin system to head off Mr. Nixon's campaign talk about a "serious missile gap." White House scientific consultant Jerome Wiesner said, "I think we ought to regard the Sentinel (thin system) as a bad joke perpetrated by Mr. McNamara and Mr. Johnson on us in an election year."

Did you ever think what a billion dollars is?—it would pay for all the 140 Model Cities programs to rebuild slums; it would build 500 brand-new grade schools; it would subsidize housing for a million families. The Pentagon wants a lot of those billions for ABM. The decision is hurtling right at President Nixon, with the biggest lobby in Washington, the military-industrial complex, behind it. The MIC is for the ABM. In a showdown between MIC and schoolchildren we wouldn't bet on the kids.

As a congressman, Melvin Laird, the new secretary of defense, proposed "limited nuclear reprisals" against the Soviets if they encroached on Western territories. He said we should let Moscow know we would strike first with nuclear weapons if it came to a showdown. This tough talk is in Laird's little-known 1962 book, *A House Divided— America's Strategy Gap*. Today he says merely that we are in a period of negotiations. The Pentagon should love Laird.

The Warren Court

APRIL 26, 1969   Any day now Mr. Nixon will send Congress the name of the new chief justice of the Supreme Court. In the long run this is more important than almost anything, more important than the shocking loss of the EC-121, for example. The Warren Court wet-nursed a social revolution; now Mr. Nixon is going to replace it. He will probably have four appointments.

Chief Justice Warren quits in June; the replacement will presumably go before the Senate for confirmation in May. Justice Black is 83; Justice Douglas, 70, has an electric heart pacer; and Justice Harlan, 69, has eye trouble. Exit the Warren Court; enter the Nixon Court.

General Eisenhower's choice of Earl Warren in 1953 was probably his single most important domestic act. Warren became one of the great chief justices of all time. In 1954, tickets to the Navy football game at the Sugar Bowl in New Orleans carried the notation, "Caucasian Race Only." In that same year the impressive, black-robed new chief justice leaned forward from the bench and read the unanimous decision that ended school segregation. And inferentially it ended an era. This decision meant not only schools—it meant shortly that blacks would have the legal right to sit where they wanted in a bus, to use common toilets in waiting rooms, to buy homes in white suburbs, to be first-class citizens. When actual rights didn't follow legal rights, there came militancy.

From then on the Warren Court was under attack. It had a built-in, bitter opposition. Whenever, thereafter, it departed from the conservative norm it was denounced and this anger was cumulative. The reason is understandable. Under ordinary circumstances the majestic Court is not a contemporary institution; normally it applies yesterday's precedents to today's problems; it lags a generation. The archaic Court in FDR's day tried to block the New Deal. But now the Warren Court was contemporary. Indeed, it often was a jump ahead of the president and Congress; it recognized the social imperative before the timid elected representatives of the people in the legislature. That has been its glory and its grief. That is why Birchite lawns sprouted signs, "Impeach Earl Warren."

If people can't get justice in law there is only one other battleground, the streets. Some think the Warren Court has been overactivist. But really, all it has done is to open doors. The doors did not have to be broken down.

Legislative malapportionment became intolerable and the Court came through with its one man, one vote decision. It is surprising how quickly this has been accepted; Barry Goldwater denounced it in 1964, and the always entertaining Senator Dirksen proposed his Constitutional Convention. But, on the whole, it has been absorbed step by step. The latest decision came April 7, when the court, 6 to 3, finepointed its doctrine of equality even further.

The attacks grew and strengthened—"soft on Communism; coddling criminals." The 8-to-1 ban on compulsory Bible and prayer reading in public schools, though supported by certain denominational leaders, shocked many. The Court was not antireligious; it was arguing that in a pluralistic society religious exercises in public schools (though sanctioned by the majority) are a threat to the liberty of nonconformists.

Warren gave his name to the Court, but actually there have been seventeen judges serving with him in all. But it is of him the public thinks. The dominant theme has been the necessity of equal rights for all, protection of the underdog, respect for the dignity of man in an agonizingly complex society. As Princeton's William M. Beaney puts it, "it seems obvious that when the Court chose to hand down decisions favorable to racial minorities, political dissenters, criminal defendants, and protagonists of unpopular causes, it could hardly expect cheers from the majority of the people."

One of the critics is Mr. Nixon. All through his campaign he complained of the Supreme Court though, like his attacks on the handling of the *Pueblo* incident, his views may shift now that he is in power. Mr. Nixon says that he wants judges who will "interpret the law" and not try "to make the law." He says, "I believe in a strict interpretation of the Supreme Court's functions." He has promised to appoint men of that view.

The trouble is, there is no clear distinction between "interpreting" and "making" the law. The Court is an extraordinary institution, part judicial, part political. It can duck the hard decisions if it wants to. It can move to the right, or left, or conduct a staying operation. Mr. Nixon can tip the balance with a single appointment. For example, he has attacked the "Miranda" decision, protecting the right of accused in certain criminal cases. The Miranda case was decided 5 to 4. No other appointment Mr. Nixon makes will be more important than his new chief justice. Almost certainly, Hubert Humphrey would have maintained the Court as a contemporary institution. Almost certainly Mr. Nixon will set it back to its old position, one generation behind.

Meanwhile, the crisis over the shooting down of the EC-121 reconnaissance plane suddenly exploded, with the gloating commentary of the North Koreans. And everybody remembered the *Pueblo*, and looked up what Candidate Nixon had said about it.

Every presidential candidate makes silly statements; the public rather expects it. Franklin Roosevelt promised to balance the budget; Kennedy pointed to a nonexistent missile gap. For Richard Nixon it was what he was going to do to get respect from other countries— particularly little ones who thumbed their noses at the US.

At his outdoor rally there would be the Nixonettes in their plastic straw hats, the release of the balloons, and then (fanfare; cheers) the Candidate, who generally promised not to let any foreign country use the American flag as a doormat (cheers; commotion). Yes, it was a good act and always got a great hand. Alas, like every other man elected president, Mr. Nixon now finds the situation greatly changed. We hope he keeps his cool.

Senate Hearings

JULY 26, 1969   Typical morning in the New SOB (Senate Office Building) . . . Hearings under way . . . Start first with Senator Mondale's subcommittee on migratory labor; subtopic, grape boycott . . . Knot outside trying to enter; inside jam-packed, hot, standing room only.

Cork floors, walls paneled, crowded press tables, hot TV lights, senators looking down on witness. Small, dark, wiry, vivid woman with hair to shoulders (like male hippie) Dolores Huerta talks rapidly, 300 to the minute with bursts of 400. After you get her wavelength you can understand.

The room fades—you're in the fields, working poor, men, women, and children, mostly Negro or Spanish-speaking, are bending over crops, the most downtrodden workers in America, the migrants. They're excluded from National Labor Law protection, they're bucking growers, courts, power structure, and Governor Reagan. If they get obstreperous, Mexican labor may be brought in.

Now they've got a union toehold, God knows how; 7,500 holding contracts with ten employers. Picket lines, police harassment, court injunctions, but after a four-year strike the boycott of table grapes is taking hold. Can they hang on? Can migrant labor organize? Nobody knows. Frightened employers have just brought antitrust suit and the Pentagon, the dear old Pentagon, has moved in to buy low-price grapes as delicacy for our boys in Vietnam. A 350-percent increase in Pentagon grape purchases will please GI Joe's palate and help keep his parents back home second-class citizens. . . .

Time to leave; what next? A larger queue outside, more cops at door. Defense Secretary Mel Laird facing Foreign Relations Committee. Five floodlights and twenty-four ceiling lights wrestle with air conditioning on 95-degree day. Cops lead out pale, fainting lad from rear standees. About thirty reporters, three tripod cameras. More paneling and cork floors.

Senator Gore (D., Tenn.) asks, five times, in view of Vietnam lull has Pentagon modified its "maximum pressure on enemy" directive? Laird ducks four times; suddenly says he's sent General Wheeler to Saigon, presumably to see about it all. Sensation. Laird adds aimlessly, "I think we've certainly turned the corner." (What corner; the same old one?) Everything's beneath the surface here. Everybody knows the war is ending. Now a great big political hand is pushing supple Mr. Nixon toward settlement and reluctant Pentagon is giving, too. Come in, come in, wherever you are; last one in's a hawk.

Let's move again. Out-of-town students waiting hopefully in line; more cops outside, more lights inside: this is your lively McClellan show. Senator McClellan (D, Ark.), scourge of radicals, is bullying unfortunate Chancellor Heyns, University of California at Berkeley. Heyns can't finish sentences; McClellan has a built-in indignation that takes off without countdown, the dour look of a Salem witch-hunter. He's a BIG CONSPIRACY man: they're gaining on us, they're getting us, they're under the bed. He kept Prexy Pusey of Harvard in rear seat three hours and never did hear him, after inviting him to testify, while listening instead to a Harvard teaching fellow who denounced student riots as all due to faculty softness. That is McClellan's idea too.

Here he goes again. Heyns's balanced presentation of life in a knowledge factory at Berkeley with 28,000 students, and firebombs, physical threats, and "swift vandalism of 100 to 300 massed individuals," includes a hint that maybe things would be better with something done about poverty, civil rights—things like that. McClellan takes off (he reminds one of Attorney General Mitchell, another stone-face). He is self-propelled with moral indignation. He's against faculty softies.

Well, we've had our fun. . . . We can't spend much time on Ralph Nader. Committee jammed, of course. He's telling McGovern committee about adulterated hot dogs (i.e., increasing cholesterol fat instead of protein). US eats 15 billion hot dogs annually. Nader wants labeling. Now it's baby food. Salt is bad for babies, he says, quoting doctors; why salt in baby food? "Not for baby but to please the taste of the mother." He says manufacturers of foods for pets offer better ingredient statements than the baby-food people. That's lucky, Nader says—millions of the poor buy dog food. . . .

Time for just one more committee pop-in before the noon quorum-call buzzer. (Actually, few are listening to Senate debates anymore; everybody's occupied making lobby deals on the ABM vote, or the surtax extension. It's the biggest auction block in years.)

No spotlight here; no cameras; handsome George Romney with eight advisers (four on a side) is talking about housing. He leans so far over the table that the microphone seems to be propping up his mouth. He's a dedicated believer in private enterprise, given a minimum of Detroit-style guidance from Washington. Bill Proxmire (D., Wis.) is the sole senator present and there's a boyish quality to both men; Romney tells about his "flowchart" and Proxmire says, "that's fine, I think that's great" . . . Few in room, maybe fifty; nice and cool and relaxed. Nobody knows how long Romney's enthusiasm can last; nobody quite believes in his housing crusade that won't cost any money. But it makes fine sales talk at the White House.

Well, that's the story. This morning we have glanced in on five hearings out of a possible nineteen in the Senate and twenty-two in the House—all going on simultaneously. They look a lot alike. Witness brings a text, then he's questioned. Sometimes he's extolled, sometimes browbeaten. Tripod cameras whir and roving photographers roam the room (in the Senate, anyway) taking background shots with windup cameras that chirp like crickets. The audience is a presence; it loved Dolores in the grape hearing; it backed Albert Gore when he needled Laird. In the McClellan spectacular oldsters seemed to like the senator, youngsters loathed him. A bit of all this may get on television or in the press. Mostly it's ignored. It's the brick and mortar of government. But it can't compete with a moon shot.

Lindsay and Muskie

JUNE 13, 1970   If Mr. Nixon is a one-term president, which seems not improbable, Democrats may make an ex-Republican president, or a man whose father's name was Marciszewski. One is a Protestant Republican who became mayor of a Democratic city; the other a Catholic Democrat who became senator from a Republican state. Each is six feet four. Meet the two: Lindsay of New York, Muskie of Maine.

. . . There was a rap on the door where newsmen were having breakfast with Mayor Lindsay the other day in Washington and a man came in with an urgent message. It was scrawled in longhand from a telephone call. The mayor read it and winced. He had been describing the volcanic pressures under the city he seeks to govern. He looked up. "Another policeman killed," he said grimly. The second that week. He went, of course, to the funeral.

Lindsay has the most fortunate face in American politics; aquiline features, fair, wavy hair, sandy eyebrows, a Barrymore profile. He is young (forty-seven), eager, earnest, and exciting with the aristocratic, rangy grace of a racehorse. He will walk this summer, head high, through the slums of Manhattan trying to keep the lid on, the way he did in the terrible summer of 1967 when cities all over the country were exploding. But not New York.

In 1970 it may be harder. Five hundred thousand kids turned loose on the streets the minute school's over, he was saying, with no recreational facilities and few jobs. Come to a Manhattan police station about one or two in the morning, he says; who is it that terrorize the streets with purse snatchings and muggings? It's the fourteen- to eighteen-year-olds. Around fifteen. I'll show you.

Reporters try to betray him into talking national politics. Everyone feels he's on a knife-edge. Representative Dick Bolling (D, Mo.), candidate for party whip, has just nominated him for Democratic standard-bearer in 1972 in a national magazine piece. Here's this golden boy, a nominating convention's dream, a Republican Kennedy—St. Paul, Yale, after eight years in Congress first Republican mayor of New York since the Little Flower; everyone knew he couldn't do it, but he did.

And so, of course, the Republicans nominated another man for mayor. Lindsay alienated the upstate conservatives. Everybody knew that cooked his goose. So he got reelected in 1969 on a fusion ticket.

But today he won't talk politics. He's against Vietnam but he won't attack Mr. Nixon. He says firmly he's not going to swap parties in a hurry. And why should he alienate the administration? He's here on a begging expedition; the way he goes begging to Albany. Every mayor of every big city goes begging. Most are bankrupt or near it. You can't bite the hand that feeds you; not now, anyway. And there's that terrible summer ahead. The administration has been cutting back city gratuities. With federal cutbacks and inflation the mayor says he probably has 20 percent less funds for the kids than last year, and think what's ahead with race, jobs, and Vietnam.

. . . So now let's look at another putative president, Ed Muskie of Maine. Lindsay and Muskie make as fascinating a contrast as there is today in politics. The scene here is a big hearing room in the Senate; it's dramatic because Nader's Raiders have just attacked this calm Yankee for being a make-believe, a false front for pretended pollu-tion-control—actually wishy-washy on the subject. Muskie is here to defend himself—if he can. He has called a special press conference.

It is a political case study to watch. Muskie, somebody said, was the only winner in 1968. Was he really that good, or was it just the contrast with the other three? Television audiences looked and liked him. It was observed that he had the loose, casual charm of Snoopy the beagle. But there was more to it; he had an aplomb that could only come from some inner reserve. Hecklers almost ruined Humphrey but Muskie just asked them to come on up to the platform. He could turn on calm like a hose that puts out a bonfire.

And that is what he is doing now. He doesn't raise his voice. The 548-page report (which only mentioned him incidentally) called him "an extremely astute politician who by temperament avoids conflict and unfavorable odds." Muskie extends his big moose-jaw in a quiet, stubborn fashion. He talks and answers questions for an hour, but sums it all up in a sentence, "I can't change the way I am." He is calm, judicial, sensible. Mister Wholesome. Most of us come away feeling his critics never touched him. Well, hardly.

The Gallup Poll asked adults to select their favorite Democratic candidate from a field of nine: Muskie got 23 percent (Kennedy 17, Humphrey 16). Then came Mayor Lindsay (10) who outdistanced four Democrats. The Harris Poll pitted Muskie as front-runner against Mr. Nixon; result—Nixon 48 points, Muskie 46 points. An extraordinary result in some ways, though more reflecting the present lukewarm attitude toward the president, perhaps, than the other way round. If the snowballing campaign had gone on a week longer in 1968 Edmund Muskie would today be our Spiro Agnew. Oh well; you say it.

Big Ed's father came over from Poland before the First World War and the immigration officer changed his name to Muskie. He lived in the small hill town of Rumford, Maine (10,000 pop.), where the family bathed once a week in a tin tub heated on the stove. It was an enjoyable, old-fashioned childhood that recalls Dwight Eisenhower's in Kansas, "We were poor but we didn't know it." His father was a tailor, "a damned good tailor," highly respected; "I worked with him, learning how to make alterations, shorten trousers."

So that's the contrast. One's the city boy, glamorous, aristocratic; the other's rural style, low-keyed, a square. Both tall, both liberal; both attractive in extraordinarily different ways. And both with political defects. Lindsay is in a dead-end street; mayor is a harder job in many ways than president; he's won the rich and the poor but not the white, working-class hard hats, the monopolistic, discriminatory building trade unions. Muskie's defect is different. He's got a personal force that would stare down Mount Rushmore; but passion, incandescence, who knows?

Nixon and the Press

OCTOBER 10, 1970   At this point in his first term of office Franklin Roosevelt had held 150 Washington press conferences. President Nixon has held 12. It has changed the whole tone here. It has made the presidency once removed.

Other Nixon officials follow the off-the-record White House pattern. The bold, direct press conference, "How about it, Mr. President?" has turned into the timid news leak, and news ooze.

Enter a new vocabulary.

Settling back in his chair the Anonymous High Official breathes heavily, glances round the oblong table, notes the poised pencils, and makes his decision: will his information be—on the record; off the record; half and half; background; deep background; very deep background; formula attribution ("usually well-informed sources")?

Everybody plays this game today in Washington; it has succeeded hula hoop and Frisbee. Does Agnew's attack on the Scranton campus unrest report represent Mr. Nixon's own views? Mr. Nixon isn't there to ask. How about the Middle East? You can get Mr. Nixon's supposed feelings filtered out from a secretary, or grab an early edition of some newspaper before the story is killed where Mr. Nixon has seen executives, or you can subscribe to *Women's Wear Daily*.

The lively Henry Kissinger is the most prolific anonymous briefer.

Press secretary Ron Ziegler brings him in: "The ground rules are as they have been in the past," says Ziegler; "'Administration officials'; no direct quotations." A reporter asks, "Are you going to give us copies to take away or just to look at?"

Ziegler: "I haven't decided that yet."

Dr. Kissinger: "You will get the text as soon as we put the verbs into it." (Laughter).

Once when the cover was a "high official source," Kissinger brightly suggested that reporters add, "with an accent."

An Eastern European reporter made surreptitious approaches to an American colleague to find out the Kissinger pitch on a recent crisis; he learned that the statement was available—no revelation of source, of course. Under this admirable arrangement everybody reads what Kissinger says except the American people. As to direct Q and A's to Mr. Nixon, that has happened only a dozen times here since he took office.

There's always the question whether it's "on or off"—the record, that is. John and Martha Mitchell have complicated that. Are comments at a cocktail buffet or at a black-tie dinner automatically "off"? The Women's National Press Club put on a recent wingding where the AG commented easily about "these stupid bastards who are running our educational institutions," and declared that with campus violence "this country is going so far right you are not going even to recognize it."

A reporter from *Women's Wear Daily* said she identified herself at the start of the conversation for an interview. She listened as the AG characterized Kissinger as an "egocentric maniac who loves to appear in newspapers with Jill St. John, but who's brilliant and indispensable when he gets back to his office." What she heard she reported.

A protest exploded instantly from the Department of Justice. Who issued it? "A Justice Department spokesman."

Martha Mitchell rises above all this. When she is in the mood, often late at night, she calls up a wire service and denounces somebody. The other morning she explained that she was speaking from her upstairs bathroom, "so John won't hear me talking to you." No off-the-record commentator, she.

Mr. Nixon is an old hand at this sort of thing. In April 1954, he spoke "off the record," as he put it, to 600 editors and guests at a convention here, urging the US to send troops into Indochina to help the French. Fortunately Ike overruled him. Of course you can't be off the record before 600 people. Mr. Nixon is still belligerent, still off the record. In Chicago the other day he briefed local editors on the Near East. What looked like inspired administration warnings to Russia promptly got into some early editions, apparently not at all to the displeasure of the White House. The official Voice of America eagerly put them out round the world. As the *New York Times* drily observed, the White House "did not deny" them, and "did not seem deeply perturbed that its tough tone was being communicated to other countries."

The other day a party of reporters had breakfast with Pennsylvania's former governor William Scranton, chairman of the Commission on Campus Unrest. It was partly on the record, partly off. The Commission's report, incidentally, is remarkably evenhanded, denouncing violence, and also the official provocations that create violence. Presidential commissions, of course, are not created to get something done but to save the president from having to do anything. The Scranton report was terribly awkward for Mr. Nixon because it urged moderation, lowered voices, and reconciliation just as Spiro was in full whoop. It was all the more awkward because tall, sad-faced Mr. Scranton, besides being an impeccable Republican, is everything the administration isn't—dispassionate, aristocratic, and magnanimous.

Well, an odd thing happened; first Governor Scranton was there and then, presto, in the same chair sat a spectral "Commission Source." We get used to that sort of hide-and-seek, of course, in Washington, but it's a bit confusing at first, like Alice interviewing the disappearing cat.

Chief Justice Burger called in two startled wire service reporters the other day for an off-the-record, not-for-attribution, deep-backgrounder on why the Court is hearing a batch of southern school desegregation cases at the start of the new term. The combative chief justice aches to have the Court understood, with some reason, but can the system stand the strain? Outside, the reporters looked at each other. How handle the story? Should they say, chummily, "It is learned"? Or start authoritatively, "An unimpeachable source in a black robe at the Supreme Court revealed today"?

Spiro Agnew ranges America chiding the press for irresponsibility. Very confusing! With "background" you omit the source, don't you? . . . Or is that "deep background"? Sorry, folks. I'm going off the record.

The Crime Men: Clark and Hoover

NOVEMBER 28, 1970   Ramsey Clark looks like a young professor, J. Edgar Hoover like an old prizefighter; Ramsey Clark is bent steel, Hoover like a wrecker's ball; Clark is married and has two children, Hoover is married to the FBI, and is a bachelor; Clark abhors wiretapping and the death penalty; Hoover favors them; Clark likes plays, Hoover, prizefights. One is forty-two, the other seventy-five; Clark thinks Hoover "petty," "self-centered." Hoover calls Clark a "softie" and a "jellyfish." Oddly enough their basic preoccupation is the same. Crime.

To John E. Hoover (J. Edgar, to you) crime is crime. He hates it. He hated it when he became director of the politics-ridden FBI in 1924, at the age of twenty-nine. He has made the FBI into an efficient, incorruptible, secretive, elite corps, which is plainly headed to becoming a national police force, in fact, if not in name. Crime, to Hoover, is breaking laws. Why people break laws is not his business. He believes crime is caused by permissiveness and by sentimental courts and by softies like Clark. Till a few years ago, Hoover also emphasized Communism. It was to the FBI what the wind is to a kite; it carried it aloft; no Congress has ever cut FBI appropriations. Recently the fear of internal Communism has rather died down, but now there is campus unrest. The 1970 Omnibus Crime Control Act carried a harvest of 1,000 additional FBI agents to add to 18,000 already existing.

J. Edgar Hoover is that strange thing in American life, an untouchable. America is cynical, mutable, skeptical; it does not allow many such figures. A Prince of the Church, perhaps; General Eisenhower while he lived; it is hard to think of many others. Hoover stands on a pedestal; presidents are wary of him; he has served eight of them. If a politician can get Hoover's approval, direct or indirect, or be photographed with the man who, because he missed a fly ball once in a baseball game has a permanently flattened nose like one of those Kremlin leaders that he so much loathes, the politician is unassailable from then on, on the law-and-order issue.

Some people thought Jack Kennedy would fire Hoover. Not a bit of it; he embraced his prestige. Bobby was attorney general, and to Hoover it was like putting a civilian in charge of the Pentagon, or a Harry Truman set over Douglas MacArthur. Hoover's mandatory retirement age of seventy came on January 1, 1965, but President Johnson waived it. That was almost six years ago. Now there is a lovely Indian summer; probably Hoover has never felt more rapport with a president or attorney general on a no-nonsense crime approach than with Messrs. Nixon and Mitchell.

Hoover's position is so impregnable that when he gets mad at a critic he can say so. He reacted testily when the Warren Commission suggested that the FBI was negligent in not advising the Secret Service that Oswald was in Dallas at Kennedy's assassination. He denounced another critic, Martin Luther King, at a 1964 news conference with women reporters as a notorious liar, and apparently had a wiretap tape on King's private life which blackmailed the Negro leader into subsequent silence. Authorized eavesdroppers have fearsome power. Now in his latest dispute he has taken on Ramsey Clark.

His sensitivity to criticism begins to raise questions. In the past month, fifteen FBI agents dropped out of the John Jay College of Criminal Justice in New York because a professor made critical comments about Hoover. Following this, eleven FBI agents dropped out of a course on "Violence in America" at American University here because the professor made some jokes about the Hoover leadership. Satirist Art Buchwald drew a deduction: it was a conspiracy by professors over the country to identify and weed out the disguised FBI agents planted with the beardless, shoeless students as undercover agents. Once the teacher sullied Hoover's name the agents indignantly departed.

People who poke fun at the FBI make Hoover writhe. Ramsey Clark has just written a book, *Crime in America*, and he looks to be a sober, rather a melancholy young man. But he mistrusts Hoover's famous crime clock and jokes about it: "What do we do when we are told there is a murder every forty-three minutes and a rape every nineteen? If that time clock applied to the Virgin Islands, everyone there would be murdered in five years, after having been raped twice."

And he criticizes Hoover: "The FBI has so coveted personal credit that it will sacrifice even effective crime control before it will share the glory of its exploits. This has been a petty and costly characteristic caused by the excessive domination of a single person, J. Edgar Hoover, and his self-centered concern for his reputation and that of the FBI."

Washington shuddered and put its fingers in its ears. The explosion came. The *Washington Post* adroitly had a reporter on hand who got one of Hoover's rare interviews; yes, two hours of it. Ramsey Clark was the worst chief he ever had, Hoover fumed; he was worse than Bobby Kennedy, who wanted more Negro FBI agents. But why should Hoover worry? He could look across Pennsylvania Avenue at the excavation of the enormous new FBI building, a block long, a block and a half wide, to be finished in 1973 or 1974 for $102.5 million, the costliest federal building. The basement corridors will hold the fingerprints of 85 million Americans already collected, and perhaps ultimately the computerized Big Brother files of Justice (civil disturbance), Internal Revenue Service (taxes and gun registrations), Defense (politically active civilian militants), and dozens of others—room for the dossiers of a nation of 200 million; all of us.

But about crime. What causes it? "In every major city in the US," Ramsey Clark says, "you will find that two thirds of the arrests take place among only about 2 percent of the population. Where is that area in every city? Well, it's in the same place where infant mortality is four times higher than in the city as a whole; where the death rate is 25 percent higher . . . where education is poorest—the oldest school buildings, the most crowded and turbulent schoolrooms." He goes on and on.

Crime is crime, says Hoover. Crime is social failure, says Clark. And those are the two views in America today; a chasm of difference as awe-inspiring as the Grand Canyon.

The Greatest Problem in the United States

DECEMBER 26, 1970　In the uproar of Grand Central Station fifty years ago the dean of the University of Pennsylvania called a redcap. "Why, Ray," he said, "what are you doing here?"—and did not wait for an answer. It was obvious what the student, Ray Alexander, was doing; he was trying to survive. He had graduated in three years with highest honors but had been denied school membership in any honorary society because he was black.

That was 1920: fifty years ago. The boy wanted to go to Harvard Law School but was strapped. He had married a girl (who also graduated in three years with high honors and later became one of the first black women to get a PhD). Some professors at Harvard gave Alexander enough academic chores to do to keep him alive and he joined the 400 in the freshman law class. It included eight black entrants, highest in history because of postwar veterans' allowances.

It was a grim business. When a white classmate said "hello" that about ended the social side. Law clubs barred Negroes, and a new black club was started that only partly filled the vacuum. To survive meant spending virtually all the time in the law library. Alexander won out. Professors encouraged his ambition to practice law back in Philadelphia. Dean Pound and Professor Williston wrote letters of recommendation to the same prestigious law firm.

Alexander got copies of the letters and replies and was told that now all would be well. His future was assured. Meanwhile on the side he was upgraded to Pullman porter, and helped A. Philip Randolph organize the $30-a-month blacks, while between times he passed the Philadelphia bar exams.

Clad in a new, conservative suit and armed with his letters, Alexander nervously went to the law firm. The receptionist stared and doubted that he had a personal appointment to see Mister Big. "Oh," said Alexander, "I do, and here are my letters from Harvard." She disappeared with letters without asking him to have a seat. Down the hall a door opened and a woman looked out, stared, and closed the door.

Alexander was still standing when Mister Big came out and greeted him. "So—you are Alexander. How nice to know you." He read the letters silently and remarked, "How nice of the professors to speak so well of you. But I am afraid there has been a mistake. I'm very sorry. We can't use you." Courteously he returned the letters, took Alexander's arm, slowly walked him to the elevator, pushed the button, and said "good-bye."

Alexander moved to the rear of the elevator and suddenly, impulsively, burst into a flood of tears, something he hadn't done since his mother died. The operator stopped the car and asked apprehensively, "Did something happen to you? Can I do anything?"

Today Judge Raymond Pace Alexander is senior judge of the Court of Common Pleas, No. 4, in Philadelphia and author and public figure. He was one who didn't quit. As Judge Alexander says in a recent issue of the *Cornell Law Forum*, most top law firms in Philadelphia today have black staff lawyers. Times have changed.

Here at the end of 1970 it is appropriate for a minute to consider that change. Without doubt, race is the greatest problem in the United States. It is so big and pervasive that generally we don't talk about it much. One American in ten is black. Russia has no such problem; neither has China. America has prosperity unparalleled in the history of civilization but the disparity of the distribution of that wealth and the agonizing racial inequality weaken the whole; we could become like a great tree with a hollow trunk.

Sometimes a climber pauses on a ledge and looks up and feels that the height is almost unscalable. But then looking down his heart leaps at the sight of how far he has come. We are in the midst of boiling social change. Here in Washington a generation ago the principal theater stopped showing plays for two years because the proprietors wouldn't admit Negroes below the second balcony. It is hard to credit that now.

When TRB was a boy the *World Almanac* matter-of-factly listed the number of lynchings each year, and there were always several hundred. Some were orgies of animalistic hate as blacks were burned at the stake. Henry L. Mencken loved to shock the unctuous and wrote that the true ambition of every gutsy reporter was to see a real lynching. . . . The new 1971 *Almanac* is just out and does not even mention lynchings.

Once a year, maybe at Christmas, we ought to stop and think how far we have come instead of how far we must go. Lest it breed complacency, it can be considered along with the 1968 Kerner Commission report, which brought an indictment of "white racism." The Negro can never forget, it said, the implications of the ghetto: "white institutions created it, white institutions maintain it, and white society condones it."

The Kerner report said that somehow the suburbs must be breached; not to do so "would make permanent the division of our country into two societies; one, largely Negro and poor, located in the central cities; the other, predominantly white and affluent, located in the suburbs and outlying areas." This, it said, would produce a garrison state. It was a powerful and probably accurate forecast. Lest we relax, remember that just last week President Nixon flatly told his press conference that he opposed using the leverage of the federal government to push racial integration in the suburbs.

Nevertheless, once a year, at this time of wreaths and carols, we might take some pride in what we have done. Other nations are smug but they can't even conceive our problem. Injustices continue but nobody can study overall statistics without seeing the direction we are going; the pressure is irreversible, short of national disaster. The boy sobbing in the elevator is still with us but remember, he did not turn to bitterness and bomb-throwing but instead broke paths for others. More break through that path every year, and there is no end in sight. So let's, for a minute, consider not how far we must go but how far we have come. Pause, friends, for station identification.

The Record of the Ninety-first

JANUARY 2, 1971   What in the world was the Senate doing in the final days of the Ninety-first Congress? Making a collective fool of itself and a mockery of the legislative process? Richard Nixon thought so; he threatened to use the Twentieth Amendment to keep Congress in virtually continuous session because it hadn't passed his welfare reform bill (Nixon didn't start pushing the bill until the eleventh hour). GOP leader Hugh Scott thought so; he accused fellow senators of dawdling, posturing, delaying. Even Democratic leader Mike Mansfield conceded the Senate was a theater of the absurd —there were "filibusters on filibusters and filibusters within filibusters."

No more to it than that? Let's take a look at what the Senate, for all its bombast, blather, and delay, was trying to do.

(1) It was trying to keep Mr. Nixon from sleepwalking the US into another Southeast Asian war. That's bad? Senators Fulbright, Cooper, Church, and others have learned something from the six years of agony since White House-Senate somnambulism gave us the Gulf of Tonkin resolution. They're not sure Nixon has got the message, or believes it. They don't trust his motives in Vietnam, Cambodia, and Laos—who does? And even if the president really does want to get out and stay out, will the Pentagon let him? So the Senate passed the Cooper-Church amendment barring US troops from Cambodia, a landmark reassertion of its responsibility in foreign affairs.

(2) It was trying to break the military's stranglehold on American policy. For years, as *Washington Post* reporter Spencer Rich points

out, Congress "has acceded with monotonous and probably disgraceful regularity to Pentagon and/or presidential requests for larger weapons systems, more weapons, more presidential authority . . . for military ventures overseas." For years, billions of dollars in military spending were whooped through both chambers with only a day's debate, without amendments, without scrutiny, without thought.

Things were different this time. The Safeguard ABM was doubted and dissected in the Senate as no new weapons system has been challenged since the big-bomber fight of a decade ago (and that was primarily an interservice rivalry). Even in the hawkish House, Chairman Mahon of the Appropriations Committee quietly clipped $2 billion from military spending requests. The Pentagon is on notice.

(3) It was trying to block the supersonic transport, which the US needs like more used-car lots. The administration's arguments for the SST were among the most specious of the session; against them, Senator William Proxmire mounted a filibuster.

Filibuster! Dirty word. Middle-aged liberals grew up hating the filibuster in the hands of southern Bilbos blocking civil rights legislation. But it depends on whose ox is being gored. What if a filibuster is the only weapon available to stand against the military state, against another Asian morass, against SST noise and pollution? And don't forget that pro-administration senators filibustered for seven weeks against the Cooper-Church amendment until Nixon could get US troops out of Cambodia.

Because they used it lavishly in the Ninety-first Congress, the filibuster now poses a moral dilemma for liberals. They can't quite look at it as they once did. But liberals thrive on moral dilemmas. And when the filibuster is abolished or modified, as it should be, it won't be Strom Thurmond or Barry Goldwater (or James Buckley or Richard Nixon) who does it. That necessary repair, too, will be done by the Bleeding Harts, Proxmires, and McGoverns. Joined by newcomers like Saxbe of Ohio, Hughes of Iowa, Schweiker of Pennsylvania, and Cranston of California, who already have persuaded the Senate to try out a set of streamlining procedures next year.

A lot of the criticism aimed at the Ninety-first Congress was deserved: the Senate's failure to act on welfare reform; the delay on appropriations bills, which rivaled old Clarence Cannon and Carl Hayden at their worst; the House's failure to pass the McGovern-Javits or Foley-Quie food stamp bills; an important consumer protection bill blocked; a stronger Equal Employment Opportunity Act held up in the House Rules Committee.

But wait another minute. The Senate blocked the nominations of Haynsworth and Carswell to the Supreme Court. Muskie's monumental antipollution bill was approved; it actually could force the closing of polluting factories, shut down auto production lines, ban cars from downtown areas. A good employment and manpower bill was passed (Nixon vetoed it, then lit the national Christmas tree; a hearty Merry Christmas to the unemployed). Congress enacted postal reform, draft reform, improved unemployment insurance, new voting rights amendments, the first population control legislation in US history, an important job safety and occupational health bill, among others.

The Ninety-first's record, in other words, wasn't quite as bad as painted. Mr. Nixon initiated some of these domestic measures, supported others, but somehow managed to cast himself as a fainéant president, a do-nothing. More accurately, a don't-really-care.

How does Nixon do it? How does he manage to make himself look so bad? He submits worthwhile proposals to Congress, no gainsaying it. But somehow there's always a news story a few months later telling how some political types in this or that department watered down the proposal or cut the funds or fired the innovator.

The other day, three of the president's domestic advisers held a backgrounder for White House reporters. They said the administration had restored "balance and stability." Proof? Why, said one, in the last six months there haven't been nearly as many ghetto riots and campus disturbances. Confronted with that kind of logic, backward reels the mind.

Whitney Young of the Urban League, after meeting with Nixon, told reporters the mood of ghetto blacks was one of frustration, hopelessness, and despair. No riots, just despair.

Arthur Burns

APRIL 17, 1971   President Nixon started his administration with an economic game plan that didn't work and had to be junked. Then he suddenly made the announcement that he was a "Keynesian," which astonished some as much as though the Hanoverian succession had embraced Catholicism. That was Game Plan II—and it hasn't worked either. Mr. Nixon embraced Keynes just when Keynesianism was going out of date—at least for the problems that beset America.

At his first press conference, seven days after he took office, Mr. Nixon abandoned, abruptly and arbitrarily, the presidential role of guiding wages and prices. It is called "jawboning," or "incomes policy." Mr. Nixon proudly said he was a supporter of a free market economy—letting competition set reasonable wages and prices.

The free market economy—laissez-faire—was outlined by good old Adam Smith in 1776 and it worked fine till they invented General Motors and the United Steel Workers union. Today maybe 40 percent of prices are controlled. The free market got Mr. Nixon's theological support at a time when it no longer existed. As Professor Robert Lekachman said, "Mr. Nixon has attached himself to an economic policy which was quite up-to-date two or three decades ago."

Well, inflation got worse and unemployment got worse. No wonder! Mr. Nixon had notified big business and big labor that the lid was off.

He set out to depress the economy and let the "free market" cure things. You would have thought he would have known about "administered prices" from the Berle-Means classic of 1932. Dr. Gardiner C. Means, a coauthor, who is still going strong forty years later, told the Joint Economic Committee the other day, "The Nixon Game Plan is aimed at a type of inflation which had already passed when it was made public."

Events slowly pushed Mr. Nixon back into an activist economic role, kicking all the way. He rapped the knuckles (gently) of Bethlehem Steel and got them to give up half of a proposed 12-percent price increase. He is now trying to jockey the hard-hat construction workers into reason under threat of dealing with lower-paid nonunion groups on government projects—no mean clout since government accounts for one third of the nation's building.

Mr. Nixon doesn't have a better friend in the economic world than Arthur Burns, the man he made chairman of the Federal Reserve System. Back in 1960 Burns warned the vice-president that a slump was coming that might defeat him unless Ike acted. Ike wouldn't act. As Mr. Nixon sadly says in his *Six Crises,* jobless rolls increased 452,000 in October 1960, and all the campaigning he did "could not counteract that one hard fact."

Every statement Burns makes today signals to Mr. Nixon that he ought to act. I have a copy of five formal talks in front of me, 1970–1971. I heard Burns deliver most of them. Contrary to Nixon's economic advisers at the White House, of whom George Shultz is top, Burns insists there is plenty of money available. Speaking slowly and emphatically on March 10 he testified, "We face a problem unknown to earlier generations—namely, a high rate of inflation at a time of substantial unemployment." Not merely Burns but the whole Reserve Board, he reported later (March 31), favor "a multifaceted incomes policy" including a Wage-Price Review Board. What is that in English?—he wants the president to step in, knock heads together, "mobilize public opinion" (Burns's words), maybe scream a little (mine). And finally, perhaps, cut taxes.

Burns is a conservative economist and liberals don't always go along with him, but he knows as much about the business cycle as any man in America and he points out the funny situation the economy is now in. It's on a hairline. Conventional fiscal and monetary remedies are doing some good—not enough. Recovery is probably on the way, but so slow. There's plenty of cash and credit, Burns insists, but the consumer is holding back. Why? This column has mentioned the circumstances before, and Burns reemphasizes them. The consumer is cautious because he's scared. He's scared of inflation; he's scared of unemployment; he isn't buying that new color TV because he's trying to stretch today's income to cover tomorrow's higher costs. Or, to put it in Burns's economic jargon: "he has cut down his current rate of spending and is accumulating liquid assets." (March 10 testimony to the Senate Banking Committee.)

Why bring this up now? Other events are thundering through

Washington. America's top icon, J. Edgar Hoover, we firmly believe, is on his way out. You can practically feel the Vietnam War coming to an end! Why then, at a time like this, talk about fusty economics? Because a quarter of America's plant capacity is idle; because the gap between actual and potential US production is now $60 billion; because there's 6-percent unemployment and because it's largely unnecessary. Restore consumer confidence and we might well have a quite spectacular recovery by year-end.

Dr. Burns deserves well of America. In June 1970, the US was on the brink of a liquidity crisis; an old-fashioned "money panic." The stock market had made a sickening, two-year drop. The administration's planned recession was taking hold. Mr. Nixon had just horrified the nation with Cambodia. Brokerage houses were failing. The wildest rumors circulated (one: Chrysler was going down, but you could substitute your own choice). Then on the weekend of June 20–21 the Fed learned that the tottering Penn Central would finally collapse.

In one of the most romantic stories of modern banking—a story that hasn't been published before—Burns and his board worked forty-eight hours to tell big banks across America that on Monday the "discount window would be kept open," and followed it next day with a suspension of ceilings on large certificates of deposit—the technical equivalent of a slug of whiskey to a heart patient. The danger of a wave of fear passed. The result without this secret effort? We don't know. Some of Washington's biggest stories are things that don't happen.

Veteran Protest

MAY 8, 1971   This is the first time I have ever made notes inside a fountain. It is a circular cement bowl and the architect must have designed it for me; the curve behind is a wonderful backrest for a man who has walked five miles, and the block in front where, I suppose, the water lilies grow, is just right for a foot brace. Fortunately they haven't turned the hydrants on yet or I would be two feet under water. A couple of exhausted marchers are lying in the basin too, with sleeping bags over their heads.

Up behind me, gleaming white, is the magnificent Capitol. Down below me on Pennsylvania Avenue where they have stopped traffic are perhaps half a million people, wandering about good-naturedly, as many going as coming, perhaps a quarter of the number listening to the speeches. The speeches come from little men standing up there on a platform while right beside me on the terrace is a battery of loudspeakers with a satanic roar that would knock a cat off a rail fence.

It is a good time for a little soul-searching. Not just about the huge crowd which constitutes a kind of folk festival, relaxed and rather gala, but about those brooding Vietnam veterans who were encamped here a few days ago down on the Mall, a thousand or so of them, and of their testimony before Congress, and of the effect it has had on the nation, and the administration, and yes, on me.

To begin with I know, at last, what an idea looks like whose time has come. It is a Popsicle tricycle parked smack in the middle of thronged Pennsylvania Avenue from which all cars are excluded. It is boys looking like Abe Lincoln with girls in serapes going around with yellow plastic bags trying to show their law-and-order respect by picking up cigarette butts and Coke bottles. It is the reverberant voice from the sky as loud as God's at Mount Sinai saying, "Please take lost children over to the press gate." It is a breeze on a scudding spring day that sends up scraps of papers like kites or runs a cardboard box along like a child's wagon, past the great equestrian statue of General Grant where a long-haired youth has climbed up and sits behind him on the crupper with an American flag upside down. It is (oh, well, I could go on like this indefinitely) suds in the fountain before the Mellon Gallery overflowing like quivery snow; the powerful voice of Ralph Abernathy denouncing the war; a sign reading, "The majority isn't silent, the government is deaf"; yes, and the brief merging of a great multitude into one personality.

This crowd was enormous, but far less impressive, really, than the quiet little band who slept on the ground in the Mall a few days earlier. They were the veterans; the ones who had really been out there. Were they phonies?—I talked to a dozen as any skeptical reporter would. Not only were they real but they gave me an awed feeling I am going to think about. . . . Remembering it, I stirred in my fountain. The cement was getting hard and the day was progressing. Naiads must have a tough time.

If I had been tapped by the draft I suppose I should have gone, too, as they did; I don't suppose I would have ducked to Canada, or been a CO. And now these boys, in their scruffy fatigues, their long hair, their provocative hippie look, and their sleeves pinned to their coats, had come back with a haunted look. They had their memories of horror and they were asking for an accounting. Why had they gone? Why had 50,000 died? Why was the thing still continuing against the evident will of the nation? Why was it necessary to save Mr. Nixon the embarrassment of saying (as the surrogate of all of us), "I am not going to be the first American president to say I lost a war"?

There will be other protests now, and they may be violent and alienate public sympathy. But these thousand or so veterans pushed the thorn right down to the quick. These were the boys Mr. Nixon said "stood tall." And, having returned, they won every engagement with an administration whose lack of grace has become a myth in its own time. They were barred at first from laying wreaths at the veterans' cemetery; they were served an injunction against sleeping on the Mall after a government appeal against them to the Supreme Court —a government that suddenly grasped its awful mistake and got the injunction dissolved at the cost of a tongue-lashing from the judge. It was a public relations disaster for the administration from start to finish. You can't win an argument with a paraplegic.

The deeper problem is, though, what happens now? What do you do with a government that fights a war that 73 percent of the public rejects (the figure may be higher since last January). At least the war has produced two pieces of literature. One was the frozen anger in that letter Captain Aubrey Daniel III, twenty-nine, the prosecutor, wrote to his commander-in-chief, in the Calley case, defending the honor of the US Army against the interference of Mr. Nixon.

The other was the scalding antiwar statement by the veterans' leader, John Kerry, to the Senate Foreign Relations committee: "The country doesn't know it yet," he said, "but it's created a monster, a monster in the form of millions of men who have been taught to deal and to trade in violence, and who are given a chance to die for the biggest nothing in history—men who have returned with a sense of anger and a sense of betrayal which no one yet has grasped." He finished and waited for questions.

"Move your microphone," ordered Senator Symington. "Which way, sir?" "To your left" (gruffly). "I wanted to see what's on your chest. That's a Silver Star?" "Yes, sir." "And that's a Purple Heart?" "Yes, sir." "With how many clusters?" "Two, sir." "That means you were wounded in action three times?" "Yes, sir."

There was a pause that made your heart leap. Senator Symington turned slowly to Chairman Fulbright. "I have no further questions," he said.

It was time to leave my fountain. . . . I walked back slowly through the throngs, up the avenue and past the White House. The little man wasn't there.

Noncandidate Kennedy

JUNE 5, 1971   He reads fast, with emotion, even passion, broadening his *a*'s. He has regular features, a handsome face that, at thirty-nine, is getting a bit heavy. He pushes the brown hair back over his right temple with a sweep of his hand. Then Teddy Kennedy sits there behind the bench in the big wood-paneled Senate committee room, chin cupped in his hand with right index finger pointed up to his ear, as Otto Kerner, twice governor of Illinois and now judge, quietly tells how his commission put together the most penetrating study of racial violence ever written in America, the one that begins: "This is our basic conclusion: Our nation is moving toward two societies, one black, one white, separate and unequal."

You can't keep your eye off Kennedy. Here is a case where the breath of gossip is actually pushing him toward the presidency. There is every reason for him not to run so soon after that wrong turn at Chappaquiddick, but his very reluctance pushes him forward. Where all the others save George McGovern are mincing words in the effort to wedge themselves into the political center, Kennedy is taking chances that only a noncandidate would take and the boldness promotes him like nothing else. When the Vietnam antiwar veterans camped in the shadow of the Capitol and an angry John Mitchell took his legal effort to oust them right up to the Supreme Court, Kennedy went down to the camp one evening and quietly fraternized. The Justice Department, to its horror, suddenly discovered that it had once more taken the unpopular course and ignominiously asked that its own motion be quashed, which the judge permitted—after giving the department a brutal tongue-lashing. (It is strange what an almost 100-percent score of mistakes like this Attorney General Mitchell has made!)

Now the topic in the high-ceilinged, cork-floored committee room is a fascinating but arcane one—presidential commissions. Presidents name commissions to sidestep trouble. These bodies could be of enormous value as the Royal Commissions are in England, a sort of fifth branch of government: executive, legislative, judiciary, regulatory agencies, and freewheeling commissions. Since 1960 presidents have named three or four a year and Mr. Nixon named five in his first year. Then when the report comes out the crisis may be nicely over.

Exaggerated? Take the last four big "social issue" commissions in our time. Kennedy (who sits alone on the bench after stony-faced Strom Thurmond in a red shirt briefly enters, and departs) recites them one by one:

The Katzenbach commission on crime (named by Lyndon Johnson) helped produce the monumental Safe Streets Act of 1968. It was one of the few implemented.

Kerner Commission on racial riots: it made its 600-page report between the riots of 1967 and those of 1968, and its indictment of "white racism" angered LBJ, who was about to quit anyway.

Violence Commission under Dr. Milton Eisenhower (1969), largely ignored by Mr. Nixon.

Scranton Commission on Campus Violence (1970) pleaded with the president to give "moral leadership"; it was denounced by Spiro Agnew as "pabulum for permissivists" and rejected by Mr. Nixon.

Kennedy is speaking and sums up these reports: all four emphasized the need for fair and just law enforcement, and the last three specifically warned against repression. All four urged vast new expenditures on social investment; the last three called for reordering of national priorities, and the last two specifically cited the need to end the Vietnam hemorrhage for tranquility at home.

And what happened? Civil rights progress stifled. (Kennedy's voice deepens with anger.) Social investments cut to the bone "by congressional timidity or presidential veto." Fear of repression fed by federal surveillance, the war continued, effective gun controls omitted even in the Nixon "law-and-order" agenda. (With two slain brothers, Ted Kennedy will never forget that last; what if he should be the third murdered? He has three children of his own, and there are thirteen of the other two.)

Kennedy sees the irony of presidential commissions. There was the testimony that sociologist Kenneth Clark gave to Kerner: there was an inquiry and a learned report after Watts; another after Harlem in 1943; after the earlier 1935 Harlem riot; after the 1919 riot in Chicago. Said Clark: "I must again in candor say to you members of this commission—it is a kind of Alice in Wonderland—with the same moving picture reshown over and over again, the same analysis, the same recommendations—and the same inaction."

Anyone with a sense of humor can get a chuckle out of the thing! Kennedy notes that the Scranton Commission, which Mr. Nixon appointed, pleaded with officials to refrain from playing "irresponsible politics with the issue of campus unrest" and to avoid insulting actions that would "exacerbate tension and encourage violence." So what happened? It was 1970 and the administration was making campus unrest its big issue. (Unsuccessful, fortunately.) A month after the report Mr. Nixon in a hostile crowd in San Jose, California, got out and stood on his car and flashed a peace sign: "That's what they hate to see," he chuckled.

The Scranton plea to eliminate "harsh and bitter rhetoric" didn't reach Spiro, of course; and only the other day the attorney general was likening irritating war protestors here to Nazi "brownshirts."

So we come back to the young man taking testimony: the question mark. America has a guilt complex about Kennedy. Mayor Daley is for him. Yet Democratic colleagues dropped him as assistant Senate leader; complained he didn't work at it. He got a college friend to take an exam for him and was rusticated for two years. In the White House—? One hat an American president wears is that of high priest: the man your boy should resemble. Kennedy has matured a lot. Make no doubt, he is a powerful, effective figure. And now the Gallup Poll says that—scandal or not—he has passed Muskie, 29 percent to 21 percent, as favorite in 1972 of registered Democrats. . . . The hearing proceeds.

Pilgrimage

J U L Y   3 ,   1 9 7 1   Business took me to Boston and I hired an Avis car for a quick private pilgrimage. The car had air conditioning and an annoying trick of buzzing after me if I left the door open. I don't mind people telling me off but things have come to a pretty pass when a hunk of machinery begins giving you orders.

The first step was Brandeis. Years back, half a century maybe, my father befriended a group of Jewish boys who wanted to form a club. He was a high school teacher in Flatbush and when nobody else came forward he, who was a stout Unitarian, volunteered. Mu Sigma prospered, spread, and, I was told, had set up plaques and inscriptions around Brandeis and maybe my father's name was mentioned.

It was a fine summer day, a week or so after commencement, and I found a splendid sculpture of Justice Brandeis, with his robes flowing, at the center of things. But my information was wrong. Here and there were plaques to the Society but no special reference to an inconspicuous high school teacher—as, indeed why should there be?—who had merely given a hand at a trying point. It was just my fancy.

I continued my pilgrimage with thoughts divided between a car that buzzed at me nastily every time I got out at a filling station, and the larger question of how little remains after a person is gone. We can't all be a Brandeis! My father bordered, I should say, on the eccentric. He wore a gold chain, a Victorian gold watch, a pearl tie stickpin and a derby, and made a practice of bringing home firewood from the trees—which he enjoyed splitting and sawing up—in an old wicker baby carriage through a respectable neighborhood. He was a poet, besides being an English teacher, and when he was getting his Ph.D. at Boston University he would sell poems to Hezekiah Butterworth of *The Youths' Companion* to help pay rent. The generation gap hadn't been invented in those days. The family relationship expressed itself, I guess, in the fact that we called him "George." At the turn of the century he had a school salary of $2000, which was adequate in Brooklyn to pay for the house with its big front porch (called "stoop" in Dutch Flat-bush) and at economic peaks to hire a maid.

Musing on these things I took the cutoff at Sagamore from Route 6 and shortly drove up to the Community Church at Onset. Onset is a modest tourists' town in a pretty setting, with its shopping street filled with seashore knickknacks; when the "summer people" leave after Labor Day it settles back to enjoy its native scallops and cranberries. My mother gave the church a little bequest and somebody had written to me something about an inscription to her in the hymn books. It was Sunday, and they would be holding services, and I thought I would go in and later on, maybe, introduce myself.

But tacked on to the church "All Welcome" sign was a paper saying that services had been transferred to Wareham. Children played on Highland Avenue. The church was closed.

I broke in through a side door and wandered moodily around the red carpeted aisles in the hushed chamber. The little stained-glass window behind the altar was donated by "The Ladies Aid: 1903–1957." Susie belonged. The altar Bible (published by William W. Harding, Phila. 1868) was given in memory of Mr. and Mrs. B. A. Atkins, presented by their brother, A. S. Atkins, and open at Ezekiel XXXIV. I brushed off the dust.

The Honor Roll "European War" had 23 Anglo-Saxon names plus Gordon Tsakiroglow. Somebody had written "(Young)" beside it, in parentheses. There was also a batch of service stars arranged to form a Cross, and one gold one in the middle. On the way downstairs was an old-fashioned telephone with a hand crank. The basement was modern and evidently actively in use by Boy Scouts. On a shelf in the minister's study was a box of elegant marriage booklets with spaces for names and dates, and transparent paper between pages, and tied with white ribbon.

Everything had stopped short—like a clock. The foot-high pile of *Newsweek*s and *The Christian Century* ended October 7, 1970.

I looked through a lot of hymnals in the pew racks knowing, somehow, all the time, that it would be like Brandeis, everybody's name there but Susie's. She lived alone in Onset, after George went, till she broke her hip. There was one other man in her life (or so we pretended), the one who went West, and we used to tease her fondly about it and she would tell us she preferred George. I thought I knew every secret she had. But once she told me something I hadn't known. She had gone up through the trapdoor into the attic and opened the old trunk and fetched out a packet of letters, from California, and walked over to Dummy Bridge and dropped them down one by one as the tide went out. She didn't explain further. It was none of my business. The letters floated away.

Well, I had drawn a blank twice. . . . I headed the car north and, in an amazing two hours was where it would have taken me a full day on the old Boston & Maine (change at Nash-u-ay, on the *FITCH*burg line). Now the highway runs right over the old railroad that cut across Grandpa Lang's farm in the '70s where the first engine scared Susie in her pinafore. But you can still hear the Bar Harbor Express roar past the South Lee depot, on a dark night, if the whippoorwills aren't too loud.

I knew just where to go. Off the highway, through the trees, up the bank and there, under the shag-bark hickory, with four generations of ancestors, are George and Susie; he 91, she 98. Across the pasture in full sight is the farmhouse where Susie was born. She is back where she started, and where he married her.

The trees made a nice sound. A chipmunk whisked by on important business. As I turned back south, I wondered what it all meant; George with his forgotten deeds at school, Susie with her aid to a closed church. They hadn't accomplished much, had they? Nothing, I guess, save that all the way back to Boston I kept wondering what I had written lately that might please them.

Press Conferences—Harding to Nixon

F E B R U A R Y 1 2 , 1 9 7 2   The first White House press conference I ever went to (the Old Timer said) was Warren G. Harding's. That was before you were born. He was the handsomest president since George Washington and some people thought he was handsomer. There he was in plus fours behind his big desk in the Oval Room with about thirty reporters asking questions, and I was a young man and my heart just went out to him. I could write home to my folks and tell them I was within touching distance of a president—a live president. They would tell that all over town. I was supposed to be a reporter but my sympathies were all against the mean correspondents, and finally he said, "Gentlemen, gentlemen, do be good to me; I want to go out and play a little golf."

That was the way it used to be. There was a relationship between the president and the press. We used to think that press conferences were an important part of the business of government.

Not any longer, though. It will be just about three months now, since Mr. Nixon held his last regular press conference, November 12. This is a kind of anniversary. In 1971 he held nine, in 1970 four, and in 1969 eight.

There used to be a friendly intimacy in these things. It was an adversary relationship, of course, but it was symbiotic, too. The president needed the press (we thought) and the press needed the president. For example, I remember one with Franklin Roosevelt. There was a great trampling of feet going in and we were all crowded in front of the big table covered with mementos and totems, with Gus Gennerich, his personal bodyguard, and a couple of Secret Service men, and smiling Marvin McIntyre and a male stenographer seated by his desk, and perhaps Miss LeHand, his personal secretary, and a couple of visitors to see the show squatted on the raised pedestal of the big French windows. The reporters stood and it took some time to get all 75 or 100 in.

FDR chats with those in the first rank before his desk. You see his head thrown back in the characteristic laugh.

"All in," says Pat McKenna.

"Well, what's the news today?" asks FDR.

Voice on left: "That's what we came to find out. We'd like a nice hot news story."

"Is that you, Fred Storm?" the president asks. "Fred, you're getting too big. There are three people trying to see around you. Here, take this chair. It's yours from now on. Is that better?"

Chorus of voices: "Much better. Thank you, Mr. President. The United Press ought not to have such big men."

Voice on right: "If it is true, as stated, that the administration intends to make its public works ultimately self-liquidating, how do you account for that statement of PMG Farley, etc.?"

FDR: "I can't see who asked that question but it sounds like the Buffalo *Evening Republican*. A man came in the other day and said, 'Is it honestly true that some of your plans will not liquidate themselves for 120 years?' I said, 'Yes, that is really true.' You see, we are making loans for planting black walnut trees which do not mature for 120 years."

And so on; if you were in the next room you would hear frequent bursts of laughter; finally when questions were exhausted it ended.

Nothing anymore like that now, of course. President Nixon is the most aloof president of modern times, maybe in history. As the secret papers printed by Jack Anderson about the Pakistan war revealed, he communicates with his top strategists through Henry Kissinger. Former Interior Secretary Walter Hickel couldn't even get in to see him.

The statistics tell the story. FDR in a little over three terms had 1,000 press conferences; twice a week before the war and once a week during the war. Mr. Truman, if my figures are right, had well over 300; Ike cut it down to 200. Kennedy in his bright Thousand Days averaged about one a fortnight. Lyndon Johnson had 158 press conferences and was always seeing individuals separately.

The funny thing is that we thought it was important to have these conferences. Yet without them the country seems to be going on much as before. The decay of Congress has coincided with the decline of critical questioning by reporters. There is nothing in the Constitution about press conferences. But in the separation of powers they are a bridge between president and nation. Something has gone out of Washington without them.

I think I am reasonably objective about it. I think more doors are open in Washington and more information available in spite of carping and criticism than in any other capital in the world. But of course in other democracies, most of them with parliaments, the opposition is able to ask the executive questions face to face. Nobody does that to Mr. Nixon now, save occasionally when he picks a TV personality.

Mr. Nixon has always disliked the press, for it interferes with his privateness. There was no chance to ask him about Carswell or Haynsworth or Lieutenant Calley. He prefers making these sudden, astonishing TV appearances of his. He agrees with the de Gaulle notion; that there should be something mysterious, aloof, awesome about the man in power, like royalty. It would diminish the mystique if Mr. Nixon held a press conference, say, and somebody asked him face to face about Bangladesh. In Truman's day we would have just gone in and asked about it. Not anymore. We can't ask why he pardoned Jimmy Hoffa, or whether he really means to try to burden the poor with a national sales tax, or why he vetoed the mothers' day-care bill. Certainly the press shouldn't be a snarling, snapping prosecutor, but in other days presidents were supposed to be asked things like that. "I try to have a press conference when I think there is a public interest," Mr. Nixon said. That was in December 1969.

Like a man who wears a top hat, an aloof president always runs some risks from the irreverent. For example, that episode at the White House last week, where a singer pulled an antiwar banner from her plunging neckline and lectured the president and guests about Jesus and the war. What audacity! Martha Mitchell cried that she ought to be "torn limb from limb." What made the thing so awful was that right in the reception for the prim *Reader's Digest* were the Reverends Billy Graham and Norman Vincent Peale. They have their own sure pipelines to heaven. When a whippersnapper from a singing troupe starts telling them about Jesus Christ and the war, you can understand why the moral foundations of the country are so shaky.

Busing

MARCH 4, 1972   The health and stability of our society over the next fifty years may well depend on the direction taken in Washington in the next few months. President Nixon has given us games and circuses in his spectacular trip to Peking but anybody can see with half an eye that the real symptoms of national peril are right here at home—poverty and racial strain. They are surfacing now in these directions: the Senate has started debate on three devastating antiblack, antibusing amendments attached in the House to the Emergency School Aid bill; the House Judiciary Committee, March 1, starts hearings on a proposed constitutional amendment to ban busing for racial balance; the president apparently has selected school busing as his emotional gut issue for 1972, as he previously used the Communist scare issue 1946–1968, and the law-and-order issue in 1970; and finally, the Supreme Court has accepted a Denver case to decide the constitutionality of segregation imposed covertly by local school districts (arguments probably in March; decision maybe in June).

Short of a national nervous breakdown, there is no chance of Congress passing an antibusing constitutional amendment and President Nixon knew it perfectly well when he summoned advocates to the White House just before he left for China. He wanted to identify himself with the Strom Thurmonds and to undercut George Wallace. He has made the same gesture time and time again. He is a naturally divisive politician who has never hesitated to spread his sails to the winds of hysteria.

In this situation two things should be noted. First, busing is a false issue. In a series of unanimous decisions the Supreme Court has never insisted on forced busing to achieve racial balance. For example, note the use of the word "one" in the opinion by Chief Justice Burger (*Swann* vs. *Charlotte-Mecklenberg*): ". . . We find no basis for holding that the local school authorities may not be required to employ bus transportation as *one* tool of school desegregation. . . ." This is typical: the courts have generally been firm, reasonable, and responsible.

The second thing to note is that the forces of reason have found a leader—low-keyed, effective, decent Walter Mondale of Minnesota. He is forty-four, the son of a Methodist minister. For sheer guts we hand it to him. He's up for reelection this fall and he's put his political life on the line. Thank God he isn't running for president. Muskie and Humphrey and Lindsay have variously evolved some equivocal or disingenuous formula on busing, Jackson has gone over to the enemy, McGovern has been staunch but rates low on the polls; Mondale and Kennedy aren't running and to that degree can speak their minds, though it could defeat Mondale for the Senate. As we have said before, we rate Mondale of presidential caliber.

For two years he chaired the Select Committee on Equal Educational Opportunity, which had heard 300 witnesses and is now shortly coming to an end. It will issue its book-length, two-year report around May 1, which should be a bible on the subject, going into side issues of segregated housing, taxation, and standards.

The legislative background for all this is dramatic, and tragic. Almost every year since Congress passed the 1964 Civil Rights Act, the battle has been fought over again. Heretofore modernists have won but now it is not certain; desegregation has washed up into the North. A year ago the Senate gave strong liberal leadership. It noted that in town after town segregation was being struck down and that this almost automatically sent up the cost to provide quality desegregated education. The need for funds is desperate. The Senate offered aid to all school districts that desegregated, whether voluntarily, by court order, or by state law.

The Senate bill went to the House and in a wild session on the night of November 4 the House harpooned the measure with what Mondale calls "three senseless and divisive amendments." It did so with Mr. Nixon's support, direct or implied. It is a tragedy for the nation that in this crucial time for the most racking issue before the country Mr. Nixon has repeatedly been ambiguous; he lamed the Justice Department's Civil Rights Division, sought to undercut the Voting Rights Act, vetoed the child development bill, nominated Judge Carswell, and is now confusing and inflaming the school-bus issue just as many districts over the country are bravely attempting to work out solutions.

The three House amendments would a) prohibit use of federal funds to support transportation to achieve racial desegregation (voluntary or not); b) prohibit any federal agency from urging school districts to use their own funds for this purpose (and ban the Justice Department from enforcing the Constitution in connected court actions); c) bar federal district courts from entering a desegregation order while any appeal is pending, even the most frivolous.

Mondale's portfolio of school improvement in various towns, with or without busing, is profoundly moving. Hoke County, North Carolina, had a triple school system: whites, Negroes, and Lumbee Indians. Now they've all integrated, black, white, and red: whites continue to progress and blacks have caught up a year and a half.

Hartford, Connecticut, bused 1,000 minority group students, picked at random, from ghetto to suburban schools. Careful analysis showed no loss to the whites and dramatic gains for the blacks.

A vast weight of expert educational evidence is that integrated education, sensitively conducted and with community support, can be better education for all—whites, blacks, rich, and poor. Kids learn from kids more than from teachers. Busing is a symbol; it isn't the real issue at all; by itself it can be either helpful or harmful. It is sad to see it turned now into a divisive, inflammatory, political code word for a presidential election like "anti-communism" and "law and order." The facts remain; the Supreme Court is not our enemy; remember that busing would be required only where it is reasonable. The Court's exact words, "busing will not be allowed to significantly impinge on the educational process." These seem plain enough and should reassure people if Mondale's courageous statements are heard.

Nixon vs. McGovern

JUNE 17, 1972   A Nixon-McGovern contest, if it comes to that, will be one of the most incongruous in American history. Few men could be more unalike. Mr. Nixon is watchful and remote, McGovern direct and open. The former distrusts youth; the latter relies on it. They do not see things alike at all. For the president, national honor is continuing in Vietnam, for the senator it is getting out. Essentially the president wants to bolster the American status quo while the senator wants to give it a big shake.

Mr. Nixon, we think, deserves well of America, uncomfortable though we find that admission in some ways. Sooner or later, somebody had to break the ice with Peking and with Moscow, and Mr. Nixon did it, and also started direct negotiation on arms cuts. It is a splendid service, we think, and it took a lifelong professional Communist-hater like Mr. Nixon to do it. The screams coming from some of the "betrayed" right-wing organizations indicate the problem. What a tizzy they would have been in if Hubert Humphrey had been elected in 1968 and tried to go to Moscow! And who would have led the denunciation? Why, presumably, Richard Nixon. Since the task had to be done he has been the right man, in many ways, to do it.

So now will an ungrateful nation reject Mr. Nixon for a second term? It will be a fascinating campaign to watch, particularly if George McGovern, the minister's son from South Dakota and bomber pilot, World War II, with Distinguished Flying Service Cross, is the Democratic nominee. The press is having a love affair with McGovern momentarily, but we don't think it will last; it is trying to make amends for having underrated the senator for so long. Also it's taking advantage of having a fresh face and a new personality to exploit.

The press is pointing out what is true, that some of McGovern's arithmetic doesn't add up. A process of collation and consolidation is going on and McGovern needs a Walter Heller. But there is no doubt, we think, of his essential purpose. There is as deep a gap between him and Mr. Nixon on economic matters as between FDR and Herbert Hoover.

Actually, in many ways, McGovern is an accidental candidate. He doesn't fit into the normal pattern. The normal candidate is the compromiser who can assume the bland, middle position required under the two-party system where each of the rival coalitions jockeys for the vital center. The system always irritates ideologues and idealists. Why can't we divide sharply between conservatives and liberals and fight it out? they demand. Well, Barry Goldwater tried that out on the conservative side, and see what happened to him. The two-party system blunts ideological frenzy, or that is the theory, anyway. The "normal" candidate, under the system, would have been Edmund Muskie, and he seemed to have the nomination in hand till he blew it, that snowy day in New Hampshire. The primary system is often ridiculed; it is a cruel business; it is an ordeal by publicity, but it winnows people out. It eliminated George Romney in 1968, and it pretty much eliminated Muskie this year. Curiously enough the calm, low-keyed, decent-looking McGovern survived.

McGovern has one big asset: he doesn't look like a run-of-the-mine politician or like any other politician you ever saw before. You may not agree with him but you feel that he is sincere, which he is. Whether this is a lasting asset for a candidate remains to be seen. He is not very eloquent; his delivery is rather dry. He does have a sense of moral outrage. He has taken positions on a lot of matters which are probably impolitic—that the federal government should not get involved in the abortion issue, that penalties for marijuana are often too harsh, that after the war there should be an amnesty for draft resisters. Former attorney general John Mitchell, who will run Mr. Nixon's campaign, is rubbing his hands gloatingly. What a chance this will be for Spiro Agnew, he reflects, or maybe for John Connally if Mr. Nixon makes the switch.

But the big things that anger McGovern aren't these but the failures, as he sees them, of the American social order. Why is it that the average man can't seem to make his voice heard in Washington? Why doesn't somebody correct the increasingly regressive tax system? Why is welfare left, for all the talk, in such an appalling mess?

McGovern has answers for these problems, such things as a "minimum income grant," which we are all probably going to be writing about shortly. It amounts to wholesale reform of the tax structure which would result in a redistribution of income. Mr. McGovern discusses these items so mildly and casually that they do not seem radical. But make no doubt of it, in the deeper meaning of the word, they are.

The question—perhaps the basic question of 1972—is whether a tide is running, whether the country has reached such a state of cynicism about things as they are, and the rules of an Establishment, that it will take a bold step in a new direction.

"Radical?" says McGovern disarmingly. "Let me say I come from the state of South Dakota where there are two-to-one Republican odds against me. I have been elected four times in that state. Ordinarily we don't send wild-eyed radicals to the US Senate from South Dakota."

Yes, he agrees mildly, the proposals to cut the defense budget, to end the Vietnam War, to reduce the loopholes in the tax law and give the middle class and the poor a better deal, "While they do represent a break with the past, I think that is what the American people want."

Does a man with these notions have a chance of election against an entrenched White House incumbent? Who knows? With unemployment almost as high as ever, with prices still rising, with 25 percent of plant capacity unused, with a deep loathing for the war, Mr. Nixon may have difficulties. Another thing to remember is that nobody really loves Mr. Nixon a whole lot; people may admire him, and certainly the banking and business interests are going to give him the biggest campaign support ever if George McGovern gets the nod, but in terms of personal popularity, whatever the opposite of charisma is, Mr. Nixon has tons of it.

One thing more should be said. If George McGovern is nominated and elected this will be one of those rare "critical" elections. They come at different intervals, about twenty-eight or thirty-six years apart, and one is long overdue—the last was FDR in 1932. McGovern believes what he says and his views mark a new direction. If the public is in the mood to elect him it almost certainly means a political realignment.

The Watergate Caper

AUGUST 19, 1972   Harry Truman's military aide, General Vaughan, got a deep freeze from a grateful client and the scandal rocked Washington. General Eisenhower's assistant, Sherman Adams, received a vicuna coat; he had to resign, of course. But now under President Nixon we have five men with electronic equipment and apparently paid by Republicans, arrested at gunpoint in the dead of night in the Democratic national headquarters, and we tend to smile at it. The very name, "the Watergate Caper," tells how funny it is. How Puritan we all were back in the days of Harry and Ike; how our sensibilities have changed. Those were pretty innocent days, weren't they? Those were the days, for example, before the Vietnam War. That has been a depressing influence. There has been an ethical letdown on a lot of things as we gradually reach moral exhaustion over the slaughter and all those bombs we are dropping on naked peasants. Ugh, let's not think of it. And the protective cynicism we have assumed over Vietnam extends into other fields of government. Hell, that's politics.

Take the dairy farmers' political action groups who contributed $72,500 to the Republican Party in the last four months of 1971 through dummy organizations, during a period when the administration first announced there would be no increase in milk price support levels, and then abruptly and inexplicably reversed itself two weeks later. Who can say that there was any connection? And what droll names some of those dummy corporations took: one was "Volunteers for Good Government," another was "Americans United for Safer Streets."

And then there was the ITT caper. We can all chuckle over that. The huge corporation abruptly reached an out-of-court settlement with John Mitchell's Justice Department allowing it to keep the Hartford Fire Insurance Company, and simultaneously it agreed to guarantee $400,000 to the Republicans for their convention in San Diego. The antitrust division suddenly and inexplicably reversed its position. The head of the division was quickly made a judge. A little later Jack Anderson published a private memo from ITT's top Washington lobbyist, Dita Beard, declaring that "Mitchell is definitely helping us, but cannot let it be known. Please destroy this, huh." Under the Federal Lobbying Act of 1946, ITT is supposed to make a report on the money it spends for lobbying, but the law is a farce. ITT doesn't even register. Dita Beard reported personal expenditures under the law in 1971 of $7,030. So that's the ITT story.

Then there was the cute trick of the Republicans of collecting $10 million in campaign funds from fat-cat contributors just before the new federal election disclosure law took effect April 7. Of course, after April 7 they could stand on moral principles about not violating their clients' right to privacy. It was hilarious. Who knows what shy and blushing oil and steel and ITT donors there are behind that sacred veil of anonymity? McGovern made public all his contributors, of course, before and after April 7, but that man is a dangerous radical, without any sense of humor.

Entertaining, eh? Well, now we come to the real laugh, the Watergate caper. Just to make it easier to follow here are the *dramatis personae:*

There's Frank Wills, the watchman, who got $5 added to his $80-a-week income for calling the police, Saturday night, June 17. And there's Ernie Prete, the straight man you need in any detective mystery, who arrested five intruders wearing rubber gloves in the seventh-floor suite of Democratic headquarters, all equipped with bugging and camera apparatus.

James W. McCord, Jr., security coordinator for the Committee to Reelect the President (CRP), one of the arrested five intruders. Fired by CRP.

Bernard Barker, head of the five; records show he made at least fifteen phone calls to CRP; had in a bank account $89,000 apparently from CRP, plus $25,000 from a cashier's check apparently intended for Mr. Nixon's campaign chest, made out to Maurice Stans, former Commerce Secretary and now GOP national finance chairman. Stans says he gave the check to Liddy (see below).

E. Howard Hunt, Jr., novelist and man of mystery, former CIA agent, former $100-a-day White House consultant; two intruders carried papers with his name, and "White House." He has disappeared.

Charles W. Colson, special counsel of Mr. Nixon, described in the *Wall Street Journal* last October as "Nixon Hatchet Man/Chuck Colson Handles/President's Dirty Work." He recruited Hunt as White House assistant. Still at work.

G. Gordon Liddy, ex-FBI agent; once ran for Congress; counsel to CRP finance committee; refused to answer questions; fired.

Hugh W. Sloan, Jr., ex-White House staff; campaign finance aide to Stans in 1968 when latter headed Nixon-Agnew finance operation as now. Treasurer of CRP. He has resigned.

John Mitchell, former Nixon campaign manager; called Democratic $1-million suit over break-in a "political stunt," then retired for family reasons.

Ronald Ziegler, White House press secretary; dismissed episode as "third-rate burglary."

Maurice Stans, national finance chairman; was initially unavailable as his secretary told reporters he is "a very busy man," who is "tightly scheduled" with "appointments every hour."

President Nixon, unlike Ike, who had 193 press conferences, and

Truman, who had 322—where reporters asked them about deep freezes and vicuna coats—has held only 26 press conferences in 3½ years and isn't asked about the Watergate caper.

Some people get indignant about things like this. They had much better relax and keep down their blood pressures. Look at the people who get excited about Vietnam. A year or two ago the kids were all hot and bothered. Now they have calmed down, thank goodness. Maybe they are learning the value of keeping quiet when they can't change things. The public doesn't want the war; the Congress doesn't want the war, but it has to be fought because the Pentagon and the president say so. The kids should learn to work within the system. Mr. Nixon is bringing the boys home—all, that is, but the 20,000 killed while he was in office. He has a slick, marvelous reelection machine and can fly in the 100 beautiful Republican pom-pom girls as often as is necessary.

The Two-Party System Is Collapsing

NOVEMBER 18, 1972   Something very strange is happening in American politics. The two-party system seems to be collapsing. President Nixon got one of the greatest popular landslides in history on Tuesday but failed to sweep his Republican Party into control of Congress. He lost Congress also in 1968, but then it was explained by the extremely close contest (though it was noted that the last time a new president won without Congress was in 1848, with Zachary Taylor). Now Mr. Nixon has triumphed spectacularly, yet his party has lost two seats in the Senate and is still a minority in the House.

The easy answer is that the public was not voting for Mr. Nixon but against Senator McGovern, and there is a good deal of truth in this. But it seems to us that it goes a lot deeper. The political parties are in disarray and since they are a vital part of our system of government this is bad news.

If a political "landslide" is defined as a popular vote over 60 percent, then there have been four in American history, all in this century, as follows: Harding in 1920 with 60.3 percent, Roosevelt in 1936 with 60.8 percent, Johnson in 1964 with 61.1 percent, and now Nixon in the over-60-percent club. The difference is that the first three won overwhelming party control in Congress and were able to govern, while Mr. Nixon's curious personal lack of charisma, or popularity, or something, leaves him facing a Congress that is hostile, though only flabbily so even here since the power still resides largely in a conservative coalition. Almost certainly this means negativism for a while, and little forward movement. This is a travesty of checks and balances; it could mean paralysis.

Another set of figures bears this out. White House and Congress have been held by rival parties in ten of the past eighteen years, and now there will be at least two more of them. Who does the voter hold responsible, anyway? Mr. Nixon can always blame higher taxes on Congress; Congress in turn can blame the White House. Curiously enough, many voters have so lost confidence in government that they seem to like it this way; they want the two branches of government to watch each other.

We are inclined to think that the country is in a state of extraordinary transition and that this is showing up in the series of divided governments in Washington. It would have been evident four years ago but for the third-party candidacy of George Wallace. Wallace got 10 million votes, or 13.5 percent of the total in 1968, which made the Nixon-Humphrey race a photo finish. But Wallace got shot last May and was eliminated and most of his votes came to Nixon. What we have now is Nixon plus Wallace, with a demoralized Congress left largely in confusion. What happens to the Democratic Party depends largely, we guess, on whether Democrats can restore discipline in Congress.

Most elections stir the blood, lift the spirits, act as a national catharsis; the country feels better after them. But not 1972. This has been the most dismal election we have ever known, with the real issues undiscussed, one candidate in seclusion and the other getting nowhere, a smell like a stopped drain from the Watergate affair, and the public largely bored. One thing we think the lonely Senator McGovern did accomplish. By his direct and passionate charge that the president does not really mean to make peace in Vietnam we think that he has compelled Mr. Nixon, willy-nilly, to make peace; we simply do not feel that with that deadly indictment pending over him the president can continue the war much longer.

The 1968 election showed the conservatives in the Democratic Party that they cannot win without the liberals; the 1972 election shows the liberals that they can't win without the regulars and office-holders. If they are unable to work out a coalition then the party—which has been the innovator and friend of the little man more often than not in this century—might as well fold.

Mr. Nixon has got his new coalition, typified by George Wallace: the alienated white underdog who is baffled and insecure in the face of turbulent economic, social, and racial change, "the most revolutionary change that man has ever lived in," said Walter Lippmann. George McGovern made a gallant fight but his moralism and supposed radicalism turned the blue-collars off. The mood of the country, as we see it, is a desire for stability, and while Senator McGovern promised reform, Mr. Nixon pledged stability; he emphasized old virtues—the work ethic, peace with honor, law and order; and at the same time he subtly played on nasty prejudices with complicated code words: no busing, no quotas, a strict contructionist Supreme Court, and free choice in housing. Though it never surfaced we believe that the race issue was a major hidden factor in the Nixon landslide.

So what are the prospects? We caught sight of one when Philadelphia's Mayor Frank Rizzo, Democrat and former strong-arm cop, hailed Spiro Agnew as "one of the truly great Americans in history." The vice-president has emerged with his new image; a man who supports all the orthodoxies with a repressive glint in his eye. His nomination in 1976 seems likely.

What has Mr. Nixon promised for the four years ahead? Very little, really; he has fought the election from his closet, the equivalent of McKinley's front porch campaign conducted by television. There will probably be two more justices on the Supreme Court, making six Nixon appointees in all. The prospect that they will be statesmen of stature is gloomy; Harding picked Taft; Coolidge picked Stone; Hoover picked Hughes; Eisenhower picked Earl Warren; but Mr. Nixon does not have men of that caliber around him; his legal associates are Mitchell and Kleindienst.

President Nixon could go either way. He is a lame-duck president; his eyes should be on history. He can, and has, done credit to himself and America by opening communications behind the Iron Curtain. We hope there will be more of it.

On the domestic side, Mr. Nixon's chief goal seems to be to keep down taxes. Four blue-ribbon presidential commissions in recent years have all urgently warned the nation that crime, violence, social decay, human waste, and racial bitterness are springing in part from a lack of public spending in essential services. There is hardly one such service that is not starved for funds, yet we have cut taxes three times in four years. Efficiency, yes; but to make taxes an absolute issue as Mr. Nixon has done is narrow and demagogic.

Kissinger Explains the Christmas Bombing

DECEMBER 30, 1972 The first Kissinger briefing on Vietnam began at the White House pressroom at 11:34 A.M. October 26 and lasted to 12:37. The room was packed. A reporter sat on the brown carpeted step under the podium. Kissinger began, "It is obvious that a war that has been raging for ten years is drawing to a conclusion." He immediately added, "We believe that peace is at hand."

Dr. Kissinger is short, rotund, chunky; wearing a blue shirt and figured blue tie; curly brown hair, conspicuous glasses that glitter. He has humor (the proposed section on international supervision, he says, "will no doubt occupy graduate students for many years to come." He has owlish face, German accent, not disagreeable (says "chust" for "just").

He is unflurried, in command of his audience, and adept in presenting the views of Hanoi, Saigon, and of his boss, the president. We are getting out of the war, he implies; with honor; Nixon has pulled it off; after four years, Hanoi suddenly (October 8) made the key concession that we had waited for; it will not require overthrow of Thieu's government.

A reporter asks bluntly if this is an election gimmick? Kissinger earnestly denies it; the communists, he says, set the deadline for agreement by October 31; and it is they, not we, who brought discussion into the open.

It is a moment of triumph. But Kissinger does not spread it on too thick; he allows himself a few witticisms but keeps ebullience under control. As he finishes his presentation it seems appropriate to ask him whether the whole agreement could not have been achieved four years before?

This sets him back a second; he spends some time answering; asks several times for a copy of Hanoi's October 8th text. It is evident that America must not be allowed to feel its sacrifices were in vain.

We admire him; what a moment! He leans on the lectern or sometimes puts hands behind him. And we ask, what now remains? Well, there are technical issues, what clauses of the Geneva Agreement apply. It can all be settled "at one more meeting." Kissinger's lips purse into a half-deprecating and demure pout that is funny and attractive. We rush to catch deadlines, bearers of glad tidings. It will put the top layer on the Nixon landslide.

So now it is two months later, December 16. The same pressroom. There is a theatrical quality to the entrance even now, though something has gone wrong. The tension is acute. It is Saturday, but the room, with TV lights, is packed. What has happened in Paris? The Nixon victory is over and the American mood is euphoric.

"I will give you as fair and honest a description of the general trend of the negotiations as I can," he begins soberly. He is more formal than before, more deliberate.

"Settlement was always within reach," he says, "and was always pulled just beyond our reach when we attempted to grasp it." It was all the fault of Hanoi. ·

Reporters' faces catch the mood; it grows grimmer and grimmer. "The president," he says, "decided that we should not engage in a charade with the American people."

He consults a red portfolio. Often there is a slight clearing of the throat when confronting a question. "We have an agreement that is ninety-nine-percent completed," he tells a reporter, "we are one decision away from a settlement."

What one decision? He has agreed not to divulge it, he says, but reporters conjecture: those Geneva accords to which the US gave consent promised *one* Vietnam, not two; but if Washington accepts that fact now then this is a civil war, not an invasion from the North, as the US has always contended; our moral justification for intervention is wiped out. This all seemed a trivial detail back on October 26, but now reporters sense the issue between Kissinger's lines: "We wanted some reference in the agreement, however vague, however elusive, however indirect, which would make clear that the two parts of Vietnam would live in peace with each other and that neither side would impose its solution on the other by force." Exactly! He keeps sidestepping reporters' questions whether this is not the basic question in the war.

A speechwriter in Mr. Nixon's 1968 campaign, Richard Whalen (*Catch the Falling Flag*), quotes the president as saying, "There's no way to win the war. But we can't say that, of course." In this instance, did Kissinger think he could slide over the difficulty? And did Mr. Nixon object? Nobody knows. But like an actor in a tragedy he repeats his line, "The risks and perils of war, however difficult, seem sometimes more bearable to them than the uncertainties and risks and perils of peace." It sounds like a translation from some sad old Roman historian.

Those are the two scenes, and what is the Washington mood now? Americans celebrate Christmas but about Vietnam there is a bewildered—almost scary—silence. The disappointment is solid. Mr. Nixon gave us peace, people seem to say; now it is snatched back; everything seems suspect; can we really believe this new accusation that Hanoi is readying another invasion?

Senator Javits, a Republican, called a press conference here last week; so many reporters appeared they had to shift rooms. He is a small, bald man; he sits far away at the head of the committee table; two huge mirrors reflect each other across the room to infinity. Deep lines from nose to chin put parentheses around his mouth. He says quietly the new bombing is a mistake. Behind him somebody has trimmed a twinkling Christmas tree.

Gentle Mike Mansfield, in another interview, says so too—the bombing is a mistake. Others join in. There are few epithets; the election is over. Muskie is terse and grim: "When Congress returns in January" he says, "it will demand an explanation."

We walk out of the old Senate Office Building. A choir in maroon cassocks fills the marble rotunda with songs of praise and hope about the Prince of Peace. Round the world shock and horror rise over Mr. Nixon's resumed bombing. But America is busy with Christmas and bombs are far off. Is a wave rising? I don't know. But I feel certain that something odd is happening; there is a very strange mood here, indeed.

Does He Believe What He Says?

JANUARY 2, 1973   In this century Coolidge, and Harding, and Hoover, and Ike, were "conservatives"; but Coolidge was passive, Harding was gullible, Hoover was impotent, and Ike never knew what it was all about. Nixon is different; he knows the political score, he is an activist and he is definitely trying to set the clock back. We think this is dangerous.

The hardest thing to believe about Mr. Nixon is that he believes what he says he believes. Can he really believe that there has been "a breakdown in frankly what I would call the leadership class in this country"?—yet that is what he told an interviewer in the glow of his election landslide. Is it possible that he believes that the nation's media are generally out to get him? Or that he thinks school busing will destroy middle-class values? Or that he thinks Americans are children—what did he say?—"The average American is just like the child in the family . . . (if you pamper him) you are going to make him soft, spoiled, and eventually a weak individual." These ideas are very difficult things to credit, yet Mr. Nixon, in his lonely aloofness in the White House, seems definitely to believe them.

There is a pattern of mean-spiritedness about the administration that sometimes seems to leap from social matters to Vietnam. Grandmotherly Dorothy McCardle (sixty-eight), society reporter for the *Washington Post* (which the White House staff is still trying to pay back for its Watergate exposures), is conspicuously excluded from a series of presidential social functions, including a Sunday prayer service, while North Vietnam, in turn, is paid off by a bloodthirsty barrage of bombs for haggling over the escalated Kissinger-Nixon peace terms.

The bomb load from Mr. Nixon is greater than that which any other small nation has endured and survived, and Communist leaders may yet come to heel. The total tonnage is approaching a couple of Hiroshimas. But the real story, we think, is not what is happening in Vietnam, savage though it is, but at home. Since it involves spiritual values it is harder to measure.

America is bemused and bewildered. After giving Mr. Nixon one of history's greatest landslides it sits back to relax; to enjoy the "peace is at hand." And then the bombing. Instead of bringing home POWs for Christmas we make new ones every day! "When I tell you I am completely confident that we are going to have a settlement," Mr. Nixon asserted in his postelection statement, "you can bank on it." Who can believe anyone anymore? It is as hard to swallow as Kissinger's lame excuse for failure: "It became apparent that there was in preparation a massive Communist effort to launch an attack throughout South Vietnam to begin several days before the cease-fire would have been declared." Correspondents searched for confirmation of this supposed buildup from US officials in Vietnam; in vain.

The revival of the war leaves public opinion groping and inarticulate, and this feeling of helplessness may turn into an attitude of indifference and disengagement and spiritual depletion that will involve other great issues before the country. As a little group of war protesters trudged hopefully back and forth near the White House on Christmas Day, they must have wondered if Mr. Nixon is, indeed, right; that the average American is "just like the child in the family." Does papa really know best?

The two great issues before America are poverty and race. Mr. Nixon as a conservative is turning the clock back on both of them. If there is no protest over Vietnam will there be any protest over curtailing housing for the poor, or enforcing civil rights for blacks? Once you create a national mood of apathy and helplessness it spreads like a plague.

Mr. Nixon's proposed new $250-billion budget will slash expenditures for a host of social welfare programs designed to aid the poor and the near-poor and he declines to contemplate raising taxes to help bridge the gulf between haves and have-nots. In reorganizing his administration the first man to feel the ax is Father Hesburgh, president of Notre Dame, for fifteen years a magnificent chairman and member of the US Civil Rights Commission. Father Hesburgh criticized the Justice Department for refusal to enforce existing civil rights statutes. He called busing a phony issue.

Last week former President Johnson recalled the civil rights crusade of the sixties, which he helped to launch. But his successor used the so-called busing issue as the successful code word in the 1972 election for an appeal to segregationists. Many think race was the great undeclared domestic issue of the campaign.

Interviewed by the *National Catholic Reporter*, a lay-edited weekly published in Kansas City, Father Hesburgh says that Mr. Nixon spent not more than fifteen minutes with the commission in the last four years. Speaking of presidential aides H. R. Haldeman and John Ehrlichman, Father Hesburgh says they are "good men, both of them" but lacking in some quality of adventure: "Take how these two guys spend their off-hours. They get together with their families and watch home movies they've taken of Nixon campaigning. Now I can think of better ways to spend my spare time."

We may be headed for quite turbulent times ahead. Indifference to poverty and civil rights will not cure them. And with an activist conservative president conspicuously failing to take Congress, let alone the public, into his confidence on Vietnam, he seems to be heading straight for a confrontation with the legislature.

It is a very strange situation indeed; we don't recall anything like it. The cabinet has been downgraded, the executive tightened and reorganized so that top staff aides no longer can be summoned to Congress but have executive immunity or, like Roy L. Ash, head of the Office of Management and Budget, don't even require senatorial confirmation; the networks frightened; reporters jailed; Supreme Court packed with Nixon conservatives; the public bemused with off-again, on-again war, and the gauntlet thrown down to a vacillating Congress over the president's right to impound funds, and to carry on an undeclared war. Can Congress put its house in order? Does it want to? We must wait and see.

Faults in the Constitution

M A Y 2 6 , 1 9 7 3   The three faults in the American form of government are all brilliantly illustrated in the fix we are in now over Watergate. By an extraordinary historical coincidence they are all present at one time. They explain why no other modern democracy has our system. They show why unless some radical change is made by legal means we shall probably be forced ultimately to make the change by more dangerous means.

The first fault is that after an election one party may control the White House and another Congress. That happened, spectacularly, last November. It has happened before, of course, and we have struggled along with it. But by a policy that seems almost crazy, Mr. Nixon in November declined to take a conciliatory line to the Democratic Congress and from the very first bullied, aggravated, and outraged his antagonist.

The second fault is the frozen four-year term. Under a parliamentary system if a credibility collapse occurs a vote of no confidence is taken for granted, then an election and a new mandate. But our eighteenth-century government lacks it. It is like a building with no fire escape. Today we have a president who probably can't govern and we are stuck with him for three years. Impeachment, resignation? —hardly likely. Quaintly enough, Mr. Nixon last week embraced the Mansfield proposal of a constitutional amendment to let the chief executive serve only one term, for six years. So if burglaries discredited him in the first year, we should have him and his Watergate clowns for five years and couldn't chuck him.

The third fault is one-man rule. The US president is a kind of elected monarch, whereas the job requires collective parliamentary team wisdom; it has grown too big for one man. It is the peculiar contribution of Mr. Nixon that he has exaggerated this isolation beyond that, we believe, of any other president. Most presidents have regular group consultations with somebody or other, normally the cabinet. Theoretically this isn't vital. If presidents were all Abe Lincolns it would be different.

The strong man for Nixon was John Mitchell. He was a kind of father figure, the second most powerful man in Washington. As we look back on Mitchell, the bond salesman, we think his advice was universally bad. We cannot really remember any exception to this. As campaign manager in 1968, Mitchell helped bring down an initial 16 percent Nixon lead over the all but mortally wounded Humphrey after the Chicago convention, to win by less than 1 percent; he was responsible for the Carswell and Haynsworth fiascoes; he backed the "law-and-order" 1970 midterm campaign, another flop; he was slapped down by his own Supreme Court on black voting rights, and on the outrageous doctrine of inherent presidential power to tap telephones without court order; and he is up to his neck now, so far as we can judge, in Watergate. What a sight it was the other day on a CBS documentary to see three flashback Mitchell interviews in which he self-righteously denied any knowledge of Watergate, followed by a fourth in which he said, yes, the lawless proposal had been discussed thrice in front of him. He brought no prosecution. That's our law-and-order leader.

It seems to us, in retrospect, that Mr. Nixon recognized the weakness of our separation-of-powers government and was trying to change it in his own way, a way we don't approve, but that we can understand because we too think it is outmoded. He tried to centralize things under his control; he tried to cow Congress for good; and he advanced doctrines of executive authority which really would have changed our system for keeps. You can't read about Richard Kleindienst as attorney general telling a Senate committee that the president has power to tell 2,500,000 federal employees not to testify, or recall the crowd at the White House arrogantly asserting that the president has the ultimate authority to spend, or not to spend, money voted by Congress (i.e., impoundment), without feeling that we were just on the verge of a change in our form of government.

Watergate has halted executive domination, we guess. At least for the time. But are we really just going back to the "old system" again, which many are demanding: the possibility of stalemate elections again with no recourse; the frozen four-year term; the built-in pressure toward presidential usurpation simply to get things done? Surely in the nuclear age this won't do. Mr. Nixon proposes a constitutional amendment for a change in presidential tenure; while we are about it why don't we explore half a dozen other amendments to give us a more flexible system.

Meanwhile the Ervin investigation commences. Some lawyers object to the procedure. They say it precludes a court inquiry and that publicity by Ervin will make it impossible to send anybody who is guilty to jail. We think this misses the point. This tremendous affair in the marble caucus room of the Senate is not the subject for a normal twelve-man jury; you and I are the jury, the nation is the jury. This is a folkmoot by America. The defendant, whether we like it or not, is the president—he and the men around him.

The role of television in this unprecedented national inquest must be noted. Television is the president's medium. It has made the modern president possible. Mr. Nixon can ask and get prime time when he wants it. He is the only man in America who can; he can speak right into your living room at will; the TV mike is more powerful than the monarch's orb and scepter; it is the symbol and instrument of his power. Save at elections, it is a monopoly appurtenance. When Senator Muskie tries to answer the president, as he did the other day, he can't get free time.

But in the Watergate probe television passes out of the president's control, for the time being. As David Wise says in his powerful new book *The Politics of Lying* (Random House), "the government has increasingly gained control over the channels of information about military, diplomatic, and intelligence events. . . . Because of official secrecy on a scale unprecedented in our history, the government's capacity to distort information in order to preserve its own political power is almost limitless."

It came within an inch of succeeding in Watergate. It is far more important now to show the nation how the system works than it is to send a few Nixon creeps and Watergate clowns to jail.

TRB Remembers

JULY 28, 1973   We're going on vacation and would like to leave some thoughts. We've seen some sad things in Washington in our time: the day they buried FDR, and the Negro woman sobbed in the crowd on Pennsylvania Avenue and made us all sob, too; the day they brought back Jack Kennedy's body and we watched the fountain playing behind the White House, a steady stream, something that you could put your hand through, something without substance, but never ending—like democracy.

We've seen stirring things, too: the night we waited under the portico of the White House and watched the grim-faced members of the isolationist Senate Foreign Relations Committee go in and come out after Pearl Harbor, in preparation for the speech next day.

Way back we remember the tear gas hissing out of the canisters when they drove the bonus veterans out from Hooverville on Pennsylvania Avenue, and a soldier had to come up and lead us down from the second floor of a half-demolished skeleton structure because we were blinded.

We can remember (or think we can) when Albert Fall came into the marble caucus room of the Senate in the Teapot Dome scandal, all shrunken and collapsed; the formerly arrogant secretary of the Interior who scorned the Walsh committee the first time he came.

We can remember Borah standing in front of the lion house at the zoo one fall day and how leonine *he* looked (like John L. Lewis), and we gave him a lift in our Model T.

Wry things, too: Calvin Coolidge with an Indian headdress on; any speech in the Senate by J. Ham Lewis; the circus midget climbing into the inadequate lap of J. Pierpont Morgan as a publicity stunt, and he thinking it was a little girl.

Yes and recently, LBJ. What a character he was!—as indigenous a folk figure as little fox terrier Harry Truman; how we interviewed him one time when he was majority leader, and he said nobody was going to treat him like a child-in-arms! And by golly, in an instant he was bounding out of his chair behind his enormous desk in a palatial room that looked like the Sistine Chapel with floating nymphs painted on the ceiling, bounding out of the chair and striding up and down the carpet with arms bent, indignantly rocking an imaginary baby.

The pay in Washington ain't much, but the show's swell. After a while, though, things begin to repeat. James McCartney writing in the current *Columbia Journalism Review* wonders how the press let the White House story on Watergate go so long. Well, here is the comment of a great reporter, the late Thomas L. Stokes ("Chip Off My Shoulder") looking back at the time he served in the White House press-room: "The irony of it all to me—the amazing disclosures that came later—was that we newspapermen at the White House sat, all the time, at the outer gate, so to speak, and had known nothing." Watergate?—no; Teapot Dome of course. McCartney and Stokes agree that the worst place to find out the scandals of an administration is in the White House pressroom: "the world of Ronald Ziegler," as McCartney puts it, "of the handout, the announcement, the statement, the official view."

Things repeat themselves in other ways. The Supreme Court has just taken another crack, five to four, at deciding what's "obscenity," already causing a Virginia sheriff to discover that the girls in *Playboy* aren't clothed and opening up a probable new chaos of "contemporary community standards." Dear me, we've seen it all before; who's this grim figure stalking about the Senate, offering to show lascivious foreign imports and asking permission to read aloud to his colleagues, in secret session, excerpts from the new novel by D. H. Lawrence, *Lady Chatterley's Lover?* Why tall, dignified, humorless Reed Smoot, to be sure, demanding to save the public morals and inspiring my favorite of all editorial captions, "Smite Smut, Smoot!"

Here's another issue coming up now, so repetitive that I have a file on it, "executive privilege." Yes, the Constitution would practically fall apart if President Nixon invited a Senate committee to the White House to tell what he knows about Watergate, let alone if he went himself to Congress to testify.

Well, old Abe didn't talk much about executive privilege. They set up a committee to watch him in 1861, a group of suspicious,

hate-ridden superpatriots ("Radical Republicans" they called them)—
the Joint Committee on the Conduct of the War. They felt they
knew how to run the war better than he did. But he didn't appeal to
separation of powers. There was talk of his impeachment. He didn't
retreat inside the White House.

One time, according to Carl Sandburg's *Lincoln: The War Years*
(Vol. 2), the committee met in secret session to consider Mrs. Lincoln's loyalty. Suddenly, as they sat, the orderly came in with "a half-
frightened expression" and, before he could speak, there at the foot
of the committee table "standing solitary, his hat in his hand, his form
towering, Abraham Lincoln stood." Sandburg says that Lincoln came
voluntarily, took oath of family loyalty, and departed.

The story may be apocryphal but there's no question that Lincoln
met with the committee many times. In *Lincoln Day by Day*, an
authoritative chronology issued here in 1960, the president is shown
to have conferred personally with the committee ten times, 1861–64.
He didn't fear loss of dignity or constitutional collapse by dealing
directly with a committee of Congress.

That's the difference between then and now; it's what we've been
mulling over in these prevacation musings. The new tone is monarchical; it varies from the bizarre to the berserk. At one minute it's the
light-opera uniforms the president proposed for his White House
palace guard. At the next it's the sinister suggestion that the people
are "children" and that the critics are subversive.

A sympathetic White House witness, under oath, quotes the president's dismay at discovering what practically everyone else already
knew: "I have racked my brain. I have searched my mind. Were there
any clues I should have seen that should have tipped me off?" Well,
the answer is yes. Furthermore for the first time in history we've had
a quasi-conspiracy to grab an election. And for the first time in history we've had burglars on the White House payroll.

Agnew—Not Like Other Men

OCTOBER 6, 1973   There he stood, tall, fastidious, handsome, the benign-looking man conservatives jubilantly recognized as one who might cut liberals down to size: "A spirit of national masochism prevails," declared impeccably groomed Vice-President Spiro Agnew in New Orleans, October 1969, "encouraged by an effete corps of impudent snobs who characterize themselves as intellectuals."

Mr. Agnew in 1969 didn't appeal for decency or mercy in characterizing his youthful opponents in Harrisburg, Pennsylvania, that same month. He declared, "We can afford to separate them [student radicals] from our society—with no more regret than we should feel over discarding rotten apples from a barrel."

Agnew speaks with few gestures and oratorical tricks. He just stands there, sleek and superior, manicured and magisterial, registering well-bred scorn. He sends editors and supporters running to their dictionaries to find what the words mean ("nattering nabobs of negativism" was a honey) and comes up with fine, resounding phrases that cause appreciative chuckles even from his opponents:

"They [the young protesters] are vultures who sit in trees and watch lions battle, knowing that win, lose, or draw, they will be fed."

His attack on the press and TV brought ecstatic praise from Tricia Nixon: "The vice-president is incredible. I feel I should write him a letter. He's amazing, what he has done to the media—helping it [*sic*] to reform itself. . . . I think they've taken a second look. You can't underestimate the power of fear."

And now, how things are changed. The vice-president is practically appealing to the House of Representatives to impeach him. The public is suddenly discovering that impeachment is about the only way under the Constitution to heave out a president or vice-president. It is so cumbersome most congressmen shudder at the very thought. But it is the so-called grand inquest of the nation. And now here we are, looking over the brink into something frightening and unknown.

Last February as the new Congress got to work, this reporter began a column, "The question is now, can he govern? Mr. Nixon stands at his peak: an unprecedented election landslide, a Gallup Poll rating of 68 percent. He is stern, taut, confident, eager to show who's boss. He looks at Congress, waiting for something to be outraged about." Yet even so, as we saw it last February there were strange portents: the evident Nixon feeling that he was being "persecuted by 'the better people.' He has an immense majority," we added, "can he govern?"

The answer is still uncertain. But it becomes more dubious all the time. There is some evidence that Mr. Nixon knew about the Agnew Maryland troubles way back before the 1972 Republican convention. But he looked at the crisis McGovern was having in the Eagleton affair and decided to let the thing ride.

Sometimes it seems that anyone who touches the Nixon administration is soiled. The *New York Times'* Tom Wicker has added it up —six congressional investigations, five grand juries, five civil suits . . . and on and on. The former cabinet is almost swept clean now and two of its former members are under indictment; and his closest former White House aides are out, and in trouble.

Now the vice-president. The man twice picked by Mr. Nixon to fill his place in office. The vice-president sounds quite noble as he tells the House that he wants it, not a grand jury, to investigate his troubles. The Constitution, he asserts, "bars a criminal proceeding of any kind —federal or state, county or town—against a president or vice-president while he holds office."

Just like Mr. Nixon who won't give up the Watergate tapes for the loftiest of reasons. And so Mr. Agnew says, "accordingly, I cannot acquiesce in any criminal proceedings being lodged against me." It is his "right and duty," he says, "to turn to the House."

This sounds fine. But what it means is that Messrs. Nixon and Agnew have an exclusive monarchical privilege under certain circumstances; they are not like other men. They transcend the law. They cannot be indicted or subpoenaed. They need not even obey the Supreme Court, unless, in Mr. Nixon's airy phrase, its judgment is "definitive." They can appeal to the labyrinthine process of impeachment which means, in Mr. Agnew's case, that instead of being tried by a hard-nosed federal grand jury of common citizens in Baltimore he may ultimately (if the House acts) go before a body of fellow politicians in the Senate, familiar with the problems of campaign donations and kickbacks, and hope that one-third of them plus one will vote "not guilty."

The atmosphere here last week was as strange as we have ever seen it. The White House carried on a Byzantine campaign to get Mr. Agnew to resign. As the rift with him widened and deepened, rumors were set afloat, and the near-desperate vice-president tried to swat them down like hornets. Obviously the White House doesn't want a discredited Agnew on its hands.

Ultimately, when the vice-president made his decision, Mr. Nixon came up with a tardy appeal not to prejudge the case. This is all very well, but under the circumstances, Mr. Nixon's own earlier failure to rush eloquently to his subordinate's defense was in itself a form of prejudgment. We believe that Mr. Agnew has already been politically destroyed.

We suspect there's something to Stewart Alsop's ingenious speculation that John Connally sees a vice-presidential vacancy looming and is angling for it. How else but to curry Nixon's favor can you explain Connally's rash and extraordinary statement that the president need not obey the Supreme Court? Through it all the public remains amazingly quiet. It is stunned and incredulous and its belief in the democratic political process may well be dangerously low. Our guess is that there are more shocks to come. We think the Watergate case will go to the Supreme Court. We suspect the Court's majority will decide against the White House. And we guess that if Agnew ultimately resigns and the president names Connally, Congress won't confirm him. In the Ninety-third Congress, we just can't see a majority of both houses, as required by the Twenty-fifth Amendment, going along.

The Era of Scarcity

OCTOBER 20, 1973 The new Era of Scarcity is coming faster than anybody thought, stimulated by the Arab-Israeli war. Your home and office may be five degrees cooler this winter because of the war, if the Arabs use their "oil weapon," which seems possible. Very likely the administration will be pushed toward rationing, which is a daunting thought when you think of how well they've handled other problems like inflation, the meat shortage, and the Russian grain deal.

The Middle East war may have shattered possible détente with Russia at the very time it emphasizes the need for it. Moscow is delivering military supplies to the Arabs, and in turn the US may very likely be asked to do the same for the Israelis. This could escalate as passions rise and hates grow. The dwarfs could pull the giants into war.

In this shrinking world where population has already outrun food and threatens to outrun basic raw materials, we do not have much time left. The US is well-heeled in many ways but quite vulnerable in others. We have 6 percent of the world population and use 33 percent of the energy. The oil shortage drives the point home; it was here before the Arab-Israeli war and now the war will accentuate it. But the problem becomes clear when there's an oil shortage. The shortage seems a complete surprise to the president. At his press conference the other day he blandly warned the Arabs that "oil without a market doesn't do a country much good" and tut-tutted them with the overthrow of the late Mohammed Mossadegh, premier of Iran, in 1953 after he nationalized Western oil companies. The comment was about as inept as some of his comments about Watergate. Iran was then producing only about 300,000 barrels a day. The man we are worried about today is pivotal King Faisal of Saudi Arabia, whose hot desert sands produce 8.2 million barrels a day. We are pressuring him to boost this to 20 million. He is friendly, but he has signaled reluctance to expand production unless we reduce support for Israel. He has never spelled out his terms, but if the Middle East oil states cut back production as they did for three months in the 1967 war there probably will be a shortage.

Faisal, incidentally, is nobody to fool with: one informed official here says his oil royalties may amount to $15 billion next year. Try as he can, he can only spend about $3 billion a year on internal improvements. In ten years he will have $100 billion and may be the world's banker.

What superpower Russia will do in the Arab-Israeli war nobody knows. No one doubts it badly wants a détente with the United States.

No one doubts it urgently wants American (and Western) technology, and will pay a price for it. No one doubts either that it has a nasty way with dissenters and is as far from democracy as many of the dictator states that are clients of the US.

Messrs. Nixon and Kissinger want to improve relations and increase trade with Russia, and this comes down to lowering tariffs to the level that we now charge "most favored nations." In Joe McCarthy's day it was the conservatives who fought closer commercial ties with Russia and the liberal intellectuals who favored them. Richard Nixon is always our favorite weather vane in things like this: ten years ago when the USSR had a disastrous wheat harvest and wanted to buy grain, our man Nixon (then a private citizen) denounced the notion as "subsidizing Khrushchev at a time when he is in deep economic trouble. It allows him to divert the Russian economy into space and into military activities that he otherwise would have to keep in agriculture."

There was a lot more beating the breast about it and it marked the difference between Nixon-out-of-office and Nixon-in-office. What is astonishing today is to see liberal I. F. Stone joining Senator Goldwater in the same theme, and John Paton Davies backing Senator Jackson against détente.

It is a genuine moral dilemma. The so-called Jackson amendment says no favored-nation clause for Russia until it liberalizes emigration for Jews. It tears liberals apart. Some want a tough line to Russia. Some, like the left-wing *Nation*, want détente: "As for Senator Henry Jackson, who aspires to the presidency," the magazine asks, "does any informed person, whether in the Soviet Union or the United States, really believe that his heart bleeds for Sakharov and Solzhenitsyn? He wants an even bigger US arms program than President Nixon dares to sponsor . . ."

We think President Nixon was right and the antidétente liberals were wrong on this one. (It's not easy to say it.) We don't think trade between nations is a good vehicle for trying to compel drastic internal reforms in one country by another. We have no illusions about freedom in Moscow but things are far better than they were under Stalin. We are glad Nixon went to Moscow and Brezhnev came to Washington. Better relations between nations often come at junctures when their material interests coincide, as they have recently between the USA and USSR. We believe in expanding trade and also in giving every bit of moral support we can to the heroic Communist dissidents. Alas, Congress seems more likely than ever to shy away from closer trade ties because of the war which could now bring the two superpowers into actual confrontation.

The dawning Era of Scarcity isn't going to be confined to oil and energy. Of thirteen basic industrial raw materials required by a modern economy, says Lester Brown in his *World Without Borders* (Random House), the US in 1950 was import-dependent (i.e., imported over 50 percent) on only four substances: aluminum, manganese, nickel, and tin. By 1970 zinc and chromium were added.

By 1985 we will have added iron, lead, and tungsten. We will be buying half of these supplies on the world market in competition with industrial rivals. By 2000 we will be import-dependent on twelve of the thirteen basic raw materials (adding copper, potassium, and sulfur). Take heart, we'll still be in the clear on phosphate!

It all sounds fairly fantastic, of course, but maybe a little less so as we conserve oil this winter. As for food, the protein war between have and have-not countries is already beginning, population experts tell us. Mankind will surely find a path, but things will be different.

James Madison on Impeachment

NOVEMBER 10, 1973   He was a small man, slight of stature, "no bigger," someone said, "than half a piece of soap," and his friends called him Jemmy. In June 1789, Representative James Madison of Virginia rose on the floor of the House of Representatives (sitting in New York), adjusted the ruffles at breast and wrist, and made certain observations about impeachment.

The legislative body listened to him intently, because the Constitution wasn't a year old yet and this blue-eyed, quiet-voiced man with the springy step knew more about it than anybody else. They were days of magnificence for a bold little country, but at the same time, everything was so new. Let's listen to Jemmy, who became the fourth president of the United States.

Suppose in days to come, he said, "an unworthy president" maintains in office an unworthy cabinet member. "Then the House of Representatives can at any time impeach him, and the Senate can remove him, whether the president chooses or not."

Yes, he continued, but "the president can displace from office a man whose merits require that he should be continued in it." That was the other side of the coin, he explained, and the modern reader will, of course, think of President Nixon and special Watergate prosecutor Archibald Cox. And what, Madison asked, "will be the motives which the president can feel for such abuse of his power, and the restraints that operate to prevent it? In the first place he will be impeached by this House, before the Senate, for such an act of maladministration: for I contend that the wanton removal of meritorious officers would subject him to impeachment and removal from his own high trust."

Madison's voice was low and friends often called to him to speak louder. Whether his wife Dolley was in the audience I don't know; after all, he was merely giving a little lecture on what the Constitution meant. He had helped draft it. "But what can be the motives for displacing a worthy man?" he asked. "It must be that he [the president] may fill the place with an unworthy character of his own. Can he accomplish this end? No," he said.

Madison was talking about the office of a possible "Secretary of the Department of Foreign Affairs" (Secretary of State), requiring Senate confirmation. But confirmation or not, Madison's words had equal relevancy: "If he could fill the vacancy with the man he might choose, I am sure that he would have little inducement to make an improper removal. Let us consider the consequences. The injured man will be supported by the popular opinion: the community will take sides with him against the president . . . to displace a man of high merit, and who from his station may be supposed a man of extensive influence, are considerations which will excite serious reflections beforehand in the mind of any man who may fill the presidential chair. The friends of those individuals and the public sympathy will be against him."

Madison went on with his methodical logic: "If this should not produce impeachment before the Senate, it will amount to an impeachment before the country, who will have the power of punish-ment, by refusing to reelect him."

The Twenty-second Amendment has of course made Mr. Nixon ineligible for another election, but his party is up for election one year from now and it may want to disassociate itself from Watergate. Anyway, that's the guide James Madison gave us some 180 years ago, as set down dutifully in the Annals of Congress, Vol. 1, June 17, 1789. They hadn't coined the phrase Founding Father then, but no better witness could be found of how matter-of-factly people then approached the process of impeachment which daunts us so much today.

A couple of months ago this fallible column reported that there wasn't a chance of impeachment. Things have changed. It has been an agonizing process of watching Mr. Nixon knock himself out. Al-ways he makes concessions and always too late. People who didn't mind "the plumbers" gasped to find that a man with a salary of $200,000 was apparently paying less tax than they; that a man who criticized welfare handouts was getting $10 million in federal funds for his Florida and California estates. Then came the firing of Archibald Cox and the resignations of Richardson and Ruckelshaus, and the White House, too late, realized the awful mistake it had made. Then came the Cox tele-vised press conference on that sunny Saturday in October.

I have seen what I regard as three supreme one-man political performances in my lifetime. First was FDR's "little dog Fala" speech to the Teamsters here in Washington in 1944. It was so funny and devastating that Dewey, who had run his candidate's special train into a quiet siding to hear it, changed his whole campaign plan. It was the only time in my life where I saw men, exuberant union leaders who had been fortifying themselves for the occasion, literally rolling in the aisles.

Next I must put in, in fairness, Nixon's "Checkers" speech in 1952. Ike was ready to ditch him at the revelation of his secret fund. (Secret fund!—it seems third-grade stuff today.) The speech was maudlin and politically superb. "Pat doesn't have a mink coat. But she does have a respectable Republican cloth coat." It brought 100,000 telegrams.

I put number three, Jack Kennedy at the Rice Hotel in Houston at 8:30 P.M., September 12, 1960, when he faced the sullen Greater Houston Ministerial Association. The Reverend Norman Vincent Peale was on the loose, giving respectable leadership to the ancient fears that beat Al Smith. In a speech cooked up with Ted Sorensen (Unitarian) and followed by questions and answers, Kennedy said, "I believe in an America where the separation of church and state is absolute." Before he finished the audience cheered. He had opened an era.

And now I have to put down number four—that press conference of Archie Cox on a sunny Saturday last month. Maybe I exaggerate. But it seemed to me he suddenly triggered off emotions that had been gathering for weeks. Here is a man of honor, the public said. Nixon had fired him, and Richardson and Ruckelshaus had quit, too.

What was it Jemmy Madison said, "the injured man will be supported by the popular opinion"?

Mr. Middle America

DECEMBER 8, 1973 Around the time you read this we may have a new vice-president. And before long he could be president. He is Jerry Ford, Mr. Middle America.

Things are so strained here that many people think any change would be an improvement. In the oil shortage, for example, Mr. Nixon's leadership capability is so eroded that he seems to be softening the full facts for the public. That's the cost of a crippled president. An executive in full command could recommend brutal remedies and absorb the consequent griping, but Mr. Nixon is forced to inch along, step by step. He may be deceiving himself, of course, when he hopefully forecasts that the crisis may last only a year, but we suspect he is temporizing. The great weight of gloomy evidence here is that the situation will get worse.

That's what investors think. In less than four weeks Wall Street has lost $20 billion in values and the near-panic is worldwide. Wall Street prices, of course, are paper values. No prediction is possible through the present murk. That's because nothing like the oil shortage has happened before; the world has never heretofore seen the sudden constriction in supply of a universal industrial essential. Talk about "one world"! A few nomads on camels living on deserts 4,000 miles away have shut down General Motors' Cadillac plants!

So how about Jerry Ford? One thing his confirmation will do, it will make it a lot easier for a number of wavering Republicans to vote impeachment-indictment if they want to. They wouldn't have done it while Spiro's old chair was vacant. And it must have some effect, too, on Mr. Nixon's lonely reveries. We don't think he will quit, but just the same the confirmation of an understudy must play some part in the equations he sets down in those neat notes he makes on that yellow pad of his.

Here are two sets of comments on Jerry Ford, a sort of personality balance sheet. Credits: He's honest. These adjectives (we think) also apply: frank, popular, modest, outgoing, loyal, uncomplicated, healthy, rational (doesn't call opponents "enemies"), decent, (wouldn't burglarize Watergate). And also solid, stable, and reliable. Oh, yes—did we say it before?—honest.

Debits: Inexperienced, limited, plodding, low-initiative, unimaginative, anti-civil rights, anti-social welfare, antilabor, anti-the Future.

Maybe we are unfair. After all Jerry Ford's job as opposition leader was to *oppose*. He undertook to put together a coalition of conservative Republicans and southern Democrats who would battle the Democrats and above all in recent days supply the one-third-plus-one to uphold presidential vetoes.

In a new role he might take a broader view. We are reminded, for example, of the magazine description of a prominent figure depicted as a mediocre machine politician, a representative of the small-town, middle-class viewpoint, a racist, a nonideological broker who lacks a grasp of the fundamental issues facing America and the world. Yes, says the article, he is an honest and devoted public servant, no doubt; but if he should become president "he would tend to drift with events and follow the path of least resistance." Jerry Ford? Not at all; the article is from *Common Sense*, October 1944, and is quoted by Ohio University historian Alonzo Hamby in his new book, *Beyond the New Deal: Harry S. Truman & American Liberalism* (Columbia). We are talking about Harry Truman.

A lot of people are getting comfort today by comparing Ford with Truman, and there is a certain parallel. Both men were professional politicians for whom party regularity was a way of life; both were squares; both were nervous with intellectuals; both started with limited outlooks and had little contact with minority groups, ghetto problems, or world affairs. "Essentially," Hamby says of Truman, "he was a party man whose career reflected the course of the mainstream of the Democratic Party in the twentieth century." Exactly; substitute "Republican" for "Democrat" in the previous sentence and you describe Jerry Ford.

Yes, under certain circumstances, Ford might make a good president. The circumstances would be an absence of major problems at home and abroad. He would be frank, restful, friendly, and would consult with a lot of people before making comfortable conservative decisions. Most of us are cheered at just the thought of returning to that kind of a world. It would be back to Eisenhower, not Truman; a caretaker president.

But this isn't 1952. Abroad we are challenged by the start of the Age of Scarcity, with oil the beginning and a dozen other essential raw materials coming after. At home we have accumulated through Vietnam a backlog of explosive social problems. They are there, you can almost hear the termites boring. It is like the day in Harry Truman's White House when the piano started to go through the floor! There is concentrated corporate power; race; inequality of income and ugly tax system to feed it; lack of rudimentary social services like health insurance; lack of gun control and as a result our incredible rate of crime-by-violence for which America is unique; and inspiring but often exasperating government that needs to be modernized at nearly every point, where rich men buy elections, Congress hands over its authority, and we haven't even got around yet to mothballing that delightful old stagecoach, the electoral college.

Ford isn't Truman. Truman's first major Senate speech lambasted rail and insurance financial manipulations. It sounds corny now, maybe, but he said that Carnegie libraries were "steeped in the blood of the Homestead steelworkers."

In twenty-five years likable Jerry Ford has never fathered a major piece of legislation; his sole big initiative was trying to get Justice Douglas impeached. In confirmation hearings the AFL-CIO found his record 94-percent antilabor; NAACP leader Clarence Mitchell attacked him on his civil rights stand. Contrast this with Truman. Labor backed him. When he left the White House he got a letter from Roy Wilkins: "You carry with you the gratitude and affectionate regard of millions of your Negro fellow citizens who in less than a decade of your leadership have seen the old order change right before their eyes."

Jerry must grow to fill Harry's shoes.

The Call of Duty

JANUARY 8, 1974   In the final analysis a country is reasonably safe if it can produce great men at great moments. The United States has a pretty good record for this: all those Founding Fathers, for example; you get bored reading about them, perhaps, but if you study the record, they were a remarkable crew. The moment came and they were touched by greatness.

In the Civil War we produced Lincoln; nobody quite knows how. He just seemed to be there waiting. In the annals of the great he ranks high. We produced him.

In the wrenching strains of recent times there have been good men, too. This reporter was there at that last great scene in the McCarthy hearings in 1954 when a lawyer from Boston, Joseph L. Welch, finally demanded of Senator McCarthy, *"Have you no sense of decency, sir, at long last?"* Joe Welch of Boston! He was a successful lawyer, but who had ever thought of him in a heroic role? He or some other decent citizen was born to be present at just that moment, and say just those words in just the right tone of quiet passion. It was the slap that finally woke the sleeping country. Greatness touched him for a minute.

And so now down to Watergate. We take a more hopeful view of the nasty mess than some, partly perhaps because we have confidence (not always sustained) that at critical moments the right person will be on hand to give us back a quiet sense of pride in America. It may be a quite unexpected person, or somebody whose duty it was to do what he did all the time, and surprises everybody by doing it.

There is, to start with, Senator Sam Ervin. He gets to seem, more and more, like a leftover Founding Father. He didn't impress people as being particularly heroic until Watergate came along. He fought desegregation tooth and nail, using every device, including the fili-buster. But he couldn't stomach Watergate. He presided fairly. He didn't shout and browbeat. He smiled. And smiled. His mysterious eyebrows went up and down and his jowls jiggled. He was quoting the Bible, or Shakespeare, or some back-home village philosopher all the time as he scored his points. It was good to feel the country could produce people like that.

There was Elliot Richardson. The former attorney general, Bos-ton Brahmin, with conservative outlook and serene self-confidence, was a kind of Yankee counterpoise to Senator Ervin. Richardson wanted to get along with the president. He was willing to make com-promises. He made too many compromises on social welfare and civil rights in order to stay on the Haldeman-Ehrlichman-Nixon team. But he had a line he would not step over and he knew just where the line was: the Brahmin line that couldn't be crossed with honor. The White House ordered him to break his word to special prosecutor Archibald Cox, his old Harvard Law School professor. So Richardson resigned. He did it with grace. Maybe you don't agree with all that blue-blood business but, let's face it, the guy has class. That's what the rest of them lack.

Time magazine nominated for its man of the year a third Water-gate figure: Judge John Sirica, sixty-nine, son of an Italian immigrant, the diminutive chief judge of the US District Court for Washington. A good choice, we thought (though we would have twinned it with another). Again we get the comforting sense of people around who are quietly ready to do their duty at the proper moment. Watergate was "a third-rate burglary" until Judge Sirica got his dogged teeth into it; then he shook it loose.

If we had been the editors of *Time* we would have split the Sirica award for the year with Katherine (Kay) Graham, publisher of the *Washington Post*. She could so easily have gone down from her big desk on the eighth floor of the paper to the noisy newsroom on the fifth floor after an exposure or two of Watergate and, almost as much by a look as by words, have said, "Hold off it, boys! I have a $200 million publishing empire at stake! The White House is ganging up on me. Let's just print *the news* after this and cut out this investigative reporting, this advocacy journalism." Fortunately she didn't. She and her team dug up the material, at considerable risk, that ended up in Judge Sirica's court.

It is comforting to pretend there will always be somebody in moments of crisis who steps out like this, with courage, with honor, with stubbornness. And then you remember all the times when nobody stepped out. Under McCarthy, think of the timid Respectables who hung back. They weren't going to risk their necks. Or in a recent case over in nearby Baltimore, when Agnew fell, evidence indicated that kickbacks by contractors to politicians had been paid for years. Why then hadn't the local newspapers exposed it? You always hope the System will correct itself; sometimes it doesn't.

After seeing John Doar the other day, the new special counsel for the House impeachment inquiry under Representative Peter Rodino, we have the feeling that he is another man in the right job. It is a tough one. He is regarded with suspicion by everybody. He is not a prosecutor, but a counsel; he is not serving the Democrats nor the Republicans, but is bipartisan; he is not seeking impeachment and not trying to prevent it, but is trying to bring out the facts, and to do it fairly. He has another job, to get an interpretation of what constitutes an "impeachable offense," a matter on which there is widest disagreement. Mr. Doar, fifty-two, a tall, lean man with large, regular features, curly hair, firm jaw, and profile like the sheriff in *High Noon*, towered eight inches above Chairman Rodino's five foot six, as he was introduced. He spent most of a brief interview with this reporter insisting that he had done nothing unusual, let alone heroic, in facing down a shower of sticks and bottles on Faris Street, in Jackson, Mississippi, thrown by black protestors bent on avenging the murder of Medgar Evers. According to local accounts, he walked out and shouted, "My name is Doar, D-O-A-R. I'm from the Justice Department. Everybody around here knows I stand for what is right. Go back, go back, you can't win this way." They looked at him. They went back.

Just kids, he explained.

Eisenhower brought him to Washington, and under Kennedy he had worked up to be assistant attorney general for Civil Rights. He has had public jobs in New York City. He is supposed to be a hard worker and a ferocious man for details. He is a registered Republican. The seventeen Republicans on the Rodino committee look at him with darkest suspicions. To us he seems to be a man trying to do his duty.

Remembering D-Day

JUNE 8, 1974   At 10:30 P.M. the loudspeaker bawls "All hands man your battle stations" and a bugle blows "general quarters," and I jump out of my berth on the heavy cruiser USS *Quincy*, Captain Senn commanding, give an embarrassed glance at the frightened young man in war correspondent's uniform looking out at me from the mirror, and say, "You fool, you damn fool, with a wife and family, what in hell are you doing here!" and go on up to the open bridge to observe D-Day. June 5–6, 1944. We are going to invade Normandy.

A couple of hours before this the chaplain prayed for us. Out in the breeze or down in the engine room men bared their heads. I looked back toward England and wondered: Something marvelous was going on. All the world's ships were coming our way. Big ships, little ships, convoys with barrage balloons tugging them ahead. British ships, Dutch ships. Free French ships. Their names mingled like a chant. The British names came down through history: the *Black Prince*, for instance, buddying up with the old battlewagons *Texas* and *Arkansas*. One transport was the *Susan B. Anthony* (sunk within hours).

"Ask and it shall be given; seek and ye shall find," said the chaplain. We hoped it was so, and it was no time for doubts. "Our help is in the Lord. . . ."

Now it is midnight. The sky is overcast. Somewhere up there the moon is one night from being full. Once it glows out and casts us in full relief in a silvery patch. Our ship is flanked by shadowy destroyers. There are only dim red battle lights. Suddenly over in France there is a spurt of tracer bullets and a falling meteor that I suppose is really an airplane. I keep thinking of home, where they are finishing supper at seven and getting ready for homework. We are probably all thinking the same thing. We talk in whispers.

Here is a wonderful thing! We are on a dark sea moving at half speed toward history and here are little pinpricks of cheery light, bobbing discreetly on the surface—a mine-swept safety lane marked so that even a landsman could follow it. They give a wonderful emotional release—somebody has been here, somebody has planned this. A sense of the immensity of this thing slowly grows.

There is no harbor ahead so we are taking our harbors with us— so-called mulberries and gooseberries, to be created by sinking old warships and merchant ships as jetties against rough weather. They are chugging out under their own power like the *Black Prince* and the *Susan B. Anthony*. We were briefed on this but we don't believe it. We will attack about where William the Conqueror sailed for England in 1066.

It is 3:00 A.M.; it is 4:00 A.M. We are six miles offshore, off what will be called Utah Beach. By now the enemy must know what's up. Bombers roar overhead. Flares drop inland. I am so wrought up I do knee bends. A thousand youngsters are on board almost as inexperienced as I. It is pathetic to hear them ask my opinion. Everything's fine, I say. Now we wait three miles offshore. All nine guns point at the beach. 5:30 A.M. There are yellow streaks in the cloud cover. Now! The guns go off and the *Quincy* bounces. Dawn finds us on Germany's doormat like the morning milk bottle.

I don't know much about battles. After an hour of this there is a certain sameness. First I am frightened and then bored and ashamed of both emotions. We are supposed to soften up shore batteries for the landing parties. At 6:00 A.M. we still bang away methodically, like a thunderbolt worked by clockwork. At 6:30 the landing craft hit the beaches. The immensity of sky and land dwarfs everything so that from here you have to hear the noise and strain at the binoculars to know a battle is going on. Maybe this is true of all battles. If you are in the middle you can't figure the score. A destroyer is hit, a mine explodes with a geyser higher than the National Press Building, a plane lays a smoke screen. Our destroyers practically walk on the beach. A little French village with a spire nestles in the cliffs.

And now runty little barges go ashore like a line of beetles. They are brave men aboard. Except for the luck of the draw I would be on one. I pick out a squarish little craft with a lace of foam in front. It is like picking out a particular ant. What would I be doing now if I were aboard, instead of Ken Crawford of *Newsweek?* Would I have the guts? God knows. The one I have picked reaches the beach, loses its foam, waddles up—I can't see her but I bet the seasick GIs are glad to exchange horrors.

Nine A.M., 10:00 A.M., noon. The cook has made a mistake. He thought yesterday was D-Day and served ice cream and cake; now it's just beans.

It is afternoon. I could sleep a week. I put on headphones in the communications room. A German broadcast denies any troops are ashore. They seem befuddled. We have attacked Dieppe and Dunkirk, they say. A BBC broadcast says we are winning. Cheers. Nobody here has any idea. Mostly it is a communications jargon, the sound of a battle: the parent voice crying out loudly and commandingly. Suddenly a quiet voice identifies itself. "I am pinned down," says the quiet voice. "I am between machine gun pillbox crossfire."

The drama is in that line of landing craft, so close to us I can almost see faces. I can see the burly skipper of the nearest and notice his arms are akimbo. He looks contemptuously at the USS *Quincy*. I bet he comes from the North River. I bet he is a tugboat captain. He sweeps the battle with an uncomplimentary eye. If he spoke he would have a Jersey accent and would take no back talk from nobody, see?—not from no warship, not from no Germans. We let go an eight-inch salvo over his right ear that must at least establish a feeling of mutual respect.

About eleven that night, double summertime, begins a great droning. An unending line of bombers comes out of England, each towing a paratroop glider. They are in single line formation, so many that they arch the sky from horizon to horizon. After the first batch comes a second, and as it passes flying high the first begins to return, without the gliders, which have crash-landed. Paratroopers in silk webs are in treetops, steeples—behind the lines. It is a cavalry charge and I have seen it. I am unable to speak. I look up, my eyes are wet. It is like a religious experience. This is my country doing this. I am doing this. *That swine—Hitler.* I am so proud.

Nixon Resigns

A U G U S T   1 3 ,   1 9 7 4   Wild scenes—the high black railing before the White House crowded with shirt-sleeved spectators peering in. They hold the bars. It's like the zoo. They extend down Pennsylvania Avenue, across the Executive Drive. Crowds like that, anxiously, wonderingly looking in, I remember that night of Pearl Harbor, 1941. Then it was crisp with reporters huddled under White House columns to watch silent senators go in to see FDR and come out knowing the worst. Some in the Pearl Harbor crowd clinging to the rails made a pathetic, gallant effort to sing "America the Beautiful," and the quavering notes made your throat choke.

Now they look in again—hot, sweating, shirt-sleeved, aghast, unbelieving, waiting for Something. They don't know what—maybe for the big black Cadillacs to roll out. Cabinet cars on the driveway.

. . . A wild scene the afternoon before. The White House pressroom; we wait for "something important," we don't know what. The regular eleven o'clock briefing isn't held; at 1:30 P.M., still nothing. "Come back at three-thirty," says press officer Jerry Warren. Action, finally, at 4:00. "Lights out, no stills!" come orders. "Don't stampede: I don't want their arms broken; they're three of my best girls."

We crush up, body to body, hearts pounding. Jerry gives out the two-page Nixon confession. I can't grasp it at first: the word "resignation" doesn't flash out at first quick scanning; odd phrases, FBI, CIA, "plumbers." What's he talking about?

Snarling, grabbing, we crowd up to get the three additional handouts; transcripts of Nixon-Haldeman taped conversations, June 23, 1972. Let's see—that was six days after Watergate. I climb out of the scrimmage across a soft-bottom chair and a couch. So what does he say? Oooh . . . minutes tick, the meaning sinks in. So this is the end, then! He admits he has held back evidence; he gets out or is thrown out. A kind of sickness of shame follows, even through journalistic cynicism.

Yes, that made the headlines across America! But that was yesterday; now it is August 6. This is the day the crowds appear looking through the bars. Reporters are back again in the White House pressroom. Word comes that the hastily summoned cabinet meeting is breaking up. We pour out into the sun by the green bank. Officials will emerge from that side portico.

We line up respectfully a little distance away, behind an imaginary rope: Germans, Orientals, British, cameramen, TV equipment holders —all watching the exit. We would believe anything. Resign? Probably animated gallows-humor. What in God's name is the nation thinking?

A lone figure appears and sees the waiting wolf pack. We advance three paces. "Hi," shouts somebody, "Mister Secretary, Mister Dent!" Dent; who's Dent? This faceless cabinet has no names; oh, that's Secretary of Commerce Dent. He disappears.

"Stand back!" shouts the lone cop. We sweep him along with us like a pebble in the stream, for now the cabinet emerges. A big jammed circle with men holding mikes and cameras aloft surrounds somebody, a man with a high, admonishing voice. It's Treasury Secretary Simon, ex-Salomon Brothers, Wall Street. "Louder, louder," shouts the fringe.

He is lecturing us; lecturing America. We shout, "How about impeachment?" he shouts back about the "economy," the administration will solve our ills. Irritation on both sides: "We've got a country to run," his vexed voice says. "Let's not have this tragedy obscure the fact that we have a determined people at work!" A photographer shouts for "a box—a box, I can't see his head."

Secretary Simon is a conservative. But the man who is coming as top economic adviser of the president is bespectacled Alan Greenspan, Wall Street consultant. Greenspan is not a conservative; he is a fundamentalist. Even in this impeachment maelstrom, I wonder about him; he is to the Economic Council what Carswell was to the Supreme Court. Can the Senate confirm him? Not likely, I suspect, if it does its homework. "Protection of the consumer by regulation," he wrote, "is illusory." He has declared the Sherman Antitrust Act "utter nonsense." He is disciple of high priestess Ayn Rand, whose church is laissez-faire. He wrote that in 1900 Standard Oil controlled "more than 80 percent of refining capacity." And that, he added, "made economic sense." Capitalism, he thinks, is "superlatively moral," but it is attacked by "welfare statists": people who believe in the Pure Food and Drug Act. This is the strange man Mr. Nixon has called to help cure our inflation in this eerie moment.

So much for economics and Simon! Scene follows scene: The tortured face of Representative Charles Wiggins (R, Calif.) on TV, the strongest defender of the president on the Rodino committee. Now, he says as he tightens his jaw to control his emotion, he will vote to impeach. He, too, is betrayed. The president has not told him essential facts, nor the public, nor his own lawyer. Fred Zimmerman in the *Wall Street Journal* quotes an ironic passage from *Six Crises:* "Hiss, a lawyer himself, had made the fatal mistake no client should ever make: he had not told his own lawyer the full truth about the facts at issue." Nor had Mr. Nixon.

Crowds peer in at the White House as the cabinet limousines roll out. Not one of them, it appears, has challenged the president face to face about resignation. The president's Gallup rating is down to 24 percent. Truman's sank to 23 percent in the Korean fiasco. That's rock bottom for presidents, the Caligula quotient. No matter who he is or what he does—Caligula, Dracula, Hitler—23 to 24 percent of Americans will support any man who's president.

THE FORD YEARS
[*1974-1976*]

Our Form of Government

SEPTEMBER 28, 1974 Arthur Schlesinger, Jr., has unexpectedly become a one-man sentry warning against the parliamentary system. He is an alert sentry. I find two articles by him in the *Wall Street Journal*, another in the *Washington Post*, and now one in the *New Republic* taking me to task. The warning comes at a sensitive moment as Nixon's imperial presidency collapses, and as the same forces that keep American presidents out of touch with reality seem to be taking effect on decent, modest, lightweight Jerry Ford.

The forces are latent in the process of making an idol of the American Priest-President, and then of pulling the idol off his pedestal. It is a cruel process. "The candidate for the presidency does well to recognize that he is running for a religious office," says Michael Novak in his new book, *Choosing Our King*. And George Reedy in his splendid little study *The Twilight of the Presidency* concludes that "some very fundamental changes are needed in the American political system"—changes that might be adapted, he suggests, from the parliamentary system.

We have seen five presidents in this century who have lost the capacity to govern—Wilson, Hoover, Truman, Johnson, and now Nixon. Will Mr. Ford be the next? He will, we fear, if he continues as he has started, unilaterally granting unconditional pardon to Nixon, making him custodian of the telltale tapes, defending the CIA in its plot to "destabilize" the government of independent Chile, and failing to find a foothold for dealing with the economy.

Leaders make mistakes abroad, too. Mr. Schlesinger spends much of his article warning that the British parliamentary system has its own faults. He deserves thanks for keeping the subject alive. We

427

intended to say, and should have made more clear, that we don't think the US is going to go parliamentary overnight, least of all on the British system. Many US political scientists have tunnel vision and only see Britain or Europe if you suggest a change in governmental style; Canada is too big and close at hand to see. But England has a unitary system; Canada, like the US, has a federal system. And we guess that if Canada had had a scandal like Watergate it would have had an almost immediate vote of no confidence, an election, and it would have disposed of the matter in two months.

Mr. Schlesinger makes the same arguments in several of his articles: the loss of a vote of confidence, for example, hasn't overthrown a British government for half a century. We are sure he is right but it is also true that the loss of such a vote just last spring in Canada produced an election. The threat of an election is always present.

To get rid of a king you kill him; to get rid of a president you impeach, or threaten to impeach, him. But to impeach you have to prove transgressions, whereas it is almost as serious for the nation to have an honorable president in the White House like Herbert Hoover who has lost his authority.

Isn't there some simpler system? Representatives like Henry Reuss, Morris Udall, and Edith Green want to initiate a presidential recall power in Congress. As Senator Mondale said last June, "We should look carefully at those aspects of the parliamentary system which can be creatively adapted to the American experience."

James Sundquist of Brookings, Charles M. Hardin of the University of Chicago, and others, agree. "Under our system," observes Sundquist, "a Neville Chamberlain who sought to appease Hitler would stay in office for his full term, even if that meant losing a war and the very freedom of the nation."

Mr. Schlesinger says the celebrated question time in Parliament isn't all that it is cracked up to be. We have heard Canadian friends, too, call it a charade. Yet we think that if a back-bencher laid down a written question to Prime Minister Trudeau demanding, "Is Canada bombing Cambodia?" and if Trudeau lied (as Nixon did), he would have been ousted almost instantly when the truth came out.

We are not trying to make debaters' points. We agree with Mr. Schlesinger that the parliamentary system is no panacea and that it may be a golden illusion for some idealists. Yet it has lessons that deserve study. One major advantage in Canada (and in other parliamentary systems) is the separation of head of government and head of state. The ceremonial head of state is Governor General Jules Leger, surrogate of the queen (salary $50,000); the head of government is the secularized prime minister (salary around $35,000, plus perquisites) who has none of the symbolism but all of the power. Never underestimate symbols, however. Every American child is brought up to revere the presidential idol; he is as sacred as the flag; Nixon always wore a totem enameled flag in his lapel (thank God Jerry doesn't). If we had our way we would have some figurehead president, with a big salary and no power, who would live in the White House and lay cornerstones to the awe and veneration of the populace, and lead worship, and we would let some shrewd political leader from Congress head the government, answer opposition questions, consult his cabinet, and fight no-confidence votes. We would secularize the chief executive.

Congress in a year or two, we think, is going right back to the habit of handing over its problems to the president. All the pressure is in that direction.

George Reedy says that he originally intended to end his book by working out "a system of parliamentary government for America." He gave it up because he decided that such a change isn't coming "without a revolution." He agrees with Arthur Schlesinger on this. But for him the failure is extraordinarily dangerous; the system "isolates the man who holds the nation's highest office and shields him from reality." It can't last. This former adviser to Lyndon Johnson gloomily predicts "a man on horseback. . . . In this probably lies the twilight of the presidency."

With all respect to the optimists, I fear we have learned little from Watergate. If an American fuehrer appears fifty years hence, some enterprising reporter will dig back in the files and remember that it all began in an administration dedicated to law and order, and that the precedent for imperial pardon was established to spare Richard Nixon a nervous breakdown.

An Incredible Year

D E C E M B E R   2 8 ,   1 9 7 4   In fifty years of Washington reporting this has been the most dramatic year I have ever known. Historians will come to it with a sense of disbelief, and for us who saw it unfold at first hand, week by week, hour by hour almost, there was the same incredulity.

That day last August in the White House, for example, when they put into our hands the transcript of the Nixon-Haldeman taped conversation of June 23, 1972; I could read it but I couldn't grasp it. Nixon instructed Haldeman to order the FBI: "Don't go any further into this case, period." Why, it amounted to a confession of obstruction of justice. Why, it meant he had been lying all the time. Why, it meant this was the end.

"This was a serious act of omission for which I take full responsibility and which I deeply regret," the statement said. Who was saying that? The president himself.

Events came like that, one after another, faster and faster, stretching through six months—some played in conferences, some on TV before the whole nation, and all centered on one theme, the unmasking, the humiliation, the ruin of the most powerful man on earth.

The year opened with the Arab oil embargo, rising inflation, Vice-President Ford on "Meet the Press" attacking critics of the president's refusal to comply with subpoenas, and President Nixon telling Congress that "there will be no recession." Cheers. But all the time the doomed man knew what was in those tapes. Eighteen minutes of them had been expunged but there was damning evidence left, and the investigators were closing in.

As we watched day by day the tension rose. Experts said there had been multiple tape erasures. The subpoena for the other tapes would be pressed in the courts. The House was turning its Judiciary Committee loose with an unknown chairman named Rodino to hold impeachment hearings. Senator Sam Ervin, that latter-day Founding

Father, had held his televised hearings the summer before. It shook the Nixon popularity rating, but always there was the other side, too: Gerald Ford and Minority Leader Hugh Scott announcing that secret data cleared the president: "I know from our conversation," Ford reported, "that the president had no prior knowledge of the Watergate break-in or had any part of the cover-up."

Ziegler told us the president intends to stay. Mr. Nixon told cheering Republicans that he would not walk away from the job to which he had been elected. Who were these men, Rodino, John Doar, Albert Jenner, whose names we heard more and more on car radios as we waited in line for hours to get gasoline before the pumps closed? The grand jury began to dribble out information about political support by ITT and the milk operators and of campaign funds secretly diverted by Bebe Rebozo, and of a $576,000 tax deduction on Nixon's vice-presidential papers. Nothing to worry about, said Jerry Ford, just efforts by "a few extreme partisans" and a "relatively small group of political activists" to "crush" the president.

The president took his case to the people, to Chicago, Nashville, Houston. That was a brutal scene at Houston, before the broadcasters' association, where I watched Dan Rather in the public panel ask him to his face how the House could pursue impeachment when you, the person under investigation, are allowed to limit access to potential evidence? I thought the crowd was going to hiss at this harsh question; the old issue of how to treat a president. Nixon, for once, faltered; it was the only time I ever saw him falter.

But don't worry—the president yielded to the inexorable demand of Judge Sirica for documents, and Jerry Ford expressed concern that the staff of Rodino's committee "may be wanting to dictate impeachment proceedings."

The last great counterattack by Nixon, the inveterate gambler, was the astonishing televised address, April 29, when he announced that he was making public 1,200 pages of transcripts of his Watergate conversations. Washington reporters stared at one another. Perhaps the old fox could exculpate himself after all; it was too risky for him to try to conceal anything (we said), and there was his statement that the tapes include "all the relevant portions"—except, of course, the profanity. That was when "expletive deleted" appeared. The president told us what was in the tapes; his lawyer told us what was in the tapes; and then we finally got the tapes and read one of the most extraordinary sets of documents in history, the president and his pals devising amoral scenarios on how to persuade, and to fool, the public. It was a shocker for those who believed in the majesty of the White House, Haldeman and Ehrlichman interrupting and contradicting the president and Dean saying, after one cover story on national security, "I think we could get by on that."

The last desperate gamble didn't pay off. Jerry Ford declared that "the new evidence, as well as the old evidence" exonerated Nixon of any impeachable offense and the president himself went to Moscow too in one of those conveniently arranged quickies Kissinger manages so well. But, on July 19, Doar asked directly for impeachment in a devastating bill of particulars, and a week later the Supreme Court unanimously told the cornered president to turn over his last tapes.

Did we, watching the thing, expect Nixon to resign then? I don't know when I reached that conclusion; in there, somewhere, of course. Before voting, the Rodino committee went on the air with its final sessions. For a while there was a little decency, a little dignity in the shameful mess. By nonpartisan votes they voted to impeach on three counts. The destroyed man resigned August 9, flew to California at once where, it would appear, he physically collapsed.

Jerry Ford, good old Jerry Ford, pardoned him September 8. For crimes identified or yet to be revealed, he gave him a "full, free, and absolute" pardon, sight unseen. He did this out of compassion, he said. He did it without an admission of guilt from Nixon and he gave Nixon custody of all his papers and tapes (an action since rescinded by Congress). Nixon gulled Ford and made a fool of him. But so what? As Nixon is pardoned the other defendants stand trial or have gone to jail.

I Dissent

JANUARY 18, 1975 Many commentators see the Watergate guilty verdicts as a vindication of the American system. Here is the prestigious *New York Times* gloating editorially: "Once more in the long march of American history it has been demonstrated that this is indeed, with all its faults, a nation governed by laws and that no man, irrespective of rank, can with impunity violate the country's basic sense of legality and decency."

A comforting sentiment, indeed—echoed across the nation as the ultimate moral of Watergate as we close the tragic story. Sorry, I must dissent.

Certainly Nixon was forced to resign, but was he found guilty by any court? (Or was Spiro Agnew, for that matter?) The existence of the mysterious and mystical imperial presidency was never more conspicuous than when the Watergate jury filed in and rendered its solemn verdict with one name omitted.

Watergate, it seems to me, shows how far our loose system can be distorted, and how easy it is for someone in the White House, surrounded by patriotic symbols, sleeping in the Lincoln bed, attacked by spiteful newsmen, to rouse the emotional support of the reverent and the innocent. "I Trust My President" said one button, even as Nemesis approached.

What Nixon left was a blueprint for how it can be done. And not many safeguards have been written, really, to prevent another Watergate. Congress passed the sweeping campaign finance reform law, which should be a help, and it may be broadened as time goes on. But the chief hope seems to be that Watergate was so extraordinary that it won't be repeated. It never happened before, did it?—and look at the honorable man in the White House now.

I don't find much comfort in the fact that Mr. Ford isn't the type who goes in for dirty tricks in his amiably incompetent administration. Two forces still push toward executive aggrandizement: the fact that separation of powers no longer works well, and the fact that accelerating world events demand prompt action of the kind that the White House alone can provide.

Our form of government is a lot different from what the Fathers expected it would be 200 years ago. And it is doubtful whether even the original pattern of the Founders would have worked very well if it had been followed. As to the first proposition, when George Washington went to deliver his initial State of the Union message in New York, January 8, 1790, he was preceded and followed by regal outriders in his fine coach-and-six, and his concept of his semimonarchical role was to give information and make recommendations to Congress and let the buck stop there. The primary responsibility for lawmaking, he thought, was on Congress. Coordinate branches of government would watch each other and perhaps stalemate each other. Delay—so what! It took four and a half days to ride from Virginia to Philadelphia, and more to New York. Things could wait.

Now we travel by jet and instead of the constitutional concept of congressional equality we find Congress relegated to second place. Nixon carried his contempt of Congress beyond anybody else and so we see a reaction taking place. Some think that with Nixon gone Congress will permanently reassert itself. Sorry, I must dissent.

Congressional government has never worked well. We have tried it once or twice, particularly after wars, and impatient people have clamored very soon for a "strong" president. If we had developed a parliamentary system (as we almost did several times) we would have collectivized leadership in Congress with strong party control, and at the White House an amiable ceremonial president would be ready to snip ribbons, throw out the first ball at World Series, ski in Colorado, and symbolize national unity.

Instead we got what chief Watergate prosecutor James Neal calls a "drift over the years to an all-powerful president." Not quite all-powerful; responsibility is still diffused. Nobody in Washington has final responsibility for the budget, nobody has final responsibility for antirecession action and, in Congress itself, the two houses squabble among themselves blocking reforms that might aid the poor or tax the big oil companies. Tax reform passed one house and failed in the other; welfare reform died in the Senate after the House passed it twice; even the antique electoral college, which the House sentenced to death in 1969, is still around: the Senate wouldn't act.

A system like this permits the establishment of what Marcus Raskin calls economic "baronies"—corporations, banks, labor organizations, public and private bureaucracies that have built compartments that separate the man in the street from any exercise of meaningful power.

Make no mistake, our system works (to the awe of foreigners), and works pretty well in normal times. Only there aren't normal times anymore; crisis is chronic. I have never, I think, seen greater anxiety and dread over the immediate future than there is in Washington at present. Domestic and global forces push reluctant Mr. Ford to action. Some think that this will all pass soon and that we shall get back to "normal."

Questions still arise. Why did we elect Nixon in the first place? He was called "Tricky Dick"; in Congress he exploited the Red Menace; he had a slush fund when he ran with Ike; when he ran for governor in California, a judge exposed his organizers' dirty tricks. In part Nixon won in 1972 because 45 percent of the eligible voters didn't vote. His "landslide" was about one quarter of the potential electorate. If it is argued that Nixon won because he had weak competition, that only shifts the issue: why is the US electoral process so unsuccessful that it fails to stir 80 million potential voters to vote?

We will stumble through somehow, no doubt. But to argue that a system of fixed terms, set elections, separation of powers, divided control, weak parties, and rival legislative chambers will produce a Congress capable of competing with the president seems unrealistic. Many feel that somehow the Watergate verdict has solved matters and that now we can relax. No future president, they feel, will yield to temptation or, if he does, Judge Sirica will be on hand and the culprit will courteously leave self-incriminating tape recordings all along his route. Sorry, I must dissent.

House of File Cards

MARCH 15, 1975   Big Brother lives on Pennsylvania Avenue in the new, block-size $126-million FBI building, which hasn't been dedicated yet but is one-third occupied.

Every capital needs a fortress at the center to symbolize police power; London has its Tower; France had its Bastille; now the US has its FBI building. It is symbolically bigger than the parent Justice Department across the way; it is the biggest building on Pennsylvania Avenue—a style of architecture that inevitably conjures up a wilderness fort, with projecting upper stories the better to shoot down on Indians or modern angry mobs. That's the "J. Edgar Hoover Building," home of Big Brother. You can get away from the Pentagon, which is across the Potomac, but this is right in the center of things. Every time I pass it in a cab it gives me the creeps.

Two congressional committees are investigating Big Brother now, one in the House, one in the Senate. In addition the Rockefeller committee at the White House is investigating Big Brother's brother, the CIA. They are twins. The law says the CIA can't operate domestically; it did just the same. The law doesn't specifically say the FBI can't use dirty tricks, hire provocateurs, spy on congressmen, slip out scandal on Martin Luther King, but it did just the same. It got its authority, apparently, from the "inherent power" of the presidency.

Almost every day now we get new details about Big Brother. The facts about the FBI that didn't come out during Watergate are coming out with the new Attorney General Edward H. Levi quietly talking to Congress. For example, J. Edgar Hoover had a private file on ex-Representative John J. Rooney, chairman of the committee that handled FBI appropriations; naturally FBI got everything it sought. Every congressman wondered if J. Edgar had a file on *him*. Three presidents, Kennedy, Johnson, and Nixon, rubbed their hands over the titillating gossip on fellow politicians that Hoover brought to them. There would be a personal call on a congressman from the director, who might say, "Sorry, but I thought you should know what we ran across about your daughter! But don't be concerned. It will never see the light. You can be absolutely confident of that."

Former FBI Assistant Director William Sullivan told the *Los Angeles Times* in May 1973 of Hoover, "That fellow was a master blackmailer. He had a file on everybody."

It is assumed that Representative Ford, when he tried to impeach Justice Douglas, got his material from Hoover.

As to the CIA, the twin Big Brother, Director William E. Colby delivered a fifty-page report to President Ford at Vail, Colorado, late in December about its illegal activities at home. And now it appears there may be an "oral addendum" about political assassinations abroad, attempted or successful. The Rockefeller group is looking into that story, aired by CBS reporter Daniel Schorr. We may not get the details right away, but wait a bit; Washington is a sieve; everything comes out in time.

Lower your voice when you go by Big Brother's home; he may have something on *you*. The building has been under way four years. It was supposed to cost $60 million. The excavation started in April

1971 and for a long while was the biggest hole in town, three stories deep and a block wide and long. Slowly the monument rose to Hoover, the monastic figure with a passion for horse-racing, who stayed in office under eight presidents and sixteen attorneys general. How the Founding Fathers would look at that building in wonder.

More than 7 million sets of fingerprints flow yearly into the FBI from local and state police, and there are records of 80 million Americans, either here or around the country. A year ago former Senator Sam Ervin said that there are over 100 "criminal history" information banks throughout the land.

Suppose your name was in a telephone conversation monitored under court order by the FBI (or without court order under former Attorney General Mitchell); you may well have a red "C" Card (cross-reference) in the index. The gray filing cabinets with six drawers bulge with three-by-five cards. There are now 58 million, with 1.3 million new ones coming in each year and 400,000 pulled out. There are 7,500 cabinets, growing at the rate of 300 a year. The electronic retrieval system is a marvel. Think of that huge building as a warehouse, wholesaling information on Americans.

The United States is programmed for fear. For years J. Edgar Hoover was the most popular man in the country, an icon, because he alleviated that fear; he was protecting us from espionage, sabotage, subversive activity, and things that go bump in the night. He was Top Cop, which meant he fought ordinary humdrum crime, but more important for his mass image he was also Minister of Internal Security, fighting Black Panthers and Communists and all wicked people. He was incorruptible, in his fashion. He was also the Compleat Bureaucrat.

Most modern nations separate the two police functions. The US should too, because they trip each other up. England has its ordinary Scotland Yard law enforcement, and it has its separate security service, MI-5. How do you investigate Watergate crimes when the FBI combines law enforcement and political intelligence? (Acting FBI head L. Patrick Gray III destroyed evidence at the request of the White House.)

A thing to remember is that an order to Big Brother to prevent disruption of internal security is a license to investigate political beliefs of leftists and radicals who may become embryonic spies and saboteurs. The theory is that innocent dupes will be infiltrated by militant agitators. J. Edgar Hoover accepted this. FBI Director Clarence Kelley seems to accept it, too. Hoover formalized it into deliberate harassment to intimidate and demoralize his domestic targets. It was done, naturally, to protect national security.

No country has had such warnings as the United States. We have seen Big Brother cowing Congress, attorneys general, presidents; we have seen him exercising unauthorized and illegal powers. For the moment there is reaction, we have ended warrantless wiretapping, the Subversive Activities Control Board, the House Un-American Activities Committee. We have thrown out Nixon. But when will the next wave of fear come? Meantime, are we really going to christen that structure the J. Edgar Hoover Building?

The Bicentennial

JULY 12, 1975   The Bicentennial, like the Fourth of July, is an occasion for justifiable flag-waving. Yet it is hard to strike just the right note. Certainly there should be a grave acknowledgment, if not overromanticized, of our debt to the Founding Fathers. And they still have things to teach us. Patrick Henry, for example, has something to say to President Ford.

An advertisement by the Richmond Corporation in the *Wall Street Journal* in May is headed "If Patrick Henry Were Alive Today" and is written by Barry Goldwater. The senator uses the space to belabor pacifism, permissiveness, and bureaucracy. Maybe that's what Patrick Henry would be saying today.

But we do know what he *did* say after the revolution and it is just as pertinent now as then; he said he favored postwar amnesty. He wasn't talking about the young men who, for reasons of conscience, wouldn't fight in a war that practically everybody now agrees was a mistake. He was talking about the Tories who wouldn't go along with the revolution. John Adams guessed that the colonists were divided in three equal parts—the advocates of independence, the Tories, and the fence sitters. Postwar bitterness could hardly have been more poisonous. With the war hardly over Patrick Henry surprised his radical followers when he urged the Virginia legislature to pass an act of "oblivion and restoration" for the vanquished loyalists. Yes, he wanted clemency and amnesty. He said that America needed the people who had left the country, and that they would make good citizens. "Oblivion and restoration." Make a note of it, Bicentennial orators and Mr. Ford.

Mobil Oil has been helpful too; it has been telling us what Sam Adams would say. Sam Adams deserves all our gratitude. He was a born revolutionary firebrand and the greatest propagandist of his time, who invented the Boston "massacre" and whose secret "committees of correspondence" around the colonies Harvard historian Samuel Eliot Morison likens to, without denigration, the revolutionary cells created by modern communist agitators. We had rather a stodgy image of Mobil and it's an agreeable surprise to find out its affinity for Sam Adams.

Something about the Bicentennial seems to tempt big corporations to frisk in print like cats in catnip. Here is a four-page color spread by Conoco in *Time* telling how Jefferson, Madison, Patrick Henry, Hamilton, Abigail Adams, and others would have rejected government controls, economic constraints, and all that. But why do they stop there? A lot of our Founding Fathers (and all reverence to them) didn't believe in our idea of democracy at all, let alone government controls. Conoco could quote John Jay: "the people who own the country ought to govern the country"; Fisher Ames who wanted government of the "wise, the rich and the good"; John Adams who regarded Jefferson's belief in the common man as sentimental nonsense; and Hamilton who wanted a lifetime president, possibly hereditary, and government by "rich and well-born." It would make a nice Conoco ad.

Finally here is the US Chamber of Commerce, caught up in the spirit of the thing in monster type in an advertisement in the *New York Times* telling us that "we have the greatest amount of freedom for the individual of any country in the world . . . of choice . . . of religion . . . of thought . . . of speech." Fine, fine; just the thing for the Fourth, to take our minds off FBI, CIA, wiretapping, and Watergate. It recalls an essay by Arthur Schlesinger, Sr., back in 1949, that America's attractive "quality of optimism" was noted by many visitors but "attained its most blatant expression, however, in the national addiction to bragging." It is gratifying to feel that the US Chamber preserves this inheritance.

One should strike a note about the Fathers that is thankfully appreciative without being jingoistically maudlin because, while they were so far ahead of their own time, they were still far from us in many concepts. The darkest side, of course, was slavery. In a moving and dignified article in the *University of Chicago Magazine* (Summer, 1975) Professor John Hope Franklin, a black, writing on "The Moral Legacy of the Founding Fathers" notes quietly one of the ugliest ironies in history, a noble Declaration proclaiming that "all men are created equal" written by slaveholders. It would be "perverse," he says, to derive satisfaction from calling attention to the flaws in the character and conduct of the Fathers, and "irresponsible" to do so merely to indulge in whimsical iconoclasm. But even today, as Professor Franklin underlines, it is a moral challenge to face the matter honestly. Over in England, in 1772, Lord Mansfield outlawed slavery in the Somerset case on the compelling ground that human bondage was "too odious" to continue. The Founding Fathers kept clear of it. At several times before and during the Revolution groups of slaves heard the word "liberty" and appealed for freedom. They were ignored.

The word "slavery," of course, does not appear in the Constitution, though it is there by indirection: the compromise of counting blacks as "three-fifths" of a person in apportioning representatives, and also in Article 1, Section 9, where it is stated by masterly circumlocution: "the Migration or Importation of such Persons as any of the States now existing shall think proper to admit, shall not be prohibited by Congress prior to the Year one thousand eight hundred and eight." We doubt if these passages from the Constitution are read at many celebrations of the Fourth.

Let us be proud, but let us not be overproud. John Gardner of Common Cause notes that "When this nation was founded, there was a Holy Roman Emperor, Venice was a republic, France was ruled by a king, China by an emperor, Japan by a shogun, Russia by a czar, Great Britain was a monarchy; and among the world powers the only government that stands essentially unchanged is the Federal Union put together in the 1780s by thirteen states on the east coast of North America."

There is also the splendidly acerb comment by E. B. White: "Democracy is the recurrent suspicion that more than half of the people are right more than half of the time."

And there is Professor Franklin's thought that "if we would deal with our past in terms of realities . . . it becomes necessary for us to deal with our early leaders in their own terms, namely, as frail, fallible human beings. . . ."

Groping for Myths

OCTOBER 11, 1975   America is confused and a little frightened and it is groping for myths to sustain it. President Ford has offered us one in dedicating the gigantic new FBI building on Pennsylvania Avenue—commemorating J. Edgar Hoover. The nation is creating another in the extraordinary rediscovery of Harry Truman—*Give 'em Hell, Harry!* as James Whitmore has depicted him—simultaneously showing in 1,500 family movie theaters across the nation, held over in many places.

Let's consider the two men.

The J. Edgar Hoover Building is the largest, most expensive, and maybe the ugliest in Washington and you can't miss it between the White House and Capitol. It was supposed to cost $60 million; cost $126 million; and its architecture is people-repellant. It honors the memory of "a pioneering public servant," President Ford explained; under his direction the FBI became "the superior professional organization it is today . . . with the best scientific crime detection facilities to serve the federal government and the American people."

Hoover, of course, is the man whom the *New York Times* editorially said in March "tried to destroy Dr. [Martin Luther] King's reputation and his marriage." Offended by some of King's views, Hoover sent anonymous material to Mrs. King. It wasn't the first time; the FBI's Operation Cointelpro (Counterintelligence Program) was set up specifically to confuse and harass dissident groups using dirty tricks. The FBI sent a spurious, threatening letter in 1969 to a black Baptist minister, Donald W. Jackson, to compel him to quit his civil rights work in Mississippi and return north. Hoover had private files on prominent people; "that fellow was a master blackmailer; he had a file on everybody," former FBI Assistant Director William Sullivan said.

On the other hand, J. Edgar Hoover was a money-honest dedicated bureaucrat, who inspired morale and élan in his beloved organization, which became a symbol of law and order for millions of anxious Americans. In fact, in many ways, the FBI is a splendid organization—so long as it is kept in control. But the man to whom the huge building is dedicated was not kept under control; presidents feared him; he became an imperial figure. Asking for 1,000 additional agents in 1970, he told a startled committee of an alleged plot by "Catholic priests and nuns" to "blow up underground electric conduits," to disrupt the government, and to kidnap "a highly placed government official"—Henry Kissinger. This was the charge against Philip and Daniel Berrigan and others, the "Harrisburg Seven." The case, of course, didn't stand up.

Public figures become legends after they die and the myth is more important than the man. President Ford lends his prestige to the Hoover myth, the symbol of law and order, the incorruptible cop, the protector against creepy-crawly dissidents from our community of shared values. It will be interesting to see if the resanctified J. Edgar Hoover icon can still do miracles.

So turn to a happier figure, Harry Truman. Can anybody doubt that his sudden revival is a deep-seated folk yearning for courage, honesty, and direction? Harry Truman was a spunky little cuss, a fox terrier of a man, who deserves to be remembered with affection and who might well inspire a great nation in time of gloom.

I was along on that famous "nonpolitical" whistle-stop trip that started out in June 1948 in a seventeen-car special with a presidential parlor car in back that, under the paint, still showed the name *Ferdinand Magellan*. That was the year, you recall, when the press was 75-percent Republican, and Walter Winchell broadcast that the official betting odds were 15-to-1 against Harry Truman. That was the year Dewey picked his cabinet in advance and lapsed into banalities. That was the year the *Saturday Evening Post* led with a story by Joseph and Stewart Alsop, "What Kind of a President Will Dewey Make?"

Press and politicians—we all lived, slept, and worked in the same traveling circus. Truman made sixteen speeches a day. Theoretically he was traveling to California to receive an honorary degree. The press relished him although we all knew that he was doomed. Nobody threatened his life; why should they? All the way west his vernacular got thicker, his folksiness greater, as he told about grandpa's covered wagon to Oregon, and produced an appropriate relative in every area he spoke. To a storm of Republican counterattacks he exclaimed at Pocatello, Idaho, "They can't prove nothing; they ain't got a thing on me!" At Davis, California, he explained to a crowd that he was going down to Berkeley "fur to git me a degree."

In those happier days, when the press threw off copy from stop to stop, writing the final penciled word on yellow telegraph sheets against the hot side of a dusty Pullman, and shouting "Postal!" or "Western!" as the train began to move, a topical song always arose spontaneously from the press car. It was columnist Tom Stokes, I believe, who saw the inner poetic relevance of Truman's two historic comments and produced what I shall always regard as the finest natural couplet in political balladry. The tune was "Oh, Susanna" and its growth traced Truman across America. Sample:

> Oh, Grandpaw went to Oregon, the dough was on his knee,
> Grandpaw went to Oregon, the West Coast fur to see.
> He got himself a partner in Cal-i-for-ni-ay,
> They bought up Sacramento on a lovely summer day.
>
> CHORUS: (*roared out*)
> They can't prove nothin', they ain't got a thing on me,
> I'm goin' down to Berkeley, fur to get me a degree.

It wasn't all cornpone, either. In his fighting acceptance speech in Philadelphia to a yelling crowd at 2:00 in the morning, off the cuff, he announced that he was going to bring the Republican Congress back to a special session and would ask them to pass laws for a national health program, civil rights, higher minimum wage and social security, and funds "to provide public power and cheap electricity."

Give 'em hell, Harry! I can still see him holding up and cackling over that *Chicago Tribune* headline electing Dewey. Somebody to dream about these dispiriting days.

Great Political Speeches

N O V E M B E R 8 , 1 9 7 5   I suppose the most successful US political speech in modern times was Franklin Roosevelt's Teamsters Union speech about "my little dog, Fala" in 1944 that devastated Dewey. After that I should regretfully have to add Nixon's "Republican cloth coat" speech in 1952 when he was fighting for his political life on the Eisenhower ticket. It was corny and meretricious and it brought in his wife, his children, and his dog Checkers, but there was no doubt about it even to some of us who were disgusted by the performance, when he finished with the pledge "to campaign up and down America until we drive the crooks and Communists and those who defend them out of Washington" he had scored a political bullseye. "You're my boy!" said Ike.

There have been other notable political addresses in recent times and some of them will be cited later on, but this is to record that Hubert Humphrey made a remarkable speech the other day in San Francisco to the AFL-CIO convention. Everybody loves Hubert. But some of us give a sigh (albeit with affection) at the thought that he might be the Democratic candidate again next year. Can't the Democrats come up with a fresh face; why should they use a retread? Yet there can be no question that after that San Francisco speech Hubert abruptly emerged as somebody to be reckoned with. Nobody takes polls too seriously at this early date for they are mostly name recognition, but momentarily, at least, Gallup has put Humphrey—the man who isn't going to enter any of the primaries—at "the top of the Democratic presidential field."

Humphrey, in what "Mr. Meany and many other onlookers considered one of the great speeches of his long career," reported R. W. Apple, Jr., to the *New York Times*, "tore the house down . . . delegates cheered and whistled and screamed . . . on the floor, delegate after delegate expressed hope that Mr. Humphrey would be the nominee . . ." and so on.

Well, there have been other powerful speeches: FDR's "Nothing to fear . . ." and his "Day of Infamy" addresses. He could communicate confidence, Arthur Schlesinger has written, by the intonation of his voice, the tilt of his head, the flourish of his cigarette holder. A cherished recollection is a speech by Ev Dirksen, a last-ditch Taft supporter, shaking the wild locks of his hair like Sargasso Sea kelp at Governor Dewey (who was backing Ike) on the convention floor and hurling studied insults at him from the podium—"you took us down the road to defeat!"—while the packed galleries cheered and booed.

There was Bobby Kennedy's brief, tragic talk on the back of a flatbed truck on the eve of Martin Luther King's assassination, and again his eulogy to his brother at the Atlantic City Democratic convention quoting Shakespeare. (He was one of the few politicians who could quote Shakespeare and get away with it.)

—Yes, and Harry Truman's acceptance speech in the stifling heat of the Philadelphia convention hall at two in the morning in 1948. . . . A game little cuss.

—And before coming back to Hubert let me include Lyndon Johnson's stirring civil rights speech to a joint session of Congress, March 15, 1965, that makes up for a lot of mistakes:

"Their cause must be our cause, too. Because it is not just Negroes, but really it is all of us, who must overcome the crippling legacy of bigotry and injustice. And we shall overcome."

Hubert Humphrey has a rugged, cartoon face, thrust-out jaw, pink cheeks, small eyes, and surprised eyebrows. He has enough energy so that if you could wire him he would light a house. A group of us asked him the other day what the Democrats should do about George Wallace. "I would treat him like any candidate who should not be a president," he said simply. Why wasn't he running himself? "I've found you can't be a good senator and a good candidate." Why does President Ford keep up his frantic pace? "He is doing it because he sees the shadow of Ronald Reagan. It is folly, because no Ronald Reagan can unseat a *president* if he *is* president. He ought to stay home and tend to the store." Asked point-blank if he thought he would make a better president than Ford, Humphrey answered matter-of-factly, "Yes."

Give Hubert Humphrey forty-five minutes to make a thirty-minute speech before a friendly audience and he is one of the most effective speakers in America. The fact is, I think, that the nation is confused and disturbed and at a time when it fears for its jobs it gets attacks on big government, when it wonders about high gasoline prices it gets denunciations of regulation, when it agonizes over recession it hears the administration leaders attack bureaucracy which they are in charge of. "It is stylish these days," Humphrey told the labor convention, "to say all the old programs that Roosevelt had, Truman, Kennedy, and Johnson had, all these programs, you know, are worn out, no good."

Then he went over the programs, Social Security to food stamps. "If it were not for the programs of Roosevelt and Truman, of Kennedy and Johnson," he cried, "this country would be flat on its back today in a massive depression."

There is something hypnotic in Humphrey's torrent, every thought repeated, every phrase given variations, the flood no more to be dammed than Niagara, sweeping receptive audiences with it: "We need leaders with a heart. We need people who care. We need people who err on the side of compassion and fair play, and we need leaders who will challenge this country, who will challenge the spirit and strength of the American people to achieve what they want. . . . The people are obviously waiting, and I say to you that they have waited long enough and they are impatient. . . . Let America sing once again and let's get back and get to work."

It is not easy in quotations to blast off chips of it, but if you yield to it it sweeps you along: "I'm not going to run away from the great dynamic leadership that I voted for when I was a young man and someone spoke to me as if he was in my heart and my mind and my soul and said, 'All you have to fear, Hubert Humphrey, is fear itself,' and who said, 'We are going to get this country going again.' "

It's powerful, moving stuff. The labor audience?—as I said at the beginning, he wowed them.

Muskie

J A N U A R Y 2 4 , 1 9 7 6 The son of Stephen Marciszewski, the tailor, answers the President of the United States on prime time this week.

Mr. Ford says his State of the Union address (January 19) is "the most important speech of my administration," for in it he outlines the program on which he will build his election campaign.

And for Senator Muskie of Maine it is a vital speech, too. He has been given an hour simultaneously on three networks for an unprecedented rejoinder for the Democratic Congressional Majority. At this writing we think it could be as illuminating to the voters on the actual issues of the election, as distinct from the froth, hokum, and personalities of the primary contests, as anything since the Nixon-Kennedy debates. It could be a new thing in American government, a regular "State of the Union Reply." How important it is depends on two men, President Ford, who now everywhere sees Ronald Reagan giving a packaged Hollywood grin over his shoulder, and Senator Muskie, sixty-one, who once ran for vice-president with Hubert Humphrey, who has just announced that he is running again for the Senate, and who recalls his tough but idyllic boyhood in Rumford, Maine, where "we bathed once a week in a tin tub heated on the stove."

The State of the Union address is a unique political art form required by the Fathers who wrote that "he (the president) shall from time to time give to the Congress Information of the State of the Union. . . ." Normally a president sanctimoniously tells the folks how lucky they are, what a good job he's doing, and how they must now all work together for splendid times that inevitably lie ahead.

President Ford last year was a glorious exception to this and will be rewarded for it by history. The poor man had been president five short months. And he looked down on the joint session and announced honestly and modestly that "the state of the Union is not good" and that "I have got bad news, and I don't expect much, if any, applause."

Whatever faults Mr. Ford may display hereafter, that fine hour will be remembered.

Just for contrast, Richard Nixon's State of the Union address in January 1974 carried the oracular promise, "There will be no recession in the United States of America." Cheers. Followed by the worst slump since the '30s. And Mr. Nixon in the midst of the tightening Watergate coil announced that he had "no intention whatever" of quitting, and was out in seven months.

A lot of people are dismissing Mr. Ford too early, we think. For one thing Ronald Reagan has tied an anchor round his own leg in this proposal to cut the federal budget by $90 billion and turn the services (and costs) over to the states. We were up in New Hampshire with Reagan, (who is an attractive, patient-spoken, ultraconservative, we thought, with a weakness for snappy box-office answers). There have been a lot of political gaffes up there in treacherous New Hampshire but this $90 billion one is the worst we can remember, and we don't see how he can get out of it even if he squirms like Houdini.

Another thing about President Ford: though his Gallup Poll rating is presently down to 39 percent, so what? Polls aren't people and Truman's, for example, was below that, and when Truman ran in 1948 daily newspapers were against him four to one. So what did voters do? They elected Harry. If we had to bet about 1976 we should think the Democrats would win this year, but it is way too early to say.

And now a word about Senator Muskie. This isn't the first time he has answered presidents. In 1970 he made two replies for his party to Nixon. The first one was after the State of the Union speech where the thrust was on environmental pollution. Muskie was chairman of a Senate committee on the subject and it was natural for him to make the response, which was polite enough and didn't repeat his earlier taunt that the administration was slogan-rich and action-poor.

A different Muskie answered Nixon's savage eve-of-the-election broadcast, November 2, 1970. All the president's paranoid rancor welled up against the crowd that had thrown rocks at his motorcade in San Jose, California. He recorded the speech in Phoenix, video-taped in black and white with harsh lights on his features like the one in his debate with Jack Kennedy, years before. He implied that political opponents were encouraging lawlessness.

Muskie's reply was quiet and powerful. Forty million people watched. It was put on back-to-back with the Nixon speech. His voice was measured and reassuring: "Something has gone wrong," he said of the Nixon vendetta: "It has been led, inspired, and guided from the highest offices of the land"; in the effort to "turn common distress into partisan advantage," he said, "they imply that Democratic candidates . . . actually favor violence and champion the wrongdoer. This," he said quietly, "is a lie. And the American people know it is a lie." It made a sensation.

Under Muskie's exterior calm there is a turbulent interior. He faced down a heckler once and an awed staff member whispered, "Geez, he's got a glare that would intimidate Mount Rushmore." His reply to Nixon really launched his 1972 presidential bid. He said he would fire J. Edgar Hoover first thing. He was "front-runner" for a year, which is as slippery a log to stand up on as any Maine lumberjack ever attempted, and he slipped off it that snowy day in the Manchester, New Hampshire, primary four years ago, tripped up by the original dirty trick, the phony "Canuck" letter.

So why does he speak for the Democratic Congress now? Mike Mansfield picked him, for one thing, because he isn't a presidential candidate—as everybody else seems to be. Besides that, his rangy six-foot-four frame reminds some of a moose—they are big, loosely hung, with a good deal of reserve power. But more important, for a year now, Muskie has known as much about the budget as anybody in Congress, and Mr. Ford's speech is on the budget. Budget Committee Chairman Muskie's effort to keep appropriations in line with revenues could be the most important thing in the Ninety-fourth Congress. It's a startling new idea. Sometimes he has seemed like Big Daddy leading a child. But he isn't a candidate—he says.

Campaigning in
New Hampshire

FEBRUARY 7, 1976   The clean-cut young man who has positioned himself on the aisle seat in the first row is ready with the first question when Jimmy Carter has finished his opening remarks at the little gathering in the hall at the University of New Hampshire, at Durham.

I have heard the same introductory comment by the candidate three times now, and I suppose it tells something of his presence and manner that it doesn't sound as corny as it reads in print afterward. He wants "our nation to have once again a government as good and honest and decent and truthful and fair and competent and idealistic and compassionate—and as filled with love—as are the American people."

He says it in a low voice and with a little catch in his throat as though it were occurring to him for the first time. The audience is silent; people don't applaud; they are impressed.

So the young man on the aisle seat stands up and asks a question, and the Yankee listeners, who maybe are Congregationalists and tight-lipped about religion, cringe a little because he is asking Carter, in effect, in evangelical jargon, "Are you saved?" That old cynic Henry Mencken, with his china-blue eyes, would rub his hands and gloat over the situation. It just embarrasses us.

He pauses for a moment that seems longer than it is, and then answers simply and matter-of-factly, "Yes, I am twice-born," and goes on quietly from there. A spark has passed between the two; they have communicated in their own way, in a language that is more familiar, perhaps, in revivalist Georgia than in snowbound New Hampshire. We go out into the waist-high drifts wondering who will be the next president and whether it could be this surprising political novelty?

I have a political activist friend in Washington who burst out against Carter with a vehemence that startled me: "He's a two-faced louse!" he ejaculated or words to that effect. My friend thinks Carter's a hypocrite; maybe he is prejudiced; deep down, perhaps, he is asking a variant of that old question, "Can anything good come out of Georgia?" Politicians are permitted a certain degree of ambiguity, and their survival requires cloudy rhetoric on occasion. In the Iowa caucus on the emotional abortion issue Carter said, yes, he was against abortion. No, he wasn't for a constitutional amendment. He added a maybe—maybe he would favor some vague federal statute on the subject. Democratic liberal candidates denounced him for cynical deviousness and Carter won the contest.

My impression is that audiences yearn to believe Jimmy Carter. They are looking for something. It is his manner and tone. He has a mop of hair like a wig turning gray at the ears, a trademark grin, a warm, friendly manner, a pietistic appeal, and a homely face of the most attractive sort that reminds one of Eleanor Roosevelt. Underneath is a first-rate intelligence and an ambition hard as nails. After Annapolis, peanut farming, and warehousing, and after leading a ten-year fight to end segregation in the local church, the local school, and the local community, he ran for office with the public support of segregationists.

Did they think they could control him? As governor he put up the picture of Martin Luther King, Jr., in the state capitol, and he has the support now of some of Georgia's respected black leaders, Andrew Young and Julian Bond. It's as odd a combination as American politics has recently seen.

At a recent rally of Democratic presidential hopefuls here Jimmy Carter stunned his audience by unexpectedly announcing that if revenue sharing of federal funds is extended (as he hopes), the money should be sent to cities, *not* states that are diverting money from poor people to marginal capital improvement projects like golf courses and parks. Wisconsin's Governor Lucey registered sharp "distress" but couldn't budge Jimmy. If he is ambiguous on some things he is obstinate on others: "sot," the Yankees call it.

Plowing around in New Hampshire's snow now, with the primary three weeks off, is Ronald Reagan. He is as surprising a candidate in his way as Carter is. At every appearance for the two days I heard him, he told audiences that the state sends "$115 million" annually to Washington and gets back only "$100 million" in services so why wouldn't it be better, he asked in his frank, likable way, to just keep the money at home and save $15 million?

At his final press conference on the trip Ted Knap, of Scripps-Howard, asked him if that extra $15 million didn't go into the army, navy, air force, and interstate highways and wasn't it a bargain, therefore, and where did he get the statistics anyway?

Ronald Reagan registered complete surprise. He explained that he had "never understood the thing that way" and that he couldn't remember where he got the figure and "if I'm mistaken," he said disarmingly, "I stand corrected." What more was there to say?

President Ford will be up in New Hampshire shortly, too, the very fountainhead of the movement for a do-less government and a politician who has staked a great deal on a bold gamble. He says in his budget that he knows of no way to get unemployment below 7 percent in the coming year and is asking for reelection on that basis. Mr. Ford deserves a good deal of credit for his frankness and the consistency of his beliefs. Mr. Ford has asked the nation to tighten its belt, lower its expectations, and accept what he calls the "new realism," which means the trickle-down theory *and* reliance on private business, not the government, to make jobs.

In essence this is what Herbert Hoover preached, but things are a lot better now. Income maintenance programs (unemployment insurance, food stamps, Social Security) have cushioned the worst recession since the '30s; the most amazing aspect of the whole affair is that there have been no riots, no bloodshed. The very programs Mr. Ford wants to curtail have buoyed us up so far. Liberal economists think it is too early to adopt the contractionary budget Mr. Ford favors, but Congress will probably take care of that, just as it gave us last year's tax cut that helped the current revival. Democrats will be wise not to underestimate Mr. Ford's appeal. He will blame Congress even while things get better (if they do). Mr. Ford has faith.

What Carter's Not

JUNE 19, 1976   Jimmy Carter has "a streak of ugly meanness—an egotistical disposition to run right over people . . . a disposition to be a sorehead"; that is the recent testimony of columnist Joseph Kraft.

He has "a vein of vindictiveness," says the syndicated columnist team of Evans and Novak; they quote "Carter's old enemies back in Georgia" as declaring that along with intelligence, discipline, and dedication there is "vindictiveness extraordinary even for a politician."

So he's mean and vindictive, and likely to be the next President of the United States! How did we get into this fix? But wait, here's contrary evidence:

Sensitive and compassionate analyst Anthony Lewis of the *New York Times* says Jimmy Carter "really does see himself fighting entrenched power, the status quo. . . . He instinctively identifies with the victims of official abuse, the poor, the disadvantaged." Yes, Lewis goes on to say, "He cares about the powerless in society—genuinely, I am convinced. . . ."

And here is an unusual character witness, eccentric iconoclast Hunter S. Thompson (*Hell's Angels, Fear and Loathing: On the Campaign Trail '72*) writing in *Rolling Stone* (of all places) June 3, "my first instinctive reaction to Jimmy Carter . . . I liked him" and who notes an extemporaneous speech Carter made in May 1974 to bigwigs in Georgia attacking special privilege; it was a "king hell bastard of a speech" (I assume this is praise); to which Thompson adds, "I have never heard a sustained piece of political oratory that impressed me more."

Let's drop Carter and look at the setting. It's one of the most astonishing political years in history. "The United States has the most elaborate, complex, and prolonged formal system of nominating candidates for chief executives in the world," say William Keech and Donald Matthews (Brookings: *The Party's Choice*). A system the late Clinton Rossiter called "a fantastic blend of the solemn and the silly." And this year more than usual. For eight years we have had split government in Washington—White House one party, Congress another—something no other nation could survive; and before Kennedy and Johnson, Ike had six years of split government.

Now there's near stalemate in Washington with Ford's forty-nine vetoes. Political parties are in decay. Loyalty has so declined that when Richard Nixon won every state but Massachusetts he still faced a Democratic Senate and House. Republicans are now weaker than at any time since the Great Depression—probably since the party started just before the Civil War.

The national mood? Cynical and penitential; Vietnam and Watergate aren't mentioned but obtrude their frustration everywhere; in 1950 three-quarters of the people thought their government was run primarily for the benefit "of the people" (17 percent said "big interests"); now only 38 percent think so and 53 percent say big interests.

Who would have thought that the Panama Canal could be an issue;

that an incumbent president could be seriously challenged; that in thirty dreary primaries only about a third of those eligible to vote would vote; or that an almost unknown former governor and peanut farmer from Georgia could be front-runner for President of the United States?

In 1972 George McGovern revealed to astonished politicians how vulnerable modern parties are to penetration by well-organized and strongly motivated groups in primaries where only a minority vote.

In 1976 there are more primaries and direct federal financial aid to ambitious political *individuals* (not parties). Jimmy Carter has shown how porous such parties are to penetration by an ambitious individual whose cause is ambiguous (unless, indeed, "love" and "anti-Washington" are causes) and who offers the sullen nation a fresh face and a striking personality, blazoned by the all-powerful news media.

Jimmy Carter planned it that way. I first met him in the snows of New Hampshire last January and liked him—and was astonished by him. I enjoyed the calculated impudence with which he told what he planned to say in his Inaugural, and reacted with the expected astonishment. I never met a candidate like that before and it was swell copy. The confrontation of southern and New England cultures was wonderful, too, when the clean-cut YMCA-type young man at Durham made the reticent Yankee ladies cringe by asking Carter straight out, had he been saved?—and Carter answered quietly, yes, that he was twice-born and what was the next question?

Carter started his campaign in September 1972 while still governor and, after his term ended, worked full-time at it. He saw the vulnerable place in the primary system—right at the start. It didn't matter if only a fraction of a fraction voted nor if the margin was minuscule, the point was to get the headline "Jimmy Carter Wins." He did that in the precinct caucuses of Iowa, first of the year, and in the tiny state of New Hampshire. Next, of course, he had to knock Wallace out in Florida, March 9, and he did. He was launched. The press grabbed him. In her remarkable series in the *New Yorker* Elizabeth Drew tells how it was done, and gives her cautious assessment of this "enigmatic and hidden man" who is asking us to take such a big gamble. He can talk about "love" and be tough and even ruthless. Was that a grin, a natural honest-to-god grin, he was giving her at one point (not the toothy smile)?

"It seems to be a natural grin by someone who might, after all, have a sense of humor about himself. It is odd," she reflects, "to spend time considering whether a grin just might be natural." Yes, she notes, Carter may have "a certain mean streak."

George McGovern fired his press secretary, Alan Baron, who was quoted as calling Carter "a positive evil, surrounded by a staff committed to no ideals, like Haldeman and Ehrlichman." This sounds silly and venomous to me. I like him and still do. James T. Wooten put it negatively in the *New York Times:* ". . . He is not a liberal, not a conservative, not a racist, not a man of long governmental experience, not a religious zealot, not a southerner of stereotypical dimensions," and from such negative deductions many, he says, have concluded "that Jimmy Carter is not entirely unacceptable as a presidential candidate."

The Incumbent

A U G U S T 7 & 1 4 , 1 9 7 6 The last time a party didn't nominate a presidential incumbent was Rutherford B. Hayes. I thought about it as I leaned back against the trunk of an accommodating elm tree on the White House lawn the other day.

We were waiting for Mr. Ford. His staff had thought up a setting whereby he would be super-presidential—a press conference outdoors with the north colonnade as backdrop. A catbird warbled in one of the trees. An ambulance shrieked down the avenue—"*Wow, wow, wow!*"

Tourists looked curiously at us through the iron rails. There is always that little group in front of the White House, rain or shine.

The president was late so I went over and sat against an elm and thought about Rutherford B. Hayes. ("B" stands for Birchard.) You remember him. He got in by a fluke and was married to "Lemonade Lucy." He lived in that big white house. He was a pleasant-faced, full-bearded, midwestern lawyer who tried to do the right things in a rather bumbling way, like Civil Service reform; not a touch of brilliance or magnetism in him anywhere. His big antagonist was another Republican, tough Senator Roscoe Conkling, the "New York Colossus," who argued that people who tried to reform the spoils system (like Hayes) were effeminate—"man-milliners, the dilettante and carpet knights of politics." They threw Hayes out.

Mr. Ford appeared at 1:30 and I scrambled back into the tight crowd, arranged like a horseshoe—about 100 reporters and camera crews and TV people. Across the way was the old granite-gingerbread State-War-Navy building now called the Executive Office Building. Fifty years ago it held all three departments. Jimmy Carter is going to shrink them all back to size again.

Questions were sharp, and personal, and without rancor, as they are in the Washington political game. It would astound other nations. Democrats had implied that Mr. Ford wasn't smart enough to be president; did he think he was smart enough? Mr. Ford standing there composedly in a striped gray suit and blue shirt (why should a man wear a *vest* on a hot day?) smiled good-naturedly. He thought he was smart enough. He is a likable figure, sandy hair and eyebrows, hands clasped calmly behind him or brought out occasionally for emphasis, not taking offense. Reporters tempted him; how did he assess Jimmy Carter? Did he think the Carter-Mondale ticket beatable? (The latest Louis Harris Poll shows Carter 66 percent, Ford 27—one of the biggest chasms in history.) "Absolutely," said Mr. Ford, registering confidence.

Yes, Mr. Ford went on, answering another question, he had pardoned Richard Nixon—and he would do it again. It brought back the episode. Mr. Ford has been in office now two years next week—August 9, 1974. A crushing question for this modest congressman of twenty-four years was what to do with the stinking mess he inherited. One Sunday morning he went to church and, on September 8, unexpectedly gave Nixon a "full, free, and absolute pardon" explaining afterward that "my conscience says it is my duty." His Gallup Poll rating plunged 21 points in one of the sharpest air pockets ever recorded, as of course he knew it would. Newspapers raged; it deprived us all of a state trial that would have been one of the gaudiest shows in history and that might still be going on in 1976. What a choice to dump on a new president. If I'd been Ford, I'm inclined to think I would have gone to church and made the same decision he did.

I got to thinking about President Ford and Rutherford B. Hayes at the press conference, and later. My hunch is that in the present day the Republicans' suicidal yen to nominate Ronald Reagan (with or without liberal Dick Schweiker of Pennsylvania) will abate and I suspect that John Connally thinks so, too. He has finally and unexpectedly come out for Ford. Does Ford have a chance to beat Carter? Oh—maybe.

Mr. Ford's strength is that they're all picking on him, and he's an underdog, like Harry Truman, and doing his best. From my point of view his two-year economic record is terrible. With a 7.5-percent unemployment rate he still vetoes the modest 3.9-billion-dollar job bill. He has so little style and brilliance that he is not able to blot out Reagan merely by flashing his incumbency. He holds only rare White House press conferences, which should be the steady link between him and the public (FDR had two a week). He has not been able to persuade the nation even yet that we teeter on the abyss of an oil shortage. (It isn't enough to say the nation won't listen; he should make it listen.)

Mr. Ford's asset is that he is an attractive man, obviously doing what he thinks is right, who says the same things in private that he says in public. Also that he is running against a man whom people haven't quite yet accepted, Jimmy Carter. Another way of putting it is that in this election Jimmy Carter is running against Jimmy Carter. It may be a close race.

I keep wondering in the Carter statements if he fully understands the Washington he's talking about; he's anti-Washington and says he's going to reorganize the government. Fine, that has been done before; it's still much the same. He says he's going to take a year of studying before submitting his big tax shake-up; the trouble is that a new president gets a honeymoon of about 180 days, and if he wants action he'd better arrive with plans in his knapsack. Governor Carter's close-knit, youthful, attractive, knee-jerk team worries me: already the *New York Times*' conservative columnist William Safire is asking about Saudi Arabia's $80,000-a-year contract with Patrick Caddell, twenty-six, the chief Carter pollster who reportedly has other lucrative clients like Exxon, Arco, Shell, and Sun. Jimmy Carter tut-tuts it.

So we turned back thoughtfully to the presidential press conference on the White House lawn the other day, with the fountain, and the government workers picnicking across the way in Lafayette Park, and the five movie cameras waiting for Jerry Ford to say something brilliant and electrifying. He didn't.

Listen to Fritz

SEPTEMBER 11, 1976   The most chilling recent book about American democracy is *The Twilight of the Presidency* by George Reedy, Lyndon Johnson's former assistant, who calmly suggests that in a generation or two we will have a Man of Destiny in Washington keeping down crime, disciplining labor, disregarding Congress, and making the spaceships run on time.

Now comes an outline of how to prevent this from happening, starting from the same agonized assumption that unless something is done right away we are going to forget the lessons of Vietnam, Nixon, and Watergate and there may be no second warning.

Above all, the remarkable book says, Congress must be strengthened to confront the executive; it is written by—guess who—a man running for the second-highest elective office of the land, Senator Walter F. Mondale.

The book is called *The Accountability of Power: Toward a Responsible Presidency* (McKay) and was apparently wrung from the senator just after he dropped his own presidential bid, November 21, 1974, and before he was tapped for the vice-presidency, July 15, at Madison Square Garden. Set down in simple and straightforward style in what must have been a trauma of soul-searching, it gives the most clear-cut view of specific executive-legislative problems of any book by a candidate since Woodrow Wilson.

It is a book, also, that most probably insures embarrassment for Mondale if he becomes vice-president; a post which, history shows, is much like that of a paralyzed grasshopper wrapped into a cocoon by a voracious spider and sucked dry at leisure, like Nelson Rockefeller and Hubert Humphrey. For Mondale sets out to tell us what the public should find out about a presidential candidate, what it should demand to know from him, and how he should behave to Congress, if he gets elected.

He is also telling how Congress should behave to the next president; he is agonizingly certain that it must redeem itself—recapture the power that the Founding Fathers bestowed on it, which it has since fecklessly dissipated. The irony is, of course, that he asks Congress to check the executive just when he is trying to leave Congress and join the executive. It's as great a switch as if George Meany joined Exxon.

Mondale's outline of what we should know about a presidential candidate comes just when millions are finally settling down to make up their minds on Jimmy Carter. Yes, he says, writing a year ago, there must be debates: "We deserve a virtual guarantee that the American people will see the candidates confronting each other over a period of two months with regularity and, hopefully, in some depth." He wasn't thinking of Governor Carter when he wrote that, he was thinking of the 1972 debateless campaign and the merchandising of the invisible Nixon.

The institution that betrayed Congress, Mondale says, is Congress. It let Nixon get away with murder. (Real murder, maybe, against hostile government heads through the CIA.) The Founding Fathers gave Congress the power to approve treaties; Congress tamely accepted the substitute of "executive agreements" that don't require approval.

They gave Congress the power to confirm appointments but instead of insisting that cabinet officials (confirmable) be in charge, Congress let Nixon set up a shadow government under Ehrlichman— the Domestic Council, the Office of Management and Budget—that was not confirmable. (When Mondale attempted to cut appropriations of the Domestic Council by two-thirds in 1973 his colleagues voted him down overwhelmingly, he recalls.)

The Fathers gave Congress the power to declare war. Nixon made secret war in Cambodia. Only at long last did Congress vote the War Powers Act.

Above all the Founders gave Congress the power of the purse. Mondale's discussion in the chapter "The Decline of Congressional Power" is the most succinct statement of the matter by an insider that I know. Where was Congress when Nixon impounded funds which, at one point, reached over 20 percent of the controllable sector of the domestic budget? The audacity of Nixon in retrospect seems incredible. He invoked the doctrine of executive privilege twenty-nine times in early 1973 (at a time when he was creating a wave of $20 billion of impoundments) and although the Supreme Court finally made him reveal the damning tapes, it did so only after recognizing the doctrine of executive privilege for the first time.

Will Jimmy, if elected, listen to Fritz? Nobody knows; but at least he has chosen Fritz from all the others as his running mate, and the blueprint for executive-legislative relations is there.

Fritz, for example, wants more "legislative vetoes," the trick of attaching conditions to presidential authorizations requiring later legislative review. It is a curb on the president. "We simply must use this device more frequently," he says. Will Jimmy agree?

He says Congress must perfect its own budget as a counterpart to the presidential budget. Will Jimmy go along?

He is angered by Congress's blackout on TV: "I am so convinced of the seriousness of this risk (presidential nomination) that I have changed my mind and now believe that licenses granted by the FCC should be for periods which in most cases exceed the terms of an incumbent administration." How will Jimmy feel?

One thing Mondale particularly hankers for. Let's get some power back into the cabinet: "I believe we need a question-and-report period along the lines of parliamentary practice," he says. He has sponsored legislation for that purpose. It might produce stronger cabinets. "I recently watched a question period during a session of the Canadian Parliament," he says, "and came away even more convinced of the validity of the process." What would President Carter think about that?

He is refreshingly frank. He attacks the Ford pardon of Nixon again. He calls the present primary system "absolutely incredible." A single, six-year presidential term?—"We should no more remove our presidents from the basic check of reelection than we should allow them to appoint their successors" he says.

As to the main point, it's clear: there's a "dangerous presidential ascendancy," says this vice-presidential candidate. Time is short.

The Electoral College

O c t o b e r   1 6 ,   1 9 7 6   If Jerry Ford piles up four million votes in New York when the ballots are opened next month and if Jimmy Carter gets four million votes plus one, Jimmy Carter gets all forty-one electoral votes. This time-honored winner-take-all system is what makes close elections such breathtaking sporting events in America.

"The electoral college method of electing a president of the United States is archaic, undemocratic, complex, ambiguous, indirect, and dangerous," reported a blue-ribbon commission of the American Bar Association in 1967. So what? Nothing was done. We all love excitement and it's titillating to live on a minefield. Whether or not to abolish the electoral college has been the longest-standing debate in American political science.

Most polls indicate a close race; Jerry has been closing in on Jimmy, aided by the *Playboy* affair, and there's a sense in Washington that anything can happen; neither candidate thrills the voters; there are no "jumpers" or "squealers," as we in the press bus used to call the excited women along the way when Jack Kennedy's motorcade went through; and they don't roll in the aisles when Mr. Ford makes one of his earnest near-beer speeches—as FDR made the Teamsters do in his overwhelming "little dog Fala" speech so long ago. No, there's a kind of bored sobriety about it all, and a patient feeling that it'll all be over soon, anyway.

So people are studying the rules of the game compiled in the Philadelphia 1787 constitutional rule book. The goal, then, was to keep the presidential selection process away from the public (you and me); Roger Sherman said that the people "should have as little to do as may be about the government. They want information and are constantly liable to be misled." They invented a cozy electoral college of the best minds which would pick a proper president, though most people today still think they are voting directly for Carter and

Ford and not for faceless electors. A candidate needs 270 electors to win. A lot of things flow out of the system including, probably, the departure of Earl Butz last week. Mr. Ford must have been reading about the Reverend Samuel D. Burchard.

Did an ethnic slur ever decide a presidential election? You bet it did, with the aid of the electoral college. The year was 1884, the candidates were Cleveland and Blaine and Earl Butz's graceless predecessor was a Presbyterian minister. It was a close race; New York State would probably decide it; New York City would decide the state, and an angry ethnic or religious group could probably decide the city. Could and did.

At a meeting of Protestant ministers for Republican Blaine, Burchard welcomed the candidate and got his name in the encyclcopedias by charging that Democrats were the party of "Rum, Romanism, and Rebellion." It was as alliterative as a Spiro Agnew speech. Blaine, of Irish descent himself, didn't hear the remark or let it go unrebuked, and his Celtic supporters turned on him passionately. Result: Cleveland carried New York by 1,149 votes out of a million; won New York's winner-take-all 36 electors and got the presidency—219 electors to 182 for Blaine. Fun, eh? And a thing like that in a close contest could happen in 1976.

You can't help feeling sorry for Butz. He's a man with a Rotarian style of oratory and behind-the-barn humor, betrayed by the tittle-tattle of a private conversation aboard an airplane after the Kansas City convention by sharp-eared John W. Dean III. Dean was Nixon's counsel, the informer with the choirboy look who first egged Nixon on and later pulled the plug on Watergate. John Dean is a character out of Shakespeare; there'll always be one of him around in great drama, always sliding through, always telling all—for a fee—always landing on his feet.

Unlike the Burchard crack, Butz's nasty slur is unprintable and attacks the whole black race. After it got out, Butz had to go. There are 15.4 million blacks of voting age in the US making up 46 percent of the population of Chicago, for example. Illinois (twenty-six electoral votes) leans to Ford. Black turnout in big cities is low but no party could shoulder a thing like that.

As to the electoral college it should, of course, be removed like that other constitutional anachronism, the vice-presidency, with direct popular voting substituted. In 1969 the House approved a constitutional amendment to end the anomaly, 339 to 70, but it got tangled up in a Senate filibuster and lost.

The college has caused some near misses. In 1968 a shift of 42,000 votes would have thrown the election into the House, which was what George Wallace (who got forty-six electoral votes) was trying to do: he told a reporter that he hoped to be the balance of power between Nixon and Humphrey and extort from one of them, as the price of his deciding votes, a voice in picking Supreme Court justices. Someday, when nobody gets the requisite majority from the Faceless Men in the college, the stick of dynamite in the Constitution will go off and the election will go into the House of Representatives. It is doubtful that we will do anything to meet the situation before then.

President Ford's Gallup Poll rating leaped after the *Mayaguez* incident. It jumped 11 percent in the sharpest gain since Nixon's 17-point leap after the Vietnam "peace" settlement in January 1973. The only trouble was, of course, that Marines were ordered to rescue the American merchantman's thirty-nine-man crew after receiving word that they were already off the island, and at a cost of forty-one lives. Release of the General Accounting Office's dry recapitulation of the incident by a House committee now is doubtless a political act. But it must be remembered that Ford boasted about *Mayaguez* in Indiana, April 23, 1976. He told an audience, "I think the *Mayaguez* incident ought to be a fair warning to any country of the decisiveness of the Ford administration." He told the nation that he had constitutional authority for the action. "I was not consulted," said Mike Mansfield.

How good is the Ford judgment in such matters? He and five other congressional hawks were briefed on Nixon's secret, undeclared bombing of Cambodia in 1969. Nixon lied to the public that he was respecting Cambodia's neutrality. Mr. Ford did not speak.

Waiting for the Last Act

NOVEMBER 6, 1976 Round about eleven o'clock on election night we will get the results from Dixville Notch, New Hampshire (unless a rival town slips in ahead); they were first in 1972 when they plumped nineteen to one for Richard Nixon and they have been organizing for months. If the Dixville Notch Republican vote is reduced this year, as seems likely, the great media projection machine will start grinding for the night's work; Walter Cronkite, albeit he wears a smile, asks his audience whether this betokens a "trend" and before long statistics and tabulations will come pouring in as the hungry univacs swallow it, and who knows the result? Maybe we will get to bed by one.

Not in 1960, though; at 2:00 A.M. there was a two-million majority for Jack Kennedy which melted to a million a couple of hours later. Along with the milkman came alternative leads from straining reporters all over America: one projecting Kennedy, one Nixon, one a toss-up for the bulldog edition. It wasn't till 12:33 P.M. Eastern Standard Time Wednesday that Minnesota fell to Kennedy, and it was over.

Dixville Notch is a ski area town and brings the circle to where the 1976 show started; a thousand eager citizens last January stamped in from the snow and sparkling stars and near-zero weather to the pastel green-and-white cinder block high school auditorium at Conway, not far from the Notch, in a scene out of Thornton Wilder's *Our Town*. Ronald Reagan threw off his fleece-lined mackinaw to denounce the Washington "buddy system" and undercut President Ford (whom *Manchester Union-Leader* publisher Bill Loeb called "Jerry the Jerk"). Meanwhile over at Durham, New Hampshire in the first of America's thirty primaries the Man Nobody Knew was telling an audience that he was born-again, that he wouldn't tell them a lie, and that he wanted to make the American government as fine (pause), as honest (pause), as decent (pause), as honorable (pause) . . . as the American people.

The American presidential courtship dance is the longest in the world and nothing is more amazing than the way supporters find logical arguments to defend the illogical system. The surprising thing is that it works in its peculiar way even in this year in which voters seem more pessimistic than usual about their ability to make things happen. They have had the aid, from the beginning of course, of the mass media and the political plenum of press pundits. How else could the ceremony progress? The ambiguity of the primaries brings in the press, who must not only report but act as referee and interpreter, and thereby participate.

Take the Iowa caucus of January 19. Governor Carter had been preparing for this for two years. Only 45,000 Democrats voted (.10 percent) and Carter got 27.6 percent of this (Birch Bayh 13 percent). Nobody cared about the numbers; he had won, hadn't he? The monster publicity machine was activated. Jimmy who? the public asked. The press responded.

In New Hampshire, February 24, one of the smallest states of the Union, the minority party gave Carter a minority of its votes—29 percent, or 22,895, which was more than Udall got (24 percent), or Bayh (16 percent). So he was a sensation. The camera crews had been prowling the drifts for weeks. New Hampshire has knocked out presidential candidates: George Romney, Edmund Muskie, Lyndon Johnson. Would it happen again? The public looks at the primaries as a spectator sport and doesn't know the names of the players: if there is a contest somebody must say who wins, and that function falls to the press. In 1972 it arbitrarily said Muskie must get at least half to remain in first place; he got 46 percent (more than anyone else), but the anchormen in TV studios and pundits in newsrooms said that this wasn't enough; although he won, he lost. LBJ's showing in New Hampshire in 1968 was below expectations, too, and both men dropped out later. Carter got a low handicap, however, as a newcomer, and was decided to have won. He went on to Florida, the state adjacent to Georgia, and beat George Wallace, 34 percent to 31 percent. He was proclaimed Front-Runner and champion.

So now we wait for the last act and look back at what went before. Past elections have been remembered by phrases: the Cross of Gold speech; the boos that became known as "Bronx cheers" at

Madison Square Garden in 1924; Teddy's "Bull Moose"; Harding's "Normalcy"; "Prosperity is just around the corner" of poor old Hoover; FDR's "little dog Fala"; Goldwater's "In your heart, you know he's right." How about 1976? It has been a silent year.

It was the first year that the government helped pay campaign expenditures, one of the few genuinely revolutionary changes in American politics in modern times. Although far from perfect, and yet to be applied to congressional races, the system is a vast improvement over four years ago; in 1972 some 153 donors between them gave $20 million to the Nixon campaign; today 32 million Americans checked off the one-dollar contribution on their tax returns for this year's campaign. After Watergate, fifteen big corporations pleaded guilty to making illegal contributions. I think we will never go back to that, no matter what changes are made in the new system.

What phrase do we remember 1976 by? It is the year Reagan constantly nudged Ford to the right, to drop "détente," to drop Rockefeller, to pick Bob Dole as running mate (Reagan himself picked Schweiker). It is the year that Reaganites introduced the bullhorns at Kansas City, when the economy had a "pause," when abortion was an issue, when there was a twenty-eight-minute gap in the TV debate; yes, when for the second time in history rival candidates stood on the same platform and confronted each other. The year of the *Playboy* interview, of the amnesiac answer on Eastern Europe. Most of the incidents seem rather negative. It has not been a vintage presidential year. But in retrospect it could appear as momentous as any, as we see the qualities of the next president confronting the overwhelming problems awaiting him. Almost certainly the big issue is the economy; for example . . . the real spendable weekly earnings of a workingman's family of four are no higher today than in 1965. . . . Almost certainly the election will be decided by how many people actually vote.

THE CARTER YEARS
[*1976-1978*]

I Solemnly Swear

JANUARY 22, 1977 Take your hat off when you write about the Inaugural. It means that democracy has come through another test. The ceremony is an American invention combining dignified and undignified things in a typical American package—parades, bands, floats, strutting majorettes clothed mostly in their own gooseflesh. It is incongruous because America is incongruous. The Inaugural is America's middle way between a coronation and a coup d'etat.

It has two big events: the ceremonial ride up Pennsylvania Avenue of the incoming and outgoing presidents forced to sit in one vehicle, though they may hate each other; and the second event—the two minutes of awed silence when the president-elect comes out on the high platform before the nation and repeats the words, "I, James Earl Carter, do solemnly swear. . . ." * It takes a very dull person indeed not to understand the almost mystical meaning of this. It is part of the thing that governs us and that makes us governable: before the words this familiar figure up there was an individual and we either liked him or didn't; but now he is president.

The words are the words that Washington repeated; the president-elect is standing before the same building where Lincoln twice appeared (with the dome unfinished). More often than not the address he delivers immediately thereafter is eminently forgettable but, on the other hand, it may not be the words but who delivers them that is important. The office has a tendency to lift even little men up.

You get an album of America in those speeches: Ulysses S. Grant, for example, (anticipating Jerry Ford on Puerto Rico) proposed to

* This column was written on January 16, before the inauguration. Actually, the new president said, "I, Jimmy Carter . . ." when he took the oath of office.

469

make Santo Domingo a state in 1873. Or Hoover, unconscious that he was already destroyed, boasting of prosperity eight months before the Crash. And FDR telling us we had nothing to fear, and Kennedy giving his "Ask not" phrase.

Every Inaugural has its own mood and flavor. Robert Sherwood, the poet, caught the essence of 1933:

> Plodding feet
> Tramp-tramp
> The Grand Old Party's
> Breaking camp.
> Blare of bugles
> Din-din
> The New Deal is moving in.

Twenty years later came the Republican restoration. That was a joyous but vindictive triumph. Suspicion of outgoing Democrats ran so high that incoming Treasury Secretary Humphrey's first order of business was to count the gold at Fort Knox. There was a protocol flap when Ike wouldn't go past the White House portico to make his ceremonial call on Truman. Jobholders quaked. Fear of the spoilsman was so intense that stores bought full-page advertisements in Washington newspapers reassuring government workers that their credit was still good. Buy now and make no payments till March, one pleaded: "We're not worried, why should *you* be?" A clothing ad said, "Bond's has complete confidence in the continued employment of present government personnel."

Let's come down another twenty years. In 1973 there was a surly undertone to the Nixon Washington festival. Antiwar protesters staged a counter-Inaugural. People thought Nixon might make some big announcement. Everything was ready. The Roost-No-More Co. had gone down the plane trees on the avenue spraying them to keep starlings off. There was no spray for dissidents.

For no good reason I found myself up in a radio perch under the ceiling of the Capitol, in a small closet on stilts holding four people; I was supposed to feed lines to the commentator. I had never looked down on the crowd before and seen it as the president did, stretching out by the acre and resembling the underside of a tapestry. You wondered what design was on the other side. Alabama's Governor George Wallace was wheeled in, just below, and the Agnews and Nixons greeted him warmly.

That was four years ago; some flags still at half-mast for Truman and a bitter wind, after the rain, that vibrated the poles. A faint throb of antiwar chants came up as Nixon talked. One mocking homemade sign said, " 'Peace is at Hand'—Henry Kissinger, October 26, 1972," in reference, of course, to his comment just before the election.

Richard Nixon is represented at this 1977 Inaugural, too, by indirection though not in person. He appointed four members of the present Supreme Court and through them he still influences affairs. He picked four remarkably like-minded conservatives, "strict constructionists," he called them. "I am proud of the appointments I have made to the courts," he said in his 1972 acceptance speech, "particularly to the Supreme Court. We must strengthen the peace forces against the criminal forces in America."

"Peace forces" was a code name for conservatives, to undo the work of the *liberal* Warren Court. The Senate rejected two Nixon appointees, of course, Haynsworth and Carswell. The present bitter confirmation controversy over Griffin Bell recalls his support of school segregationist Carswell and brings back the Nixon echo. Just last week the four able and high-minded Nixon justices lined up again together in a split decision. It was a procedural matter in a zoning case with racial implications. Along with Potter Stewart (an Eisenhower appointee) the Nixon justices carried the day.

Every presidential Inaugural has its own mood under the bands and gaiety, and the one today, I think, is uncertainty. It is wonderful to be rid of Watergate and Vietnam, and Jerry Ford helped us to do that. But what about the man we elected? His selection of Bell has raised a row with the blacks, and his skimpy plans for stimulating the economy have upset organized labor. Liberal economist Walter Heller in Senate testimony last week rather scornfully referred to Carter proposals as "being 'realistic' and 'pragmatic' to the point of being downright modest." The United States is not out of the woods yet. Our allies are counting on American recovery to lift them from the slump. Yet we are further from our high-employment goals now than a year ago; the operating rates of manufacturing are barely above a year ago, and industrial production is limping along at rates no higher than those it first reached three years ago. Senators Humphrey and Javits have introduced a two-billion-dollar bill for programs to reduce youth unemployment. Almost certainly the Democratic Congress will demand greater federal effort. . . .

The crowd hushes, the black-robed chief justice steps forward, and Jimmy Carter takes the oath. Does that end anything? No, it is just the start.

Report Card

JUNE 11, 1977   How's Jimmy Carter doing? My impression is that he's doing pretty well. We hardly knew him when we elected him, and we elected him by a slight margin. He's not turning out the way many expected, which disappoints some and pleases others. He's still surrounded by a kind of fog which makes final judgment unwise. But a lot of things are clearer than they were. Some misapprehensions have been corrected. One was that he is a stiff-necked fundamentalist who couldn't yield to opposition and would just dig in his toes. On the contrary, he is now criticized for being too pliant on a number of issues and for making unnecessary compromises as on the $50 tax rebate to stimulate the economy. It is a little too early to say yet; he's been in office less than five months, but a definite style has appeared. The staff and advisers are settling down, the administration that got elected as an enemy of the Establishment is now the Establishment. The political honeymoon (which was never too ardent) is over, but the Gallup Poll says the public still likes him, the figure being 66 favorable, 16 hostile, and 18 percent no opinion. That's about par for a newcomer at this stage of the game. President Carter seems to be taking hold.

Foreign affairs always tempt a president because he needn't consult Congress all the time. One thing you must say about Jimmy Carter, he has plunged right in. A striking characteristic is his firm, his formidable self-confidence. His representatives have been all over the world—Africa, Asia, Middle East, Geneva, Latin America—setting forth the Carter activist foreign policy. His wife goes out as his vice-president returns, and UN Ambassador Andrew Young and cabinet members are all around. There is a touch of the dilettante in some of this. Mr. Carter wants to emphasize human rights, except to the dictatorships with which we are allied and to whom we sell our arms: Iran, South Korea, the Philippines. The Russians didn't understand Mr. Carter's emphasis on human rights before the SALT talks and the first session failed. Now they have been revived with less talk of ideology.

I give Carter points for proposing gradual troop withdrawal from South Korea; for slapping down Major General John Singlaub who criticized this; for trying to find a way out of the Jewish-Palestine deadlock; for overtures to Fidel Castro; for making a last effort to prevent global plutonium proliferation by embargoing sales of sophisticated breeder reactors abroad. Jimmy Carter is a new type of president who is being appraised round the world and who seems to have handled himself well at the London summit talks. There is a moralistic fervor about him which always threatens to get out of hand, and that caused some uncomfortable anticipations in the campaign, combined with the toothy grin and the thought of having a president called "Jimmy"; but I think he and the nation are now achieving a working relationship. And in the speech on foreign affairs the other day at Theodore Hesburgh's Notre Dame, the sincere fervor was evident; it was a "we-love-everybody" kind of speech with more reaffirmation than innovation, but its sincerity and idealism rang true. He told them, incidentally, that the United States is now cured of the "inordinate fear of communism." Good thing, if true.

It's on the domestic side that Carter's real ambiguity appears; George McGovern says he doesn't act like a liberal; the *Wall Street Journal* says he's no conservative; bewildered citizens ask what these terms mean. The problem is that nobody can define them. The issue arises over the economy. We have had the worst slump since the 1929 crash, double-digit inflation, agonizing unemployment, now it's getting better. Economists are divided, some of them want more federal stimulus, the bulk of them appear to be holding their breaths in a wait-and-see attitude.

The old maestro, Arthur Burns, chairman of the Fed, preaches magic: it's now a matter of "business confidence," he says, pulling at his pipe; it's mysterious, it's psychological; it's econometric metaphysics; if the Carter administration will just hold off and utter a few comforting runes this intangible "business confidence" will be restored. Maybe in time even the Dow-Jones index will get the word.

For the layman it's terribly confusing. President Carter has given some stimulus to the economy. His tax measure the other day, for simplification-and-reduction, cuts about $5 billion a year in taxes from those with low- and middle-class incomes. They will have that much more to spend. His top economic adviser, Charles Schultze, a certified liberal, worked out an ambitious stimulus package, including an $11.4-billion tax rebate, at the start of the administration. Now Schultze has been vetoed. The budget deficit has been running about $60 billion but the president wants to cut it down to $45 billion; in fact to balance the budget by 1981.

House majority leader Jim Wright of Texas gave a breakfast group a rule-of-thumb figure the other day—for every 1 percent of unemployment, $16 billion is added to the budget. It works the other way, too; if unemployment comes down a point the cost of unemployment and relief falls drastically. Since last fall unemployment has fallen from 8 to 7 percent, and economist Schultze hopes it will decline another one and a quarter points this year, even without pump-priming.

Sometimes in his speeches Jimmy Carter sounds like Jerry Ford, sometimes he sounds like Franklin Roosevelt, sometimes he sounds like both together. He told a press conference that the rate of inflation is "directly tied to the degree of responsibility of the federal government in handling excessive spending." He told the United Automobile Workers convention that "it's not legitimate spending on human needs that causes our deficits." It all depends on the tone of voice in which you say "spending."

When all is said and done, however, Jimmy Carter has heaped vital programs on Congress—tax, energy, social security, welfare, public works, and many others—more than they can handle. Legislative mastication is under way. There are disagreements; there may be vetoes. On the whole, prospects are good for constructive results.

Eight Million Illegal Immigrants

JULY 30, 1977   A German employer who knowingly hires illegal aliens may pay a fine as high as $20,000 or spend five years in jail. The moment of truth has come for President Carter; he must decide whether to include penalties for employer violators in the new immigration enforcement package he is bringing out shortly.

Failure to enforce immigration laws is a scandal. Illegal immigrants are pouring in over the Mexican border and the number already here about equals the total of US unemployed, around eight million. Still they come. It is partly a problem of the economic slump; it is partly the bigger problem of rich and poor nations.

Global population explosion—like nuclear proliferation—is a big, hazy problem that nobody wants to face. Maybe we won't face it, which is one way to deal with a problem. But we can at least sense what it means to let things slide. We got a glimpse of it when New York had its blackout, and outsiders watched the looting in comfortable chairs, by color television, with after-dinner coffee. Black and Hispanic teenagers were showing their contempt for the society that imposes on them a 40-percent unemployment rate. And many of the jobs they don't have are taken by illegal aliens here not only in New York but in other cities. In particular the blacks, who have been trying to fight their way up since slavery, are faced with a new illicit tide of low-wage competitors.

The population of the United States is only about 5 or 6 percent of the world's four billion. Five percent uses around 30 percent of all the world's energy. Can we maintain this fantastically favored position? Nobody knows. Are we morally entitled to it? That again is a matter of opinion. But at least the United States, like most of the prosperous Western nations and like Japan and, yes, China, has imposed a voluntary slowdown of population. As standard of living has gone up growth of population has come down. It takes the pressure off diminishing global resources.

But this isn't true of the poorer countries. Every twenty-four hours the population equivalent of the city of Des Moines is added to the world population. If it goes on like this teeming Spaceship Earth will have another four billion passengers in thirty years. But this isn't going to happen, says Lester R. Brown, president of the privately funded Worldwatch Institute. He is sure of it. Hopefully he believes that world population growth will continue to slow down. (It's now around 1.9 percent.) Other demographers, less optimistic than Brown on voluntary restraint, note grimly that there's always pestilence, famine, and war—the hideous riders who follow hungry hordes through history.

So let's come back to President Carter. For months he has delayed issuing his package of recommendations for getting illegal immigration under control. I understand that it should now come shortly. Meanwhile, a House committee under Chairman Joshua Eilberg (D, Pa.) starts hearings this week on employer liability. Bills on this have passed the House before; the problem is the Senate.

Here are two big countries side by side, the United States and Mexico. The natural increase of US population has slowed down to .59 percent. Legal immigration, under laws which are the most generous of any industrial nation on earth, raises growth to .9 percent. But this doesn't include illegal aliens, and immigration of one sort or another, legal or illegal, probably now supplies half of the total US population growth.

On the other side of the Rio Grande is Mexico. It hasn't enough jobs for its workers nor food for its hungry; as population has soared to 62 million it has taken to importing food, not exporting it. It has huge foreign debts. Inflation is about 30 percent. The estimated growth rate of 3.5 percent, higher than India's, will double its population in twenty years and make Mexico City the biggest city on earth, twice the size of London. What's the answer? Why, Mexico has oil; that will help. But meanwhile the pressure to get into the United States is almost irresistible.

"I believe that the rich countries will increasingly be *invaded* by those in the poor world who cannot find employment and attempt to seek it elsewhere," says Jan Tinbergen, Nobel laureate in economics. The periodical press is becoming aware of this. In June, Gene Lyons in *Harper's* ("Inside the Volcano") forecasts an eruption. Farm workers earn less than $15 a month, he says, and Mexico has the largest external debt in relation to gross national product of any nation in the world.

"What Illegal Aliens Cost the Economy" is outlined in alarm in *Business Week* (June 13) which figures that one year's illegal influx from Mexico will offset the entire job-creating effect of the administration's stimulus package.

Many think the Mexicans' silent invasion can't be stopped; the US is not prepared to take the steps necessary. Certainly the pathetic army of border officials at present can't do the job. One proposed solution is to help make Mexico more prosperous, give it economic aid and stimulate jobs that will keep workers at home. This theory is advanced in the current issue of *Foreign Affairs* by Professor Richard R. Fagen, who argues that it's the only hope:

"If such programs are not forthcoming," he declares, "all the electronic gadgetry, registration cards, fines to employers, and forced deportations that the US can muster will not keep Mexicans at home."

It's a question: is America stern enough? In Europe, France has sent back her laborers from Southern Europe; Germany has given tickets to Turkish labor battalions. But they are hard-boiled about this. The US is a nation of immigrants; presently six to eight million illegals are believed to be here and by one estimate about a tenth of Mexico's population lives illegally in the United States.

So that's the choice for America and it's a big one. A Gallup Poll in April found 82 percent favored punishing employers who knowingly hire illegals. But how firm is this feeling? How strong is Carter?

The Ford administration issued a 244-page report on illegal aliens. It found that they compete "particularly with the minimally skilled and underemployed" (like New York looters). The illegals produce "underground communities of people whose existence depends on evading and avoiding contact with the law and with government in any form." Will America do anything about this, or let it slide?

Silent Cal

AUGUST 6 & 13, 1977   Fifty years ago a vacationing president rode down a mountain to a semiweekly press conference and created a political mystery that has lasted to this day.

Calvin Coolidge normally offered little news at Rapid City, South Dakota, but today Everett Sanders, his private secretary, told reporters in the news shack that there would be a statement at noon. In the executive office the president finally broke a long silence; he dictated a ten-word sentence and asked that twenty-five copies be made, cut into neat, two-inch slips. At noon reporters lined up and he handed out the slips without comment.

They glanced, gasped, gagged, demanded amplification, got none —and stormed for the wires. The statement read, "I do not choose to run for president in 1928." It was August 3, 1927.

After the conference Coolidge didn't say a word on the subject to an astonished senator who had watched the show and who rode with him back up the mountain; not a word to his wife Grace at lunch, where he chatted on other subjects. He went off to his customary nap, savoring every moment of nondisclosure with impish relish. (He sometimes had a mordant gleam like that in the beady eye of a parrot before it tweaks you.) Grace Coolidge learned about it from the visitor after Cal departed. "Now isn't that like him!" she exclaimed.

Why did he decide not to run? His reelection was sure. Republicans were dominant. The "Coolidge boom" had begun. He was not merely popular, he was a media-manufactured folk myth, Silent Cal, with more jokes about him than about the Model T. He had taken the oath by kerosene lamp, hadn't he? He represented perseverance, prudence, and parsimony which sanctified the nation's own recklessness and extravagance as it started on the greatest, gaudiest binge of all time. He had a Vermont twang, accentuated by chronic obstructed nasal passages into a kind of quack. America mimicked it. It had no problems that it was prepared to recognize and it gloried in Cal's afternoon nap that symbolized serenity. He, like the nation, was snoozing on a volcano, but who in 1927 saw the Crash, and Hitler, ahead?

Sophisticates were certain there must be native shrewdness behind this Puritan facade; there wasn't. It was just that he rarely said anything. We in the press corps saw him twice a week at news conferences and we quoted "the White House spokesman." We saw the commonplace, respectable mediocrity that we had turned into a legend. Public speeches were sententious and dull; he told us that "when many people are out of work unemployment results." Germany was going down the drain, and our former allies suggested easier terms on war debts. No, said Coolidge: "They hired the money, didn't they?" At home he accepted the gross disparity of income of workers and farmers. When they couldn't buy the goods they produced, the Crash came.

There was another side to the drab little man, though. When he greeted the returned hero Lindbergh, the day before leaving for the Black Hills, I watched his face; for a second the constrained self-consciousness disappeared; and the smile was as sweet as a wild strawberry you find unexpectedly on a rocky Vermont pasture.

With a folk figure like Cal to relish, the nation had just what it wanted. Some stories are unreliable, like the one about putting his rocker on the front portico of the White House so he could watch the streetcars better. But he had a pawky, rather cruel sense of humor—expressed, for example, by pressing all the desk buttons and stepping aside to watch guards and secretaries rush in. Columnist Tom Stokes told me once that Cal dropped the family cat into a Thanksgiving hamper with a live turkey, one time, to see what would happen. Senator Lodge sarcastically called him the kind of man who lives in a two-family house. He did, in Northampton; and paid $36 a month rent.)

The summer pressed down on Washington half a century ago like a damp, hot thumb; nothing was air-conditioned. At press conferences Coolidge stood behind his desk and picked up questions written in advance. This time we had all asked about the third term. He picked them up sheet by sheet and put them down without comment; finally he found another subject and answered briefly. Then he went off to the Black Hills.

Life had hit Cal hard as a boy. At twelve he kneeled with his beloved sister, Abbie, to receive the final blessing of his mother on the rock-ribbed farm. Then Abbie suddenly died. In Washington his younger son Calvin developed blood poisoning from a tennis blister on the White House court. It was before antibiotics. To the Puritan it was somehow retribution. "I do not know why such a price was exacted for occupying the White House," he wrote. "When he went, the power and glory of the presidency went with him."

There was another episode, too, of a different kind—almost comic. He was petulant in private, given to tantrums; chief White House doorman, Ike Hoover, said he was worse than Teddy Roosevelt. His link to happiness was Grace Goodhue, his wife, with charm, warmth, sparkle, and bottomless admiration for him, yet relishing his oddities, too. She had come to hate Washington.

On the first day at Black Hills she hiked with Jim Haley, veteran Secret Service man, and returned at 2:15, just as a search party was organized. They had a grim delayed lunch, probably with a tantrum after it; a few days later Haley was shifted. Mike Hennessy wrote with a smirk in the *Boston Globe* that the new guard was "not as striking a figure" as Haley; "hard to lose in a hike, always on time for his meals."

I offer these clues to a fifty-year riddle. Suppose that after a week everyone has forgotten the Haley incident but Cal; he regrets his petulance, his peevish dismissal, his words with Grace. He has thought it over and made up his mind. So he rides down the mountain composing a statement that, even so, is ambiguous; doesn't say "Won't"; says, "Don't choose." He rides the ten miles that bright morning in the big car, relishing the fact that he holds all the cards, that nobody else knows, that he can change history. He gets wry satisfaction in confiding to nobody; in planning a kind of surprise nosegay for Grace in his queer, crabbed fashion—the announcement of departure. And so—

It is noon, now August 3. He is at his office. He tells his secretary, "Tell those newspaper fellers to come in."

Senator Byrd

OCTOBER 8, 1977   See Senator Byrd. He's a strong man. He plays the fiddle. He guides the Senate. Once he was just a kleagle. Then he became a senator. Then he beat Teddy Kennedy for Senate whip. Now he lectures the vice-president. Now he tells President Carter to fire Lance. President Carter fires Lance. What will Senator Byrd do next? Nobody knows. But watch him.

In the feudal system when the emperor's power diminished the barons' power increased, and that is the way things are done in Washington with presidents. People have been studying the unknown President Carter for eight or nine months, speculating about him and noting the extraordinary narrowness and provincialism of his staff, and then he blew it in the Lance affair. Maybe he will make a fast recovery; I hope so, because we are all involved and live under a presidential system where everything goes to pot if we have an ineffective chief executive. By the end of the year the Carter legislative record almost certainly will look better than it does right now. In the meantime the other power centers have enlarged as the White House power center contracted; the seldom-smiling Mr. Byrd is probably the most powerful man in the legislative branch, excepting House Speaker Tip O'Neill of Massachusetts, and the word of Congress is growing more important.

Somebody had to explain to the White House that Congress is not the Georgia legislature. Five days after the Carter Inaugural Byrd took the surprising step of publicly criticizing the president for not consulting Congress more. That matter was straightened out quickly. Then in June Press Secretary Jody Powell told the press after a setback of the energy program in a House committee that Mr. Carter was "deeply concerned" and that the "oil companies, the auto companies, and their lobbies have won significant preliminary victories" and that deregulation of natural gas was a "rip-off of the American consumer." The observation was probably right but ill-timed; the real legislative problem was the Senate, not the House. Byrd told the press that Carter was "overreacting"; that it was "only the first pitch in an energy ball game that may go ten innings or more."

Mr. Carter gracefully yielded in part, and consulted his stiffly independent Senate leader more and more. Who else was there to consult? The parochial White House staff misappraised every development in the Lance affair. Somebody had to remind the president that he was *president;* that it is a national responsibility; that it is above friendships and self; that it requires sacrifices, sometimes cruel; that there is only so much presidential power and it must be spent wisely. In short, Byrd at the White House told Carter that Lance should go and the sooner the better. In a day or two Lance was gone. It was impressive advice from a formidable figure, one of the most curious figures in Washington.

Carter and Byrd have much in common. Each is a born-again Baptist. Each is a proud, one-time poor southern boy; each is hell-bent on consolidating and legitimizing his new status. Each, also, is intensely disciplined and a little self-righteous. Each has struggled to "make it," but Byrd has struggled harder.

Byrd has fought his way up and, like many self-made men, finds it hard to forgive weaklings who can't rise. He's a po' white kid from a gloomy holler in West Virginia; an orphan; a garbage collector of scraps for his pigs; a boy who pulled his forelock to the nice people; a high school graduate (valedictorian) with a primitive attitude toward race; a Klan organizer; a butcher who learned how to cut meat from a manual; a scholar who waited sixteen years to start college after finishing high school; a law degree after ten years of night school while in Congress (*cum laude.*) That's a success story. He lives in a modest house in a Virginia suburb with the woman who shared the days when they couldn't afford even a refrigerator—just a half orange-crate nailed outside the kitchen window. He hates socializing.

Robert Byrd hasn't stopped growing—or adapting, anyway. He threw in his lot with the southerners when he came to the Senate; he regrets the Klan experience ("a mistake," he says) but some of his raw attitudes at the start of his almost thirty years in the Senate sound almost obscene today; of the Warren Court—"the Marxists, in their own godless scheming, could hardly have asked more from our Supreme Court than they have received." He was sorry for Martin Luther King's murder, of course but, after all, he was a troublemaker;

as for the protest mobs—"I have two pistols in my home. I intend to protect my family." He voted and filibustered against the civil rights bills; was a Vietnam hawk.

But Byrd has mellowed a bit in the interval; he has moved from far right to moderate-right and after all, he's a powerbroker and parliamentary technician, not an ideologue. Some of his attitudes contrast extraordinarily with earlier ones; he's "gone national," just as Lyndon Johnson did, and regrets some old positions, but still hasn't told the president whether he's for the Panama Canal Treaty.

Senators underestimated him. Working hard on details for fellow senators was what he did during dreary years for customers as a butcher. He was collecting political chits all the time. He suddenly knocked out the surprised Teddy Kennedy for the number-two Democratic spot as party whip in 1971. (It was a dramatic little struggle: he had the decisive proxy of his patron, the dying Richard Russell, which wouldn't count if Russell expired. Russell was still breathing when he used it, and died within four hours. The vote was actually 31 Byrd, 24 Kennedy.)

One thing Byrd has that no other senator has—a fiddle. At the Washington Press Club party last year Mr. Carter was there and so was Byrd; both performed. The president had wisecracks; Byrd hoedowns, rousing tunes with proper hoots. A formidable figure with few traces of humor, a big brow, big nose, commanding eyes, a man who learned that a Senate leader makes himself powerful by making himself useful, whose former unction has turned to aggression, was bringing down the house with "Goin' Up Cripple Creek" and stirring hillbilly tunes. It was a smash.

Last week the dour majority leader lectured the vice-president sharply from the Senate floor for making an allegedly inappropriate parliamentary ruling. No harm done; they kissed and made up. Where does the Carter-Mondale-Byrd relationship go from here? Nobody knows.

Terror

O CTOBER 29, 1977   Susanne Albrecht betrayed her godfather with a bouquet of roses. "Here's Susanne," came the familiar voice over the intercom and the gate was opened. She entered with her roses and two members of the West German terrorist group and they gunned down Jurgen Ponto, chairman of the Dresden Bank, her father's friend.

She believed in a Cause, of course. So did the two men and two women who hijacked the Lufthansa jetliner last week, flew to Somalia, murdered the kneeling pilot, threatened the eighty-six passengers and crew, and finally were overwhelmed by the German commando team. The commandos blew the door off the jet with a bomb that blinded like a lightning flash and stunned like a thunderclap and gave just the gasp of time needed for rescue.

Susanne Albrecht was well-educated, upper-class, highly motivated, and "sick of eating caviar," as she said. So she added one more crime to what's been going on in Germany and elsewhere. The supreme judge of the Berlin high court was murdered; West Germany's chief public prosecutor was murdered; banker Ponto was murdered; industrialist Hans-Martin Schleyer was kidnapped and his guards murdered. This has been going on for ten years.

Now comes the second part of it, in Germany and other countries. Terrorists are caught, tried, and imprisoned and then, in order to release them, their reckless gangs undertake more spectacular terrorism, seizing innocent victims and demanding the release of the prisoners. Mostly they lose, sometimes they win: Israel defeated air terror at Entebbe; Dutch marines rescued a hijacked train; now German commandos have achieved another thrilling rescue (and probably saved Helmut Schmidt's government). But two years ago Germany freed five terrorists to rescue a kidnapped politician, and last week Japanese terrorists made blackmail pay; Tokyo liberated six jailed terrorists, threw in six million dollars in ransom, and bought off 156 passengers whose lives were at stake. The terrorists disappeared into the silence of Algiers. Their victory encourages every other outrage, of course.

What is society going to do about events like these which leave it seething with helpless fury? The question is still unanswered even though the Somalia rescue was successful. Theoretically, of course, we shouldn't pay ransom. We know intellectually that it will simply produce more crimes. When the life of only one man was at stake (Schleyer) a West German poll showed 60 percent against yielding to terrorist demands, only 22 percent for it. But when the dreadful stakes were the women and children on the Lufthansa jetliner, a later poll showed a tie, 42 percent to 42 percent. What a damnable choice to be confronted with, to be sure, in this elegant modern age!

Certain things begin to stand out. There is no doubt any longer that there always will be an absolutist faction which holds individual life in contempt, which justifies ends over means, which clutches at martyrdom for no matter how tawdry a cause. There always will be a Susanne Albrecht with her roses.

Another point: The world has grown so small now that nations must cooperate in these matters in spite of themselves. Moscow is as much opposed to hijacking as Washington. There has been no hijacking from the US to Cuba since Castro made a no-landing agreement. Surely there are sanctions that can be taken against nations which accept air pirates or which don't install adequate electronic security checks, tedious and irritating as they are.

We know more, too, about the psychology of terrorists; that a quite close relationship can grow up between them and the passengers they have abducted; that the enforced intimacy of the adventure makes them take a human interest, after all, in the victims who seemed merely pawns at first. Weariness can also produce a letdown. The government that bargains with them should stretch matters out; employ every circumstance as a basis of further negotiations; put back, if possible, the deadline originally imposed. The West German government let two deadlines go by without capitulating.

It begins to look, too, as though nations must organize specialized strike forces for such emergencies. At Entebbe, at the Dutch railroad train, and now again at Somalia, the spectacular surprise attack was successful; the need is for sudden weapons that blind and stun.

The worst thing that could come out of Somalia would be the idea that the problem has been met. The more that society becomes mechanized the more vulnerable it is to urban, guerrilla-style terrorism. This, in turn, is likely to produce a counterferocity in the public. It seems to me that West Germany has so far shown remarkable restraint in the face of the stepped-up provocation.

Probably a more serious problem lies ahead, not only for Germany but for the world. It is disagreeable to be the bearer of bad news but it seems to me that we are in a countdown to a crisis that we are even more reluctant to face than the energy crisis: the time when terrorists will have nuclear bombs. This could bring about a quite new kind of world in a very short time.

Will they get them? The authoritative Mitre report (1977) sponsored by the Ford Foundation (Ballinger Publishing Co.) noted that "the past few years have seen an upsurge in the size, sophistication, and capabilities of terrorist groups." Plutonium, it says, "would be vulnerable to theft, diversion, and misuse at all stages following its separation at reprocessing plants" (the kind of plants Jimmy Carter wants delayed). Of course "less skilled terrorists" couldn't make a Grade-A bomb "but even an inexpertly assembled terrorist weapon might well have a yield equivalent to a few hundred tons of chemical high explosive." Yes, it said, the threat "must be taken seriously."

The Office of Technological Assessment of Congress last April said that a small group including a "jack-of-all-trades" might put together a modest bomb if it had stolen the fissionable material. As to civil liberties, it noted, it would be hard to preserve them if a real threat of nuclear blackmail developed.

When Isolationism Died

DECEMBER 10, 1977   It's a Sunday like any other. Going on Christmas. Brown packages hidden in closets. Outside brisk and snappy. Children go to Sunday school. Newspaper jammed with advertisements. All about the new upsweep hairdo. Wanamaker's advertised white shirts at two dollars (regular two-fifty and three-dollar values—better come early). Morning news pretty good: Russians counterattacking around Moscow; maybe they'll hold out after all. After lunch the telephone rings. And it's never, ever, the same again . . .

"Hey, heard the news? The Japs have bombed Pearl Harbor!"
"No! You're crazy. Hey, Ernestine . . ."

Everybody of my era knows where they heard the news, December 7, 1941. Try us out. That's what separates generations. The stadium was crowded to watch the Redskins and at the half the loudspeaker began to blare. Will Lieutenant General Smith call his office? There's a telephone call for Commander Russell! It went on and on. Veteran *New York Times* photographer George Tames wondered what was up; called his office; got the news. He went to the Japanese Embassy; iron gates barred; a gray-white smoke rising from burning papers in the rear. There was a two-way traffic jam on Massachusetts Avenue of cars gawking at the embassy.

It's an anniversary to remember not because a war started but because a madness ended—isolationism. I have a personal feeling because I was one of the gawky boys who volunteered in Mr. Wilson's dream to make the world safe for democracy. We won; there was the exhilaration of the Armistice, and then the Lodge fight against the League. Wilson forlornly asked the nation to remember the "dear ghosts" of boys left on Flanders Fields. There was a majority, never a two-thirds majority, for the League. Soon the whole crusade was derided. The Nye committee showed it was all a plot by munitions makers.

Senate isolationists defeated the World Court, too. Again there was a majority, 52 to 36, but this was seven short of two-thirds. Borah and Johnson left the Senate chamber laughing and rejoicing.

Isolationism came down through the start of World War II. It weakened when England fought alone and when Hitler madly attacked his surprised partner Stalin. But Colonel Lindbergh wrote an open letter to Americans through *Collier's*: France was defeated, he said; Great Britain was being defeated; the US would be defeated too, if it joined the fray. No distinction between Hitler's and Churchill's moral aims.

On Thursday, December 4, three days before Pearl Harbor, the isolationist *Chicago Tribune* and *Washington Times-Herald* published a top-secret US position paper laying out logistic and supply plans for an imagined invasion of Germany with five million Americans in 1943. It was the kind of thing all war offices prepare, but the newspapers charged it showed a Roosevelt plot.

And so the day of trial came, thirty-six years ago. Most of it still is quite incredible.

It is incredible because we had broken the Japanese code and never should have let the surprise occur. A little Army officer who was a demon at cryptography had unscrambled the imperial code under "Operation Magic" and was giving the Army, Navy, and State Departments translations of Tokyo war orders before the Japanese troops got them. We knew an attack was coming. Where, we didn't know. We knew that Japan had sent a so-called peace emissary to Washington to fool us and mask the surprise, and we played along with it; it was a double game of make-believe. We had warned Army and Navy commanders November 24 of a probable attack; we had sent a more urgent warning November 27. But mental blockage is more powerful than reality; the attack would be on Malaya, Dutch East Indies, Philippines, Guam—not Hawaii.

Then the following mishaps occurred. Tokyo dispatched a fourteen-part message to the Japanese Embassy in Washington December 6 of which the first thirteen parts were decoded for the State Department before the Japs got them. "This means war," FDR said solemnly to Harry Hopkins as he ate dinner from a tray. There might still be hope in the fourteenth section, however. Oddly enough the Japanese transmitters called it a day before sending the fourteenth section, which had the sting in it (though it didn't mention Pearl Harbor). They sent it next morning. General Marshall, Chief of Staff of the Army, didn't get the fourteenth section till he came in from a Sunday horseback ride at 11:30. He sent another alert then.

More curiosities occurred. A Japanese midget submarine was detected about 3:50 A.M. off Pearl Harbor. The US minesweeper *Condor* took action. But it didn't report the incident till 6:00 A.M.

Electronic equipment picked up Japanese planes winging to attack at 7:00 A.M. just as supersensitive electronic equipment is supposed to do. The watch officer didn't do anything; it must be a flight of American B-17's.

General Marshall decided to send his Sunday alert to US commanders; contact with Hawaii had temporarily been interrupted, so he used Western Union and RCA cables. The crucial message was delayed hours in transmission. Finally a motorcycle courier started out with it in Hawaii to military headquarters. Unaccountably bombs began to fall and he jumped into a ditch.

As background to all of the above, the Hawaii commanders, Admiral Kimmel and General Short, were barely on speaking terms from interservice jealousy: the big battleships were tied up two by two for fear of sabotage. The airplanes were on the ground. Antiaircraft guns were wrongly placed and there was no effective air patrol by either service. Absolute surprise. The Pacific fleet was canceled out—eight battleships and three cruisers sunk or disabled.

Yes, I remember the day. I went to the White House and stayed—until 1:00 A.M. A crisp night, nearly freezing; trucks with early Christmas trees coming down Pennsylvania Avenue; a misty moon climbing the trees over the old bronze cannon in Lafayette Park. Cabinet meeting at 8:30; Congressional leaders at 9:00.

We went out to stand on the front portico of the White House—a little stone stage among the columns. One senator was Hiram Johnson. (Borah, who called it a "phony war," was dead). Johnson looked straight ahead, didn't speak to us or we to him. We were awed.

Behind the iron rails on the avenue a little crowd looked in at us. It tried to sing "America the Beautiful."

The Economic Report

FEBRUARY 25, 1978   There's nothing more agreeable of a winter evening than to curl up before a good fire with the tables of statistics of the president's Annual Economic Report. Let the gale howl. Let the snow fall. I have here Table B-28, "Civilians employed and unemployed by sex and age, 1947–77." A page or two later is the equally fascinating Table B-49, "Consumer Price Indexes by expenditure classes, 1929–77." You see what I mean?

Some people may not agree. Sheer poetry, I call it, with a little sex and romance thrown in. It's what you bring to these things; to illustrate, let me cite an advertisement that I ran across the other day from a *New York Times* published in the early '20s about Van Raalt stockings:

"Enhance the charm of those few silken inches of hose that twinkle 'neath your skirt by wearing Van Raalt silk hose." The picture shows a demure young lady with the hemline a little under halfway to the knee and those few silken inches twinkling away at a great rate. (I try to be exact in those things:—in 1921 the hemline started eighteen inches from the ground and fashion showed it was steadily rising; to where one could only speculate with awe.)

The close connection between Van Raalt and Table B-29 (employment by age and sex) is immediately evident. Women, of course, were going to work. As they took jobs they cast off their draperies. Some of the bolder ones even discarded stockings when they went bathing at Brighton Beach. Thirty years ago (the table shows) females "20 years and over" numbered 14,354,000 in the American working force, or about 24 percent; last year it was 33,199,000, or over 36 percent of the present working force. That's a social revolution in anybody's book of statistics; from one woman worker in four to one in three. Where it will climb to—how far those "few silken inches" will rise— one can only ask with awe.

The statistical tables show women are still discriminated against. Unemployment by sex is always a little higher among female workers; they are let out first.

Take another example, this time race. Ugly racial riots flared across the nation ten years ago, the worst in history. The impartial government tables pin down and compare the job discrimination in various ways; we all know about it, but there's a certain cool brutality in seeing the facts numerically expressed. Example: teenage unemployment in 1954 was 13.4 percent for whites and 14.4 percent for blacks, about the same. Now look at the figure in 1977—for whites it's 15 percent, for blacks it's 37 percent. Or compare figures on income ("in 1976 dollars"); in 1959 some 18.5 percent of all white families were below the poverty line but this has dropped to a gratifying 9.4 percent in 1976. Black families? The decline is gratifying, too, but the two base figures start from a much higher point; in 1959 some 50.4 percent of all black families were below the poverty line; now it's 26.4 percent.

The storm cries outside, so put another stick on the fire and look at some more figures. Only remember that these aren't just statistics; they are men and women. Here's another table. Why are the farmers so unhappy at present? It affects our politics and our relations abroad. First note one of the most extraordinary figures in the whole 381-page book: the percentage of farmers to total US population. When I came to Washington the farm lobby was, past all doubt, the most powerful in the city. You can see why; as late as 1929 farmers made up a quarter of the nation (25.1 percent). But now (1977) they have dropped to 3.6 percent. Has crop production per acre declined? Just the reverse. It has doubled. In short, the American farm has been mechanized. It's the wonder of the world. Can you look at that column of numerals without seeing Old Boss at the top being milked by hand, and at the bottom yielding her lactic stream to an electric pump?

On the subject of farmers, you can see why they're sore right now. Table B-94 puts it as pithily as it can be put. Using the "1967 = 100" formula, the price received for all farm products has declined from 185 to 183 from 1975 through 1977 inclusive, but the price "paid by farmers: all items, interest, taxes and wage rates" has risen from 180 to 202. No wonder they're sore.

It's not merely farmers who have seen living costs kick over the traces. Medical costs have doubled in the past ten years. That's why there's all this talk of federal health insurance. There are vital odds and ends of information in many tables. You can trace the growth of the welfare state, for example. Down to 1940 the government paid nothing for old age, survivors, disability, and health benefits; now it's a cool $105 billion. That's a revolution, too, statistically expressed. The revolution has come partly because the American population is getting older: people over sixty-five made 5 percent of the population in 1929, Table B-26 says; today it's around 11 percent.

Random items: The last time the federal budget was in the black was way back in 1969, and the time before that, 1960—both times for small amounts. A thing that surprised me is that federal workers (those miserable bureaucrats) have diminished since 1968; yes, there are fewer of them today, whereas state and local officeholders have jumped by three and a third million in the same time.

You can play the game yourself. There's something for practically everybody in here. One thing puzzles me in the section on "Corporate Profits and Finance" (profits by industries, business failures, bond yields, and the like for thirty years). How does the yield of stocks compare with times past? I found that the ratio of yield to price (currently 8.90) has been higher in the past three years than at any time since 1953. You would think that yield would make stocks a bargain, wouldn't you? Maybe Wall Street knows something we don't know. Stock prices have tumbled about one-fifth in value since President Carter took office.

Some of us will always brood over statistics. Here's a table from the World Bank, for instance, giving "Indicators of Comparative Standards of Living" for thirty nations. I always wondered about telephones in Iceland; seems they have 417 per 1,000. (We have 695, and the Russians only 66.) Our per capita output is two and a half times Russia's. And we have 571 TV receivers per 1,000, to Russia's 208. How can they get through those long winter nights?

Tax Time

APRIL 8, 1978   Of all the rituals of American democracy I think the annual self-flagellation of citizens in filling out their income tax forms (deadline April 15) is the most impressive. I suppose nobody hates to pay taxes more than I do. But I go through my Form 1040 once a year, by custom, with reasonable honesty, and send my contribution on to the federal bureaucrats, grumbling at every step of the way. We carry the self-inflicted mortification beyond any other nation. Why do we do it? Let's face it, because we accept Oliver Wendell Holmes' saying that taxes are the price of civilization; because, at heart, we trust our government to administer the money with a reasonable degree of competence and evenhandedness; and because, finally, we trust our neighbors—yes, we believe that they are doing their share too and, on average, will be as conscientious as we are, or maybe more so.

It is well to have the grizzly ordeal come in the spring, the time of hope. Everything looks brighter then. We couldn't stand it in November. Taxes come up with the tulips.

Having made this unpopular genuflection to the income tax, let me add that I think that anything that weakens this unique relationship between Americans and their government is subversive in the ultimate sense. By the middle of this month 85 million individual income tax forms will have been received by the Treasury, with a vernal tide of about $186.8 billion dollars. Some 2.3 million corporations will have contributed another $60 billion. Of these returns about 2.5 percent will be audited. No doubt the fear of such audits propels the process along. But it would not survive for a minute without the additional ingredient: confidence in the ultimate fairness of the government and of fellow citizens.

It is the ingredient of confidence that is challenged now from many directions. During the campaign candidate Carter called the tax system a "disgrace to the human race" which was a rhetorical way, I suppose, of promising that he would make reforms if elected; so far these reforms haven't appeared.

Confidence in the tax structure is attacked from many sides. For six years Representative Charles Vanik (D, Ohio) has compiled an annual study of corporate tax loopholes. Last January he examined 168 of the biggest US companies and found that 17 of them had paid nothing in effective federal income taxes in tax year 1976. These 17 companies (listed in the *Congressional Record* of January 26) had combined worldwide net incomes of $2.9 billion. No US income tax. Forty-one other giant companies (listed by name) paid less than 10 percent in effective federal income taxes in 1976, Vanik reported. IRS Commissioner Jerome Kurtz, in a TV appearance last week, agreed that corporations are paying a smaller proportion of all taxes than they used to; individuals are paying a higher proportion. Tax loopholes for corporations and affluent individuals, he acknowledged, have grown: Kurtz called it "an increasing number of abusive shelters." How much escapes? "We have some estimates of a $200-billion subterranean economy," Kurtz said. He put a comfortable face on it, however: "Two hundred billion dollars is a very high number, but in a two-trillion-dollar economy it's certainly not overwhelming," he said.

It may not be overwhelming in a world of cash and balance sheets, but in a tax system that rests on intangibles like faith and fairness, it could be said to be destructive.

Another attack on the unique American tax system is inflation. If we cherish the progressive income tax, we must do something about this. Consumer prices rose in February at an annual rate of 7.2 percent and the average worker's buying power, according to the Labor Department, declined at an annual rate of 2.4 percent. The consumer was caught between higher prices, a Social Security tax boost, and graduated income taxes. Consider the example of the luckless Jones family. The Jones family has four members, and back in 1955 Mr. Jones earned $15,000. His sympathetic employer matched inflation with wage increases, dollar for dollar, over twenty-one years. This produced a fine income of $32,900 in 1976—an increase of 120 percent. But the higher salary pushed the Jones family from a 22-percent tax bracket into a 36-percent bracket. Its tax soared from $1,540 to $6,600. That's an increase of 330 percent. The unfortunate family doubled its nominal income but it is now 11 percent worse off in purchasing power than in 1955.

Most American families, despite inflation, are better off than they were. But old people, pensioners, those on fixed incomes aren't; and now comes last week's warning signal that for one month, anyway, the average worker's buying power declined. If a Washington politician isn't aware of the dynamite in that signal he is very stupid indeed.

The most dangerous attack on the tax system in our time was made by Richard Nixon, who undertook to warp the Internal Revenue Service into a political appendage. On September 11, 1972, John Dean handed to IRS Commissioner Johnnie Walters an "enemies list" of 490 McGovern aides and supporters for investigation. Four days later, at the White House, H. R. Haldeman told Nixon that Dean was "moving ruthlessly" on the investigation "through IRS."

The attack on the integrity of the IRS, I think, was the worst breach of faith of Richard Nixon. As contrasted to this, John Kennedy, and, after him, Lyndon Johnson, called in the IRS regional commissioners and district directors and addressed them emphasizing their bipartisanship. On the third floor of the IRS building, down the hall, is a small plaque proudly commemorating the visit Kennedy made to the office—the only visit of any president. An income tax form tells about a citizen's family, debts, social status, payments, donations, contributions—it is hard to imagine any document more entitled to privacy. Information is recorded and stored on tapes in a bank of IRS computers in Martinsburg, West Virginia. David Wise, in his chilling book *The American Police State*, shows how Nixon and his crew deliberately set out to make the IRS the equivalent of the FBI and CIA, an instrument of social control. The Special Service Staff (SSS) had files on Jimmy Breslin, Mayor John Lindsay, Coretta King, columnist Joseph Alsop, the Ford Foundation, the American Civil Liberties Union. There were dozens of lists—"audit them, investigate them" were the orders. The sullen bureaucrats resisted. Nixon had three IRS commissioners in five years. And at the end of it all it was disclosed that Nixon himself paid only $792 in taxes in 1970, and $873 in 1971, having deducted half a million for donating his vice-presidential papers in an improperly backdated gift. Something to think about on April 15.

A Puff for Jimmy

APRIL 22, 1978   There is a funny attitude of condescension toward Jimmy Carter in America. I do not recall anything like it. It is a national attitude of deprecation, of disparagement. "You know Jimmy," we say with a helpless shrug. Then we point out his inadequacies.

For example, the Panama treaty vote is scheduled to come up this Tuesday. Right down to the wire it is a touch-and-go thing. And even if it is passed, the DeConcini reservation (arrogantly asserting the US right to intervene after the year 2000 to keep the canal open) may cause Panama to reject it. Why hasn't Jimmy Carter prevented this embarrassing situation? Doesn't he have the art of leadership? It is true, of course, that when he started the drive to ratify the course approved by four presidents the polls showed the public against any treaty at all. It is also true that the Constitution gives 34 senators a veto power over the 535 members of Congress. But so what? Look at the unsavory deals Carter made to get the first Panama treaty approved by one vote. Why does he have to demean himself?

Or take energy. An anniversary comes up this Thursday (April 20).

A year ago April 20 Jimmy went before a joint session of Congress and insisted that something had to be done right away about oil imports. We imported more than $35 billion worth of oil in 1976, he told them: "Our trade deficits are growing." In his flat, uninspired voice he called it "the moral equivalent of war." It is a matter of urgency, of "patriotism and commitment," he said. He outlined an energy program that he called "fair, reasonable, and necessary." He said that "If the American people respond to our challenge we can meet these targets."

It is a year later now; no energy bill. Why didn't Carter get Congress to act? What's the matter with the man; he's president isn't he? Last week he spoke to the American Society of Newspaper Editors here. Oil imports this year will cost $45 billion, or $10 billion more than last, he told them; the unfavorable trade balance has sent the dollar into a skid; the failure to come to grips with the situation promotes inflation. He did not belabor Congress. He read a little lecture on economics.

"Our security depends on it; our economy demands it," he said.

The problem is, of course, that to do something drastic about energy—to do something drastic about inflation—requires self-sacrifice. America hasn't taken drastic action because there has been a failure of national will, expressed through Congress and sublimated, in part, in deprecating Jimmy Carter.

The attitude is contagious and has jumped the Atlantic. "Europeans View Carter as Weak, Unskilled Leader," says a story in the *Washington Post*, datelined Bonn, Germany. That's about the decision to postpone manufacture of the neutron bomb. It has caused a great flap all around the world. Moscow mounted an extraordinary barrage against the N-bomb from behind its own megaton weapons (which slaughter 10 million at a shot) and called it "capitalistic, cannibalistic, barbaric." West Germany, by contrast, wailed because Carter had decided *not* to make the bomb. West Germany and NATO wanted to be pressured into taking the bomb but wouldn't promise to deploy it.

In his simple way the president declared at Yazoo City, Mississippi: "I don't believe the neutron bomb is more wicked or immoral than the present nuclear weapons we have and the Soviets have as well."

Nevertheless, because it is a "clean" bomb its manufacture might encourage that final catastrophe, nuclear warfare. So Jimmy decided to hold it up to see if Moscow would make concessions, and to see if NATO and West Germany would share responsibility. Result? Horrid outcries about the "ineffective" Jimmy Carter. The Germans were particularly bitter; a *Baltimore Sun* dispatch explained that "the deferral avoided forcing Mr. Schmidt [Chancellor Helmut Schmidt] to take a public stand on whether or not Germany would accept the weapon on its soil." But at the same time the German press denounced "Mr. Carter's 'flight from political action.' "

The rage at home was even greater. Columnists Evans and Novak, who despair over Jimmy nearly every week, declared that he "seems to have succumbed to Soviet pressure." The *Wall Street Journal* editorial (April 11) rejoiced that if Jimmy Carter wouldn't become an activist, at least there was another power in Washington. "Happily, the Founding Fathers gave us more than one branch of government. If the administration cannot come up with processes that produce cogent decisions, Congress will have to bear more responsibility than usual."

Congress has been trying to produce a cogent decision on the matter of energy for a year, come this week.

The president got some support. For example, James Reston of the *New York Times* noted that after all the arguments for and against "these handy little atomic weapons," Carter had paused, temporized, and thought about compromising. "And a good thing, too," Reston added.

Jimmy Carter is a most unusual president. He made a lot of mistakes. He overpromised himself in the election. When he came to office he sent up an impossible load of bills apparently thinking that you pressed a button and a law rolled out like a pop bottle from a vending machine. Another thing, Jimmy Carter is low-keyed, not electrifying. I thought of that again last week while he was addressing the editors. There were no lively gestures, no rhetorical embellishments, no fireworks. He was just Jimmy Carter, working hard, sounding earnest, honest, and idealistic.

He has aggravating character faults, too. He doesn't respond to brutal detractors; he doesn't lash out at Congress nor lose his temper. By now he ought to have a rousing persecution complex like most presidents, but he doesn't; he is probably the most temperamentally secure chief executive of modern times.

A Gallup Poll shows an interesting thing about him. It is not that

49 percent approve, 34 percent disapprove, but that the feeling about him is so uniform, the same division seems to run through all the categories: rich-poor; whites-blacks; Protestants-Catholics. He doesn't inspire wild hatred or passionate support. He is just a hardworking man doing the best he can, trying to rouse the country to greatness. It is terribly irritating. What can critics do but condescend to him?

E. B. White Defines Democracy

APRIL 29, 1978   Here I get worked up about the absurdities of Washington, and am just prepared to denounce them, when along comes E. B. White who wins a Pulitzer Prize (which he should have received twenty-five years ago) and my typewriter rattles off into nostalgia. The first time I met E. B. White was at the White House, and he had a stomachache.

There has been a linkage with White for forty years, all to my advantage. Henry Ford brought us together. He invented the Model T that stood seven feet high with the top up and that was as incredible to its generation as the solar system (it had a "planetary" transmission, incidentally, that seemed to link it to celestial bodies). I drove one of them down to Washington from Boston on a trip that took three days. The temperature was ten above zero and all we had to protect us as we hurtled along at twenty-five miles per hour were the snap-on isinglass side curtains and the warmth seeping up through the slits in the floorboards from a red-hot exhaust pipe. (When we shuffled the newspapers with our galoshes we could see the pipe glowing. Don't ask me why the papers didn't catch on fire; I don't know.) When I got to Washington I found I could park the car all day long on the Ellipse behind the White House.

It turned out that E. B. White, a shy young genius, whom I out-

[TRB won a Pulitzer Prize Special Citation at the same time E. B. White did.]

rank in seniority by one year, had taken a trip across America in his own Model T with a classmate, Howard Cushman, at about the same time I was first driving. Like every member of the cult he learned in no time how many turns to give the grease cup on the elbow joints, how to calculate mileage by inserting a dipstick in the nine-gallon tank immediately under the front seat (after removing the seat), and how to get the motor started by hand-cranking.

I didn't know E. B. White until I submitted a piece to the *New Yorker* in 1936, nine years after the last Model T had come down the production line but when a million or so of the nimble little things were still moving about the countryside. My piece touched White and recalled his store of reminiscences. With my research and his artistry it came out as "Farewell, My Lovely" and subsequently infiltrated all the anthologies. There could be no rivalry in such collaboration; first of all White was an essayist unsurpassed in the English-speaking world, and second, we were both serving the same beloved memory, prompting and reminding each other of Model T's little oddities.

In case you haven't cranked one recently this is how it went: "Leave the ignition switch off, proceed to the animal's head, pull the choke [which was a little wire protruding through the radiator], and give the crank two or three nonchalant upward lifts. Then, whistling as though thinking about something else, you would saunter back to the driver's cabin, turn the ignition on, return to the crank, and this time, catching it on the down stroke, give it a quick spin with plenty of That. If this procedure was followed the engine almost always responded—first with a few scattered explosions, then with a tumultuous gunfire, which you checked by racing around to the driver's seat and retarding the throttle. Often, if the emergency brake hadn't been pulled all the way back, the car advanced on you the instant the first explosion occurred and you would hold it back by leaning your weight against it. I can still feel my old Ford nuzzling me at the curb, as though looking for an apple in my pocket."

Things got lively in Washington in December 1941 and White, whom until then I hadn't met, wrote me that he was coming down to do some stuff for *Harper's*. There was war in Europe, our neutrality was giving way, and Japan was invading China. It was Roosevelt's last press conference before Pearl Harbor. As I wrote to my parents right *after* Pearl Harbor, "E. B. White was down last week—how long ago that seems! I showed him around and found him an extraordinarily shy fellow, small, with a stomach trouble that made him nearly pass out at the White House press conference." As a matter of fact I proposed to take him up to meet FDR behind his big totem-laden desk after the conference, relishing the thought of being the intermediary at such a meeting. But when I took his elbow White rejected forward movement with vehemence. He was feeling ill. In fact this tensely wrought, fey man could, and did, induce illness at critical social moments through his career (like mounting a platform or receiving a public honor). He amusingly tells of it in his *Letters of E. B. White.*

It is improbable people like E. B. White who lift up the hearts of a nation in time of war and show us why we must nourish artists as we do gunboats. Something was created in the war called the Writers' War Board and in the *New Yorker*'s "Notes and Comment," July 3, 1943, issue he noted that it had asked him for a statement on "the Meaning of Democracy." What an opportunity for sententious utterance! "It presumably is our duty to comply with such a request, and it is certainly our pleasure," he wrote in an unsigned rejoinder:

"Surely the Board knows what Democracy is. It is the line that forms on the right. It is the don't in don't shove. It is the hole in the stuffed shirt through which the sawdust slowly trickles; it is the dent in the high hat. Democracy is the recurrent suspicion that more than half of the people are right more than half of the time. It is the feeling of privacy in the voting booths, the feeling of communion in the libraries, the feeling of vitality everywhere. Democracy is a letter to the editor. Democracy is the score at the beginning of the ninth. It is an idea which hasn't been disproved yet, a song the words of which have not gone bad. It's the mustard on the hot dog and the cream in the rationed coffee. Democracy is a request from a War Board, in the middle of a morning in the middle of a war, wanting to know what democracy is."

Young writers, top that. It made FDR roar with delight. It is a mixture of the colloquial and the lustrous so compounded that you don't see how he does it. James Thurber mentioned "those silver and crystal sentences that have a ring of nobody else's sentences," his sensitive ear "that not only notes the louder cosmic rhythms but catches the faintest ticking sounds."

In short, E. B. White could write a note to the milkman that would leap out of print. But if the Pulitzer committee thinks he will step up like a good boy to receive his belated accolade they are, I think, mistaken.

Jimmy Parts the Red Sea

SEPTEMBER 30, 1978 They were just sitting there, Sunday afternoon, having coffee in the Legion Hall press headquarters when ABC's Sam Donaldson burst up the stairs. The summit was over—the summit they had blown up and down in hope and gloom for thirteen days. There would be a briefing in Washington at 9 P.M., Carter at 10:30, with the others. *Others?* they roared. What others? Begin, Sadat, everybody! All hell broke loose. There was a two-way rush to telephones and cars.

Eight miles away at Camp David, Hamilton Jordan caught the president's eye through a window. Carter gave a big, jubilant thumbs-up. Just then came the damndest crack of thunder ever heard. Maybe it's legend—I don't know; already it's part myth. But it was no myth what happened at the parking lot outside the Legion Hall: 100 crazy cars trying to nose out simultaneously through a narrow channel: pelting, pouring rain; gutters wouldn't hold it; everybody soaked to the bone; Dave Garcia of ABC using a fruit box as an umbrella.

So that's when I picked it up. Why was it like Pearl Harbor, December 7, 1941? That was on a Sunday, too. This time the NBC News interrupted with a flash—the summit's over, Carter on at 10:30. Telephone rings . . . White House calling . . . briefing at 9:00. Yes, I'll be there.

The floor of the briefing room slopes slightly like a theater, seats 150; it fills up with reporters—exhilarated, excited, electrified. Ice-cold Brzezinski doesn't chew gum; his jaws seem to be reacting as he keeps his cool; he presents the intricate timetable to reporters struggling between cynicism and euphoria. He is clear, precise, incomprehensible. Modalities . . . what are modalities? Jody Powell, only man in the room wearing a vest (let alone coat), says if we leave immediately we can see them arrive by helicopter on the South Lawn.

The lovely White House glows luminously. Grass is thick, springy. Harry Truman's balcony looks down, and the porch where I saw FDR give his fourth Inaugural, in January 1945. (They lifted him around like a potato sack. The bare boughs had snow on them.) Now it is mild, muggy; a moth darts in the lights, the fountain plays at the far end; over behind looms the great floodlit Monument, ethereal as a dream. Distant planes at the airport sound like subway cars. I try to make notes in the dark. This setting, those stage-scenery trees—it isn't real; anything can happen; is happening. The moon peekaboos down. (There was a moon, too, at Pearl Harbor; a crescent, and it saw grim senators go in to FDR and come out still grimmer.)

The pop-popping of a helicopter; the huge hulk lands delicately on the lawn, giant blades rotate with another little eggbeater on the tail. "United States of America," it says. The door opens: there they are—Carter, Begin, Sadat; incredible; everything's incredible. A little applause. Moon comes out full. We dash for the pressroom.

This is prime time, Sunday night, three networks; ABC showing something called "Battlestar Galactica" with ray guns; poof, you're killed. Suddenly they are giving an instant replay of the South Lawn landing we have just witnessed. A miracle, that is, too! Carter starts; always the potential Sunday school teacher, he says "prayers have been answered beyond any expectations." Swarthy Sadat gives testimony next ("let us join in prayer to God Almighty"); tough little Begin follows, ex-terrorist, dedicated, looking more and more like Felix Frankfurter. He praises God; Jewish teachings; "*habemus pacem*"; the "Jimmy Carter Conference"; *Shalom, Shalom*. He is in high fettle. They all praise Jimmy. They are all born again. What an unlikely trio for a revival: Muslim, Jew, Christian. The first two are so happy they ham it up—look (cheers), they are hugging each other!

Outside on the front lawn as I come away I pause to hear Senators Jackson and Percy giving a floodlit interview after just leaving the East Room. They are nonplussed, prompting, corroborating, babbling.

Next day, 11:30 A.M., Monday, September 18—Vance gives the briefing. Sadat's foreign minister, Kamel, has resigned. Again there is irrefutable testimony how Carter worked at Camp David, hour by hour, night and day, urging, cajoling, persuading. Punch-drunk reporters begin to get a sense of the thing. Yes, it is real. The Red Sea has parted; Jimmy Carter is leading them through, with a wave of "ifs" on either side. Vance goes fifty minutes. More modalities.

So here I am, finally, in the press gallery for Carter's talk to the joint session of Congress, where this thing must stop. Again the atmosphere is crucial. I have watched many times; this is noisier, more high-spirited—like a birthday party. In the president's gallery, flaxen-haired Amy rotates rapidly to shake out her ringlets. Sadat and Begin enter, with girlish-looking Mrs. Carter between them. The applause rises, and rises; crests in an ovation. The clerk shouts: "Mister Speaker, the President of the United States!" Sixty seconds of applause. He hails Sadat, Begin, more applause, standing; the frame of no other government could create a scene like this. Men's summer suits are tan, beige, light blue; the carpet is figured red and green; an occasional woman's dress . . . the big chamber vibrates; even Carter's anointed delivery can't dull it. He ad-libs a bit; uses a teleprompter, addresses four vital audiences simultaneously—Congress, the nation, Sadat and Begin, and the people of the Middle East. He tries to wall in Begin and Sadat with flattery till they can't escape. He is folksy—"the three of us together." He hails Vance (huge applause). And he ends movingly: "Blessed are the peacemakers, for they shall be [called] the children of God." A great moment.

Begin and Sadat love it; they do their act again, they embrace, they hug. . . . I have seen everything.

So now, what do we say about Jimmy Carter? He is the despised kid at school who stepped up to bat and clouted one over the fence, bases loaded. He is so easy to underestimate. Enemies didn't hate him; they patronized him. He is soft-spoken, a poor speaker, almost unctuous; America has never had a president quite like him, perhaps. He will have more ups and downs. He is facing an inflation-recession now and doesn't know the answer, I think. (Nor does anybody else.) The post-Summit agreement may collapse. Those polls may sink again. But how hard he is trying.

Strout's Far-from-Last Word

RICHARD L. STROUT *gave the following speech in Washington when he was awarded the prestigious Fourth Estate Award by the National Press Club in October 1975 for his distinguished service to American journalism.*

On a happy occasion like this the speaker, I believe, is supposed to strike a forward-looking and inspirational note. I hope I can do as well as Senator Kenneth Wherry of Nebraska in a speech in Missouri in 1940. This notable orator was discussing the future of China, and the American Dream, and he wound up in a great peroration to a wildly cheering audience,

"With God's help we will lift Shanghai up and up—ever up . . . until it is just like Kansas City!"

That was part of America's innocence, something that has been lost, I believe, in the half century I have been in Washington.

In 1923 I drove down from Boston to Washington in a towering seven-foot Model T, and it took three days. That was the car where you measured your gasoline by getting out, lifting the front seat, and sounding the tank with a yardstick.

I could park my Model T all day long on the Ellipse behind the White House with plenty of room and no parking ticket.

It's hard to reconstruct 1923 today. There wasn't any Pentagon; the "State, War, and Navy Building" beside the White House still held all the State Department and parts of the other two agencies; Harry Truman hadn't put the porch on the back of the White House, and there were sculpture groups in front of the Capitol that you will note in old prints—Columbus Discovering America, and a Pioneer, or somebody, staying the tomahawk of a ravishing Indian from a settler maiden—what Mark Twain called the "delirium tremens" style of sculpture. They lasted from 1853 to 1961.

There were other differences in the country. Population was half today's; you could buy four tokens on the trolley for thirty cents, and though the postage stamps didn't carry pretty pictures, they cost only two cents.

I always wanted to be a big spender, but I never thought it would come by buying bread, and bacon, and postage stamps!

As a journalist I note, too, that in 1923 there were sixteen different makes of motor cars commonly made and sold, and there were also some sixteen different daily newspapers published in New York City.

Today the number of automobile manufacturers has shrunk to five; and the number of New York newspapers has shrunk to five, too. Big changes! I may add that *Time* and *Newsweek* hadn't been invented yet, nor the *New Yorker*, and *Life* was a comic magazine, edited by Benchley.

Warren Harding was president. I went to my first press conference and there, standing in plus fours behind his desk in the Oval Office—so close that I could touch him—was the handsomest president since George Washington. I was pretty naive. I had all the appropriate feelings of a youngster, standing in awe before his Leader. In fact, I remember my hostility to my blasé colleagues, crammed around the desk, asking sharp questions.

I have total recall: "Gentlemen, gentlemen," he pleaded at last, "please go easy on me—I want to get away for some golf." (I add that to the utterances of Great Men.) There was quite a lot going on that I didn't know about in the Washington of 1923. There was "the Little Green House on K Street" where the benign president got away from The Duchess and played poker and where Prohibition Commissioner Haynes arranged to have Internal Revenue guards with pistols and badges deliver liquor in Wells Fargo Express wagons. (That was 1625 K Street; the "Little House on H Street" was 1509 . . .)

Mr. Harding's girl friend, Nan Britton, visited him in the White House and they made love on the closet floor amid the rubbers and galoshes while Secret Service man Walter Ferguson guarded the corridor and shooed off the suspicious Duchess.

Those were gaudy days. I can't help looking back at them wistfully. Yes, there was corruption then, but it was of a more innocent sort, I think, than nowadays. The Teapot Dome scandal broke in 1923, unraveled by reporters like Tom Stokes and Paul Y. Anderson (the Woodward and Bernstein of their day) and I covered it; yes, in the very same marble Senate Caucus Room where, half a century later, Senator Ervin heard the Watergate story.

The chronological cycle of events has led to the promulgation of Strout's Law. There's a major scandal in American political life every fifty years: Grant's (that you all remember) in 1873; Teapot Dome precisely fifty years later in 1923; and Watergate punctually after that in 1973. Nail down your seats for 2023!

It is instructive, I think, to recall that despite the Grant and Harding scandals the public elected Republicans again in the next presidential election. Strout's Law doesn't cover that, but it is a not unlikely event next year.

I must get away from Harding, one of my favorite characters. But I can't refrain from saying that one time when reporters who had covered the 1920 "Front Porch" campaign were having a reunion in the National Press Club (then located in the Albee Building), an awed servant rapped on the door of their private room and announced that the president of the United States was outside and would like to join them. They welcomed him, and the lonely president spent a quiet evening there, free of The Duchess.

Harding's successor, Calvin Coolidge, had an association with this Club also. The tight-lipped little Yankee—who took the oath of office by a kerosene lamp in a little village in Vermont from his father, a justice of the peace—laid the cornerstone of this building in 1926. I remember he had a mason's trowel with a dab of mortar on it, the size of a butter pat. If he had been working on the Club's present face-lifting, the work would be going even slower than it is.

I have seen the presidents come and go. In 1923 two ex-presidents were living in Washington, jovial Bill Taft as chief justice, and Woodrow Wilson, who was just a wraith, lived on S Street until 1924. For a Washington reporter over the years the presidents are mileposts; there have been eleven in my time. You go to bed one night, it seems, a reporter, and wake up to find you are a pundit!

(I am surprised to find how many people mistake longevity for profundity.)

Harding I have mentioned: he was the handsome, genial, vulgar fellow whom Alice Roosevelt Longworth appropriately called a "slob."

Calvin Coolidge found duties so easy that he napped in the afternoon; it was said of him that he was weaned on a pickle.

There was Herbert Hoover, a towering figure in many ways, caught in an economic Greek tragedy he never understood.

FDR, elected four times—the greatest president of my time: a superb combination of Machiavelli's lion and fox.

Harry Truman, a spunky little fox terrier of a man.

Charming, bumbling Eisenhower, who gave us a caretaker government just when we wanted it, but who had the good sense to look at the clock, not to try to turn it back.

JFK, a fairy-tale prince, who gave us a brief, bright Camelot—but who, alas, sent "advisers" into Vietnam.

Lyndon Johnson, an elemental force, who exclaimed one time when I was interviewing him that he was no "babe in arms," and jumped up to my amazement, pacing the floor, rocking an imaginary baby in his arms.

And then there is Richard Nixon. Of them all, I may say, he was the only one I actively disliked, right from the start. He was a flawed and insecure man, I think, who said once, you remember, that "the American people are like a child."

And finally, it's refreshing to add, we have Jerry Ford, an accidental and attractive figure, the least devious of them all, whose crashing virtue is that he isn't Richard Nixon, but who sometimes seems to have difficulty in distinguishing between Running and Governing.

Looking back over a reasonably fruitful lifetime, I sometimes ask what the satisfactions are of being a newspaperman. It isn't well paid; a lot of my good friends have dropped off into other jobs always, it seems, to their financial improvement. But journalism has rewards. You meet a lot of odd people. It flatters your vanity, too, to know things before other people do. Besides that, I think there is generally a feeling of commitment. You can look back every now and then with a feeling of having coined a good phrase; of having explained an involved problem; of having—let's face it—exposed something that needed exposure.

I mentioned the liveliness of the job. Two of my happiest recollections were traveling with Harry Truman on his famous 1948 whistle-stop campaign across America, and with Nikita Khrushchev in a similar trip in September 1959. Truman was imaginatively and wonderfully corny the further west he got, explaining to crowds that it was a nonpolitical trip and that he was "going down to Berkeley fur to git me a degree." When adversaries dredged up some scandal or other about the party, he exclaimed, "They can't prove nothing, they ain't got a thing on me." Tom Stokes put the two lines together as a chorus to the tune of "Oh, Susanna:"

> They can't prove nothing, they ain't got a thing on me!
> Oh, I'm going down to Berkeley fur to git me a degree.

The Khrushchev trip in 1959 was the most hilarious I ever was on. We had hundreds of reporters and photographers from all over the world: the scene I remember best was when we invaded a supermarket outside San Francisco. We simply wrecked the place. Photographers are a special breed. One climbed up on a pyramid of glass coffee jars; it collapsed. For safety's sake I got over onto the checkout counter. There was one woman, an unfortunate customer I suppose, prostrate on the floor and people simply stepped over her. "She fainted," we told a photographer later. "Oh," he replied brightly, "I thought she was dead."

"Why were you fighting with the butcher?" we asked another.

"I just don't know," he replied in an injured tone. "He attacked me. I didn't do anything to him. I just stood on his meat."

There were other, graver scenes.

On the morning of D-Day, off the Normandy coast, I watched the troops go ashore and then, amidst the flashing and banging, out of the west from English bases came an endless line of airplanes, each towing a glider, as far as the eye could reach! I felt such a feeling of exultation and of pride, as I have never felt before. The line kept coming— indomitable, invincible, implacable American planes, American gliders, American paratroopers. While it was still coming, the earlier planes began returning, this time without their gliders. They had crash-landed with their paratroopers behind the enemy lines!

And one final memory of the past: On the night of Pearl Harbor, December 7, 1941, I was one of the reporters huddled under the White House columns on the portico. Under a slight moon grim senators in overcoats rolled up in their cars, to hear FDR tell them the horrid news. Some were isolationists who had said this was a "phony war." They came in silent and went out silent, and behind the iron fence a small crowd watched that, toward midnight, made an effort to sing "America the Beautiful." Nobody could sing "America the Beautiful." It quavered badly. It made me cry.

The crowd was out there, too, when they brought Jack Kennedy's body back. That crowd haunts the place. It always appears. It was out there when President Nixon fired Special Prosecutor Archibald Cox. It is an actor in the drama. When it materializes—silent, steady, patient, watching all night—you know great moments of history are occurring.

Let me come now from the past into the present. One thing that strikes me, as it may you, is how many things that we knew couldn't happen have happened. I don't mean merely physical accomplishments, like putting a man on the moon. These are the easy things. We can walk on the moon but we can't walk in Central Park. I am talking about other things that were "impossible:" a Roman Catholic couldn't be elected president. Schools couldn't be desegregated. Federal budgets couldn't be expanded in a recession. Birth control couldn't be discussed publicly. Public welfare was "socialism." U.S. troops couldn't be kept in Europe in peacetime. Oh yes, and there was a more pervasive myth: Americans couldn't lose a war.

This has been an extraordinarily fascinating half century from Teapot Dome to Watergate. It was marked, I think, America's coming of age. We have lost our innocence. This is a trying process but we have, I think, a more realistic view today of the world we live in. We supposed that when we became a world power our moral superiority and our wealth would lead the world to better things. There was the Utopian evangelism of Woodrow Wilson; I would not sneer at this idealism; on one hand it led us to the Marshall Plan; on the other, into the Vietnam War.

In just a few years we have lost our illusion of omnipotence. We have lost the safety of distance. In a shrinking world we have to reach an accommodation with the nuclear bomb. Some of our seemingly endless resources threaten to give out.

Nearer at home we have suffered a series of humiliations. I don't just mean Watergate, I mean the thought that behind our back government forces were playing with poisoned darts with the idea of assassinating foreign leaders! In brief, I think we are a decent people suffering a sharp recession in our spiritual standard of living; we are temporarily living above our material means, and below our spiritual means.

The problems that we faced in the past fifty years seem relatively simple, I think, compared to those ahead. I don't envy the upcoming generation! We brought a new grandson home the other day. I held him while I was reading a paper last night and he gingerly flicked open one eye, took one glance, and closed it again as hard as he could. The story I was reading said the "CIA had opened 215,000 letters to and from the Soviet Union in a twenty-year program that was not merely illegal but worthless." "Sonny," I said, "I don't blame you!"

I don't mean to say that these new problems are insoluble; I do feel that the clock of history has speeded up. The pace of history is overtaking our capacity to adjust. The margin of error is shrinking.

Take the global picture, for example. There are 4 billion people on earth, and the birthrate is such that population will double in thirty-five years. That's not a long time, really; about the time from Franklin Roosevelt till today. Every year the population of an East and West Germany combined is added—that's 73 million; every twenty-four hours the aggregate of 200,000 more people, the equivalent of a new, instant Des Moines, Iowa (God help us); in the short time we're sitting here, population will expand 8,000 (a good reason for limiting this talk). And where will this doubled population go? Who will feed them? My friend Lester Brown, the demographer, simply says he thinks they won't be fed; population won't double. Pestilence and war and Nature will take charge of human fertility, if people won't, he thinks.

(And while I'm about it, let me toss off a thought; the Population Explosion is everybody's baby.)

Here's another solemn thought. Of all the people on earth today, only five percent are Americans, and yet we consume one-third of all the energy, one-third of the food, and enjoy one-half of the world's income. I ask you, in all simplicity, can a disparity like this last? Personally I think it can't, and I think much of the news in the next fifty years is going to turn on whether we yield to the inevitable graciously or vindictively.

Cheer up; don't despair! But note that the planet is so restless already that it spends $240 billion annually on armaments—to "protect" a world population, most of whose citizens earn less than $100 a year.

Here at home my impression is that a good many injustices are slowly being ameliorated. When I was a boy, the *World Almanac* every year published a table of lynchings; that dreadful table has long since disappeared. Racial injustices continue but my impression is that they are not growing worse, but more visible. Yet the potential instability of our society constantly impresses me. One person in eleven in the world's richest country is below the "poverty" line. And about one American in eleven is nonwhite. One thing is certain, if we ever have social turbulence, the weapons are right there: there are 24 million handguns available, with a couple million more added each year.

I don't offer these pessimistic appraisals with the idea of sending you away steeped in gloom. After the Sick Sixties we are halfway through the Uncertain Seventies. There is something to be said, I think, for a little salutary anxiety from time to time. We are fed up with idiot optimism, the smirking assurances that Mr. Nixon, for example, gave about the budget just before the 1973 inflation which produced the comment, "If he had been the captain of the *Titanic* he would have told the passengers that he was stopping to take on ice."

One of my favorite worries is about our form of government. I have always favored the parliamentary system, like Canada's, as more flexible than our separation of powers. What other country, for example, could have a one-year deadlock over the energy crisis between president and Congress! Our 200-year-old government is slow-moving and sprinkled with roadblocks and vetoes. But when the crunch comes, as Watergate showed us, we have to get decisions from somebody and we automatically turn to the president and his power, I believe. The power of the president inevitably grows. We encourage a kind of mysticism, a religiosity about the presidency. It is a santification of the office and deification of the man, and I think it is dangerous.

I have meant to be challenging in this talk, which has ranged from presidents I have known to problems of the future. So let me end with some comforting reflections. We have escaped most of the dangers that might have engulfed us.

Though we criticize America's "materialism," there is no more generous or idealistic nation on earth. There is no more stunning statistic than that we have made the leap from a median elementary school education for everybody to a median high school education, and done it in a few years.

I have criticized the American government, but I believe there is no more open capital in the world than Washington; few secrets, thank God, are kept long and, as a working journalist, I get tremendous satisfaction from this. It is not so much the occasional News Leaks, it is the steady, persistent News Ooze.

So I come back, in the end, to the American Dream. We should make affirmation of our belief guardedly, with the spare reserve of E. B. White's definition of "democracy":

"Democracy is the recurrent suspicion that more than half the people are right more than half the time."

I have advice for fellow journalists. I hope they will stay committed. I hope they will retain their curiosity—their interest; yes, and at their heart a touch of anger. When the adrenaline runs low, when the little flame of anger flickers out, I think it is time for the reporter to think about going into some more remunerative form of work!

I agree with Ronald Steel: "America's worth to the world will be measured not by the solutions she seeks to impose on others, but by the degree to which she achieves her ideals at home."

So let me end with a quotation from that tough old Yankee historian Samuel Eliot Morison, who was not given to sentimental trivialities:

"If the American Revolution had produced nothing but the Declaration of Independence it would have been worth while. . . . The beauty and cogency of the Preamble, reaching back to remotest antiquity and forward to an indefinite future, have lifted the hearts of millions of men and will continue to do so:

" 'We hold these Truths to be self-evident, that all men are created equal, that they are endowed by their Creator with certain inalienable Rights, that among these are Life, Liberty, and the Pursuit of Happiness.'

"These words," said Morison, "are more revolutionary than anything written by Robespierre, Marx, or Lenin, more explosive than the atom, a continual challenge to ourselves, as well as an inspiration to the oppressed of all the world."

Index